Legal Data for Banking

Legal Data for Banking

Business Optimisation and Regulatory Compliance

Akber Datoo

Registered office
John Wiley & Sons Ltd, The Atrium, Southern Gate, Chichester, West Sussex, PO19 8SQ, United Kingdom

For details of our global editorial offices, for customer services and for information about how to apply for permission to reuse the copyright material in this book please see our website at www.wiley.com.

Wiley publishes in a variety of print and electronic formats and by print-on-demand. Some material included with standard print versions of this book may not be included in e-books or in print-on-demand. If this book refers to media such as a CD or DVD that is not included in the version you purchased, you may download this material at http://booksupport.wiley.com. For more information about Wiley products, visit www.wiley.com.

Designations used by companies to distinguish their products are often claimed as trademarks. All brand names and product names used in this book are trade names, service marks, trademarks or registered trademarks of their respective owners. The publisher is not associated with any product or vendor mentioned in this book.

Limit of Liability/Disclaimer of Warranty: While the publisher and author have used their best efforts in preparing this book, they make no representations or warranties with respect to the accuracy or completeness of the contents of this book and specifically disclaim any implied warranties of merchantability or fitness for a particular purpose. It is sold on the understanding that the publisher is not engaged in rendering professional services and neither the publisher nor the author shall be liable for damages arising herefrom. If professional advice or other expert assistance is required, the services of a competent professional should be sought.

Library of Congress Cataloging-in-Publication Data

Names: Datoo, Akber, 1978-
Title: Legal data for banking : business optimisation and regulatory
    compliance / Akber Datoo.
Description: Chichester, West Suxxex, United Kingdom ; Hoboken : Wiley, 2019.
    | Includes index. |
Identifiers: LCCN 2018061435 (print) | LCCN 2019005061 (ebook) | ISBN
    9781119357209 (ePDF) | ISBN 9781119357223 (ePub) | ISBN 9781119357162
    (hardback)
Subjects: LCSH: Financial services industry—Law and legislation—Data
    processing. | Law offices–Automation. | BISAC: BUSINESS & ECONOMICS /
    Finance.
Classification: LCC K1066 (ebook) | LCC K1066 .D38 2019 (print) | DDC
    346/.082—dc23
LC record available at https://lccn.loc.gov/2018061435

Cover Design: Wiley
Cover Images: © T33kid/Shutterstock,
© Titima Ongkantong/Shutterstock, © Akber Datoo

Set in 10/12pt WarnockPro by SPi Global, Chennai, India
Printed in Great Britain by TJ International Ltd, Padstow, Cornwall, UK

10 9 8 7 6 5 4 3 2 1

Contents

Preface

I first encountered the capital markets and investment banks in the late 1990s. Thrust into a trading floor environment straight from a computer science degree at Cambridge University, there was a lovely mix of mathematics, business and adrenaline on that Fixed Income Derivatives Trading floor that I fell in love with and which set the path for derivatives to be the one constant in my future professional career.

During my lifetime, technology has been a game changer in every aspect of our lives, not least the workplace and business, with the increasing reliance on computers, the internet and smartphones, to the increasing data-enabled world and digital economy.

The investment banking and finance industry recognised this in the late 1990s and early 2000s, using technology to scale and grow business. But amongst the innovation and embracing of change, I encountered in-house legal teams and external lawyers who were seemingly oblivious to the empowerment offered by process refinement, systems and data. The legal profession is quite rightly a conservative one in approach – one certainly does not want lawyers to be overt risk takers, rather trusted advisers and counsel through the risks that are taken in order to succeed in business, and to balance legal and commercial risks as required. However, I felt the balance was wrong, and resulted in far too many missed opportunities to unlock business value through legal change.

After wonderful years at Warburg Dillon Read (UBS by the time I had left!), including meeting my lovely and dear wife Naila during my time in New York, I decided to go back to study, curious through my engagement with in-house lawyers at UBS, particularly through industry initiatives such as FpML and Swapswire (now Markitwire). There surely had to be a way to optimise business operations and achieve through the medium of legal data, and I was hoping to find this out via a journey through the legal profession.

I was fortunate to practise law at Allen & Overy LLP, a magic circle law firm, with an outstanding derivatives and capital markets practice. I worked alongside some of the brightest minds, many of whom had worked on key foundational industry documentation, such as drafting the original ISDA Master Agreement in a mythically smoky room in 1987.

It was only, however, during my secondments to the legal teams of Royal Bank of Scotland (RBS) and Credit Suisse, the latter during the midst of the Financial Crisis and the Lehman Brothers collapse, that the importance of the legal data really struck home.

Deciding that the time was right, with the regulatory impetus in many ways forcing the financial industry to recognise the importance of legal data and systems – especially given that the financial instruments at the heart of the Financial Crisis were, in many ways, nothing more than contractual obligations – I decided to pull the two strings together, legal and data, founding D2 Legal Technology (D2LT) in October 2011.

Over eight years later, we are truly seeing legal data come to the fore, through the intersection of Fintech, Regtech and Legaltech. It may be over a decade since Richard Susskind raised the spectre of technology replacing lawyers, with his sensitively titled book *The End of Lawyers*, but the arrival of commercially viable artificial intelligence solutions has, quite suddenly, begun to make the vision look ever more real. The question arises, though: Have organisations truly understood the new digital agenda – or how to respond to digital disruption? This is not just about the use of automation to reduce headcount or drastically minimise fees. It is about delivering business value and, critically, bringing legal teams out of the ivory towers and fundamentally into the business mix. This requires not only the use of technology, but also a critical examination of the business need, and the current processes used to try and meet that need. Legal data is at the heart of this.

The new model should be about using digitisation to become data driven in order to add business context to legal activity. Particularly within the specialism of financial services, the new legal digital agenda is a chance to bring legal counsel further into business and use digitisation and data connectivity to achieve hyper-awareness both pre- and post-trade. With real-time recognition of key events and how they may affect a position, an empowered legal team can drive new and measurable value. The greatest risk is inaction.

This book is my humble attempt to bring together some of the foundational building blocks required to empower the capital markets business through legal data. As a result, both technologists and lawyers will find some sections in the book basic for them and so they are probably best skipped over. However, I hope all readers, be they students, legal practitioners, technologists, business analysts, traders, risk professionals, regulators or academics, will find something of use in this journey on the digitisation of the law.

Akber Datoo, London – 20 February 2019

Acknowledgements

First and foremost, a special thank you to my parents for their continual support and encouragement in every walk of life. Without you, I would not have been able to finish this book, especially without the recent trip to France when it finally took proper shape. No thank you can ever be complete enough to acknowledge your role as the best parents a son could ask for.

I would also like to thank my dear wife Naila for her love, patience and support as I have been writing this book, together with my wonderful son and daughter, Abbas Hassan and Fatema Zahra (who have convinced me that I have missed many a trick in failing to cover the more important topics of football and fairies in the chapters to follow). Abbas Hassan and Fatema Zahra really are the best children a father could have – fun, loving and caring – and I have missed out on so much whilst writing!

I would like to thank all of the staff at D2LT, especially Jessica Bryant, Katie Oliver, Peter Newton, Jason Pugh, Michael Wood, Subhankar Ghosh, Carol Lance and Adrian Jenks, who have endlessly reviewed and assisted with various parts of the book, providing their expert views and feedback, as well as checking for accuracy and correctness. Many thanks to Emma Patient, Senior Counsel at HSBC, for her meticulous review and comment on Chapter 7.

I have been fortunate in the time invested in me by a number of managers and colleagues, such as Jeffrey Golden at Allen & Overy, Ulku Rowe and Kirren Basavaraj at UBS. Your time and effort to guide and develop my knowledge has been invaluable.

My colleagues and clients, including Colin Hall Nicholas Sainsbury and Vasan Siva (Credit Suisse), Amir Mehdi, David Todd and Laura Muir (Barclays), Sam Hooker, Vivienne Chan and Jillian Melton (HSBC), Simon Berkett (Macquarie), George Simonetti, Lee Cummins, Richard Paolini and Josh Luber (Wells Fargo) and Ciarán McGonangle (ISDA) – thank you for all the legal data adventures we have been through, many of which form the foundation of parts of this book.

Finally, but not least, thank you to Wiley for making this book a reality. In particular, thank you to Thomas Hykiel (with whom I shared the initial idea – I am grateful for his enthusiasm and support), Kari Capone (Manager), Elisha Benjamin (Project Editor), Banurekha Venkatesan (Production Editor) and Gemma Valler (Commissioning Editor).

1

The Role of Data in a Financial Crisis

This first chapter serves to provide context for the rest of the book – setting out the causes of the 2007–2008 Financial Crisis (the Financial Crisis) that swept the global financial markets well over a decade ago and has substantially impacted the banking and finance industry as we know it today. It was this turbulent period that provided the impetus for the substantial body of financial regulation that has been introduced over the last 10 years, as well as the enhanced legal data requirements that this body of regulation imposes, extending beyond the business and operational needs for such legal data.

In subsequent chapters we will further examine the Financial Crisis through various lenses, as some of the more pertinent aspects of recent financial regulation (such as regulatory capital requirements, margin for uncleared derivatives and recovery and resolution planning) are considered in detail. It is impossible to adequately consider legal data within the banking industry without reference to the Financial Crisis. The substantial regulatory change that has occurred affects how banks conduct business; therefore, legal data, once initially important for business optimisation and business processes, is now mandated for regulatory compliance.

For the purpose of this book, any reference made to the 'Financial Crisis' should be taken to mean the financial crisis of 2007–2008 and its subsequent impact. In the context of this book, by legal data, we are usually referring to legal agreement and/or legal opinion data, or that representing financial rules and regulations.

The Financial Crisis – Looking Back

The world of finance has undergone a tremendous period of change, including much retrospective questioning and attempted diagnoses, since the Financial Crisis. Albeit with the benefit of hindsight, the seeds and signs of impending trouble were undoubtedly present and grew in the build-up to the dramatic events of 2007. Many of the effects of the issues that came to light during the Financial Crisis unexpectedly compounded each other, catching out investors, dealers, banks, regulators and politicians.

Most put the cause of the Financial Crisis down to the rapid expansion of the securitisation markets and a backdrop of accommodative monetary policies serving to heighten the value of the housing market prior to 2007. Sub-prime borrowers were encouraged to take out more and bigger mortgages – in effect, creating an inflated 'housing bubble'.

Some also attribute the Financial Crisis to finance professionals who lost track of the risks they were generating by entering into securitised deals, compounded by a lack of regulation. Bank regulation in respect of the level of capital that banks need to hold based on the Basel Accords played a part in encouraging unconventional banking practices to optimise regulatory capital treatment, contributing to the Financial Crisis. The repeal of the Glass-Steagall Act removed the previously mandated separation of investment banks and depository banks, effectively providing a stamp of approval for a universal risk-taking bank model. Financial firms were allowed to move significant amounts of assets and liabilities off-balance sheet, into complex structures such as structured investment vehicles (SIVs), having the effect of masking the real risks, in particular, capital and leverage involved, only to be unmasked and unravelled during the full force of the Financial Crisis. Furthermore, the over-the-counter (OTC) derivatives market was substantially unregulated, however, it increased exponentially in volume and complexity. From supposedly being a risk-mitigant tool at heart, their usage quickly became a significant source of systemic risk in the midst of the Financial Crisis.

Overall, the explanations given for the Financial Crisis are still hugely contested. Perhaps this is because of the undeniable complexities of the subject and the banking system as a whole, leading to an oversimplification of its causative features, or maybe it is because of the tendency to lay blame or scapegoat on particular actors in the financial markets.

It is crucial, however, to remember that banking is ultimately about taking risks. Without the assumption of risk by those financial firms best placed to assume and manage the risk, there is no banking business and therefore no financial intermediation system. The issue was the inability to identify activities that were too risky for the banks to undertake, both by the banks themselves and by their regulators.

Within the financial markets, there was a natural incentive for the underpricing of systemic risk by financial institutions. Absent regulation, they were not commensurately burdened with the costs of the broader systemic risks, fostering and, in many cases, rewarding risky behaviour. Through the Financial Crisis, the public at large ultimately bore the burden of the market failure, due to the 'too big to fail' view of the largest financial firms.

Regulators' forecasts of serious problems and 'dire prophesies' years in advance of the Financial Crisis were largely ignored, partly because of the successful lobbying by the very financial institutions that are today either bankrupt or had to be rescued with government funding. For instance, the failures of the two federal agencies (Fannie Mae and Freddie Mac) were preceded in 2005 by a successful $2 million campaign by Freddie Mac to lobby Congress from restricting their own investments in higher-risk mortgages. These same agencies, banks and other institutions provided assurances that their lending practices (including those enabling loans without adequate documentation) were 'safe' based on evaluations of past data.

Data played a significant role through a failure to provide business intelligence on the underlying causes of the Financial Crisis, occurring not only at the individual firm level but also at the broader industry and supervisory level, and being unable to aggregate and derive the required intelligence in relation to the rising systemic risk beforehand. At the individual firm level, it is a significant failure that the data available and used to supposedly optimise the business decisions, in fact, could not even ensure survival in many cases.

Given this, it is welcome, and not surprising, that a number of the regulatory responses to the Financial Crisis have been to increase the banking data requirements, from transaction to trade and legal agreement-level reporting.

There have been issues identified concerning:

- the scope of data available (i.e. that within the shadow banking system, such as hedge funds and the OTC derivatives market);
- the understanding and governance of the data available;
- the quality of the data; and
- the way in which the data was used to derive the required business intelligence.

To better understand the role data should have played prior to the Financial Crisis, and needs to play going forward, from both business optimisation and regulatory perspectives, it is worth considering in more detail some of the causes of the Financial Crisis.

Causes of the Financial Crisis

The economic backdrop of the financial system is particularly crucial to explaining the onset of the Financial Crisis. Some commentators attribute the start of the Financial Crisis to the American Federal Reserve's change of policy post-2001. In the wake of the *dot-com* bubble bursting, the American Federal Reserve lowered their interest rates to 1% in an attempt to keep the economy strong. The implication of this low rate was a low return on investment for investors, causing them to limit their investment activities, but also an increase in borrowing. Many banks used this abundance of cheap credit as leverage. Essentially, this involved borrowing to amplify the outcome of a deal; using debt to, for example, buy larger quantities of a product than cash flow would otherwise allow and then selling that product for a huge profit, even after the cost of interest (see Figure 1.1).

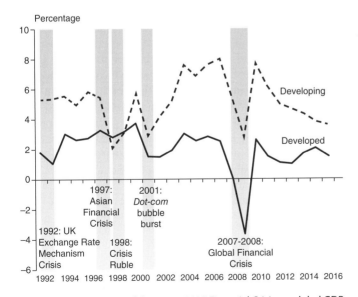

Figure 1.1 The impact of the 2007–2008 Financial Crisis on global GDP growth

The monetary policy increased financial institutions' willingness to take on risky assets, driving the demand for collateralised debt obligations (CDOs) and collateralised loan obligations (CLOs). These combined risky mortgages together with other financial assets before *slicing* them into different tiers, or tranches. Each slice – or tranche – would be made up of securities with different financial terms, meaning that they could then be marketed to investors based on the presumed level of risk. These tranches were prioritised such that the most senior tranche related to the lowest risk assets – offering safer assets, but a lower return. The most junior tranches would relate to the riskiest assets (and offer the highest returns), and if underlying assets defaulted, the tranches affected first would be the most junior ones, rising to more senior tranches as the level of losses increased. The aim was to construct a portfolio of well-diversified assets and reduce risk through diversification. However, the quality of the CDO/CLO depends on the quality of the assets in the portfolio and most importantly, on the correlation of different tranches, which is managed by a CDO/CLO manager.

Furthermore, there was an increased use of synthetic products – for example, a synthetic CDO where the underlying asset, such as a mortgage, is instead replaced with a synthetic equivalent, such as a credit default swap (or other derivatives). With a limited number of actual assets to meet the demand of these products (surely another data metric of note in assessing the build-up of systemic risk), these synthetic products thrived, being cheap and easy to create. In fact, synthetic issuance jumped from some $15 to $60 billion in the space of a single year in 2005, valued notionally at around $5 trillion. For example, the value and payment stream of a CDO would be replaced with premiums paying for 'insurance-like'[1] credit default swap protection on an underlying reference asset(s) from defaulting. This allowed speculative views to be taken on the underlying assets, even when they didn't ultimately exist. These assets hence offered a way to obfuscate the true risks being introduced into the global financial system and amplified, for example, the sub-prime mortgage bubble. The data available – used by the regulators and market participants – was incomplete, inaccurate or simply not fully understood in terms of the caveats to it (partly due to the sheer complexity of financial products and engineering).

In 2006, interest rates in the USA started to rise in an attempt to control inflationary pressures. This meant that homeowners began to struggle to make mortgage payments, especially in respect of sub-prime mortgages that had grown in the previously easy credit/low-interest-rate environment. Bank traders started to feel the impact of declining interest in CDOs/CLOs based on the growing issues with the underlying assets. There was therefore a repackaging of this risk by splitting out the problematic parts and creating new CDOs/CLOs with them – with large commissions and fees continuing to be paid both to traders and the CDO/CLO managers. Ironically, in many cases, the banks selling the CDOs were actually the investor, lending most of the funds to their clients in order to purchase them. This was a clear failing in the data aggregation to understand the vicious circle being

---

1 With apologies to the legal and regulatory correctness of this statement!

created, partly driven by the opacity of the inherent synthetic derivatives in these products, which increasingly formed a part of the more and more complex financial product engineering. Consider the CDO-cubeds that were created, a CDO that invested in CDO-squareds (which are CDOs that invested in other CDOs). As Les Leopold states in his 2009 book *The Looting of America: How Wall Street's Game of Fantasy Finance Destroyed our Jobs, Pensions, and Prosperity and What We Can DO About It*:

> *But what if you can't sell all the bottom tranches of the CDO-squared securities? You guessed it. You form another pool of these untouchables … and tranche away again.*

The modelling assumptions that had been used to manage the risk and diversify it ultimately failed in the Financial Crisis and could not sustain the plummeting asset prices at the very heart of these products. This left financial firms holding boxes of worthless (or close to!) CDOs/CLOs that could not be sold or used as collateral, despite rating agencies' seals of approval (yet another data shortcoming exposed in the Financial Crisis). This undermined the credit rating agencies' data, relied upon by investors to determine the level of risk, leading to a loss of confidence in the market. The Financial Crisis also exposed the potential effect of conflicts of interest, with the very same credit rating agencies that the banks relied upon to create the CDOs/CLOs being paid by the banks to provide the credit ratings that acted as a seal of approval to investors.

As the Financial Crisis started to unfold, financial institution traders, finding it harder to shift the CDOs/CLOs containing elements backed by riskier assets, would split these elements out and create new ones that effectively bought these 'toxic parts'. By creating new CDOs/CLOs, they were able to earn their commissions, with the CDO/CLO managers buying these new CDOs/CLOs with the traders' banks themselves lending most of the money to buy them. Effectively, the bank selling the CDOs/CLOs was itself the customer. As a higher and higher proportion of these CDOs/CLOs failed to sell, again they would be sliced up and the worst bits sold into new CDOs that the traders created, recursively self-dealing.

The OTC derivatives market was identified as one of the chief villains in the global crisis (Warren Buffet had famously previously labelled them as 'financial weapons of mass destruction' in 2003). As largely unregulated, bilateral arrangements, OTC derivatives were somewhat of a black-box to regulators. Their complexity resulted in significant information asymmetry between those using such products and the regulators. The well-documented derivatives troubles of Bear Stearns, AIG and investment banks post-crisis ultimately showed the lack of understanding of their inherent risks for even the supposedly most sophisticated of users. Derivatives originally came into being as a means to manage risk, as a protection against a possible catastrophe or market event. For example, farmers would enter into a contract where they would agree to sell their crops at a certain time in the future for a predetermined price. This meant that should the crops be negatively affected by bad weather or disease, the farmer could ensure he or she would still make money and a good living. But what started as a way to hedge risk could also be used as a speculative tool. The issue is that when packaged products become so complex that no one truly understands their underlying level of risk, they cannot be reliably used for the purposes of safely generating returns. Many banks who entered into derivative contracts did not know or understand the full extent of their liabilities. Moreover, the number of derivative contracts that were entered into, accumulating these risks, was huge and sufficient to cause financial disruption with the backdrop of the other market stresses developing.

An underlying problem at the heart of the Financial Crisis was that new instruments in structured finance (including derivatives and securitised and collateralised debt instruments such as syndicated loans, collateralised mortgage obligations and credit default swaps) developed so rapidly that the market infrastructure was not prepared when those instruments came under stress. Because of the complexity of many of these products, investors were unable to make independent judgments on the merits of investments, and the risks of aggregate effect market transactions were obscured. Moreover, regulatory requirements such as record-keeping and reporting were insufficient and fragmented, as they had not had time to be developed, nor did regulators ever realise the seriousness of the situation. Many commentators argue that regulators mishandled the Financial Crisis. They failed to exercise proper oversight of financial institutions and were unable to keep economic balances in check. According to *The Economist*, lax capital ratios proved to be the most significant regulatory shortcoming: regulatory rules prior to the Financial Crisis failed to define capital strictly enough, enabling banks to smuggle in forms of debt that did not have the same loss-absorbing capacity as equity. Essentially, banks were too highly leveraged and operated with insufficient equity to protect themselves in the event of disaster. Had they been in place, regulators could have been made aware that systemically vital institutions were without adequate capital and that the market was at risk of collapse. The problem is that, as explained by the economist Brian Wesbury, the onus could never have been on the dealers trading with these instruments. He describes the financial climate in the run-up to the recession as being like a system of traffic lights and argues that when a traffic light is green, you will never see a driver get out of their car to check the traffic light at the adjoining junction is red so that it is safe to cross the intersection. Likewise, when interest rates are down to as low as they were, it is only natural that banks and investors will leverage and make the most of seemingly good opportunities. The onus should have been and – even more so – is now on the regulators to ensure that the system and its inherent risks are properly managed.

The chasing of short-term profits and individual incentivisation schemes encouraged an unsustainable level of short-term risk-taking and reliance on financial modelling. Simply consider AIG. This major insurer of debts via credit default swaps placed 'blind faith in financial risk models' and for a few years their small elite staff of financial modellers generated large incomes for the firm (and equally large bonuses for individuals). However, that later turned into decimating losses for AIG as the mathematical credit risk models developed, and the data they provided, were ultimately incorrect. There was significant underestimation of the likelihood of sudden large events, which are especially important in the credit markets as the tail of a distribution is key in predicting the defaults that typically have a low probability of occurrence and a failure to consider inter-related systematic risks.

In fact, the regulatory community had itself not been alert to the growing systemic risks and if anything was misled by the data, in terms of scope, timeliness, accuracy and aggregation. In an article entitled 'Market-based risk is changing banking', the then leaders of the banking and capital markets sector of the FSA claimed:

> From 'hold what you originate' the business model of banking is shifting to 'underwrite to distribute, and buy what makes sense to hold.' Banks are shifting to market-based risk management [...]. Traditionally, banks originated loans to customers, which they held on their balance sheet until maturity. Banks still originate loans, but aim to reduce their exposure, either by selling participations in the loan to other investors – not all of them necessarily banks – by securitising the loans, or by buying credit protection in the derivatives market.
>
> At the same time, banks are buying exposures to credits not only through purchases of participations in loans originated by others, but also through selling credit protection and buying collateralised debt and loan obligations (CDOs and CLOs) [...]. Regulation supports this move towards market-based risk management. Under Basel 2 and the Capital Requirements Directive, capital regulation is moving in the direction of economic capital. Capital is now assessed in line with risk, and the new capital regulation framework gives much more adequate recognition for credit mitigation factors such as derivatives and securitisation. (Financial Times 2007)

Ultimately, of course, it is hard to argue, post-crisis, that the recognition of these factors was, in fact, misled. In most cases, the data available did not allow recognition that, rather than dispersing the risks, many turned out to be concentrated in entities that were unable to bear them. For example:

- Conduits and SIVs held the assets with substantial leverage coupled with maturity and liquidity risk – therefore very vulnerable to classic bank 'runs'.
- Banks ended up with indirect exposures (through contingent credit lines, reputational risks and counterparty credit exposures) to many of these vehicles (despite assuming, from their knowledge of the risks and supporting data, that the risks had been transferred away).

Systemic Financial Contagion

The seriousness of the onset of financial contagion demonstrates the importance of the regulatory landscape in avoiding future systemic failures in the financial sector. Once the Financial Crisis had fully started to take hold, the market was overwhelmed with firms trying close-out trades at the same time. However, different financial institutions were also inter-related and dependent on each other, as they had all been borrowing from and transacting with each other. Cross-default clauses in financial contracts, which will be discussed later within this text in detail, demonstrate part of the problem when it comes to the interconnectedness of financial institutions. Standard default and termination clauses in financial contracts mean that if a party to the contract fails to perform its financial obligations, the other party can terminate the arrangement. Cross-default clauses put a party into default if they default on another obligation under a separate contract with a third party. This can have a domino effect; if one party defaults under one relationship, other defaults are triggered elsewhere.

Additionally, when – during the Financial Crisis – counterparties started to default and could no longer rely on failed institutions' promises to fulfil their commitments, financial institutions began to lose trust in one another, causing them to withhold short-term credit. This became known as the *credit crunch* – a crisis caused by a sudden reduction in the availability of liquidity in the financial markets. Gokay (2009) describes the credit crisis as being comparable to a heart attack:

> *Every modern economic activity depends for their day-to-day activities on continuous borrowing and lending. […] If it is not dealt with properly, the whole system immobilizes. That is why all those governments rushed to interfere, pouring billions of dollars into private banks, hoping the recipients will use the cash to start lending and borrowing again.*

Financial contagion can occur on both a domestic and an international level and can be observed via co-movements in exchange rates, stock prices and capital flows. However, this is not a problem that can be resolved purely by the inflow of more capital into the market. It is not likely that the financial sector will ever start trading or lending again with the same relaxed attitude, even once liquidity has fully improved. Moreover, the influx of regulatory requirements is now seemingly a thing of permanence.

The Legal Data Consequence

Each of the identified vulnerabilities that helped cause the Financial Crisis or increase its intensity (lack of capital, liquidity risk and so on) catalysed banking regulatory reform. Such regulatory reform has included the introduction of:[2]

- The US Dodd–Frank Act
- The Basel Committee's Third Accord
- The European Market Infrastructure Regulation (EMIR)
- The Alternative Investment Fund Managers Directive (AIFMD)
- The Market Abuse Regulation (MAR)
- The Markets in Financial Instruments Regulation (MiFIR)
- The Foreign Account Tax Compliance Act (FATCA)
- Client Assets Sourcebook – Client Money and Assets Rules (CASS)
- Margin for Uncleared Derivatives Regulation
- Securities Financing Transaction Regulation (SFTR)
- Recovery & Resolution Regulation [such as Recordkeeping Requirements on Qualified Financial Contracts (QFC) and the Bank Recovery and Resolution Directive (BRRD)]

Accordingly, the sector has been hit by a torrent of new regulatory requirements. Many of the above regulations mandate, or indirectly require, a number of data

---

2 This list contains a number of overlaps and inconsistencies, and has a focus on US and EU regulation, but is intended to present a good picture of the coverage of regulated themes, rather than anything remotely approaching a comprehensive list.

reporting requirements, from the reporting of transactions to that of key contractual terms. Ultimately, many financial instruments, and therefore their consequences that need to be better understood, managed and regulated, simply consist of a series of complex contractual obligations – or legal data. It is this legal data that is the subject of this book, seeking to demystify and provide guidance on some of the challenges that exist in ensuring this data on the contractual obligations is complete, accurate and ultimately useful, from the perspective of business optimisation, operational management or regulatory compliance. Increasingly, there is criminal liability attached to ensuring operational effect is given to meeting regulatory mandates, significantly increasing the burden of reliance on legal data by senior management at financial institutions, such as in the context of the treatment of client assets and money.

It should be noted that the post-crisis regulatory response, whilst large-scale in the changes made to the fundamental banking infrastructure in many parts, has also brought out and increased differences in standards and expectations globally. There is also an increasing need to maintain data on the regulations themselves and to be able to understand the cumulative impact for an impacted firm – yet again, a significant data challenge. In an ever-increasingly globalised world, this also, with the prospect of regulatory arbitrage it brings, raises the challenge for supervisory bodies utilising data to be on top of the consequences of regulation.

Bibliography

Associated Press (2008) 'Bush administration ignored clear warnings', *Associated Press*, 12th January 2008

Berkshire Hathaway Inc. (2003) 2002 Annual Report

Dewar, Sally and Huertas, Thomas (2007) 'Market-based risk is changing banks', *The Financial Times*, 8th May 2007

Gokay, B. (2009) 'The 2008 world economic crisis: Global shifts and faultlines', *Global Research*, 15th February 2009

Greenberger, M. (2010) 'The role of derivatives in the financial crisis', Financial Crisis Inquiry Commission Hearing, Washington, DC

Jameson, R. (2008) 'The blunders that led to the banking crisis', *New Scientist*, 27th September 2008

Morgenson, G. (2008) 'Behind insurer's crisis, blink eye to a web of risk', *The New York Times*, 27th September 2008

Murphy, A. (2000) *Scientific Investment Analysis*, 2nd edn. Quorum Books: Westport, CT

Murphy, A. (2008) 'An analysis of the financial crisis of 2008: Causes and solutions' (http://dx.doi.org/10.2139/ssrn.1295344)

The Economist (2013) 'The origins of the financial crisis: Crash course', *The Economist*, 7th September 2013

United Nations Organisation (2017) 'Global context for achieving the 2030 agenda for sustainable development: Sustained global economic growth', Development Issues No. 8 (www.un.org/development/desa/dpad/publication/development-issues-no-8-global-context-for-achieving-the-2030-agenda-for-sustainable-development-sustained-global-economic-growth/)

Wesbury, B. (2014) 'The real truth about the 2008 financial crisis', *TEDxCountyLineRoad* (YouTube video)

Yost, P. (2008) 'AP IMPACT: Mortgage firm arranged stealth impact', *Associated Press*, 20th October 2008

Zuckerman, G. (2009) *The Greatest Trade Ever: The Behind-the-Scenes Story of How John Paulson Defied Wall Street and Made Financial History.* Broadway Books: New York

2

The Law, Legal System and Basics of Contract Law

This chapter will be trite for any legal student or practitioner, however, we hope invaluable for those approaching this text without formal legal training or experience. In order to fully appreciate and ensure legal data helps to ultimately unlock business value, one needs to understand the context of the law, the legal system and – of particular relevance in respect of the banking and finance industry – the basics of contract law (given that financial instruments are at heart, simply a series of contractual obligations).

This chapter starts with a discussion of the differences between civil and common law systems concerning choice of governing law, before explaining the different requisite elements of valid and enforceable legal contracts, followed by a discussion of how contract law sits alongside other relevant areas of law.

Chapter 3 will provide details of financial instruments themselves, before considering the fundamentals of 'data' in Chapter 4.

Legal Systems and Traditions

We will begin by outlining some of the most major legal traditions before delving into the legal systems most commonly used in the world of international finance, namely English and New York law. The term 'legal system' refers to the content or body of the law generally, along with the means by which it is enacted and adjudicated. A 'legal tradition', on the other hand, is a less specific term, referring to the general similarities shared between a family of legal systems. Contemporary legal systems that exist around the world today can be primarily categorised into a number of different traditions: civil, common, religious or even a combination of these. The legal system of a jurisdiction is resultant of its individual history and the legal evolution it has undergone over a period of time. As a result, all jurisdictions encompass unique variations. So, it is important to bear in mind that, whilst legal systems are capable of being broadly categorised into one or more of a number of legal traditions, any categorisation does not promise to describe the intricacies individual to a particular jurisdiction entirely. It is useful to understand the main legal traditions to achieve an overall feel of how the law works as a whole, before considering the more particular elements of an individual legal system.

A key example is the British common law tradition. Many British colonies replicated the British legal system at the time (major legal traditions tend to be associated with the original legal system as it then existed rather than as it exists today). As such, the legal systems used in countries such as Australia, India, Canada and the USA – although now individually unique – follow the same legal tradition due to their Anglo-Saxon roots. The English common law is now the most widespread legal system in the world, with 30% of the world's population living under it, according to Professor Philip Wood.

Common and Civil Law Traditions

Although legal systems can vary greatly, most jurisdictions mainly follow one of two major legal traditions: common or civil law. In common law systems, judicial decisions previously made in similar cases are of primary importance. These judicial decisions, which collectively form a body of case law, are used as precedents to be applied in the decisions of new cases. In contrast to civil law systems hold case law to be of secondary importance, subordinate to statutes. Statutes are written laws passed by the relevant legislative body of the jurisdiction in question and will specify matters capable of being brought before a court, the procedure by which this should be done and the appropriate consequences. As such, judicial decisions in civil law systems are primarily made from codified compilations of statutes. To fully understand the differences and similarities between common and civil law traditions, it is beneficial to start by tracing back the historical context of both.

The common law emerged during the Middle Ages in Anglo-Saxon England. At the time, the English monarchy would issue 'writs'. A writ was essentially a royal order commanding an individual to act or abstain from acting in a particular way. Each writ provided a specific remedy to a specific wrong. However, writs were limited in their ability to cover all situations and achieve justice, because they were so rigid in their application. In an attempt to overcome this issue, further appeals to justice could be made directly to the King. While originally exceptional in nature, by the time of King Henry II (in the latter part of the 12th century), the use of writs had become a regular part of the system of royal justice in England, evolving into the establishment of the courts of equity (also known as the 'Court of Chancery', because it was the court of the King's Chancellor). The function of the court of equity was to hear complaints and formulate appropriate remedies based on the *equitable principles of fairness*. These equitable principles were founded on many sources of authority, including Roman law and the philosophy of 'natural' law. These decisions were collected and published, making it possible for courts to apply past decisions to current cases to achieve a degree of consistency, impartiality, transparency and therefore *fairness*.

Today, the common law and equity are now administered by the same court. Equity is only applied at the discretion of the court and is used on the basis of a number of general principles known as *equitable maxims*. Some key examples include the maxims: 'Equity follows the law', meaning that equity cannot override the common law or statute; 'Equity looks at the substance, not the form', meaning that equity will look at what something is rather than what something is called; 'He who seeks equity must do equity' or 'He who comes to equity must come with clean hands', meaning that a party wanting to use equity must act fairly towards their opponent for it to apply; and 'Delay defeats equity', meaning that failing to claim equitable rights within a reasonable period of time will prevent a party from using equity.

Historically, the courts of equity have shown a greater concern to enforce promises than to uphold a bargain. One significant difference between contract and equity are the remedies available. Unlike legal remedies such as damages, which are granted to a successful claimant by right, equitable remedies are given at the discretion of the court and can include an injunction, specific performance, rescission, rectification and so on.

The civil law tradition started to emerge at the same time as the common law. Originating in Roman law (which required codification due to its intricacy), the civil law tradition later spread into continental Europe, where it was applied in the colonies of imperial powers such as Spain and Portugal. Due to the codified nature of a civil law system, its uniformity promised a higher degree of certainty for citizens and judges than that offered by the common law. The political and social climate required such certainty in those regions in respect of the protection of property and the rule of law.

Whereas the common law operates as an *adversarial* system, the civil law operates as an *inquisitorial* one. This distinction is important because it assists in explaining the different approach of each system in the event of a case being brought before a judge. Under an 'adversarial' system, each side to a dispute presents its opinion. The judge – who acts as an arbiter or referee between each side – then analyses the case law that presents similar (but not identical) fact patterns. By doing this, the judge can apply the law in light of the arguments presented by both sides to deduce a result. This means making inferences by reference to general principles. The legal premise that underpins this system is that the argumentation between two opposing sides will lead to the best determination of the truth. Importantly, common law judges are also able to propose new rules to cover facts that have not yet presented themselves. Under an 'inquisitorial' system, in contrast, a judge or the court is actively involved in investigating the facts of the case. The premise underpinning this system is that the truth is best discovered through an impartial inquiry. Though the judge plays an active part in investigating the facts of the case, the judge must still work within a framework established by the codified laws that have been put in place. So, because the law within a civil system is designed to cover all eventualities, the implication is that the judges have a more limited role. Instead, they take a more investigative role. Consequently, judges have less scope to shape the law than the legislators who draft it.

In practice, many legal systems use a mixture of features from both traditions. After all, both systems utilise similar sources of law – both employ statute *and* case law, neither rely on one instead of the other. The central distinction is that they approach regulation and resolve issues in different ways. As already outlined above, although statute is of importance to both, civil law codes systematically and exhaustively consider statute before turning to jurisprudence, whereas common law uses case law as its core set of rules and uses statute to complete it. As such, the English legal system is comprised of a combination of both common law and statutory law (albeit the latter operating at a more substantive, prescriptive level).

Within banking and finance, new codified laws are intermittently issued by various government agencies in the UK. For example, the Bank of England Prudential Regulation Authority (PRA) has issued EU prudential rules for banks, building societies and investment firms, including the EU Capital Requirements Directive IV (CRD IV) – an EU legislative package in accordance with Basel III. It is these rules and regulations that will be discussed later in this book.

Governing Law

As we have already established, different jurisdictions have different and unique sets of laws, although we can trace some similarities between them due to broader legal traditions. When parties enter into a contractual relationship – especially in the context of an international transaction where a contract is likely to be connected with more than one jurisdiction – it is commonplace to decide which laws will apply via a 'governing law' clause.

A governing law clause specifies the legal rules that will govern a contract (e.g. the laws of England and Wales). This is relevant to the way in which a contract will be interpreted and the enforceability of the provisions of the contract. The courts of a particular jurisdiction may sometimes intervene in a contract to apply their own laws (notwithstanding a governing law clause, essentially an expression of the laws which the contracting parties are seeking to apply). For example, the courts may apply their own consumer protection or insolvency laws, above and beyond the terms of the contract. Conflicts of law, detailing the interaction between governing law clauses and the rules of private international law, can be very complex.

Without such a governing law clause, in the event of a dispute relating to a contract, the parties would have to determine which set of laws would be used to interpret the obligations of the parties, before being able to resolve the actual matter at hand. Accordingly, the governing law seeks to help frame the specific rights and obligations of the parties flowing from it (considering the possible overarching applicable non-contractual rules and regulations).

The choice of governing law will be a function of both the scope and reach of the rules and regulations of a particular legal system. Some laws are more 'extra-territorial' than others (e.g. US tax law) – meaning that they will be a function of the location in which the relevant parties or assets are located.

When a party considers its choice of governing law, the following considerations need to be taken into account:

1) Reputation – particularly for providing fairness and certainty.
2) Popularity – in the context of banking and finance, its use in international commercial and financial contracts.
3) Accessibility of competent and experienced lawyers (for the purposes of initially putting contractual arrangements in place, as well as for dispute resolution in the event of a dispute under the contract once it has been entered into).

As an aside, it should be noted that in certain circumstances, there may be merit in one system of law applying to specific clauses in a contract and another system applying to the remainder. This can have a significant impact from a banking regulatory perspective; for example, contractual requirements on termination stay provisions under recovery and resolution, or the operational requirements of client assets and money regulation. In common law, the term 'dépeçage' is usually used to refer to a single contract, which provides that different laws shall govern different parts. Dépeçage can arise in the OTC derivatives context, which will be explored in Chapter 3, where an International Swaps and Derivatives Association (ISDA) Master Agreement governed by English law is used, for example, in conjunction with a New York law-governed Credit Support Annex. This may be done if the party providing collateral over which security is being taken is located in the USA, as well as the collateral itself, and therefore would be preferable to be governed by New York law.[1]

Why Does the Common Law Dominate the Financial Sector?

Even with the best intentions, a contract is unlikely to cover every single contingency and disputes will from time to time inevitably arise. Ultimately, the respective benefits and drawbacks of the laws within different jurisdictions impact upon the choice one might make with regards to the governing law. With this in mind, parties need to think carefully about their choice of governing law.

Some might argue that the civil law system is more stable than common law systems, because laws are stated explicitly and are therefore easier to discern. If we turn back to the origination of the civil law tradition (as discussed above), its *raison d'être* was to codify the complexities and intricacies of Roman law to ensure its usability from the perspective of both citizens and the judiciary. As such, in some ways, it could be said that parties entering into a contract may be enticed by the certainty of entering into a contract under a civil law system. In civil law countries, contracts and penalty clauses are strictly enforced. This means that, if a party has acted illegally, a civil law court will remedy the situation. However, there is a downside to this. If a party has acted immorally or in bad faith, but not *illegally*, a civil law court may not be able to remedy the wrong since statute will not specifically cover it. This makes it possible for parties to more easily structure unfair transactions, even though they conform to the letter of the law, thereby offering weaker protection to investors.

The common law system offers predictability, transparency and flexibility, unlike its more rigid and prescriptive civil law counterpart. Because judges can quickly adapt the common law and without the need for legislation to be amended, a great deal of benefit can be derived from the flexibility of the common law. Judges are not strictly bound by the clauses of the contract and have greater freedom to interpret them, meaning they can determine whether the parties acted in accordance with the *spirit* of the contract and not just the black letter of the law. A good example of this would be penalty clauses (which specify sanctions for failure to abide by the terms of the agreement). Under the US common law system, penalty clauses are generally inapplicable because the judge determines whether a contractual promise has been broken and, even if it has been, can alter the contractual penalty. Under the English common law, a contract with penalty clauses is typically accepted as valid – therefore offering a degree of certainty – *unless* it is for an illegal purpose or is otherwise contrary to public policy. Both these approaches provide an additional safeguard and makes it clear that parties should contract not just to the letter of the law, but with a more holistic view in mind.

Different legal systems differ in their attitude to debt, credit and insolvency. Some favour the debtor, some favour the creditor and others offer a balance between the two. Both the English and US common law systems are generally creditor-friendly in respect of insolvency issues, whereas Napoleonic systems tend to favour the debtor, with Roman-Germanic systems falling in between.

---

1 Note that a governing law is related to, but distinct from, the contractual jurisdiction. Contractual jurisdiction clauses specify the courts that (the parties want to) have the right to adjudicate disputes relating to a contract.

The Dominance of English and New York Law for International Finance

English and New York law are significant in their dominance as the governing law for documentation used for international finance. Even where another governing law is chosen, the drafting tends to conform to an international standard, reflecting the City of London or New York usage. Much of this is for the reasons detailed above. Documentation for complex project financing looks similar wherever the underlying project is situated. It might even be said that 'the [global financial] markets have created a kind of global law by contract'. That said, the divergences in regulatory standards post-crisis have eroded into the benefit of this.

A distinction must be drawn between US and New York (or other state) laws. US law is the *supreme law of the land*, meaning that all other (state) laws are subordinate to it and it binds judges (in every state). US law is comprised of different forms of law, the most important of which being the US Constitution. States may grant their citizens broader rights, so long as they do not infringe on any constitutional rights, in the form of state law, which can vary significantly from one state to the next. New York law is a source of state law under the Constitution of New York (which in turn is subordinate only to US law). Both New York and English law operate common law systems, so there are certain inherent similarities. As was the case for many British colonies, US law was initially derived from the English common law system. It subsequently diverged over time, both in terms of substance and procedure, and now also incorporates some features of the civil law system.

As already established, the choice of law can have an impact on the outcome of a case. This is true for even seemingly minor reasons such as stylistic word choice. For example, English contracts tend to use the wording 'best endeavours' to oblige a party to commit to an absolute obligation, whereas 'best efforts' is generally preferable under US law. Using terms that differ from the specific wording provided above increases the risk that the courts will deem the parties to have implied a different meaning. As a further example, many US states require that for indemnity terms to be enforceable, they must be clearly visible, whereas English courts do not require this. A more major difference would be the implied duty of good faith imposed by many US states, which is not matched under English law. This means that parties to a US contract may be able to recover damages for unfair dealing or lack of good faith, whereas damages would not be available in the English courts under the same circumstances.

Contract Formation

To understand the contractual obligations formed within financial instruments, it is important to consider contract formation. For simplicity, this has been limited to consideration of English law (although the differences under a New York law analysis are not regarded as substantial for the background this provides for the text as a whole).

English contract law is based on a combination of both common law and statute. As such, two (or more) parties may enter into a contract, and they may agree to whatever terms they wish. However, these terms are limited to the extent that if there is a disagreement further down the line and the case is taken to court, the outcome of the disagreement will be judged based on precedent from similar, past cases, as well as the rules stipulated by statute. Case law stipulates the elements that are required for the formation of a valid and enforceable contract, and these are discussed below. Note that there are many specialist areas of contract law, such as shipping and insurance contracts, as well as contracts of employment. In many important ways, these areas depart from ordinary contractual rules, since they are governed by additional legislation enacted for this purpose. It should also be noted that this is increasingly the case in some aspects of banking and capital markets contracts.

The highly regarded English law academic, G. H. Treitel, defined a contract as: 'an agreement giving rise to obligations which are enforced or recognised by law'. The agreement encompassed by a contract, as a general rule, has no prescribed form. This means a contract may be written or spoken (or even present via conduct), so long as it is communicated and so long as it is intended to be enforceable by law. Certain contracts, such as oral contracts, however, are more challenging to enforce as there is no clear record of some of the necessary elements of a contract required for enforceability. Treitel's definition can be broken down into three distinct parts: an agreement, (an) obligation(s) and legal enforceability. This maps nicely onto the following elements, which are recognised and enforced by the courts: (1) offer and acceptance; (2) an intention between the parties to create binding legal relations; (3) consideration; (4) legal capacity of the parties to act; (5) genuine consent of the parties; and (6) legality of the agreement. The first three of these elements will be explained in some detail below.

Offer and Acceptance

A contract requires that an offeror makes an offer, which is then accepted by an offeree. A valid offer must be clear and certain, communicated to the offeree and open (it must not have lapsed, have been revoked or have been rejected, as discussed at a later stage in this chapter). Whether an offer has been made is to be judged objectively: 'the alleged offeror will be bound if his words or conduct are such as to induce a reasonable person to believe that he intends to be bound, even though he, in fact, has no such intention'. As such, an offer may be made formally in writing or informally by words (with some exceptions, such as interests in land or guarantees, both of which must be written), or conduct. The typical process of entering into a financial derivatives contract highlights the way in which agreements can be entered into without a written contract – at least initially. OTC (or off-exchange) derivatives trading is done directly between two parties, without the use of an 'exchange' (an organised market purpose-built for the trading of financial products such as securities, commodities, foreign exchange, futures and options). OTC derivatives transactions often take place over the phone, and the written contract follows later. The contract is entered into from the moment the parties agree to the terms over the phone. Of course, oral contracts are riskier, as there may be practical problems of proof when trying to enforce an oral contract in the courts, but oral contracts are still generally accepted as legally binding nonetheless.

An offer can be distinguished from an 'invitation to treat'. Whereas an offer is 'an expression of willingness to contract on specified terms, made with the intention that it is to become legally binding as soon as it is accepted by the person to whom it is addressed', an invitation to treat is merely an expression of willingness to enter into negotiations. The best way to understand this is to think of an invitation to treat as a preliminary stage to reaching an agreement, where one party is trying to ascertain whether another party would be willing to contract and, if so, upon what terms. An invitation to treat is apparent from the intention of the person making it, as revealed by their words and/or actions, together with the surrounding circumstances (although note that the words used by the parties themselves are not themselves conclusive. An offer may indeed be an invitation to treat or vice versa, as was shown in *Clifton v Palumbo* and *Spencer v Harding*). For example, when an individual walks into a supermarket and sees goods displayed on a shelf, or walks past an advert on a billboard, these scenarios constitute invitations to treat rather than offers. In the case of *Fisher v Bell* for example, the defendant was charged and convicted with the criminal offence of offering a knife for sale as he displayed a flick knife in his shop window with a price tag on it. Statute had made it a criminal offence to offer such knives for sale under section 1 of the Restriction of Offensive Weapons Act 1959. The conviction was, however, quashed on the basis that goods displayed in a shop window in this manner are not contractual offers, but rather invitations to treat.

Offers can be categorised as unilateral or bilateral. The famous example of *Carlill v Carbolic Smoke Ball Co* shows how a unilateral contract is formed as purely one-sided without the offeror having any idea as to whether it will be taken up and accepted or by whom. A good example of this would be a lost-and-found scenario, where a reward is offered to anyone who can find the missing item. The vast majority of commercial contracts, however, are bilateral contracts, which are negotiated on a promise-for-promise basis between two parties. Acceptance must be communicated by the offeree (or by an authorised third party and maybe by conduct) in response to the offer. It must also be a mirror image of the offer, so that the offer and the acceptance match. If, in the reply to an offer, there are new terms introduced and/or variations to the terms are made, the reply cannot be an acceptance. Instead, it may constitute a counteroffer.

In the complex world of banking and capital markets today, it can be difficult to determine the precise stages of offer and acceptance. This was shown in the case of *New Zealand Shipping Co Ltd v AM Satterthwaite & Co Ltd (The Eurymedon)*. Lord Wilberforce gave the judgment that it is only the precise analysis of this complex of relations into the classical offer and acceptance, with identifiable consideration, that seems to present difficulty, but this same difficulty exists in many situations of daily life. He gave numerous examples of this point in action, including: sales at auction, supermarket purchases, boarding an omnibus, purchasing a train ticket, tenders for the supply of goods, offers of rewards, acceptance by post, warranties of authority by agents, manufacturers' guarantees, gratuitous bailments and bankers' commercial credits. These are all examples which show that English law, having committed itself to a rather technical and schematic doctrine of contract, in application takes a practical approach, often at the cost of forcing the facts to fit uneasily into the marked slots of offer, acceptance and consideration. Note however, that Lord Diplock was of the view that it is only exceptional cases which cannot be analysed in this way.

In a commercial context, the words 'subject to contract' are often used by parties who are negotiating as to the terms of a contract to indicate that documents passing from one to another are not intended to be offers capable of acceptance so as to form a binding contract. This is the case when, for example, a bank enters into a loan agreement with another party and uses a term sheet. A term sheet is a document that outlines the terms by which the bank makes the loan and it therefore typically contain the words 'subject to contract', in order to make clear that the term sheet is itself not legally binding and that the parties do not intend a contract to come into being until they have signed the relevant contract (with the terms contained in the term sheet being more of a guide or indicative expression of the terms).

There are six ways in which an offer can be brought to an end before acceptance:

1) revocation;
2) rejection by the offeree;
3) lapse of time (where expressed to be for a certain period);[2]
4) occurrence of a terminating condition;
5) death (if the offer is dependent on the offeror personally); and
6) insanity, incapacity, insolvency or impossibility.

Legal Relations

Not every agreement leads to a binding contract that can be enforced through the courts, who deal with legal duties only (as opposed to moral ones). The requirement of an intention to create legal relations assists in removing cases that have no place in court. When an offer is made, it is made with the intention that it shall become binding as soon as it is accepted by the person to whom it is addressed, whether that be an individual, a group of people, or the world at large – the offeror is bound if it is accepted. Where the agreement is a commercial one, there is a presumption that the parties intended to enter into legal relations. This means that the party bringing an action to a court of law does not need to have to prove intention in order to succeed; the court will presume its existence. However, this presumption can be rebutted if a contrary intention is expressed.

'Legal capacity' is the ability of a contracting party to enter into legally binding relations, without which a contract is invalid. Parties will still have legal capacity if they do not have full knowledge of the relevant subject matter, are illiterate or unfamiliar with the English language, and consequently are unlikely to be released from their contractual obligations. Parties will not have legal capacity if they are minors or are mentally incapacitated (although this does not mean they are exempt from entering into legal relations). Ultimately, parties to a contract must genuinely consent, and there must be no duress (duress being the threat of violence or unlawful constraint). It can be easy to assume such matters are not relevant for the modern-day banking industry, but there are timely reminders of the importance of these items from cases such as *Hazell v Hammersmith* and *Fulham London Borough Council*, where a House of Lords decision on an *ultra vires* point, the power of a local council to enter into 'derivative swap transactions', was found to be missing (albeit there were a number of political factors at play which transcended some of the legal contractual analysis itself).

Consideration

Consideration refers to 'the price for which the promise is bought' and is a requirement for a valid and enforceable contract. This was defined by Lush J in *Currie v Misa*: 'a valuable consideration in the sense of the law may consist either in some right, interest

---

2 The relevance of this in modern-day finance can be seen, for example, through the differing 'adherence' windows for ISDA protocols.

or profit or benefit accruing to one party, or some forbearance, detriment, loss or responsibility given suffered or undertaken by the other'. An individual wishing to enforce a contract must show that they have brought something to the bargain which has value in the eyes of the law. Value may be brought either by conferring a benefit on another person or by incurring a detriment at their request. In practice, this cannot include, for example, gratitude or love, things already done in the past, or the promise to perform a pre-existing duty. However, there is no requirement that the consideration is *adequate*, so long as it is *sufficient*. What this means is that consideration need not be market value, so long as it has *some* value.

Guarantees and Indemnities

Guarantees and indemnities are a means by which creditors protect themselves from the risk of default. A guarantee is a secondary obligation, contingent on the obligation of a third party, who promises to ensure that the third party fulfils its obligations and/or promises to pay the amount owed by the party if it fails to do so itself. An indemnity, on the other hand, is the contractual promise of a third party to accept liability for loss. It is a primary obligation because it is independent of the obligation of the party to the beneficiary of the indemnity under which the loss arose. Guarantees and indemnities constitute informal gratuitous promises, as they are not supported by consideration. An informal gratuitous promise may, however, be formalised by being made under seal as a *deed*. A deed is a document containing all the terms of the agreement but requires an additional execution formality beyond a simple signature. It must be signed in the presence of a witness and sealed and delivered as a deed, as per section 1 of the Law of Property (Miscellaneous Provisions) Act 1989. Guarantees and indemnities, for example, are often executed as deeds to avoid these issues surrounding consideration.

Enforceability of Contracts

So, whilst most contracts can be either written or oral and still be legally enforceable, some agreements must be in writing in order to be binding. Other contracts – along with deeds – that are required to be in writing by statute include contracts of a lease of more than 3 years, contracts for the sale or disposition of land, the transfer of shares in a limited company, bills of sale (Bills of Sale Act (1878) Amendment Act 1882) and promissory notes (ss 3(1) and 17(2) Bills of Exchange Act 1882), regulated consumer credit and consumer hire agreements (Consumer Credit Act 1974), the assignment of the benefit of contractual rights (s 136 Law of Property Act 1925), the assignment of a number of intellectual property rights (ss 90(3) and 222(3) Copyright Designs and Patents Act 1988) and guarantees. For a deed or other instrument to be rendered invalid by an alteration that was not approved by all the parties to it, the party seeking to avoid the contract must show that the alteration was one which was potentially prejudicial to that party's legal rights or obligations (*Raiffeisen Zentralbank Osterreich AG v Crossseas Shipping Ltd* – a space left blank in a guarantee was later filled in, but the guarantee was regarded as enforceable since alteration did not change the liabilities under it).

Importantly, the elements required for a valid and enforceable contract as described above are used to protect the parties. Term sheets (see above) are also used for the protection of the parties by precluding the possibility of misunderstanding or dispute but are not contractual *per se*. Through the addition of various representations and warranties, coupled with due diligence, the context of the agreement is set such that the impact of the contractual obligations of the agreement being entered into is clearly understood.

Auction Sales

As a general rule, an auctioneer's request for bids is an invitation to treat. An offer is only made once a bidder places a bid, which the auctioneer is free to either reject or accept. An offer can be withdrawn at any time before acceptance, which means that a bidder may retract their offer up until the point that the auctioneer's hammer falls. There are some exceptions to this; namely, where there is an auction without a reserve. In this case, when the auctioneer states the auction will be without a reserve, a unilateral offer is made. The highest bidder accepts this offer when they make their bid. Modern-day finance does often utilise such mechanisms as auction sales (e.g. credit derivative swap auction sales).

Battle of the Forms

Offer and acceptance should be mirror images of one another. When two parties negotiate the terms of a contract, each party will want to contract on the basis of its own terms and will try to ensure that it is their terms that prevail. That is the very essence of the contract negotiation process. The rule is that offer and acceptance should be mirror images of one another, but this can give rise to what is called 'a battle of the forms' where, when it comes to execution, two different contracts, 'forms', in terms of the precise wording, have actually been executed.

Two problems surrounding this 'battle of the forms' may arise over the course of commercial negotiation if the traditional process of offer, counteroffer and acceptance is applied, which may cause unwanted legal effects:

1) There may, in fact, be no contract at all, because of the absence of a mirror offer and acceptance.
2) There may be a contract referable to the last set of terms to be sent before performance.

In the situation outlined in (1), a contract does not exist, which if unknown to the parties is clearly significant, given the impact of such a finding if that occurs after the parties have continued dealing, both on the basis that their own version of the 'form' is correct.

It may be possible to obtain payment on a restitutionary basis so that the receiving party would not be unjustly enriched by the receipt of goods that have not been paid for. It was decided in *Butler Machine Tool Co Ltd v Ex-cell-O Corporation Ltd* that if the variance is insignificant, the offeree can impose a variation without drawing the offeror's specific attention to it. If the variation is significant, however, and would affect the price, it must be drawn to the attention of the offeror as it would be regarded as a new offer.

When a contract is referable to the last set of terms sent before performance, as outlined in (2), the 'last shot' invariably appears to be the significant document in determining who wins (or loses) the battle of forms, because of the possibility of acceptance of this counteroffer by conduct.

In the context of the ISDA Master Agreement, Global Master Repurchase Agreement or other standard industry pre-print contracts, it is not uncommon for parties to protect against a change by the counterparty to the standard terms, which has not been noticed by the party, by including wording that it is the parties' intention for the pre-print wording to apply, and any changes to the pre-print itself not specifically acknowledged shall not be effective.

Principal and Agent

The 'principal–agent' relationship is an arrangement in which one entity legally appoints another to act on its behalf, which is allowed so long as there is no conflict of interest. A good example of this is the relationship between a fund manager and an investor. When an investor buys a financial product, the fund manager becomes his or her agent and so must manage the assets of the investor in order to assist in maximising the returns on their behalf. This principal–agent relationship can be entered into for the purpose of any contract (Figure 2.1).

In the case of a large asset manager, it is common for the asset manager to act for a large number of underlying funds, each of which may have a need to enter into derivative transactions with an investment bank. Since each fund has a separate legal identity, and typically the assets of the funds are separate (or ring-fenced) from others, separate documentation is required in respect of each such fund, such as the ISDA Master Agreement and any relevant annexes to it. In the case of an asset manager acting for thousands of funds, this can be a massive documentation exercise. Given that many of the credit terms the asset manager will require for each fund are likely to be similar, except in the case of commercial items relating to the difference between the individual funds themselves, a drafting trick is often utilised in such scenarios, where a single ISDA Master Agreement

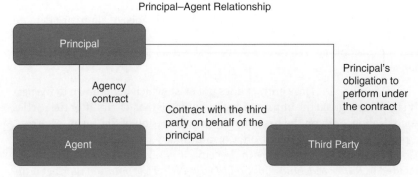

Figure 2.1 A principal entering into a contract via an agent

(see Chapter 3) is in fact put in place, however, where the asset manager is expressed to act, not as principal, but as an agent on behalf of each of those funds.

So, one physical ISDA Master Agreement is executed, that references several investment funds in an annex to the agreement. The ISDA Master Agreement makes it clear that each of the investment funds thereunder is, in fact, entering into a legally separate and distinct ISDA Master Agreement with the investment bank, therefore creating sometimes thousands of actual agreements,[3] and that the asset manager is simply acting as an agent to simplify the documentation drafting and execution process (although as the asset manager of the funds, it will clearly have some 'asset manager' responsibilities which it provides for the funds and are relevant to the funds' meeting of their contractual obligations under the derivatives transactions).

It is important to highlight how many problems this 'drafting trick' to deal with documentation issues has caused the banking industry. Much of this relates to the difficulty firms have had in storing this documentation, being caught between the single physical agreement and the fact that it actually creates many individual agreements. With the storage of the agreements themselves being problematic, it will come as no surprise that the issues are amplified when it comes to ensuring the actual terms of the agreements, the legal agreement data, is properly understood and provided to various downstream stakeholders. Additionally, in many cases, the due diligence surrounding the funds, and additional data items (such as identifiers in the credit hierarchy), have been inadequately set up by institutions, resulting in major multi-million-dollar credit valuation adjustments, operational losses, incorrect netting treatment for regulatory capital purposes and – more generally – sub-optimal risk management.

Contract Law and Important Overlaps

To this point, we have only really considered one area of law – contract law. This is the regulation of contracts and their enforceability between legal entities. As the law of promises, it is the backbone of the financial markets. Loans, bank deposits, derivatives, insurance policies and guarantees are all examples of contracts, creating agreements between parties to them – promises to perform in a particular manner in exchange for another promise. We now briefly detail the other key areas of law and some overlaps with contract law.

Tort

Contracts are voluntary obligations, distinct from tort – which covers non-criminal 'wrong-doing' leading to a right to compensation. It does not involve agreements, rather

---

3 This is typically achieved by inserting a preamble to the schedule to the ISDA Master Agreement where parties acknowledge the separate liability of each investment fund. For example: 'Separate Agreement for each Party B. This Agreement constitutes a separate agreement between Party A and each Party B listed in Appendix 1 hereto separately and not jointly, with the same legal force and effect as if Party A had entered into a separate ISDA Master Agreement with each Party B. No rights, remedies or obligations arising as a result of a transaction between Party A and one Party B in any way give rise to any rights, remedies or obligations with respect to another Party B.'

in many cases it regulates relations between parties where there is no such relationship framework set up (or such framework is not sufficient). Tort seeks to regulate civil wrongs. In the financial markets, this mostly relates to misleading, dishonest or fraudulent behaviour (which can in some – and increasing! – cases, attract criminal considerations).

Property

The law of contract creates rights *in personam*, whereas the law of property creates rights *in rem*. Rights *in personam* refer to the personal rights attached to a specific person; this includes contractual rights, torts against a defendant and licences. Rights *in rem*, in contrast, refer to property rights of possession or ownership. Rights *in rem* are enforceable against the world, whereas rights *in personam* bind only the parties to the contract. Of course, financial instruments – contracts that concern the creation of a financial asset and corresponding financial liability – often concern property.

Criminal

This regulates behaviours in order to protect society, with an emphasis on punishment and, in the case of individuals, potential penalties of imprisonment. Typically, criminal penalties are imposed regardless of whether a victim has been compensated or not.

Corporate liability determines the extent to which a legal person can be liable for the acts and omissions of natural persons employed and/or engaged by a corporation. It should be noted that more and more criminal justice systems now include criminal sanctions against legal entities.

Post-crisis, there are increasing criminal offices in order to address much of the public and regulatory concern over trust, standards and culture in the banking industry that played a part in the Financial Crisis. For example, in the UK, the Financial Services (Banking Reform) Act 2013 provides that senior managers of banks and building societies may be prosecuted by the PRA or Financial Conduct Authority (FCA) for taking a decision that causes their institution to fail. For the offence to have been committed, at the time the decision was made the senior manager must have been aware of a risk that its implementation would cause the institution to fail. In addition, the senior manager's conduct in relation to the decision must fall significantly below what could reasonably be expected of someone in their position.

Constitutional and Administrative Law

This covers the rules of a state, its functions and its relationship with its citizens. When a bank applies for a licence in order to start business or the regulator punishes the bank for failing to comply with the law, these relationships between the state and the market belong to public and administrative law. Financial markets are severely regulated, exacerbated by the public backlash post-crisis. In most cases, the regulation from this area of law takes precedence over contractual arrangements. The recent regulation has had a tremendous impact on the nature of contracts put in place between parties in order to be compliant with regulation. As well as mandating certain contractual terms, regulation may imply certain terms in financial contracts (it is for this reason that the regulatory framework is considered in the context of legal agreement data).

Note the impact of EU law, which is the regulation of matters within the scope of the European Union.

Equity and Trusts

This covers wills, mechanisms of ownership of property and an overarching set of fairness requirements.

Bibliography

Barry v Davies [2000] EWCA Civ 235

Boulton v Jones (1857) 2 H & N 564

British Steel Corporation v Cleveland Bridge & Engineering [1984] 1 All ER 504

Broome v Antler's Hunting Club 595 F.2d 921, 923

Butler Machine Tool Co Ltd v Ex-cell-O Corporation Ltd [1979] 1 WLR 401

Carlill v Carbolic Smoke Ball Co [1893] 1 QB 256

Chappell v Nestle [1960] AC 87

Clifton v Palumbo [1944] 2 All ER 497

Collins v Godefroy (1831) 1 B & Ad 950

Currie v Misa (1874–75) LR 10 Ex 153

Dainow, J. (1966) 'The civil law and the common law: Some points of comparison', *American Journal of Comparative Law*, 15(3), pp. 419–435

Don King Productions Inc v Douglas 742 F.Supp.2d 786, 791 (S.D.N.Y. 1990)

Dunlop Pneumatic Tyre Co Ltd v Selfridge Ltd [1915] AC 847

Felthouse v Bindley [1862] EWHC CP J 35

Fisher v Bell [1960] 1 QB 394

Gibson v Manchester City Council [1979] 1 WLR 294

Golden, J. (2010) 'The future of financial regulation: The role of courts', in I. MacNeil and J. O'Brien (eds), *The Future of Financial Regulation*. Hart Publishing: Oxford

Hazell v Hammersmith and Fulham London Borough Council [1992] 2 AC 1

Hyde v Wrench (1840) 3 Beav 334

McCormack, R. (2010) *Legal Risk in the Financial Markets*, 2nd edn. Oxford University Press: Oxford

Micklitz, H., Stuyck, J., Terryn, E. and Droshout, D. (2010) *Cases, Materials and Text on Consumer Law*. Hart Publishing: Oxford

New Zealand Co Ltd v AM Satterwhaite & Co [1974] UKPC 1

Payne v Cave (1789) 3 TR 148

Poole, J. (2012) *Textbook on Contract Law*, 11th edn. Oxford University Press: Oxford

R v Clarke [1972] 1 All ER 219

Raiffeisen Zentralbank Osterreich AG v Crosseas Shipping Ltd and others [1999] All ER (D) 313

Re McArdle (1951) Ch 669

Sauter Automation Ltd v Goodman (Mechanical Services) Ltd (1986) 34 BLR 81

Smith v Hughes (1871) LR 6 QB 597

Spencer and others v Harding and others (1869–70) LR 5 CP 561

Stilk v Myrrick [1809] EWHC KB J58

Storer v Manchester City Council [1974] 1 WLR 1403

Taylor v Laird (1856) 1 H & N 266

Tetley, W. (1999) 'Mixed jurisdictions: Common law vs civil law (codified and uncodified) (Part I)', *Uniform Law Review*, pp. 591–618

'The common law and civil law traditions', The Robbins Collection, School of Law (Boalt Hall), University of California at Berkeley (www.law.berkeley.edu/library/robbins/pdf/CommonLawCivilLawTraditions.pdf)

The Economist (2013) 'What is the difference between common law and civil law', *The Economist*, 17th July 2013

Thomas v Thomas (1842) 2 QB 851

Treitel, G. (1999) *Law of Contract*, 10th edn. Sweet & Maxwell: London

Warlow v Harrison (1859) 1 E & E 309

Wood, P. (2008) *Maps of World Financial Law*. Sweet & Maxwell: London

3

Structured Finance and Financial Products – Derivatives

This chapter will mainly provide an overview of OTC derivatives financial instruments, both in terms of the products and then the documentation used for them. It is of course only one example of financial instruments, however, it provides a useful context for the remainder of the text, both in terms of background understanding, as well as for examples of legal agreement data considerations. They are also important trading products, for which close-out netting is a significant commercial consideration, due to the regulatory capital impact netting can have on the exposure of a firm to its counterparty – an item that will be considered in the context of legal opinions and legal opinion data in Chapter 6. Additionally, these products were found to be a major component of the Financial Crisis, and therefore the legal agreement data aspects of these products have become the focus of much regulatory reform post-crisis.

Derivatives

Derivatives contracts are agreements to receive, make or provide payments and/or assets at a time or times in the future, with the value being derived from the level and/or value of a different underlying asset. Such underlying asset might be an interest rate, asset or index, or even decisions made by parties to the contract. In many regards, derivatives instruments are similar to the underlying, but allow a mechanism to take a very similar synthetic position. For example, an airline may enter into a commodity derivative, where the underlying is oil, allowing it to effectively 'lock in' the price of its fuel at a future date in time, without worrying about storage or transportation costs. One can both increase and reduce exposure to an underlying via the use of derivatives.

Uses of Derivatives

There are a number of uses of derivatives that are important to bear in mind when considering these products:

1) **Hedging.** This allows market participants such as corporates, asset managers and dealers to manage (hedge) risks, for example, the market risk, due to factors such as interest rates, foreign exchange rates and commodity prices.
2) **Investment opportunities and speculation.** Since derivatives allow parties to take positions on either side of a market for an underlying, they enable profits to be made from anticipating such movements.

3) **Indirect investments in an underlying.** Derivatives provide an alternative to investing directly in the underlying assets, typically with lower transaction costs.
4) **Cash flow management.** Derivatives allow parties to change the nature of a position or instrument and create appropriate payoff patterns in line with their broader risk appetite.

The derivatives market is subdivided into two – the listed market and the OTC market (see Figure 3.1).

The simplest derivatives products are on the listed market and traded on exchanges. This is a financial marketplace where parties can trade standardised contracts, such as options and futures, at a set price. To become an exchange-traded product, the product needs to have reasonable trading volume, standardisation and price discovery (i.e. the 'market' price can easily be determined from interaction with market participants, buyers and sellers of that product). Exchanges nowadays also have a central counterparty clearing function, which guarantees the performance of parties to the exchange, reducing counterparty risk (see Chapter 6). Traditionally, trading on exchanges took place on a physical floor, with a face-to-face auction process; however, this has today been replaced or complemented with systems-based, electronic trading. The costs of exchange-traded derivatives tend to be lower than those of OTC derivatives.

OTC derivatives describe trading activity that does not take place on an exchange. Since the 1990s, this market has grown exponentially, primarily due to the use of OTC derivatives as hedging instruments and investment vehicles. Unlike exchange-traded products, OTC derivatives allow parties to customise the product to meet specific needs, such as size and maturity. They are also typically traded bilaterally and through private arrangements. As a result of this, certainly pre-Financial Crisis, the market was not well reported or transparent, and unlike exchange trading, parties take on credit risk on the other. Many participants in the OTC derivatives market do not have the strongest credit rating, and therefore, in the absence of credit mitigants such as collateral, counterparty

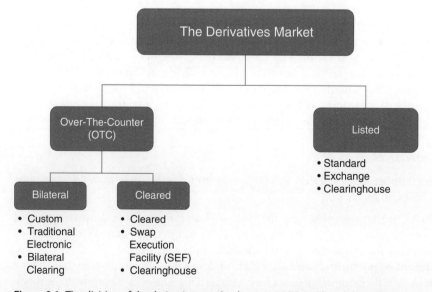

Figure 3.1 The division of the derivatives market between OTC and listed derivatives

risk considerations are a strong feature of the OTC derivatives market. There are a small number of investment banks that dominate this market, and their large size and inter-connectedness meant that these became viewed as 'too big to fail' (see Chapter 10).

The Financial Crisis caused a significant reduction in the total notional amount outstanding of OTC derivatives post-crisis (see Figure 3.2), with banks having reduced their balance sheets and reallocated capital, as well as being incentivised by regulation to move away from the use of OTC derivatives. It should be noted that compression exercises have also played a part in the reduction of outstanding notional amounts.

For the last two decades, and accelerated by mandatory regulation pre-Financial Crisis, there has been a growing trend in centrally clearing OTC derivatives. This primarily reduces counterparty risk. In many ways, this results in an OTC derivative taking on a number of features of exchange-traded products. It is possible to clear an OTC derivative that is not liquid enough for exchange trading; however, it needs to have a certain degree of standardisation and liquidity for it to be centrally cleared.

An increasingly large part of the OTC derivatives market is collateralised, whereby the exposure between counterparties is mitigated. This provision of collateral reduces counterparty risk, however, it introduces additional risks, such as liquidity, legal and operational risk (see Chapter 7 for a further description of the use of collateral in the context of OTC derivatives).

In this text, we focus on the OTC derivatives, rather than the exchange/listed part of the derivatives market, since this is the more complex part (see Figure 3.3) where the legal data issues continue to be most pronounced, although many of the considerations are also applicable to the others.

Market value of OTC derivatives falls to its lowest level since 2007

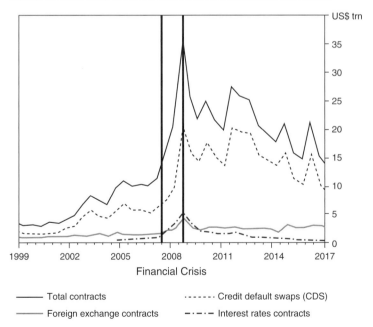

Figure 3.2 Outstanding gross market value in trillions of US dollars [adapted from BIS OTC derivatives statistics (Table D5.1) (2017)]

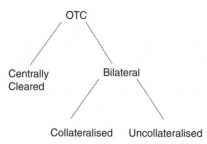

Figure 3.3 The continuum of complexity across the derivatives market

Derivatives – Product Families

Derivatives can be broken down into five main product families:

1) **Futures.** These are standardised contracts between two parties, the 'buyer' and the 'seller', where the parties agree to transact an agreed underlying asset at a predetermined price on a future date.
2) **Options.** These are agreements between two parties giving the right, but not the obligation, for one party, the 'holder', to buy or sell an agreed underlying asset at a predetermined price in the future.
3) **Forwards.** This is an OTC version of a futures contract that is customised to meet the individual needs of the parties.
4) **Swaps.** These are agreements to exchange a series of financial obligations (such as cash flows and/or assets) at specified future dates, according to predetermined conditions. A swap transaction can be thought of as a series of futures/forward contracts.
5) **Swaptions.** A swaption is a combination of a swap and an option transaction. It gives a holder of the option the right (but not the obligation) to enter a swap transaction with another party at a given time in the future.

Derivatives – Asset Classes

A derivative product derives its value from an underlying asset. These underlying assets can be classified into a number of different classes and subtypes, such as:

- **Interest rate derivatives.** Here the underlying value is affected and/or associated with interest rates. They are also known as fixed-income derivatives. This also includes bond futures and options.

- **Foreign exchange derivatives.** Currencies form the underlying, facilitating a transfer of one currency to another. The basic trading types in this asset class are similar to those under the interest rate asset class.
- **Equity derivatives.** The underlying is an equity product such as a share or a share index.
- **Credit derivatives.** A credit derivative is a product in which a party (the credit protection seller) agrees to pay the other party (the credit protection buyer) contingent upon the occurrence of a credit event with respect to a particular entity (called the reference entity). The credit event refers to an incident that affects the credit of the reference entity, such as the cash flows of a financial instrument issued by it. This could be, by way of example, filing for bankruptcy, failing to pay or debt repudiation.
- **Commodity derivatives.** The underlying is a commodity asset. This can be regarded as the oldest derivatives asset class. Due to the large range of possible commodities, they tend to be subdivided into smaller groups, such as agricultural, energy, precious metals and industrial metals.

For OTC derivatives, ISDA has published a series of definitional booklets, within the different asset classes. Generally, and broadly, each set of definitional booklets provides relevant terms for documenting a particular type of derivative transaction within an asset class. For example, the 2014 Credit Derivatives Definitions are intended for use in documenting credit derivatives and the 2006 ISDA Definitions are drafted primarily for use in documenting interest rate and currency derivatives. This provides a framework for documenting a transaction and various possible standard elections for the economic terms of the transaction itself (the parties are also free, of course, to amend the terms of the relevant definitions or include additional provisions). The terms of the definitional booklets typically represent the result of an extensive industry consultation process through various working groups, although they are not appropriate for the terms of all transactions without amendment or additional provisions.

Example – Interest Rate Transaction

Due to it being one of the easier products to explain, we will now analyse an interest rate swap transaction as an example. This is a simple example, of an exchange of one set of cash flows for another, without any exchange of principal between the parties – with an underlying of 'interest rates' to the derivative transaction. One of the reasons for entering into such a transaction is often the desire to change from one funding method to another. Rather than buying or selling interest rate swap transactions, one refers to buying 'payers' (who pay the fixed rate) and 'sellers' (who receive the fixed rate).

To illustrate this, imagine ABC plc has borrowed £100 million under a loan arrangement from XYZ Bank. Under this loan arrangement, ABC plc is required to pay an interest-only payment to XYZ Bank every 3 months for the next 5 years. This payment is based on the 3-month GBP London Inter-bank Offered Rate (LIBOR) index. ABC plc will not know the specific LIBOR applicable until the time of the related payment.

This creates a degree of uncertainty for ABC plc and exposure to changing interest rates. Accordingly, ABC plc enters into an interest rate swap, a fixed–floating swap transaction with an investment bank dealer. Under the terms of this interest rate swap, every 3 months, ABC plc will make an interest-only payment on £100 million to the investment bank dealer based on a fixed rate of 4%. In return, they will receive from the investment bank dealer an interest payment based on the LIBOR at the relevant time of payment, which ABC plc will use to make its due payment under the loan with XYZ Bank. The interest rate swap has effectively allowed ABC plc to convert its floating interest rate obligation into a fixed interest rate obligation and also mitigated its exposure to rising interest rates (see Figure 3.4).

At the end of each 3-month period, the fixed rate payer, in this case XYZ Bank, pays a fixed amount. This amount rarely changes, other than by small amounts due to differing length payment periods. On these dates, the fixed rate buyer, ABC plc, pays an amount that changes based on the level of the floating rate index, 3-month GBP LIBOR. As shown, the floating rate payments for the first two payment dates have been determined and are 'fixed', while the floating rate payments in the future are still unknown. For the swap transaction, the parties may have agreed to use the 3-month GBP LIBOR as published on Reuters LIBOR01. Such items have been standardised in ISDA definitional booklets as referred to above (in this case, in the 2006 ISDA Definitions).

Unlike other simpler financial transactions, not all details of the swap transaction are known at the point of trade, most importantly, the 3-month GBP LIBOR for each point in the transaction. Each such floating rate is set when the rate is published (referred to as a 'rate-setting event'). Each time such a rate-setting event occurs, the trade becomes more certain, and there is less market risk attached to it. Each payment period is referred to as an accrual period. The floating rate is set a number of 'spot days' prior to the start of the accrual period, although – unlike many other LIBORs – there is no delay for GBP LIBOR.

Most swaps are traded at par, meaning that they are traded such that the fixed rate is adjusted so that the overall value of the swap is equal to zero. Thereafter, the value of the

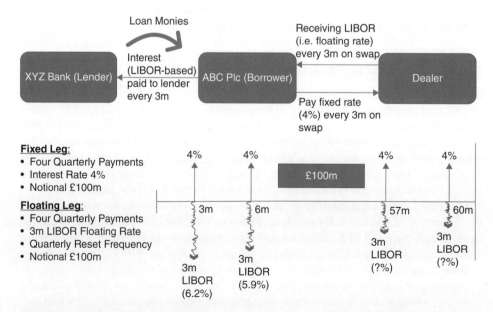

Figure 3.4 Interest rate swap cash flows, hedging interest rate risk that a loan borrower is exposed to under a floating rate (LIBOR-based) loan

swap will fluctuate based on the expected future cash flows, in particular in this case, the yield curve predicting the reset rate applicable to future floating rate payments.

At a very high level, in order to price the swap at a point in time, each leg of the swap (i.e. the fixed rate leg and the floating rate leg) is viewed as a series of future cash flows (as if each leg was a bond) and summates the present value of each of those cash flows. In practice, the calculation can get more complex, needing to know the exact number of days between each payment date (which is based on the day-count convention the parties agree on), taking into account various valuation adjustments known as XVAs: credit valuation adjustment (CVA); debit valuation adjustment (DVA); funding valuation adjustment (FVA); collateral valuation adjustment (ColVA); capital valuation adjustment (KVA); and margin valuation adjustment (MVA). Aspects such as counterparty credit risk in the transaction, as well as funding, collateral and capital considerations, all need to be taken into account.

The XVAs

The rise in importance of legal agreement data in respect of master trading agreements has very much arisen post-crisis from the rapid realisation that factors such as counter-party risk, funding risk (e.g. relating to collateral) and capital costs were not fully considered when pricing trades (with the primary focus of trading desks being to accurately price for the market risk of the transaction). The Financial Crisis exacerbated the effects of many of these factors, the key input to calculating many of which is detailed in the underlying legal master and collateral agreements but has not been historically thought through when putting documentation in place, or sufficiently captured as legal agreement data. It is this previously ignored and complex XVA aspect of trading documentation that has brought legal agreement data to the fore when compared, for example, to other types of banking instruments (e.g. loans).

- **Credit valuation adjustment.** This reflects the cost of mitigating the credit risk that the bank faces to the counterparty on a derivative contract. It is the difference between the risk-free and the credit-risky values of a netting set (see below), where the credit-risky value takes into account the possibility of the counterparty's default. CVA is the expected loss or value of counterparty credit risk.
- **Debit valuation adjustment.** This is the opposite of CVA, in the sense that it reflects the credit risk the counterparty faces towards the bank. It stems from a liability due to a negative exposure that would give rise to a gain if a firm were to default. (There is some debate over the relevance of firms 'pricing in' their own default probability when assessing counterparty risk.)
- **Funding valuation adjustment.** This refers to the funding cost that arises when the trade and collateral terms on a client trade are misaligned from the terms on which an OTC derivatives dealer will hedge the derivative with the client in the market. For example, if the dealer posts cash collateral on the hedge and does not post collateral from the client-side transaction, the dealer would need to raise the cash itself as part of its usual funding operations – with an associated funding cost.
- **Collateral valuation adjustment.** This assigns a value to the embedded optionality that may exist in a collateral arrangement, giving an ability for a posting party to select the 'cheapest to deliver' or 'best to deliver' collateral. This also takes into account the

choice of discount curve for collateral, which may differ from the trading currency discount curve.

- **Capital valuation adjustment.** This is the incremental cost of holding regulatory capital in respect of a trade.
- **Margin valuation adjustment.** The margin requirements for uncleared derivatives mandate the provision of initial margin for derivatives trading on a gross basis and held with a third party in a segregated account (not rehypothecated). Accordingly, this initial margin is a 'sunk cost' in respect of a trade on each contract, which the MVA reflects.

Documentation of OTC Derivative Contracts

We can now focus on bringing together the aspects of contract law covered in Chapter 2 and the aspects of derivatives we have included in this chapter, and look at the documentation of OTC derivatives.

The ISDA trade association (previously known as the International Swaps Dealers Association) was formed in 1985 and has undertaken a considerable amount of work to standardise the documentation used for the trading of OTC derivatives. This has undoubtedly helped to make the global derivatives markets safer and more efficient. The fundamental output has been the development of the ISDA Master Agreement documentation, which creates a master netting agreement (see Chapter 6 for further details on close-out netting) and a wide range of related documentation materials, such as the product definitional booklets. At the time of writing, ISDA has over 900 member institutions from 69 countries. These members comprise a broad range of derivatives market participants, including corporations, investment managers, government and supranational entities, insurance companies, energy and commodities firms, international and regional banks. In addition to market participants, members also include key components of the derivatives market infrastructure, such as exchanges, intermediaries, clearinghouses and repositories, as well as law firms, accounting firms and other service providers. There are other, typically national associations, who have published local OTC derivatives master agreements, such as the Fédération Bancaire Française (FBF) who publish the FBF Master Agreement; and Bundesverband Deutscher Banken who publish the German Master Agreement for Financial Derivatives Transactions (Deutscher Rahmenvertrag für Finanztermingeschäfte, DRV). We focus in this section on the ISDA-published documentation, although the local master agreement variations have many similarities in terms of structure and provisions.

Historically, parties to OTC derivatives transactions would document each transaction in a separate, comprehensive agreement. As an independent agreement between the two parties, these were quite lengthy documents, setting out not only the economic terms of the relevant transaction, but also terms relating to the general legal and credit relationship between the parties. As a result, in addition to the economic terms of the transaction – that are specific to a transaction – these general legal and credit terms had to be negotiated each time the parties entered into a transaction. To address this, a framework 'master agreement' was created – the ISDA Master Agreement – that sets out the ongoing legal and credit relationship between parties and provides that each transaction entered into by the parties can be governed by that master agreement. This avoids the repetitive process of individually documenting all terms for each individual trade – and most importantly, opens up the possibility of close-out netting (described in the following section).

The parties to an ISDA Master Agreement can, of course, agree to amend the terms of their master agreement at any time after it is put in place, should there be a need to change the general legal and credit terms. To aid broader contractual standardisation, and ease negotiation, ISDA published a pre-print form of the Master Agreement, as well as a pro-forma Schedule. The pre-print form is intended to remain unamended. In many ways, this serves as a menu of options for the parties to elect from, in terms of the legal and credit terms. Parties are then expected to select and insert the relevant options applicable to the two parties seeking to trade OTC derivatives within the Schedule.

There are currently five published versions of the ISDA Master Agreement, specifically:

- 1987 ISDA Interest Rate and Currency Exchange Agreement
- 1987 ISDA Interest Rate Swap Agreement
- 1992 ISDA Master Agreement (Local Currency – Single Jurisdiction)
- 1992 ISDA Master Agreement (Multicurrency – Cross Border)
- 2002 ISDA Master Agreement[1]

It is the 2002 and 1992 (Multicurrency – Cross Border) versions that today dominates the documentation portfolios of market participants, although other versions do exist. For the purposes of this text, we concentrate on the 1992 Multicurrency version, and then briefly describe the main differences with the 2002 version.

The ISDA documentation has been built on a modular architecture, with a number of key building blocks which have very much allowed the industry to grow in a highly efficient and flexible manner, with these modules evolving for market participant needs over the last 30 years. This architecture is itself evident in the structure of the ISDA Master Agreement, consisting of two parts as described above: the printed form and the Schedule.

Close-Out Netting

It is often said that the primary purpose of a master trading agreement is to facilitate close-out netting. Where two parties have more than one outstanding derivatives transaction between them, at any particular time, some may be profitable to a particular party and others profitable to the counterparty. In other words, the mark-to-market of the transactions between the parties may be both in-the-money and out-of-the-money to a particular party. This creates counterparty credit risk (essentially the risk of loss to a party due to the counterparty's default prior to the termination of a trade) for 'in-the-money' transactions. In the event of the insolvency of the counterparty, a party may not recover any or only some of the owed sums from the insolvent estate of the counterparty. However, the party would still owe the insolvent estate the mark-to-market of the out-of-the-money transactions. This is known as cherry-picking – where a debtor has a number of contracts with a party and the debtor 'cherry-picks' such that it assumes profitable agreements and rejects unprofitable agreements.

---

1 Note, ISDA have recently additionally published specific Irish and French governing law versions of this 2002 preprint.

Close-out netting is a key way in which to control the counterparty credit risk in cases where there are both in-the-money and out-of-the-money transactions. It overcomes the fundamental issue with counterparty credit exposure that a positive value of a financial instrument to a party corresponds to a claim on a defaulted counterparty, whereas in the event of a negative value the party is unlikely to be able to 'walk away' from the claim of the counterparty (this means that if a party is owed money and the counterparty defaults, then it will incur a loss, whereas if the party owes money, they cannot gain from this situation by being released from the liability to the counterparty). Close-out netting, one of the key components and advantages of a master trading agreement, allows a party to offset in-the-money transactions with out-of-the-money transactions. This credit risk mitigant is recognised for regulatory capital purposes for prudentially regulated firms (see Chapter 6), since regulators view it as being helpful in reducing systemic risk in the financial markets and it is therefore a key aspect of the legal documentation of the ISDA Master Agreement (and other master trading documentation).

The regulatory capital of close-out netting can usually only be obtained if legal opinions have been obtained by firms in support of it. It should be noted that many jurisdictions recognise the enforceability of close-out netting, but it is less than certain in a number of other jurisdictions. The ISDA Master Agreement does, however (as do most other industry master agreement forms), contain a number of elements designed to try and assist with the likelihood of a jurisdiction recognising the close-out provisions it contains as being enforceable, such as the single agreement concept, flawed asset provisions and close-out mechanism (including the availability of the automatic early termination election). These are often fondly called the 'three pillars' of a master agreement (upon which close-out netting is based).

Single Agreement Concept

By its terms, each ISDA Master Agreement (inclusive of the pre-print, Schedule and any annexes such as the Credit Support Annex to collateralise the trading relationship), together with any trade confirmation, including any relevant definitional booklet applied to the trades, entered into between two parties, forms a single agreement. There are a number of potential benefits to this single agreement approach, including:

1) Parties can elect to net payments across transactions if they are due on the same day and in the same currency (known as settlement, or payment, netting). This reduces 'daylight risk'.
2) Parties can collateralise their trades based on their portfolio of trades rather than on individual trades (and therefore the net rather than the gross transaction exposure) (see Chapter 7).
3) Upon a default or other termination event with respect to one party (the 'defaulting party'), the other party can terminate all the outstanding transactions, value them and net out the amounts owed by the defaulting party from any amounts that may be owed to the defaulting party, reducing exposure between the parties.

The concept of it being a single agreement, and not a series of agreements, reinforces the argument that a liquidator or insolvency practitioner cannot break the 'single agreement' in order to cherry-pick profitable transactions. The single agreement concept is contained in section 1(c) of the 1992 ISDA Master Agreement.

Flawed Asset Provisions

A flawed asset provision seeks to 'flaw' an asset (in the case of the ISDA Master Agreement, the obligation to make payments or deliveries by a non-defaulting party under transactions to the ISDA Master Agreement) without terminating the transactions and, therefore, avoid the step of crystallising a mark-to-market loss (if the non-defaulting party was out-of-the-money). This is done by adding a number of condition precedents to the obligation to make payments and deliveries. In the case of the 1992 ISDA Master Agreement, the flawed asset provision is contained in section 2(a)(iii). Section 6(c)(ii) should also be noted as the flip-side of section 2(a)(iii), with section 2(a)(iii) providing the condition and section 6(c)(ii) operatively suspending performance upon an occurrence of the condition.

Close-Out Mechanics

This generally involves the termination of all transactions between an insolvent and a solvent counterparty, by aggregating the values of each of those transactions and replacing the transaction payment amounts with a single sum representing all transaction payment amounts. By replacing the various payments with a single amount, this again assists with the argument against an insolvency practitioner or liquidator seeking to cherry-pick certain transactions, since the individual transactions no longer exist, having been replaced with a single close-out payment. This will be considered in greater depth in relation to close-out netting in Chapter 6.

Collateral Credit Support Arrangements

Parties to an ISDA Master Agreement may also enter into a collateral credit support arrangement in order to manage the credit risk due to the exposures that arise between them under trades governed by the relevant ISDA Master Agreement. This is considered in detail in Chapter 7. Such arrangements might be annexes to the ISDA Master Agreement or standalone agreements (albeit tightly coupled to the ISDA Master Agreement).

Trade Confirmations

Confirmations are the documents in which the parties record those economic terms (although they are not necessarily the documents that 'create' the trade – that is often the electronic or verbal engagement between traders, the confirmation merely then 'confirming' the terms of the trade so agreed).

The ISDA Master Agreement itself provides that the agreement includes the Schedule and the documents and other confirming evidence (each a 'Confirmation') exchanged between the parties confirming individual transactions. Further, each Confirmation is identified (or should be identified) either in its own terms or through another effective means as a Confirmation, and state that it supplements, forms a part of and is subject to the ISDA Master Agreement between the parties. In this way, the provisions of the agreement govern the transactions documented in Confirmations.

The use of Confirmations to document the economic terms of transactions again illustrates the modular architecture of ISDA documentation.

Confirmations come in two forms:

- **Long form.** A long-form Confirmation itself contains, in full, all the terms necessary to document the economic terms of the transaction.
- **Short form.** A short-form Confirmation does not contain all the terms necessary to document the economic terms of the transaction. It relies on, and incorporates, standard terms and provisions that are already contained in another document (or documents), such as a set of ISDA product definitions (see above). This enables the use of shorthand terms in the Confirmation and avoids the need to set out in full various operational provisions. The terms and provisions contained in that other document should broadly reflect market practice. Therefore, completing a short-form Confirmation should be a quicker task than completing a long-form Confirmation.

The distinction between a short-form and a long-form Confirmation is in many ways a function of the development of new derivative transaction products. When a market in a new type of derivatives transaction has developed, ISDA has traditionally published a long-form Confirmation for use in documenting that type of transaction (e.g. the 1997 Confirmation of OTC Credit Swap Transaction, prepared for use in documenting a credit default swap, which at the time was a relatively new type of transaction). Then, when a new asset class market matures, and a consensus has developed among those active in that market, ISDA traditionally takes the step of preparing a set of definitions (in the case of the example, the 1999 Credit Derivatives Definitions), together with one or more short-form Confirmations, typically provided at the back of the definitional booklet. Until the market has matured and that consensus has developed, it would probably not be possible to gain market traction for a standard set of asset class definitions. Over time, these definitional booklets are updated by ISDA to reflect changing market standards[2] (e.g. the subsequent publication of the 2003 and 2014 Credit Derivatives Definitions).

It should be noted that the term 'long-form Confirmation' is also used to describe the case where an ISDA Master Agreement has not been fully negotiated between the parties and, instead, the parties agree to use the pre-print form, with only a handful of specific terms agreed between the parties (at a bare minimum for a 1992 ISDA Master Agreement, this would be the 'dated as of date' of the Master Agreement, the Termination Currency and the Governing Law). It can be common, where there is an underlying urgency to trade, to operate using this form of 'long-form Confirmation', in order to deem an ISDA Master Agreement in place to govern the trade. It does often, however, mean that the credit and general legal terms between the parties are sub-optimal. It is therefore common for dealers to only agree to such a deemed ISDA Master Agreement as a temporary arrangement, and to insist on an ability to terminate any trades under such a deemed ISDA Master Agreement, in the event that a fully negotiated ISDA Master Agreement is not put in place within a certain time period. Given that trade confirmations are normally drafted by business operations teams rather than legal teams, long-form Confirmations deeming an ISDA Master Agreement in place cause

---

2 Or in some cases, to try and push for a change to such standards, typically driven by regulation.

considerable difficulty for many financial firms in terms of record-keeping and data management. This is partly due to the different business processes (and controls) in respect of such deemed agreements. Wording to deem an ISDA Master Agreement in place is provided in the User's Guide to the 1992 ISDA Master Agreement, as follows:

> *This Confirmation evidences a complete binding agreement between you and us as to the terms of the Swap Transaction to which this Confirmation relates. In addition, you and we agree to use our best efforts promptly to negotiate, execute deliver a Master Agreement (Multicurrency – Cross Border) in the form published by the International Swap Dealers Association,[3] Inc. ('ISDA'), which such modifications as you and we shall in good faith agree. Upon the execution by you and us of such a Master Agreement (the 'Agreement'), the Confirmation will supplement, form a part of, and be subject to the Agreement. All provisions contained or incorporated by reference in the Agreement upon its execution shall govern this Confirmation except as expressly modified below.*

Protocols

Despite the excellent work done in preparing the building-block documentation, such as the master agreements, credit support arrangements and definitional booklets, there have been a number of unforeseen events, sometimes market driven (e.g. the adoption of the Euro) or regulatory (the requirement for stays to termination rights under the BRRD regulation), that have meant that market participants have had to amend *en masse* the terms of their trading contract portfolios.

Protocols are a multilateral contractual amendment technique used by ISDA (and subsequently by other trade associations such as the International Capital Market Association, ICMA) to address a number of cases where such large-scale changes are needed for the contract portfolios of market participants. They have been used to amend at the master and/or collateral agreement level, as well as trade confirmation level. For the purposes of this text, we mainly concentrate on the former.

The development of an ISDA protocol followed the historic decision by 11 European countries to abandon their national currencies in favour of a new single European currency. This introduction of the Euro raised issues in relation to derivatives transactions entered into under ISDA Master Agreements, where the transaction was agreed before the start of the third stage of the European Economic and Monetary Union (EMU) but continued after 1 January 1999. There was market concern regarding the treatment of such transactions, and the industry consensus was that some simple amendments to the terms of these transactions would help to eliminate any remaining uncertainty. In particular, these amendments would seek to (a) at the ISDA Master Agreement level, confirm continuity of contract; and (b) at the trade confirmation level, confirm applicable successor price sources, clarify payment netting between participating currencies, provide new and amended definitions for Euro, ECU, ECU Settlement Day, Business Day and Banking Day, and create an allowance for adjustment to bond options in the light of redenomination of underlying bonds.

---

3 Note the subsequent name change to the International Swaps and Derivatives Association.

The amendment of all affected ISDA Master Agreement and Trade Confirmation contracts to incorporate such amendments would have been extremely time-consuming and expensive if undertaken through bilateral negotiation between all counterparties – to the point of impracticality due to the tens of thousands, if not more, of contracts involved. Furthermore, due to the use of a standard set of amendments in the protocol text rather than each amendment being individually drafted and negotiated, it would encourage a consistent approach for market participants and standardises the contract wording the industry uses as a whole.

Accordingly, the protocol mechanism was created with the launch of the 1998 ISDA EMU Protocol. This is effectively a club of sorts, whereby the rules of membership accession are that each member of the club contractually agrees that its contracts with any existing member, or any future member, are amended in line with the substantive terms of the amendment. Thus, a member of a protocol only needs to sign the protocol adherence letter (i.e. one single contract that is with the organisers of the protocol, in this case ISDA) rather than an amendment letter with each member of the protocol (or even an amendment letter in respect of each affected contract with a member).

In terms of operational details, any prospective member can (e.g. a dealer or OTC derivatives market participant) indicate its participation in the protocol arrangement by sending a set form adherence letter to ISDA's offices. The EMU Protocol actually allowed, within the adherence letter, the prospective member to specify which five standardised amendments it wished to make with other protocol adherents. Amendments would only be made in areas where an election made in its adherence letter matches that made in an adherence letter submitted by one of its counterparties. The amendment and adherence process, among other matters, was set out in the protocol itself, which was then publicly published on the Association's website, along with a form of the adherence letter. The names of the adhering parties were listed on ISDA's website. Protocol adherents therefore needed to monitor the ISDA website to determine which of their counterparties have adhered, and to check for matching elections.

The success of this ground-breaking effort was reflected in the fact that more than 1,100 firms became adhering parties to the protocol. At the time of writing, this protocol mechanism has now been extended, by ISDA alone, to close to 100 protocol areas, ranging from amendment of trade confirmations, master agreements, credit support arrangements, as well as non-ISDA-sponsored documentation. In some cases, the effect of the protocol is not only to amend existing terms but also, in some, to deem the agreements in place.

There are essentially five methods of effectively adhering to the terms of a protocol:

1) **Traditional.** Any relevant elections are made on a hard document. A physical copy of the protocol adherence letter is executed and sent to ISDA (or the relevant protocol coordinator).
2) **Electronic.** This was provided by ISDA as an option from August 2012 onwards. Election adherence is made online via the ISDA website by each party individually.
3) **Bilateral Demand.** The parties do not actually adhere to the formal protocol but agree to amend their documentation bilaterally as if they had both adhered to the protocol (this can save on the administrative fees payable to the protocol coordinator).

4) **Bilateral.** The parties simply use the wording of the substantive protocol but put this into a bilateral amendment (although this would allow them to tailor and tweak the operation in a bespoke manner).

5) **ISDA Amend.** This is a joint service provided by IHS Markit and ISDA through which market participants could engage via a secure online platform to provide the relevant details needed for certain protocols, first used for the 2012 Dodd–Frank Protocol. Unlike previous protocols, where amendments or supplements were effected solely through the delivery of an adherence letter by each party to the underlying document to be amended, the 2012 Dodd–Frank Protocol included additional bilateral delivery requirements in order to effectuate the addition of supplemental terms. Each party wishing to adhere also needed to deliver a completed questionnaire to another protocol participant for the addition of supplemental terms to be effective with respect to that protocol participant. ISDA Amend sought to deal with these additional bilateral delivery requirements.

The initial EMU Protocol solved a substantive practical drafting issue faced by the industry, but the underlying amendments made by the protocol were reasonably uncontroversial and left little scope for substantive negotiation between the parties. Over time, the use of the protocols has extended beyond this, into areas of commercial negotiation (such as collateral terms with a valuation impact), requiring bilateral exchange and consideration of questionnaires (e.g. in the case of the ISDA 2016 Variation Margin Protocol). The issues this can create in the legal agreement data context will be considered in Chapter 7.

Figure 3.5 illustrates the various issues that need to be taken into account and integration points with other systems and processes for some of the more complicated protocol considerations when considering business processes.

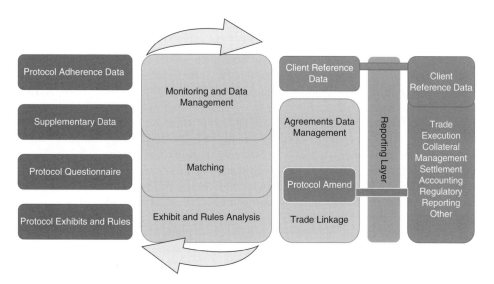

Figure 3.5 Managing the business process in relation to protocols

Brief Guide to the 1992 ISDA Master Agreement (Multicurrency – Cross Border)

(Note that paragraphs of the pre-print are referred to as 'sections', paragraphs of the Schedule as 'Parts' and within the Credit Support Annex as 'paragraphs'.)

Preamble:

The preamble to the pre-print introduces the concept of a 'dated as of date' to be agreed between the parties. This is to be distinguished from the execution date of the agreement. Rather, it is the date of the first transaction between the parties that is intended to be governed by the ISDA Master Agreement. This means that the provisions of the Master Agreement are applied retrospectively to transactions predating the agreement instead.

Section 1 – Interpretation:

Sets out the fact that the definitions are found in section 14 and that they also apply to the negotiated Schedule part of the agreement. Section 1(b) confirms that in the event of inconsistency, the provisions of the ISDA Schedule override those of the pre-print and that the terms of a confirmation override both those of the ISDA Schedule and the pre-print. This is a fundamental point to be noted when considering the terms and their data representation for downstream consumers of the legal agreement data. Finally, section 1(c) confirms the 'single agreement concept' and that the transactions are entered into by the parties in reliance of the fact that the Master Agreement and trade confirmations form a single agreement and that, but for this fact, they would not otherwise have entered into any transactions between them. This is a statement of intention between the parties to establish 'connexity'. Connexity is a term of art from the law of set-off, meaning contractual interdependence between otherwise independent transactions. This is considered important in some civil law jurisdictions.

Section 2 – Obligations:

Section 2(a)(i) provides that the parties will make payments and deliveries as required under transactions between them, specified in the related trade confirmations. It should be noted that anything can constitute a transaction governed by the ISDA Master Agreement, and there is no standard limitation on the types of transactions that can be entered into under its trading framework. Although one can negotiate limitations (typically in the Schedule), this is rare, and trades are normally linked to a master agreement by specifying the master agreement, typically by reference to the parties and the dated as of date, at the point of trading through the trade confirmation. This does, however, cause a number of financial firms severe difficulties in terms of being able to link trades (where the front-office trading systems are the 'golden source' of the data) with the correct master agreement as referenced in legal agreement systems. Trade confirmations are typically drafted by a middle office/operations-type function that is fairly removed from the legal function. Data consumers of these areas (e.g. risk and collateral) then receive inconsistent input data.

Section 2(a)(iii) is the key 'flawed asset provision'. By virtue of this clause, the parties' obligations to make payments and deliveries set out in the trade confirmations are qualified in a number of respects. Firstly, the obligations of the parties are made conditional on the fact that there is no outstanding Event of Default or Potential Event of Default with respect to the other. The reason for this is that such an event might imply the defaulting party may be in trouble, therefore offering a means by which the non-defaulting party can avoid any further increase in their credit risk. Secondly, this clause can also be used to avoid termination of transactions under the master agreement via the close-out mechanism (trying to remedy the issue rather than bringing the trading relationship under the agreement to an end). It should be noted that this clause has been the subject of much recent case law, calling into question the effectiveness of the suspension under this section of the ISDA Master Agreement.[4]

As discussed above, section 2(a)(iii) attempts to ensure an insolvency practitioner or liquidator is unable to 'cherry-pick', enforcing certain transactions whilst refusing to perform others. This section allows such an attempt to be met with the response that 'the other party's obligations are not due'.

Section 2(c) deals with settlement or payment netting and not close-out netting. See Chapter 6 for a more detailed explanation of netting – both settlement and close-out. Under the 1992 ISDA Master Agreement, by disapplying section 2(c)(ii) in the Schedule, payment netting can be applied across transactions. In practice, there can be operational constraints in applying this broadly across transaction types. It should be noted that there is often a disconnect in the legal agreement position on payment netting with the operational reality between the parties.

Section 2(d) contains tax gross-up provisions. This requires a party, subject to certain exceptions, to gross-up in respect of taxes other than those imposed as a result of a connection by the recipient with the relevant taxing jurisdiction (defined as 'Indemnifiable Taxes'). No gross-up is required where the additional amounts would not have been required but for (i) a failure to provide specified or reasonably requested tax forms/information or failure to notify of a tax representation being inaccurate or (ii) the failure of a payee tax representation (other than as a result of a change in law of an action by a taxing authority after the date of the relevant transaction).

Section 3 – Representations:

Section 3 contains a number of representations that are deemed to be given by the parties at the date of entry into the agreement and repeated each time a transaction is entered into. Many of these are quite standard for banking agreements, such as the fact that the party is '*duly organised and validly existing under the laws of the jurisdiction of its organisation or incorporation and, if relevant under such laws, in good standing*'. The parties can, of course, insert further representations within the Schedule. Whilst asking a counterparty to provide representations might flush out potential problems with the trading relationship between the parties, the giving of such representations will not – of itself – cure such problems. It is primarily about the allocation of risk. The giving and receiving of representations is, however, not a substitute for proper due diligence (and parties should only give them if factually correct!). If any representation is untrue or misleading in any material respect, this amounts to an Event of Default (the 'Misrepresentation' Event of Default defined in section 5(a)(iv), which entitles the other party to close out all outstanding transactions, or alternatively it may claim damages for breach of contract, seek to rescind the relevant transactions or claim damages in lieu of rescission).

---

4 See, *inter alia, Lomas v Firth Rixson, Marine Trade SA v Pioneer Freight Futures Co Ltd* and *Metavante v Lehman.*

Section 4 – Agreements:

Section 4 provides for the parties to provide information as detailed in the Schedule or any Confirmation, to maintain authorisations or consents needed in respect of the agreement, to comply in all material respects with applicable laws and regulations if failure to do so would impair its ability to perform under the agreement, to give notice of any failure of a payee tax representation and to pay any stamp taxes in respect of its execution or performance of the agreement.

Section 5 – Events of Default and Termination Events:

Both Events of Default and Termination Events are key provisions relating to the termination of transactions, and in some cases the trading relationship between the parties under the agreement. Section 5(a) sets out the list of standard Events of Default and section 5(b) the list of standard Termination Events. These can be disapplied or added to, as needed, within the Schedule.

There are some important differences between an Event of Default and Termination Event, which are detailed through other sections of the ISDA Master Agreement.

- An Event of Default is generally regarded as implying some degree of fault or culpability on the part of the defaulting party, whereas Termination Events are normally regarded as no-fault-based. This drives a number of the differences between the consequence of an Event of Default or Termination Event occurring.
- If a close-out occurs following an Event of Default, all transactions between the parties under the Master Agreement are terminated, whereas if a Termination Event occurs, it is only those transactions that are affected by the Termination Event that are terminated. As such, a close-out after an Event of Default represents more of a cessation of the trading relationship between the parties.[5]
- It is only the non-defaulting party that can close out following an Event of Default, whereas, under certain Termination Events, either party may be entitled to terminate affected transactions.[6]
- If the obligations of both parties are affected by a Termination Event (i.e. there are two Affected Parties), both parties are responsible for calculating the close-out amount, and the payment is based on the average of the two amounts calculated (so that, in effect, this represents the mid-market value). In contrast, with an Event of Default, only the non-Defaulting Party calculates the close-out amount, and it can therefore use its side of the bid/offer spread such that the calculation is more favourable to it.[7]

Section 5(a) – Events of Default:

Section 5(a)(i) – Failure to Pay or Deliver. This is the most fundamental of the Events of Default in the Master Agreement, given that it covers the parties' obligations to make payments and deliveries under section 2(a)(i). Given that this might be due to administrative errors which can easily be cured, the standard wording allows a 3-day grace period, from the point of time at which notice of the failure to pay and/or delivery is given.

---

5 See definition of 'Terminated Transactions' in section 14 of the 1992 ISDA Master Agreement (Multicurrency – Cross Border).
6 See sections 6(a) and 6(b) of the 1992 Master Agreement (Multicurrency – Cross Border).
7 See section 6(e) of the 1992 Master Agreement (Multicurrency – Cross Border).

Section 5(a)(ii) – Breach of Agreement. This Event of Default covers breaches of the agreement, other than a failure to pay or deliver, a failure to notify of a Termination Event, or certain tax agreements. In this case, there is a 30-day grace period to cure before the event is an Event of Default.

Section 5(a)(iii) – Credit Support Default. This covers (other than in accordance with its terms) the expiration, termination, default or repudiation of any Credit Support Document, where a Credit Support Document is any separate guarantee, collateral agreement or similar document that has been entered into to 'support' the obligations of the parties under the Master Agreement. This Event of Default is therefore designed to catch a default under such a Credit Support Document which, given that it 'supports' an obligation of the parties under the agreement, is important like the supported obligation itself. The specific Credit Support Documents can be specified by the parties in the Schedule.

Section 5(a)(iv) – Misrepresentation. This Event of Default caters for the scenario that a representation (other than a tax representation) of a party or a Credit Support Provider (which are parties specified in the Schedule, typically the providers of the 'support' under a Credit Support Document) is incorrect or misleading in any material respect when made or deemed to be repeated. An exception is made for the tax representation, since the remedy for a breach of these representations is that the financial burden of any then resultant withholding tax is placed on the party in breach.

Section 5(a)(v) – Default under Specified Transaction. This Event of Default is intended to catch significant defaults by a party to the Master Agreement, the specified Credit Support Providers or other parties specified for this purpose (as defined by the parties as a 'Specified Entity in the Schedule' – typically a related entity within the group) occurring in relation to derivatives transactions, but that are not governed by the specific ISDA Master Agreement. This provision means that if the parties have entered into derivatives transactions under another agreement, for example, a local German Master Agreement, the DRV, a close-out of such other agreements can be accompanied by a close-out of the ISDA Master Agreement. The derivatives products under which the default must occur are limited to 'Specified Transactions', which are defined in section 14 of the pre-print (but can be amended as needed in the Schedule).

Section 5(a)(vi) – Cross Default. Such clauses are very common in finance documents, allowing termination of an arrangement in the event that there is a default by a party under other banking arrangements. Such a default is likely to lead to a domino effect under other arrangements. Without such a clause, the creditor would be unable to force its way to the negotiating table during any restructuring discussions, or even take any positive enforcement action until the default under another arrangement has actually led to a default under the specific agreement (which may, of course, be too late, leaving the party at the end of a potentially long line of creditors).

The Event of Default is triggered upon acceleration of debt (amounts which are or may become due by acceleration) and debt amounts maturing (amounts due but unpaid):

> *(1) a default, event of default or other similar condition or event, howsoever described [...] under one or more agreements or instruments [...] relating to [...] in aggregate amount of not less than the applicable Threshold Amount [...] becoming, or capable of becoming [...] due and payable [...] or (2) a default [...] in making one or more payments on the due date thereof in an aggregate amount of not less than the Threshold Amount [...].*

The accelerated debt wording can be a focus of negotiation between parties on the basis that it should only apply to borrowed money that is not only capable of being accelerated but has actually been accelerated.

Unlike other Events of Default, Cross Defaults only apply if specified as being applied by the parties in the ISDA Schedule. This Event of Default is anticipatory in nature, occurring if there is a default by a party to the ISDA Master Agreement, Credit Support Providers or other parties specified for this purpose (as defined by the parties as a 'Specified Entity in the Schedule' – typically a related entity within the group) under another agreement in respect of 'borrowed money' – essentially money that has been paid on the basis that it will be repaid at a future date.

The precise type of obligations covered are defined through the term 'Specified Indebtedness', which is defined in section 14 of the pre-print document but can be amended by the parties in the ISDA Schedule. The definition covers loan arrangements and debt issuances, for example, through a corporate bond issue, as well as where the repayment obligation is as guarantor rather than principal. It typically excludes amounts due to trade creditors and financing arrangements which do not involve an actual exchange of money, such as a repo transaction. Debt instruments exchanged for assets would similarly not be included, or most derivatives transactions. It is common for financial institutions to exclude obligations in respect of deposits received in the ordinary course of a party's banking business, from the definition of 'Specified Indebtedness' in the Schedule.

It is important that the 'Specified Entities' for the purposes of Cross Default are carefully considered. They should include all affiliates relevant to the creditworthiness of a party to the ISDA Master Agreement. The fact that a party has allowed a default to occur in respect of its subsidiary (that is material in respect of the party's credit standing) may be a sign of an impending credit issue that may ultimately affect the counterparty under the ISDA Master Agreement.

The Threshold Amount is usually specified as a fixed amount or a percentage of shareholders' equity. It is important, if Cross Default is selected, to insert a Threshold Amount in the Schedule, otherwise, it will be set to zero, and the 'domino-effect' Event of Default might be triggered by a tiny failure to repay borrowed money.

Section 5(a)(vii) – Bankruptcy. This Event of Default details a number of insolvency-related events in relation to parties to the agreement, Credit Support Providers and any 'Specified Entities' for this purpose. The wording in the pre-print is drafted to cover insolvency proceedings across different countries in which parties may be located. A close-out netting opinion may indicate a need to amend this wording in the ISDA Schedule for a particular party (type) to the agreement.

Section 5(a)(viii) – Merger Without Assumption. This Event of Default is triggered when a party undergoes a merger, consolidation, amalgamation or other similar event, without transferring its obligations under the agreement to the resultant entity. The aim of this Event of Default is to capture events where a corporate event occurs that leaves the counterparty facing an entity with a greater risk of default under the agreement, as it has transferred assets out of the entity, but not necessarily all obligations.

Section 5(b) – Termination Events:

For the purposes of the descriptions below, the party referred to as 'a party' is the party to which the Termination Event occurs and not the 'innocent' party. It should be noted that unlike Events of Default, Termination Events may be relevant to – and therefore lead to the termination of – some but not all transactions. This is done through the definition of 'Affected Transactions' in the context of Termination Events. For example, a change in law may result in certain types of FX transactions between the parties becoming illegal, but may not affect, for example, interest rate swaps.

Section 5(b)(i) – Illegality. This Termination Event occurs if the payments and/or delivery obligations, or other material obligations under the agreement, become unlawful for a party.

Section 5(b)(ii) – Tax Event. This is triggered upon an event that would create, or create a substantial likelihood of, a withholding tax obligation on future payments.

Section 5(b)(iii) – Tax Event Upon Merger. This is triggered by the imposition of withholding tax as a result of a merger or transfer by a party of its assets to another entity.

Section 5(b)(iv) – Credit Event Upon Merger. This is triggered where a party undergoes a merger, consolidation, amalgamation or events similar to this, resulting in the counterparty facing a materially weaker party in terms of its creditworthiness. Many parties seek to amend this provision in the Schedule by adding a more objective test to the degradation of creditworthiness than 'materially weaker', for example, by reference to debt ratings of the parties issued by credit rating agencies. This may create contractual contingent liabilities that are relevant from a liquidity perspective for firms that are prudentially regulated (see Chapter 9).

Section 5(b)(v) – Additional Termination Event. The parties may insert Additional Termination Events in the Schedule. This is recognised in section 5(b)(v). (Despite there being no equivalent 'Additional Event of Default' section in the ISDA pre-print, the parties can also include such provisions in the Schedule.) It is important that any such Additional Termination Events specify who the Affected Parties and Affected Transactions are, as this will have implications as to who may designate termination in respect of such an event occurring, as well as the transactions that are covered by that event. Parties may seek to include Additional Termination Events that are based on a rating downgrade of the counterparty (see Chapter 9).

Section 6 – Early Termination:
This is a key clause of the ISDA Master Agreement in that it deals with the close-out mechanisms and the calculation of the amounts payable in a close-out situation.

Section 6(a) – Right to Terminate Following an Event of Default. This clause gives the right for a non-defaulting party to terminate. If an Event of Default has occurred and is continuing, the non-defaulting party may choose to notify the defaulting party that all transactions (under the agreement) will be terminated on a specified date, the 'Early Termination Date'. This Early Termination Date may not be more than 20 days after the date such notice is given. This section also allows for parties to specify the 'Automatic Early Termination' election in the Schedule. If selected by the parties to apply, an Early Termination Date will be deemed to occur immediately (and automatically) upon the occurrence of certain (or the moment immediately before) insolvency events. This election is typically selected when required to be based on the close-out netting opinion for particular jurisdictions of a party to the agreement and the insolvency laws of such a jurisdiction (rather than the governing law of the agreement).

Section 6(b) – Right to Terminate Following Termination Event. The Affected Party (which is defined in the context of each Termination Event in section 5(b), including any Additional Termination Event defined by the contract parties) is required to notify the other party of the Termination Event promptly upon becoming aware of it. Certain

Termination Events, such as an Illegality under section 5(b)(i)(1) and where there is only one Affected Party, require the Affected Party to, as a condition of its right to terminate, use reasonable efforts to transfer within 20 days of its notice of a Termination Event, all of its rights and obligations to another office or affiliate to attempt to avoid the Termination Event. The right to terminate following a Termination Event is for:

- either party in the case of an Illegality;
- the 'Burdened Party' in the case of a Tax Event Upon Merger;
- any Affected Party in the case of a Tax Event or an Additional Termination Event where there is more than one Affected Party; and
- the party that is not the Affected Party in the case of a Credit Event Upon Merger or an Additional Termination Event where there is only one Affected Party.

Like with the right to terminate following an Event of Default, the terminating party designates an Early Termination Date which may not be more than 20 days after the date such notice is given. Only 'Affected Transactions' under the agreement, rather than all transactions under the agreement, are, however, subject to termination.

Section 6(c) – Effect of Designation. This section contains the key flawed asset provision. Subsection (1) makes it clear that once an Early Termination Date has been correctly designated, the close-out provisions apply regardless of whether an Event of Default or Termination Event has subsequently been cured or is still continuing. Subsection (2) is the flip-side of section 2(a)(iii), reinforcing the fact that no amounts are now payable under transactions governed by the agreement; rather, all payments are now made in accordance with section 6(e). Accordingly, any insolvency practitioner or liquidator attempting to cherry-pick profitable transactions only will be met by a claim that the asset (the profitable transaction) is flawed or worthless, since it expressly provides that no moneys are due to the defaulting party in the circumstances.

Section 6(d) – Calculations. This section details the various calculations that are required to effect the close-out of transactions, and the statements parties are required to provide showing the detail of the calculations.

Section 6(e) – Payments on Early Termination. The agreement allows two measures of payments on an early termination ('Market Quotation' or 'Loss') and two methods of payment on early termination ('First Method' and 'Second Method'). Under the Market Quotation payment measure, the amount payable on a close-out is determined by reference to quotations from leading market dealers, which are based on the cost of the hypothetical entry into by such a dealer of replacement transactions reflecting the intrinsic value of the terminated transactions to the party (but excluding unpaid amounts). Under the Loss payment measure, the determining party determines its losses and gains by reference to rates and values on early termination (and there is no need to consider unpaid amounts as they would be included in the losses and gains). The parties are expressly required to make a reasonable determination in good faith. First Payment Method is often known as 'limited two-way payments'. It works on the basis that all the positive and negative replacement values and unpaid amounts (if a Market Quotation payment measure), or losses and gains (if a Loss payment measure), are aggregated to give a net figure – however, the amount is only payable if it is due to the non-defaulting party and not if it is due to the defaulting party. Such a provision is disliked by regulators on the basis that it is a 'walk away' clause. It is, in fact, a condition under most prudential regulation (see Chapter 6) – for being able to treat exposures as net for capital adequacy purposes under a Master Agreement – is that parties do not select such a payment method, and consequently almost no financial firms elect First Method. The second payment method is known as 'full two-way payments'. It involves the same calculation as under the first method, however, the net amount calculated is payable by a party, regardless of whether it is due to the non-defaulting party or the defaulting party.

Section 7 – Transfer:

This section restricts the parties' ability to transfer (whether by way of security or otherwise) to a third party, thereby creating an intervenor – which might destroy mutuality, which is a key requirement for close-out netting in some jurisdictions. The section also prevents, subject to certain exceptions, transfer of any interest or obligation in or under the agreement without the consent of the other party.

Section 8 – Contractual Currency:

This details that each payment under the agreement will be made in the relevant currency specified for that payment.

Section 9 – Miscellaneous:

This section contains a number of standard boilerplate provisions for finance agreements.

Section 10 – Multibranch Parties:

This section allows the agreement to cater for parties with branches in different locations. The trade confirmation details which branch is obliged to make/receive particular payments and/or deliveries. It allows the parties to specify, in Part 4(d) of the ISDA Schedule, whether a party is acting as a multibranch party or not. By virtue of this section, the obligations of a multibranch party are the same as if the party had entered into the transaction(s) through its head or home office.

Section 11 – Expenses:

Details that a defaulting party will, on demand, indemnify and hold harmless the other party for and against all reasonable out-of-pocket expenses incurred by reason of the enforcement and protection of its rights under the agreement or any Credit Support Document.

Section 12 – Notices:

Contains details of how parties may give notice to each other under the agreement, and conditions on effectiveness.

Section 13 – Governing Law and Jurisdiction:

Section 13(a) states that the agreement will be governed by and construed in accordance with the law specified in the Schedule (anticipated to be in Part 4(h) of the ISDA Schedule, based on the pro-forma Schedule provided by ISDA). The 1992 ISDA Master Agreement was designed to be governed by either English or New York law and, accordingly, the majority of ISDA Master Agreements are so governed. Other governing law types are likely to be unsuitable without a number of amendments to the documentation. At the time of writing, ISDA has just published Irish and French law versions of its 2002 ISDA Master Agreement.

Section 14 – Definitions:

Contains a number of key definitions used in the pre-print of the ISDA Master Agreement, as well as for use within the ISDA Schedule. The parties are, of course, free to amend these definitions as required in the ISDA Schedule.

Legal Agreement Data Considerations in Respect of the ISDA Master Agreement

The modular form of the ISDA Master Agreement and standard elections as laid out in the Schedule pro-forma does help hugely with the standardisation of legal agreement data but requires a number of key terms to be well defined and their interrelation to be well understood. It does also require controls to manage cases where provisions are amended in ways that would not have been expected by the pro-forma, for example, use of party definitions other than 'Party A' and 'Party B', or extending the scope of a cross-default provision other than through the use of the 'Specified Entity' definition in respect of section 5(a)(vi).

Unfortunately, to date, the Master Agreement has been negotiated by market participants without enough consideration of the legal agreement data requirements to subsequently track the agreed position, as truly required for operational and business needs. The regulation post-Financial Crisis has identified this shortcoming and is gradually forcing, through regulatory reporting requirements, firms to have much more detailed understanding of the specific terms in the Master Agreement, particularly in respect of netting (both close-out and payment) and termination rights of parties.

Additionally, many firms struggle with the true linkage of trades to the Master Agreements that actually govern them. In one case, a major investment bank assumed that if there was more than one Master Agreement in place between the parties to a trade, the Master Agreement with the latter date should be used, on the assumption that the earlier ones were, in fact, legacy and likely dormant. This assumption that the later Master Agreement governs the trades is not always true. There may be a need for parties to have alternative terms, for example, for particular trades (interest rate and currency swaps being under one set of terms, and equity derivatives under another), and therefore there may be more than one ISDA Master Agreement that is a valid selection for a particular trade. Firms have also struggled with this linkage because of the manner in which trades are attached to the Master Agreement at the point of trade, typically some time after the Master Agreement framework has been put in place. There is a significant disconnect between the manner in which transactions are described in trading systems as compared to legal agreement systems (the latter typically being far more detailed and granular, making assumptions about which classes of trades might be governed by a particular master trading agreement, despite the fact that this is not always necessarily true). This has wreaked havoc for trade reporting, regulatory capital and collateral management purposes, with many firms suffering from poor data quality in this area.

It is also not uncommon for larger firms to have multiple systems for storing Master Agreement terms for different purposes (e.g. close-out netting being separate from the store of terms for liquidity reporting purposes). This has led to duplicative legal agreement data stores with the inefficient overhead of capture of terms for multiple systems. The burden ultimately has led to a number of data governance issues (e.g. poorly defined terms and a real disconnect between the producers, stewards and consumers of legal agreement data).

Bibliography

Bank for International Settlements (BIS) (2017) 'Statistical release: OTC derivatives statistics at end June 2017' (www.bis.org/publ/otc_hy1711.pdf)

Firth, Simon (2003), *Derivatives: Law and Practice*. Sweet & Maxwell Ltd: London

Gregory, J. (2010) *Counterparty Credit Risk – The New Challenges for Global Financial Markets*. Wiley: Chichester

Harding, Paul C. (2010), *Mastering the ISDA Master Agreements: A Practical Guide for Negotiation (The Mastering Series)*. FT Prentice Hall: Great Britain

Henderson, Schuyler K. (2009), *Henderson on Derivatives*. LexisNexis UK

ISDA (1998) EMU Protocol, 6th May 1998

ISDA (2006) 2006 ISDA Definitions

ISDA (2014) 2014 ISDA: Credit Derivatives – Definitions

Lomas & Others [as joint administrators of Lehman Brothers International (Europe)] v JFB Firth Rixson Inc & Others [2012] EWCA Civ 419

Lomas v JFB Firth Rixson Inc [2012] EWCA Civ 419

Marine Trade SA v Pioneer Freight Futures Co Ltd BVI and Armada (Singapore) PTE Ltd [2009] EWHC 2656 (Comm)

Metavante v Lehman (2009) Case No. 08-13555

Re Southern Brazilian Rio Grande Do Sul Rly Co Ltd [1905] 2 Ch 78, 83

Zapeda, Rodrigo (2014), *The ISDA Master Agreement: The Derivatives Risk Management Tool of the 21st Century?* Kindle Edition

4

Data, Data Modelling and Governance

In the first part of this chapter, we define and discuss the concept of 'data', before going on to detail the different forms of data, and data models that can be used to represent information and hold data. In particular, we consider the structure of a database, and how this can be effectively put to use in a commercial context in order for businesses to be able to maximise the value of their data across a firm (or more specifically, in the context of this book, legal data).

It is crucial that well-developed reference data principles are applied when considering legal data (be it for legal agreement or legal opinion data). One of the issues financial firms face currently is that legal data stores have been developed and built with little beyond technical legal expertise, failing to understand basic data governance and modelling principles and techniques. As a result, this has severely limited the ability to use such data for business, regulatory and operational purposes.

What is Data?

The term 'data' refers to facts or pieces of information that can be used for reference and analysis. Data can exist in a huge variety of different formats; as text, electronic memory or even as facts in a person's mind. It is important to draw a distinction between 'data' and 'information'. Data refers to raw facts and statistics, whereas information refers to a subset of data that is accurate, timely, organised and specific to a purpose. Information can therefore be characterised by the way in which it is presented so as to give it meaning, use and relevance. In short, information is data that has some sort of utility.

A large amount of data is created, stored and processed in the ordinary course of business: for example, records and files, emails, accounts, logs, tweets, customer details, reviews, trade or sales information, employee details – the list is endless. Moreover, the proliferation of data in business is increasing all the time. Not all of it, however, is utilised to its full potential – as usable information. The value of data lies in the information that can be obtained from it and the value of information lies in the actions that can be taken from such information. For example, from a collateral agreement, a party can determine the types of collateral that can be delivered in the event that the counterparty's exposure increases. This can be used to determine the 'cheapest to deliver' or 'best to deliver' collateral asset and therefore optimise business resources. Data is one of the most valuable assets in any business and is core to achieving strategic goals. However, it is of little benefit if it is not collected and collated in an efficient and usable way. The quality and consistency of the information extracted from data is key to unlocking value within businesses. Ultimately, data is not just an IT issue – it should be understood from the perspective of a business need and response. Far too many lawyers and legal departments have failed to recognise this in the context of legal data, ultimately resulting in a failure to meet the needs of the businesses they support, who increasingly rely on systems to help them manage their business processes, certainly not legal contracts, documents or opinions, but rather, the data and information it may contain relevant to the business context and process.

The role of data in the crisis has already been identified, however, in the context of the banking industry, legal data remains a significant problem area, particularly in respect of the contractual obligations that represent the financial instruments of the industry. This has been recognised through post-Financial Crisis regulation such as BCBS 239 (see Chapter 5) and recovery and resolution planning (see Chapter 10). The main issue is that much of the legal data in the banking industry is either significantly unstructured in nature, or there are issues with the governance and usability of the structured data representing it (including that of data definition, quality and accuracy). We now consider what is meant by the terms 'structured' and 'unstructured' data and how this data is collected and collated in a way that is beneficial to a business. After all, data is only as good as the business process that collects it.

Unstructured vs Structured Data

The term *unstructured data* refers to data that is not stored in a predefined manner. This includes forms of data such as Word documents and other text files, audio and video files. The term 'structure' is somewhat imprecise because structure, while not formally defined, can still be implied. Data that is 'structured' may still be characterised as unstructured if its structure does not assist in generating usable information. So, it would not be technically correct to categorise data as either structured or unstructured (although on a practical level we do this all the time); instead, it should be viewed as a continuous spectrum where data may be completely unstructured, semi-structured or even highly structured.

What matters is not the structure itself *per se*, but the utility the structure provides (really, in the context of any associated business processes). Unstructured data constitutes a vast majority of data in the world today (believed to be as much as 95% – and increasing). It is a generally accepted belief that the amount of data in the world is roughly doubling every year, so one can come to the conclusion that the quantity of unstructured information is growing at an increasing rate, meaning that in approximately 2 years' time there will be more unstructured data in the world than is in existence today. Social media and the internet of things (IoT) are significant contributors to the explosion of data that we are seeing. So, the challenge for firms in today's world is to work out how to transform data (both past, historically created data and data created in the future) into a useful and reliable structure so that it is possible to obtain actual, actionable insights into business processes and tasks at hand. To ignore unstructured data in today's fiercely competitive marketplace would be at a great opportunity cost to any firm. Part of the fundamental philosophy of big data, which we touch on next, embraces the unstructured 'messiness' of data that is not precisely structured or accurate – abandoning such ideals due to the advantages that large data sets with these properties offer over smaller, better-defined data sets.

Big Data?

Big data is a blanket term for collections of data sets that are enormous in size and complex, such that their processing using traditional data management means, such as relational database management systems, is problematic. Big data is regarded as meeting a number of the following characteristics (often referred to as the 'Vs' – traditionally focusing on the three characteristics of volume, variety and veracity, although we have included an oft-mentioned fourth here, velocity):

- **Volume.** This is the main characteristic that makes data 'big' – its sheer volume. Note that what is 'big enough' to be big data is not a static concept. It is dependent on whether the data in question can be ingested, processed and analysed in a timely manner, meeting the business requirements of that data set. This can also evolve as technological processing capability increases.
- **Variety.** The data types and structure (if any) of the data are not wholly consistent. A large part of big data sets typically consists of data that is unstructured, with no perfect representation or data about what it is to define it.
- **Veracity.** This refers to the trustworthiness and accuracy of the data, such as whether it is representative of what it represents. Big data aims to overcome any such limitations through the sheer volume of data that is available.
- **Velocity.** The (high) speed at which incoming data needs to be analysed to derive value from it. (Note that the methods to analyse massive amounts of data and extract the intelligence and knowledge it contains are referred to as data science.)

Often, big data is messy and varies in quality. It helps where a sense of general direction is satisfactory, rather than understanding and exactitude, essentially exchanging the characteristic of accuracy at a micro level for insight at a macro level. This can cause issues in the context with legal data. Often, for a particular problem, the data set may just not be large enough to satisfactorily overcome the messiness – for example, a small hedge fund's portfolio of trading agreements. Additionally, the standard expected of the legal profession[1], and therefore of the impact of legal agreement data, may be at odds with the general insight it brings. However, when one considers trade and market data, and the data sets available through the regulatory trade reporting requirements, one is much further into big data territory. Of course, the trade and market data needs to be considered in the context of the governing legal agreement (and its end 'business data'). Legal data, in isolation, is unlikely to unlock much business intelligence and value other than efficiencies of the legal process and function.

Legal Agreement Data as Unstructured Data

A legal contract would probably fall somewhere towards the 'unstructured' end of the spectrum, since most contracts are typically executed and then stored as an image-based PDF or other similar format in a file store with no way of easily searching for each file bar the name it is saved under or via the location it is saved in (such as a client file). The documents can typically be digitised to reveal the individual characters

---

1 Just consider replacing probable cause with probabilistic cause!

in the document (see Chapter 11 for a discussion of optical character recognition (OCR)). What makes it unstructured in nature is the difficulty of conducting precise searches based on certain key terms or outcomes. Although it may be possible to search by document name (which may include the counterparty name or date of execution, or may be stored in some form of alphabetised filing system), or across the raw text of the documents, the point to note is that it is not structured to its full potential. Merely finding a set of contracts by the name of the counterparty, the date of execution or by reference to a keyword is often of little use in checking the implications of a contract due to regulatory changes, for example. If a related business process has not been implemented, then there is probably no fully accurate method to search for contracts containing a 'Material Adverse Change' clause or for master trading agreements with particular governing laws (e.g. to determine the impact of an event like Brexit), or for those master trading agreements that have a valid, up-to-date and robust legal opinion, which can be relied upon to treat exposures under the master agreement as net rather than gross for regulatory capital purposes (see Chapter 6).

Stepping back for a moment and looking at the natural structure of text, one can see that it will typically have a linguistic structure (both syntactic and semantic) and will almost always appear within an envelope of descriptive information (such as date, publication name and author's name). It is information ('metainformation' or 'metadata') that can be used to index documents for storage and retrieval, as is the case with contracts stored in Portable Document Format (PDF) on a computer system or server and saved under a particular name.

Formal documentation inherently contains metainformation by its very nature: for example, a letter will tend to contain a welcome salutation, date and signature, an insurance claim form will have a standardised set of fields and a contract will contain certain key terms and provisions, such as details of the contractual parties and a governing law. Documentation is typically broken up into parts and annexes/schedules, each of which contains paragraphs/clauses, that – for ease of drafting – tend to deal with, either alone or as a group, particular commercial and operational concepts. Such clauses usually contain the same type of comparable information. It is this compositional structure of a contract that assists with its data structuring, data extraction and data generation. Given that parties to a contract would (or at least should!) have intended to give operational effect to the contractual terms, where there are standardised systems to help manage a type of financial contract – for example, payment and collateral management systems – one would expect there to be some standardisation in how operationally the contractual obligations are ultimately managed. The larger the volume of particular types of a contract, the greater the likelihood of such standardisation due to the practical logistics of operationally managing and running that type of business.

Confidentiality, Personal Data and Data Protection

It is important to recognise that data may be subject to a duty of confidentiality, which will have implications with respect to the storage and use of the affected data. From the English law[2] perspective, this is mainly a matter of contract between the party providing the information and the recipient, although it should be noted that there is a common

---

2 In some jurisdictions, there is criminal liability in respect of a breach of bank secrecy/banking client confidentiality (e.g. under the Banking Act in Singapore).

law duty of confidentiality to a client under English law. There is typically an implied contractual term in the contract between a bank and a client for the affairs of the client to be kept confidential. In *Tournier v National Provincial and Union Bank of England* the basic duty was described by Atkin LJ as follows:

> *It clearly goes beyond the state of the account, that is, whether there is a debit or a credit balance, and the amount of the balance. It must extend at least to all the transactions that go through the account, and to the securities, if any, given in respect of the account, and in respect of such matters it must, I think, extend beyond the period when the account is closed, or ceases to be an active account… I further think that the obligation extends to information obtained from sources other than the customer's actual account, if the occasion upon which the information was obtained arose out of the banking relations of the bank and its customers, for example, with a view to assisting the bank in coming to decisions as to its treatment of its customers… in this case, however, I should not extend the obligation to information as to the customer obtained after he had ceased to be a customer.*

This common law duty and any further contractual agreements with respect to client confidentiality is subject to an increasing number of exceptions. The common law duty itself is subject to exceptions for cases where disclosure is made with the consent of the client; is required by the interests of the bank; is required by law; or if there is a duty to the public to disclose. There will also be exceptions under regulations (e.g. the cooperation banks are required to give to the FCA and other regulators under the Financial Services and Markets Act 2000 (FSMA 2000) as part of the investigatory powers of HM Revenue & Customs and on criminal matters).

It is common for clients to require certain data information to be expressly treated as confidential, or to limit the use of the data by a financial firm. In the trading context, asset managers may insert confidentiality provisions into master trading agreements such as the ISDA Master Agreement, requiring the identity of underlying funds to not be disclosed to sales and trading functions in banks, and limited to those that need to understand the identity of those underlying funds from an operational and processing perspective. This can create significant issues in the legal agreement data context. Although the legal and documentation teams will typically be able to have access to a legal agreement database, there may be other departments, such as sales and trading, that may also have access to the documents and any related legal agreement data. This would be a breach of the confidentiality provisions agreed with the asset manager. Accordingly, in some cases, an identifier is often used in such systems rather than the name of the underlying fund entities, although where the actual documents are stored in the database, this may require a process to redact relevant details in the legal agreement database. As there will be some departments (e.g. compliance and operations) that need to identify the client, there will also need to be a way of mapping the identifier to the actual client, linking the legal agreement data to client data – of course, subject to the required security and access privileges.

It should be noted that some jurisdictions also have strict bank secrecy laws and regulations, although these are treated as outside the scope of this text (but may have a significant impact on the manner in which legal agreement data is managed).

Subject to the above detailed client confidentiality in the banking context, as between corporates, the protection of data and the delineation of the scope of its potential use is mainly a matter of contract between the parties.

In contrast to this, where the client is a natural person, there is significant regulation in order to protect the fundamental rights of that person. In particular, the General Data Protection Regulation (GDPR) became directly applicable in all EU Member States on 25 May 2018, although the Member States have legislated for this individually as permitted, for example, in the UK, under the Data Protection Act 2018 (also in effect from 25 May 2018). The GDPR covers 'personal data', broadly defined as 'any information relating to an identified or identifiable natural person'.[3] The GDPR is concerned with the processing of personal data, which would include storing or using the personal data. It seeks to provide a core set of data protection principles for personal data processing, providing that it must:

- be processed lawfully, fairly and in a transparent manner;
- be collected for specified, explicit and legitimate purposes and not further processed in a manner inconsistent with those purposes;
- be adequate, relevant and limited to what is necessary for the relevant purpose;
- be accurate and, where necessary, kept up-to-date;
- not permit identification of the individuals to which it relates for longer than necessary for the purpose for which the data is processed; and
- be processed in a manner that ensures its security.

It should be noted that the GDPR has very broad applicability, including in relation to data of natural persons stored in the legal data context (e.g. the names and contact details of contract signatories stored in a legal agreement). Unlike the previous regime, data processors have obligations and liabilities under the GDPR.

Accordingly, the GDPR requires parties to review current contracts, which will need to be renegotiated where necessary to ensure they implement the requirements of the GDPR in respect of personal data sharing and governance, appropriate allocation of responsibilities and liability for compliance with the GDPR. The impact of this for financial firms cannot be underestimated, given personal data flows throughout the very heart of such organisations.

Databases

A database is simply an organised collection of data (or 'data store') in relation to a particular theme or topic that is stored and accessible electronically. A relational database is a data store containing one or more related tables each given a name, which is referred to as a 'schema'. Each table holds information about certain 'entities' – these might be objects, people or things about which data can be collected. In the case of a database of OTC derivative transactions, the entities might be the specific legs or their cash flows. Entities are comprised of 'attributes' which describe their characteristics. For example, a transaction which is to be recorded is an entity and things like counterparty ID, transaction type, start date, notional amount, termination date and other defining features of a transaction will be its attributes. A database provides a means

---

3 Article 4(1) of the General Data Protection Regulation.

of storing information. It is essentially a structured collection of different data sources such as schemas (the structure of a database expressed in a formal language), queries, reports and so on, allowing the user to see all records stored in the database via tables. These schemas and tables in a relational database are sets of data values, which can store any number of data sets and a database can contain many schemas and tables. As such, databases enable the easy access of information as well as the easy management of data.

There are a number of benefits to using a database. To start with, vast amounts of information can be stored. Financial firms have large numbers of counterparties and subsidiaries of counterparties with whom they trade, and with each counterparty there will be thousands of different types of transactions, meaning there is a huge number of payments and deliveries of certain assets that need to be understood and managed day to day. Firms must be able to store the details of every single transaction which takes place, relating to when amounts and assets need to be paid and/or received, delivered and/or received, generating a large amount of data. The use of a database means that queries can be run to search for specific records or groups of records, making information more accessible. Furthermore, reports can be produced from the data stored and queries run, as well as supporting trend analysis in relation to the data. This is important, especially where there is a vast amount of information, as it can be difficult to search for specific features where a table cannot fit onto one page or screen. Databases also mean that data can be extracted and exported into, for example, a usable spreadsheet or Word file, or other forms such as charts and heatmaps.

So, each table within a database contains the number of records, attributes and values. Before setting up a database, this record structure must be decided, and it is this structure/data model that will enable search and report functions. So, how are databases structured? We first introduce this concept, although we return later in the chapter to the concept of data modelling and how best to represent data in a structured format.

Given the subject of this text, let us use the example of a database of legal opinions (see Chapter 6). A record is made up of lots of individual pieces of information called 'fields'. Our record structure can be created in the form of a table containing a number of columns having 'field names' covering areas such as the law firm providing the legal opinion, whether active or not, the type of legal opinion, the date the opinion is provided and its cost (both in terms of amount and currency) (see Figure 4.1). Each

Field Name	Data Type	Format
Law Firm Providing Opinion	Text (VARCHAR)	Up to 50 characters
Active	Boolean	Y/N
Legal Opinion Type	Close-out Netting or Collateral Enforceability (VARCHAR)	Close-out Netting or Collateral Enforceability
Date Provided	Date	DDMMYYYY
Cost	Number	INTEGER(5)
Cost Currency	Currency ISO Code (VARCHAR)	ABC (VARCHAR(3))

Figure 4.1 Record structure for a legal opinion database

Field	Data
Law Firm Providing Opinion	Dhalla, Khimji and Dolea
Active	Y
Legal Opinion Type	Close-out Netting
Date Provided	01122014
Cost	50000
Cost Currency	USD

Figure 4.2 Example legal opinion record

legal opinion will result in data that can be recorded in each field (referred to as a column) and each field name will correspond to a 'data type'. The data type for each field name will determine what sort of information will be input under each field name; for example, the data type for the 'date provided' will be 'date', whilst other data types may be alphanumeric, currency or a simple yes/no (referred to as 'Boolean'). Data type is important as it ensures that the data stored is usable and makes validation simpler; if a numeric field (e.g. the cost of a legal opinion) was stored in a text field, the database would not easily facilitate the addition of individual figures to automatically generate a total (e.g. of amounts spent across multiple opinions with a particular law firm). The length and format of each field type can then be determined as, for example, 'up to 7 characters', 'DDMMYY', 'Y/N', 'up to 5 numbers', and so on. This necessitates, when setting up a database, that two things be considered: (1) what information is being stored (which should consider the business process that requires this information) and; (2) what data validation needs to apply? Once these questions have been answered, it is possible to make effective decisions about the record structure. See Figure 4.2 for a sample record structure in action. A key field is a unique identifier for each record and, as such, a table should always contain a key field (although this might not be displayed in the 'front-end' of the database). In the context of the above example of legal opinions, it may make sense to select the law firm name as the key field, or, if not unique (i.e. a law firm might provide more than one legal opinion), to apply a unique identification number.

Relational Databases and Flat Files

A relational database has multiple tables which are connected via keys (see Figures 4.3 and 4.4 for an example of a relational database and record). In contrast, a database in which data is stored in a single table is known as a flat file (see Figure 4.5).

Relational databases were originally proposed by the English computer scientist Edgar F. Codd in 1970, who showed that data relationships could be represented in this way. Each entity type that is described in a database has its own table, with rows representing each entity and columns representing attributes. Each row in a table has its own unique key, so that the rows in a table can be linked to the rows in other tables by reference to the unique key of the row to which it should be linked (the details of different types of keys are covered later in this chapter).

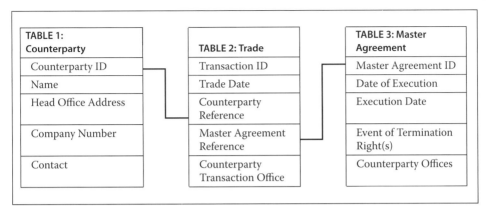

Figure 4.3 Example legal opinion relational database structure

Counterparty Record 1	Trade Record 1	Master Agreement Record 1
123456XYZ	888888	7777777
ABC Bank	01/01/2017	02/12/2010
44 Bank Street, Frankfurt, Germany	123456XYZ	08/08/2020
987654321	7777777	Non-payment; Material Adverse Change; Insolvency; Cross-default
Phillip Chymiy	London	London; Frankfurt

Trade Record 2
181818
23/12/2016
123456XYZ
7777777
Frankfurt

Figure 4.4 Example database table records

For example, a capital markets derivatives transaction database may contain three tables: a table containing counterparty details, a second table containing the economic terms of transactions and a third table containing information as to the Master Agreements in place. Rather than inputting all data manually in a flat file, using a relational table it would be possible to select the counterparty from some sort of drop-down menu, it would then be possible to select the Master Agreement under which the trade has been made, before inputting the trade details.

One limitation of relational databases is that each item can only contain one attribute. So, we end up with a multitude of different tables: the counterparty details are stored

Transaction ID	Trade Date	Counterparty Transaction Office	Counterparty ID	Counterparty Name	Head Office Address	Company Number	Contact	Master Agreement ID	Date of Execution	Event of Termination Right(s)	Counterparty Offices
88888	01/01/2017	London	123456XYZ	ABC Bank	44 Bank Street, Frankfurt, Germany	987654321	Phillip Chymiy	7777777	02/12/2010	Non-payment; Material Adverse Change; Insolvency; Cross-default	London; Frankfurt
181818	23/12/2016	Frankfurt	123456XYZ	ABC Bank	44 Bank Street, Frankfurt, Germany	987654321	Phillip Chymiy	7777777	02/12/2010	Non-payment; Material Adverse Change; Insolvency; Cross-default	London; Frankfurt

Figure 4.5 Flat file equivalent of the database table records shown in Figure 4.4

in one table, the trade details in another, the Master Agreement details in another, the collateral details in another, the netting details in another, the legal opinion details in another, and so on. Flat file databases, on the other hand, store key values in one row of data. For example, a flat file table would contain the counterparty name, address and company number together as one record, making it a far more convenient option for very small data sets, especially when the data coverage is limited to one conceptual entity. As the coverage expands beyond that, a flat file database will need to be populated with an increasing amount of duplicate data. Flat file databases cannot enforce relationships between different pieces of data. Flat file databases can be converted into relational databases through the 'normalisation process' (described below).

The benefit of a relational database is that they are simple, robust, flexible, scalable and compatible in managing generic data and able to scale to cover multiple data entity types as well. Under a flat file database (see Figure 4.5), each time a trade is made with the counterparty ABC Bank, for example, a number of fields relating to the counterparty and the Master Agreement in place with it would have to be filled out manually and duplicates would have to be created. Because this method is a manual one, it is not time-efficient and increases the risk of mistakes. For example, when a user manually enters the name of the counterparty as 'ABC Bank', there is a risk that the counterparty name may be misspelt or that one user may enter the counterparty name in capitals and another user may enter the counterparty name in lowercase. If there is no consistency in the way in which the information is input into the tables, when a user needs to search for all trades entered into with a counterparty, the search function would not be validated; in searching for 'ABC Bank', it might not be possible to easily search for trades entered into by 'ABC BANK PLC' and 'abc bank'. Hence, important trade information could be lost within a large collection of data on a database because of a lack of consistency. Repeating data unnecessarily in this way is called 'data duplication'. A relational database offers a better solution, as it means that multiple tables can be set up which link together; when a user enters a trade into the system with the counterparty 'ABC Bank', they can link to a separate table containing a list of all counterparties and search for the 'ABC Bank' entry, which is then selected and will ensure consistency across all trades with that counterparty. Reducing data duplication also has the additional benefit of reducing the amount of data which needs to be stored, thus making the database smaller. However, in order to achieve this, relational databases must be internally complex. For example, a relatively simple statement could have dozens of potential query execution paths; if a bank is trading with thousands of different counterparties and each counterparty has offices in a number of jurisdictions, the number of entries for each counterparty alone could be massive, let alone the huge number of trades.

Data in a relational database is readable by executing Structured Query Language (SQL) queries in a database management tool (e.g. TOAD) to extract and present the data as required. SQL can be thought of as a language for managing data in a relational database. It can assist with the extraction of data from multiple tables in the database, but requires an understanding of the database structure, including the various 'key' (e.g. primary and foreign) relationships.

For example, the SQL statement 'Select Trade_Date, Counterparty_Reference from Trade_Table where Transaction_ID = 989272' would, in respect of the Trade_Table shown in Figure 4.6, give the following result: 15/03/2018, 567315AZX.

Transaction	Trade_Date	Counterparty_Reference	Master_Agreement Reference
888888	01/01/2017	123456XYZ	7777777
989272	15/03/2018	567315AZX	2041781
125789	12/11/2013	380360BAE	8861210
803606	03/06/2018	781978DAP	5049356

Figure 4.6 Example Trade_Table transactions

For very large databases, the main concern is scalability. As more and more tables are created, their scalability requirements can grow exponentially large. Almost all relational database systems use SQL as the language for querying and maintaining the database. A database object is an aspect of a database that can be used to manage and hold data. Examples of this are:

- Tables (as explained above, providing an ability to store rows of data);
- Indexes (data structures that allow quick location and retrieval of data in the database – without having to search each row of a database table – by creating and storing an index data structure);
- Sequences (provides a set order of operations/functions to be performed on a set of data);
- View (saves the way – 'the view' – in which data is presented and viewed; and
- Synonyms (an alternative name for a database schema object).

Data Model

The issue that we must turn to now is *how* data can be structured to optimally support its best use. A data structure – or *data model* – is an abstract way of organising data so that it can be used efficiently by those to whom the data is relevant (data consumers). It does this by organising the data available and standardising how different pieces of data relate to both one another and to the properties of real-world business objects or 'entities'. In short, data models determine the structure of data. The important thing to grasp is that data models describe the structure, manipulation and integrity aspects of the data stored in database management systems (DBMSs). Examples of DMBSs are MySQL, PostgreSQL, Microsoft Access, SQL Server, Oracle and FoxPro. Data models do not describe the unstructured data, rather they organise the various elements of the data so that usable information can be obtained from it. There are numerous methods of data modelling views methods available (see Figure 4.7), each using different diagram conventions and styles; some examples include VHDM (very high-level data model), HDM (high-level data model), conceptual, logical and physical data models, which we now explain.

Very High-Level Data Model and High-Level Data Model

These simply seek to provide a structure from which other, more detailed data models can be viewed. The audience for such levels of detail are the business world and they

Data Model Feature	Conceptual Data Model	Logical Data Model	Physical Data Model
Entity Name	√	√	
Entity Relationship (how entities relate to each other)	√	√	
Attributes/Characteristics (details of entities)		√	
Primary Key		√	√
Foreign Key		√	√
Table Name			√
Column Name			√
Column Data Type			√

Figure 4.7 Comparing conceptual, logical and physical data models

would typically be no more than one page, setting out business areas, subject areas, applications and possibly stakeholder viewpoints. These are only really required for larger data modelling exercises. The notation used for the VHDM is far less important than for other levels of data model. The HDM builds on the VHDM, seeking to introduce core terms and definitions and business logic. It is still aimed at business users.

Conceptual Data Model   This is a combination of concepts and facts (with semantic formulations defining them) about what is possible, necessary and obligatory in the 'subset' of the real world (see Figure 4.8). It presents a view of reality in the way it is seen by a

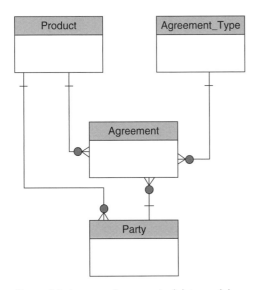

Figure 4.8 An example conceptual data model

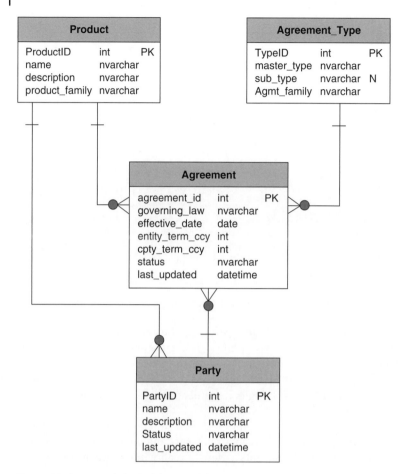

Figure 4.9 An example logical data model

business. Accordingly, it provides concise details about the business and the terms used by the business. The conceptual data model identifies high-level key business and system entities and their relationships that define the scope of the problem to be addressed.

Logical Data Model This involves the refinement of the conceptual high-level business and system entities into more detailed logical entities (see Figure 4.9). It provides details of concepts in a manner that can be understood by end users of the data but is closer to the way in which the data is organised 'physically' in a database than the conceptual data model. The logical data model is an intermediate design step between conceptual and physical levels. It is meant to be both platform and database management system-independent.

Physical Data Model The physical data model (see Figure 4.10) deals with internal IT design, including hardware, software and tools, and the implementation in the technical environment. A physical data model is dependent on the specific database management system (even the specific version of it, and configuration choices for an instance of

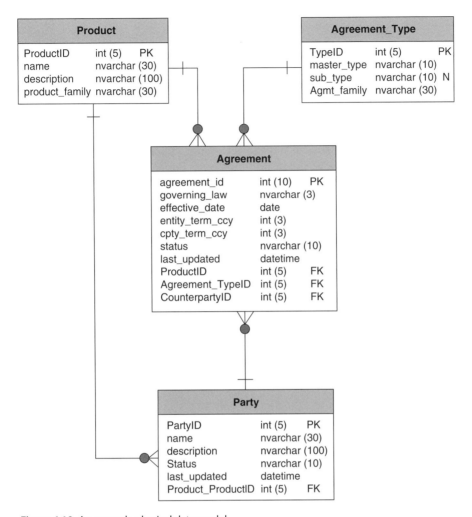

Figure 4.10 An example physical data model

a database) and is therefore sometimes called a database scheme. It will involve details of tables, index construction, modes of referential integrity (declarative or procedural), constraints, views and physical storage objects such as table spaces.

As can be seen from the visual representations of these three types of data model (Figures 4.8–4.10), complexity increases from the conceptual to the logical to the physical data model. It is for this reason that one starts with the conceptual data model (to ensure an understanding at a high level of what the different entities in the data are and how they relate to one another); we then move on to the logical data model (to understand the details of the data without worrying about how it will actually be implemented), before finally addressing the physical data model (providing details on how to implement the data model in the database of choice).

In order to ensure that the legal agreement, for example, conveys the correct meaning through to its structured data form of representation, it needs to consider an understanding of the ever-changing regulations at play (and what they mean for the information needed from the agreements) and the key ingredients in the formation of a valid and enforceable contract. Typically, business data stewards (so in the context of a legal agreement, the legal department) provide the business requirements for data and information and then data architects, analysts and database administrators (who collaborate with software developers) are responsible for the design of the data model. While lawyers do not need to be involved in the physical design of database systems, they do need to be involved in the conceptual data models that define these database systems. Communication between the subject matter experts (in this case lawyers) and IT is necessary to achieve the desired outcome. For example, lawyers can help determine items such as: What is an agreement? Does it need to have two parties, or is it possible to have a contract with a single or three parties? Can contracts have annexes or schedules or link together?

Database Relationships

A 'primary key' or 'key field' is a field which is unique and therefore enables the identification of every and any record in a particular table (each such database table row, often referred to as a 'tuple'). Without a primary key, there is nothing to uniquely identify a record and so all records would have to be manually searched if a field needed to be found. There are two types of primary key:

1) simple; and
2) compound/composite.

A primary key is made up of a single field only (e.g. a counterparty ID), whereas a compound primary key combines two or more fields to create a unique value. It is not always possible to identify a single client agreement from simply the type of agreement entered into (this is therefore not a primary key). However, every agreement might be uniquely identified from a legal agreement ID (a primary key). In contrast, a combination of agreement type, the counterparty to an agreement and an execution date might uniquely enable an agreement from a firm's agreement portfolio to be uniquely identified – this is therefore a composite key, requiring three fields to be combined, to uniquely identify an agreement in a table holding details of agreements.

When databases have a large number of records, it can take a long time to search for values using a primary key. As a solution to this problem, fields can be indexed for faster searching in a similar way to an index contained in a book. This is what is known as a 'secondary key' and is achieved by setting fields to be 'indexed' when setting up the database table. It requires a 'cataloguing'-type process to be undertaken.

A foreign key links database tables together, creating relationships between them. It represents one field (or a combination of fields) in a particular table and uniquely identifies and references the primary key of another table, thereby establishing a link between them. Stated differently, a foreign key is defined in one table, but refers to a primary key in another table (see Figure 4.11). In the example below, 'Party' has a primary key called 'PartyID'. The agreement table has a foreign key, 'PartyID', which uniquely references it. The table containing the foreign key is called a child table, and the table containing the primary key is called the parent table. The foreign key's purpose is to identify a particular row of a parent table. Accordingly, it is usually required that the foreign key is

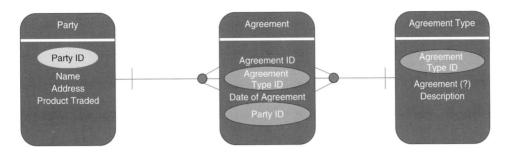

Figure 4.11 The use of primary and foreign keys, shown in an entity relationship diagram

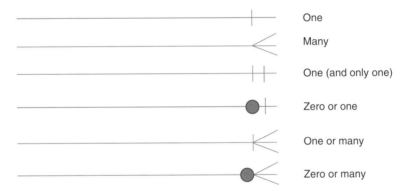

Figure 4.12 Symbols used to express relationships in an entity relationship diagram

equal to the primary key in a parent table row, or else has no value (i.e. a 'null' value). This is a referential integrity constraint between the two tables. It is common to require that every non-null foreign key corresponds to a row of a parent table to avoid data issues.

Where there is a link between entities, this is known as a 'relationship'. These relationships (Figure 4.12) can be shown in the form of an 'entity relationship diagram'. As part of the entity relationship diagrams, there are different stylings of the lines between the entities to represent the relationships (known as 'cardinality' and 'ordinality').

These relationships take the form of one-to-one, many-to-many and one-to-many.

A one-to-one database relationship (Figure 4.13) shows where an entity may only be linked to one other entity. For example, the defined business view might be such that a

Figure 4.13 An example of a 'one-to-one' relationship

Figure 4.14 An example of a 'many-to-many' relationship

company can have only one registered office, and a registered office can only relate to one company.

Many-to-many database relationships (Figure 4.14) show where a number of entities may be linked to a number of other entities. For example, in the example here, each department must be managed by one or more employees, and each employee may be the manager of one or more departments.

Many-to-one or one-to-many are preferable to many-to-many relationships. In the example of Figure 4.14, although one would be able to – from the database – determine who managed a department in the past and which departments were managed by a particular employee in the past, one cannot, due to the many-to-many relationship, put any dates to this management assignment. This can be 'resolved' through the addition of a new entity type and relationships. This process is referred to as 'resolving the many-to-many relationship'.

In order to make a many-to-many relationship either a many-to-one or a one-to-many relationship (Figure 4.15), an extra entity is usually added to the database design.

Normalisation   This is the process of organising data in a database (Figure 4.16). It involves the process of restructuring the tables in a relational database in order to ensure that database usage results in unambiguous data and operates as intended. It is a method of refining the initial table design and assisting with the relationships

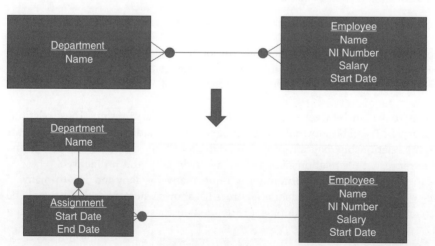

Figure 4.15 Adding extra entities to convert a 'many-to-many' relationship to a 'one-to-many' relationship

Client	Client Contact	Contact Number	Transaction	Mark-to-Market
Fund 786	Abbas	+44 7765434574	Interest Rate Swap	$240,000
Fund 110	Naila	+1 1987543123	Credit Derivative	$120,000
Fund 5	Fatema	+44 7712345678	Interest Rate Swap	$250,000
Fund 14	Peter	+44 7798765432	Cross Currency Swap	$32,000
Fund 12	Oana	+46 9876450987	Credit Derivative	$32,000
Fund 1	Jason	+41 9870965432	Commodity Derivative	$100,000
Fund 66	Damian	+1 6458654274	Credit Derivative	$50,000
Fund 1	Jason	+41 9870965432	Commodity Derivative	−$10,000

Figure 4.16 A database consisting of one table prior to normalisation

Client	Client Contact	Contact Number	Client	Transaction	Mark-to-Market
Fund 786	Abbas	+41 9870965432	Fund 786	Interest Rate Swap	$240,000
Fund 110	Naila	+1 1987543123	Fund 110	Credit Derivative	$120,000
Fund 5	Fatema	+44 7712345678	Fund 14	Cross Currency Swap	$32,000
Fund 14	Peter	+44 7798765432	Fund 12	Credit Derivative	$32,000
Fund 12	Oana	+46 9876450987	Fund 1	Commodity Derivative	$90,000
Fund 1	Jason	+41 9870965432	Fund 66	Credit Derivative	$50,000
Fund 66	Damian	+1 6458654274	Fund 5	Interest Rate Swap	$250,000
			Fund 1	Commodity Derivative	−$100,000

Figure 4.17 The database in Figure 4.16 post-normalisation

and columns that are incorporated in each table. It can increase data duplication, but does not introduce data redundancy – which is the unnecessary duplication of data.

To illustrate the normalisation process, in Figure 4.16, the table is used for the purpose of keeping track of a certain group of transactions and the current mark-to-market. However, there may be circumstances whereby a client's trade may need to be deleted (i.e. that trade might be terminated or reach expiry), which would result in the deletion of their client contact data. The normalisation process would understand this issue and solve the problem by dividing this table into two tables, one with information about each client and the transaction entered into and another with each transaction and the related profit made, as seen in Figure 4.17. The two tables would be linked through keys, but can be maintained separately.

XML stands for eXtensible Markup Language. It can be viewed as a tool allowing the storage and transfer of data that is both software and hardware independent. It is a form of markup language, like HTML (Hypertext Markup Language), a process in which a document can be annotated in a way that is syntactically distinguishable from the text of the document itself. Both HTML and XML are 'descriptive' markup languages, in that the markup is used to label or 'tag' parts of a document, rather than to provide instructions on how to process parts of a document (as is the case with other types of markup language, such as PostScript). This decouples the structure or form of a document from its specific presentation. The founding idea behind HTML and XML is, however, significantly different, with HTML designed by computer scientist Sir Tim Berners-Lee to mark up a document in relation to how it should be presented (specifically, on the World Wide Web), whereas XML was designed to provide a means of marking up a document to help define what the data in the document is. It is often referred to as a 'meta-markup' language. Unlike HTML, XML tags are not predefined by the standard, rather the author of an XML document is required to define both the tags and the document structure itself. Many systems contain data stored in different formats, which makes transfer of data between such systems difficult. XML provides a means of storing data in simple text form, and allows a manner for it to be transferred from one system to another and shared, through the use of the tags to help ensure each system is given details of the document contents.

XML vs Relational Databases

XML[4] databases present an alternative to relational databases, allowing data to be specified and persist in XML format. Both XML documents and relational databases store data and enable data extraction. Relational databases are typically preferable if handling large volumes of data but do not represent data in a way that both machines and people can read. Because XML documents can be read by both people and machines, they are therefore termed as 'self-describing'.

Extract, Transform, Load

In order to give a sense of the broader processes involved in legal data management, we now detail the extract, transform, load (ETL) process (Figure 4.18). There are many software tools that provide all three of these processes together.

1) **Extract.** Data is extracted from data sources. These data sources may be homogenous or heterogenous and can be stored in relational databases or flat files, but can include other data structures. Overall, the extraction phase converts the data into a single format prior to transformation processing.
2) **Transform.** Refers to the process where data is transformed for storage into a consistent format so that it can be used for querying and analysis. A series of functions is applied to the extracted data in order to prepare it for loading into the end target. Otherwise, data may require aggregation in order to produce total figures, joining with data from other sources, transposing, translating coded values or selecting only certain columns to load. This step may involve both reformatting and cleansing of data.
3) **Load.** The data is loaded into the final target database, which will be an operational data store, mart or warehouse.

---

4 Although perhaps outside the scope of this text, beyond simple XML text there are also related technologies such as XML Schemas (XSD) and XML Transformations (XSL), which complement XML text documents by adding value in the areas of validation and processing.

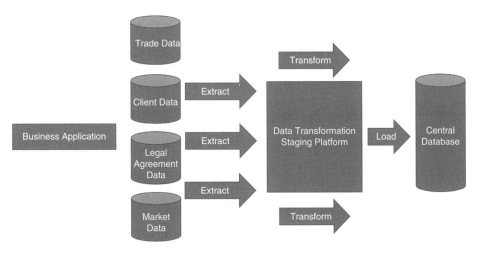

Figure 4.18 Illustrating the extract, transform, load process

ETL gained popularity in the 1980s as data warehouses were developed. Firms began to use multiple application databases to store different types of business information. The ETL process offered a manner of obtaining data from these separate stores and transforming it as required to be able to combine the data into a central database.

For legal agreement data, an ETL layer is often used to avoid repetitively capturing data multiple times, when it can be formulaically expressed and automated. For example, a legal agreement may specify a rating agency code range, as a condition for certain events to occur, such as the loss of rights of rehypothecation over collateral. Rather than capturing this agreement data multiple times, one for each level in the rating agency scale, it is common for an ETL process to be used to generate each of the rows of data required in an end target database table.

When designed properly as part of the end-to-end data management process,[5] the ETL step can enforce data quality and consistency, provide data validation and assist with the lineage of data (i.e. where it comes from), and help understand its impact on other data assets across a firm.

We now examine the importance of successful data management within a firm. Key to this successful data management are those responsible for the management, storage and security of the data – these varying roles are discussed, before a brief consideration of the relationship between good data governance and regulatory compliance in the wake of the Financial Crisis.

Legal Data Governance

Data governance is the delegation of authority, control and decision-making over the management of data assets. As such, data governance is best understood as the managing of data as an asset, using a framework of accountabilities and processes.

---

5 Note that ETL tools are usually part of a suite of functionality offered by a master data management (MDM) tool. This provides, through a combination of architecture, technology and business process, a method of providing authoritative master data throughout an enterprise.

Importantly, data governance is not a function performed by those who manage information and, as Ladley in his excellent text on data governance so adamantly explains, 'It is *never* an IT program'. Data governance is a business process separate from data (or information) management. It is crucial in our understanding of data governance to emphasise the formation of a framework, undertaken by different roles and levels of accountability. Whilst not a function performed by those who manage information – it refers to making sure that information is managed properly. The 'bucket and water' analogy is an effective method of explaining this concept. Chief Information Officers (CIOs) are responsible for information management; they ensure that the *bucket* is fit for purpose, is the right size for the amount of water, and is clean and water-tight. Chief Data Officers (CDOs), however, are responsible for the *water* contained within the bucket, by ensuring that the right amount of water is collected, that the water is clean and of good quality. The CDO is responsible for what happens to the water, making it available when it is needed.

At a minimum, a data governance framework should include policies to mandate:

1) how a firm will manage its data;
2) the roles and responsibilities of those involved in the management of data; and
3) the basic processes to ensure clarity, consistency and coordination.

Data Governance Roles

Definition of Roles
Having established that data governance concerns a framework of accountabilities and processes, it is clear that certain roles and responsibilities need to be assigned to individuals within firms in order for them to work. Enterprise data management theory typically defines the following roles: (1) the *data trustee*, (2) the *data steward* and (3) the *data custodian*.

The Data Trustee
The data trustee is ultimately responsible and the overarching guardian of a particular data domain, defining the scope of the data domain, tracking its status, and defining and sponsoring the strategic roadmap for the domain. They would ultimately be accountable for the data, but would typically delegate the day-to-day data governance responsibilities to data stewards and data custodians within the firm.

The Data Steward
The data steward is a subject-matter expert (for legal data purposes therefore probably a lawyer) who defines the data category types, allowable values and data quality requirements. Data stewardship is concerned with taking care of data assets that do not necessarily belong to the steward(s) themselves, but which represent the concerns of others (potentially a business unit, department, set of data, or even the needs of the entire firm). It is essential that a data steward understands data management concepts in order to be able to ensure that the value of a firm's legal contract data is realised. This is particularly important as it is the data steward's role not just to manage the data, but also to ensure that the data can be used to draw business conclusions and make decisions. Data quality involves fitness for a purpose (else the

data will not be of the requisite quality from the data consumption perspective). This includes ensuring data quality and the protection of data assets (e.g. by keeping them up-to-date and complying with the increasing regulations which are being brought in to deal with data issues in the increasingly digital environment regarding data security and privacy).

The Data Custodian

Data stewards and data custodians are both accountable for data assets, however, the former is from a business perspective and the latter from a technology perspective. They both play crucial and complementary roles in respect of data governance.

Data custodians are typically part of IT, managing access rights to the data and implementing controls to ensure their integrity, security and privacy. They are accountable for the technical control of the data and are concerned with issues such as availability, continuity and back-up/restore of data.

Why is the Outlining of Roles so Important?

Industry-wide, there is a lack of ownership, accountability and responsibility regarding (1) the storage of legal contracts, terms and conditions and (2) the key legal terms required by an institution's internal and external consumers (both in terms of what these key terms are and the accuracy of the data captured). As noted by Murphy (2013), it goes without saying that market trading necessitates significant operational complexity: '[t]rades have to be recorded and confirmed, payments have to be made and options sometimes have to be exercised. Trades terminate, are restructured, or novated to third parties. Moreover, the business has to be accounted for and regulatory capital is required for many risks'. Not only do these processes generate a large amount of data, '[t]he processes for fulfilling these requirements are often fallible, and the resulting operational risks can be substantial'. Data governance is the key starting point for curing these issues. In particular, a formal statement of roles helps to establish a hierarchy to enable issue resolution, monitoring and direction setting.

The Relationship Between Data Governance and Regulatory Compliance

Regulatory compliance is a hangover from the Financial Crisis, but it is widely acknowledged that while regulations were put in place to safeguard against future collapses, the cost – and effort – to comply is high. What makes regulatory compliance so difficult? The problem is that regulations are complex and ever-changing, data is inconsistent and resides in a multitude of different systems, compliance reporting is complex and requires an army of analysts to complete, current processes are not scalable or sustainable, technology is not user-friendly and, finally, cross-departmental collaboration is challenging at best.

The secret, however, to making the inevitable pain of regulatory compliance easier to bear is data governance. After all, it is, as described by Ladley (2012), 'a set of best practices that optimize, secure, and leverage information as an enterprise asset by aligning the objectives of multiple functions'. Data governance has the potential to master data management, build business intelligence, improve data quality and manage documents. The potential for value-added, particularly in the financial sector, is immense.

There are a number of regulatory requirements where compliance can be aided with the assistance of data governance. Regulators expect firms to show that the data used by a firm is trustworthy and increasingly demand a demonstration of clear ownership, lineage, quality and security, as well as being able to show progress by regulatory reporting data governance maturity in these areas, especially when the data relates ultimately to financial stability, such as for risk aggregation purposes (see Chapter 5 and the discussion of BCBS 239). But the struggle for many financial institutions is that data governance is currently a series of manual processes, hastily glued together through emails, SharePoint sites, spreadsheets and End User Development Applications (EUDAs). Financial firms have previously failed to implement data governance as an ongoing framework and clearly the aforementioned 'cut and paste' method is not effective, scalable nor sustainable. As is the case in other areas of business, embracing purpose-built technology can help promote automation, repeatability, transparency and collaboration across the institution through integrated data governance processes and reporting.

End User Development Applications

EUDAs are applications that evolve somewhat outside the main control of a firm's IT department and instead are developed by business users. EUDAs normally take the form of (amongst others) Microsoft Excel spreadsheets and can be created easily and quickly by non-IT staff – in some cases they can support critical business operations such as valuation models. Such applications have often arisen due to business users becoming frustrated by the speed at which IT departments are able to service their requests or by the lack of flexibility in existing IT systems. Consequently, they have reverted to developing their own solutions. From an end-user perspective, EUDAs can provide significant benefits as they allow users to directly manage, control and manipulate data when responding to circumstances such as new regulations. However, from a data governance perspective, the creators of EUDAs may not appreciate how the data is managed within these applications, since they are often not subject to the same development, monitoring and reporting scrutiny and control as traditional applications developed by IT departments. As a result, there is a strong risk that such applications will contain data errors and are vulnerable to unauthorised change by other members in the firm.

This clearly creates conflict between IT departments and those developing EUDAs, which gives rise to two challenges. Firstly, given the scale of legacy EUDAs, it is not practical to simply remove these applications since many support critical business processes. Secondly, it may not be viable to convert these applications into the existing corporate IT systems due to the cost and timeframes involved. Therefore, since firms rely so heavily on EUDAs for financial reporting purposes, the solution is that firms must place tight data governance principles at the heart of EUDA development. Such a task would require collaboration between the end users developing the applications and those in the IT departments, to ensure that the practical solutions can be created but within a robust and secure data governance framework.

We begin with a brief summary of the concept of taxonomies before going on to consider their use within the legal data context, including examples and issues that have been found within major global financial institutions.

Contractual Taxonomies

The term 'taxonomy' refers to a scheme of classification; it is a term that is derived from the Greek words '*taxis*' meaning 'arrangement' and '*nomos*' meaning 'managing'. It therefore involves constructing mechanisms by assigning names and categories, and making judgments as to how to map different concepts and terms to these categories so as to systematically classify things. For example, animals may be classified into kingdom, phylum, class, order, family, genus and species. So, a taxonomy may classify animals into vertebrates and invertebrates, before categorising them further into reptiles, fish, mammals, birds, amphibians, insects, crustaceans, arachnids, molluscs and so on, then into exact species. However, this is not to say that living organisms *must* be classified in this way. Alternative means by which they may be classified might include whether they are living or extinct, the number of legs, whether they are hot or cold-blooded, plants or animals, and so on. Ultimately, there is no single way by which any taxonomy should be represented. Whilst this affords a great deal of flexibility and means that specific taxonomies can be constructed with a specific purpose or set of data in mind, it also means that taxonomies must be thought through clearly and can change over time as use function changes.

Why Classify and What Purpose Do Taxonomies Serve, Particularly with Regard to Legal Data?

A taxonomy creates a framework in which to work. It allows classification to be conducted within the framework of that taxonomy. Without this, there is no standard way, in the legal context, of reviewing a set of legal agreements (or the data within them) in order to then manage the need for the particular agreement to be made known (e.g. operational purposes such as making payments or deliveries, or risk management) or details of the terms within it.

Taxonomies need to be distinguished from metadata – although they both need to work together in order to make content searchable, recognisable and, ultimately, useful. A taxonomy organises information and the metadata describes it. Defining and using a taxonomy also facilitates the categorising of content and assets using a controlled vocabulary. This can then be used as an integration reference point between a legal data system and other business systems. It is this integration, or mismatch between data definitions, that is particularly problematic in the context of legal data in the financial services industry.

Historically, the storage of legal agreements and the data contained within them has been somewhat of an afterthought. Even with a subsequent investment in systems to try and assist, firms have struggled with this – in fact, implementing a system without the underlying taxonomies is similar to purchasing an expensive bookshelf, only then to throw the books at the shelf and wonder at the lack of subsequent organisation. It is the taxonomy, classification, that ensures the books are usefully organised within a library.

Accordingly, there will be a number of taxonomies that are required in the context of legal data, the most important being:

- agreement type;
- agreement clause; and
- legal opinion (in this regard, see Chapter 6).

As a set of principles, it is useful to consider the following guidelines when developing a taxonomy. The taxonomy should:

- give specific uses defined for each of its inherent classification dimensions (e.g. defining the contract status, or whether it is an agreement for which a close-out netting determination is relevant);
- follow a logical hierarchy and be understandable;
- conform to other published taxonomy standards when possible (although there are few of these of note in the context of financial services documentation, any implied industry standard taxonomies should be borne in mind);
- not be redundant to other defined metadata;
- not nest further than four or five levels if possible (this is more a question of practicality than anything else); and
- be system-agnostic.

By way of example, one agreement type taxonomy at a major investment bank consisted of a single-dimensional list of some 520 agreement types. An agreement could only be tagged to one of the listed types, including:

- ISDA Master Agreement
- 1992 ISDA
- 1992 ISDA Master Agreement
- 1992 ISDA Maaster Agreement (intentional misspelling)
- 1992 ISDA Master Agreement (Multicurrency Version)
- 1992 ISDA Master Agreement (Single Currency Version)
- 1992 ISDA Master Agreement (Multicurrency or Single Currency Version)
- Amendment Agreement

It does not take much to quickly understand the issues such a poorly thought out agreement type taxonomy can create.

Leaving aside the erratic entry, one of the issues is that many agreements could fit into each of these categories. Where consumers of the legal data therefore try to search for all ISDA Master Agreements using the tag 'ISDA Master Agreement', the results are inaccurate and incomplete. The issue results from additions to the agreement type list to meet new 'use cases' for agreement types, without considering the impact on existing use cases.

One common issue even when such taxonomies are created is failing to plan for their maintenance. For example, a new agreement type may become relevant to those consuming the legal agreement data (e.g. the new Credit Support Annexes in response to the mandatory margining requirements for uncleared derivatives), or a new type of clause may emerge (e.g. a 'Brexit clause'). It is also all too easy to simply amend the taxonomy without revisiting the specific use cases of the taxonomy dimension affected, and ensuring that this is taken into account. There may be a tactical need to develop the taxonomy in a particular manner, however, after a while, such tactical fixes may become, in total, unmanageable, or cause legal data held to lose its business value. Ultimately, it is crucial that the correct data governance is applied to the management of the taxonomies (see the section 'Legal Data Governance' earlier in this chapter).

During the implementation of the taxonomy, there will no doubt be cases which do not sit neatly within the defined taxonomy. This is to be expected, given the range of documentation types and the variety of information they contain. Although one might amend the taxonomy if required, the more important matter is to define a process by which such cases will be managed, and the ultimate users of the legal data can work with the process and its ultimate impact on them as consumers of the legal data.

ISDA Clause Library

In October 2018, ISDA instructed D2 Legal Technology (D2LT) to create a foundational agreement clause taxonomy and clause library for the ISDA Master Agreement. This initially began as a proof of concept, focusing on five initial clauses, namely Payment Netting, Termination Currency, Set-Off, Credit Event Upon Merger and Automatic Early Termination. After its success, this initiative has at the time of writing, been extended to further clauses from the ISDA Master Agreement, and likely to be extended into other parts of the documentation architecture thereafter.

This taxonomy and clause library can be seen as a basic building block to connect various initiatives, such as the ISDA Common Domain Model (see Chapter 12) and document generation / negotiation platforms (see Chapter 11), as well as more broadly, allowing better management of regulatory and market change. Figure 4.19 below shows a number of the possible benefits and applications of this taxonomy and clause library.

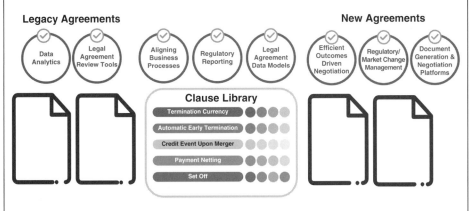

Figure 4.19 Applications and Benefits of the Taxonomy and Clause library
Source: © D2 Legal Technology/Akber Datoo

Other Non-legal Data Taxonomies

In order to unlock the inherent value in the legal data, the legal data in particular needs to correctly link with client and product data. Therefore, the presence and development of client and product taxonomies are crucial to the management of legal data. For example, the representation of a master agreement requires detailing the counterparty, including its type (e.g. corporate vs hedge fund or supranational) and the trades that are governed by the agreement (and their type – e.g. OTC derivative transactions vs repurchase transactions).

Bibliography

Aiken, P. and Allen, D. (2004) *XML in Data Management: Understanding and Applying Them Together*. Morgan Kauffmann: Burlington, MA

Askham, N. (2015) '*Why are there so many different data governance definitions?*' (http://memphis.edu/)

Bray, T., Paoli, J., Sperberg-McQueen, C. M., Maler, E. and Yergeau, F. (2008) 'Extensible Markup Language (XML) 1.0 W3C Recommendation', 26th November 2008

Carruthers, C. and Jackson, P. (2017) *The Chief Data Officer's Playbook*. Facet Publishing: London

Codd, E. (1970) 'Relational completeness of database sublanguages', in *Database Systems*, pp. 65–98. Prentice-Hall: New York.

Collibra (2016) 'Data governance: The secret to sustainable regulatory compliance' (www.collibra.com/data-governance-secret-sustainable-regulatory-compliance-gated/)

D2 Legal Technology LLP (D2LT) Industry Survey (2013) – OTC Master Trading Agreements – Legal Documentation Systems and Processes Survey Results

Datoo, A. (2015) 'Legal contract data: The new reference data challenge for financial firms', *Journal of Securities Operations & Custody*, 7(3), pp. 253–259

Datoo, A. (2017) *GDPR and Big Data – Friends or Foes?* GDPR Report, 24th July 2017

Definition of XML, Merriam Webster (www.merriam-webster.com/dictionary/XML)

Elgendy, N. and Elragal, A. (2014) 'Big data analytics: A literature review paper', in P. Perner (ed.), *Advances in Data Mining: Applications and Theoretical Aspects*. Springer International: Cham

EMC (2014) 'The digital universe of opportunities: Rich data and the increasing value of the internet of things' (www.emc.com/leadership/digital-universe/2014iview/index.htm)

Gordon, K. (2014) *Principles of Data Management: Facilitating Information Sharing*, 2nd edn. BCS Learning & Development: London

IBM (n.d.) 'What is big data' (www.ibm.com/software/data/bigdata) [accessed 20 August 2017]

IBM (2013) 'Infographics & animations: The four V's of big data' (www.ibmbigdatahub.com/infographic/four-vs-big-data)

Information Commissioner's Office (2017) 'Overview of the General Data Protection Regulation', 20th October 2017

Inmon, W., O'Neill, B. and Fryman, L. (2007) *Business Metadata: Capturing Enterprise*. Morgan Kauffmann: Burlington, MA

Ladley, J. (2012) Data Governance: How to Design, Deploy, and Sustain an Effective Data Governance Program. Elsevier: Boston, MA

Mullins, C. (2012) *DB2 Developer's Guide: A Solutions-Oriented Approach to Learning the Foundation and Capabilities of DB2 for z/OS*, 6th edn. IBM Press: Indianapolis, IN

Murphy, D. (2013) *OTC Derivatives, Bilateral Trading and Central Clearing: An Introduction to Regulatory Policy, Market Impact and Systemic Risk*. Palgrave Macmillan: Basingstoke

Prentice, S. (2012) 'From data to decision: Delivering value from 'big data' (www.gartner.com/doc/1966716/data-decision-delivering-value-big)

Tanwar, M., Duggal, R. and Khatri, S. (2015) *Unravelling Unstructured Data: A Wealth of Information in Big Data*. IEEE: New York

The Data Governance Institute, 'Governance and Stewardship'

Tournier v National Provincial and Union Bank of England [1924] 1 KB 461

5

BCBS 239 – Legal Data in Risk Aggregation

In the banking context, the specific importance of data to ensure risk management and global financial stability has been recognised primarily by the Basel Committee on Banking Supervision through BCBS 239. This chapter first seeks to lay out the contents of, and reasoning behind, the BCBS 239 principles on risk data aggregation and reporting, before discussing how firms can successfully achieve compliance and the problems they may face in doing so, focusing on, as relevant, the legal data context.

What is the Basel Committee on Banking Supervision and BCBS 239?

The Basel Committee on Banking Supervision (BCBS) was founded in 1974 and was comprised of regulatory authorities from the major G-10 countries (the G-10 being made up of industrial countries which consult and cooperate on economic, monetary and financial matters), as a forum for Member States on banking supervisory matters. The original aim of the BCBS was the enhancement of financial stability by improving banking supervision worldwide. BCBS 239 is a set of principles published by the Basel Committee in January 2013 for effective risk data aggregation, seeking to strengthen the risk data aggregation capabilities of systemically important banks, as well as their internal risk reporting capabilities. The Financial Crisis showed the inadequacies of the IT and data architectures of these systemically important institutions in the financial system, ultimately leading to the view that they were unable to manage risks properly. For example, most institutions struggled to assess their true exposures to Lehman Brothers and other casualties of the market events in 2007–2008 as the key information required was siloed across different department systems and processes, resulting in wholesale fragmentation and a near impossible task to collate the relevant information quickly across numerous legal entities within a large investment bank.

Risk data aggregation is defined in the BCBS 239 document as 'defining, gathering and processing risk data according to the bank's risk reporting requirements to enable the bank to measure its performance against its risk tolerance/appetite. This includes sorting, merging or breaking down sets of data'.

The Basel Committee, in publishing the principles, heavily recognises the link between the ability for banks to aggregate risk data and improving their 'resolvability'. In particular, resolution authorities need timely access to aggregate risk data to understand the correct course of action to restore financial strength and viability when a key financial institution comes under severe financial stress, for example, in finding a suitable merger partner. Although focused on global systemically important banks (G-SIBs), as outlined in the Basel Committee's document, 'it is strongly suggested that national supervisors also apply these Principles to banks identified as Domestically Systemically Important Banks (D-SIBs) three years after their designation as DSIBs'. Firms identified as G-SIBs in 2011 and 2012 were required to fully adopt the BCBS 239 principles by January 2016, however, at the time of writing, the fourth report on progress published by the Basel Committee found a wholly unsatisfactory level of compliance, with only one G-SIB fully compliant within the deadline timing.

The main issues behind the BCBS 239 drive can be summarised as follows:

- Immature data processes and infrastructure (which meant that 'data struggled' to correctly influence critical decision making in the Financial Crisis).
- The data required for critical risk assessment came from multiple sources, requiring many manual processes in order to aggregate.
- Bank boards and senior management were 'blindsided' by lack and/or inaccuracy of the data available, with the data lifecycle escaping senior scrutiny.
- Poor risk models (reflecting also the underlying poor data), with mistrust at the highest levels of management.
- Lack of definitions of roles and responsibilities in respect of key risk data, mainly due to non-vertical ownership.
- The potential value of the aggregate risk data is not recognised (due to the underlying issues with the data) and therefore neither is its capital optimisation potential.

The Principles

The 14 published principles cover four closely related topics, summarised below.

A) **Overarching Governance and Infrastructure**
1) Governance:
Risk data aggregation and risk reporting practices should be subject to strong governance arrangements.
2) Data Architecture and IT Infrastructure:
Firms should design, build and maintain an infrastructure that works both in normal conditions as well as at times of stress and crisis.

B) **Risk Data Aggregation Capabilities**
3) Accuracy and Integrity:
Data should be accurate and aggregated on a largely automated basis to minimise errors.
4) Completeness:
The principles should be applied across all material risk data and should facilitate data to be viewable by business line, legal entity, asset type, industry, region – as may be required to observe risk concentrations, exposures and emerging risks.

5) Timeliness:
   It should be possible to generate the data in a timely manner while also meeting the principles relating to accuracy and integrity, completeness and adaptability. (Note that the precise timing depends on the nature and volatility of the risk being measured and its materiality to the risk of the organisation as a whole.)

6) Adaptability:
   Firms should be able to generate aggregate risk data to meet a broad range of on-demand, ad-hoc risk management reporting requests, including requests during crisis situations, requests due to changing internal needs and requests to meet supervisory queries.

C) **Risk Reporting Practices**

7) Accuracy:
   Risk reports should accurately and precisely convey aggregated risk data. Reports should be reconciled and validated.

8) Comprehensiveness:
   Risk management reports should cover all material risks, with the depth and scope matching the complexity and size of a given business.

9) Clarity and Usefulness:
   Risk reports should be clear, concise, useful and meaningful to the recipients.

10) Frequency:
    The frequency of the data and reports should be set by the board and senior management and meet the needs of recipients. The frequency should increase in times of stress.

11) Distribution:
    Procedures should be in place to allow for rapid collection and analysis of risk data and timely dissemination of reports to all appropriate recipients.

D) **Supervisory Review, Tools and Cooperation**

12) Review:
    Supervisors should periodically review to ensure compliance with the first 11 BCBS 239 principles. This includes testing a firm's capabilities to aggregate data and produce reports in both stress/crisis and steady-state environments, including sudden sharp increases in business volumes.

13) Remedial Actions and Supervisory Measures:
    Deficiencies should be addressed in a timely manner.

14) Home–Host Cooperation:
    Supervisors should cooperate and have appropriate information sharing between home and host supervisory authorities, assisting with the robustness of a firm's risk management practices across operations in multiple jurisdictions.

A Detailed Review of the Principles

The principles detail the need for the identification, assessment and management of data quality risks as part of an overall risk management framework, with the bank's board and senior management needing to review and approve the group risk data aggregation and risk reporting framework, ensuring adequate resources are deployed. It is made clear that roles and responsibilities should be established, as well as ensuring that there are adequate controls throughout the lifecycle of the data and for all aspects of the technology infrastructure. The role of the business owner includes ensuring data is correctly entered by the relevant department and kept current and aligned with their data definitions, ensuring that risk data aggregation capabilities and risk reporting practices are consistent with firms' policies.

In order to do this, the paper details that banks should establish integrated data taxonomies and architecture across the banking group, including information on the metadata, as well as use of single identifiers and/or unified naming conventions for data including legal entities, counterparties, customers and accounts. There should also be a 'dictionary' of the concepts used, such that data is defined consistently across an organisation. This is then expected by supervisors to be used as the starting point to measure and monitor the accuracy of the data, and to develop appropriate escalation channels and action plans to rectify poor data quality.

There is also a drive towards a golden (i.e. single and authoritative) source for each type of risk data, however there is a need to reconcile the risk data with other sources, including accounting data where appropriate, to ensure that the risk data is accurate.

The paper specifically details the fact that critical risks include, but are not limited to, aggregated credit exposures to large borrowers, counterparty credit risk exposures (including, for example, derivatives), trading exposures, positions and operating limits, liquidity and operational considerations that are time critical (e.g. systems availability and unauthorised access). Supervisors expect banks to consider accuracy requirements analogous to accounting materiality. For example, if omission or misstatement could influence the risk decisions of users, this may be considered material.

The speed at which data is expected to be pulled together is most notable, requiring a comprehensive review of the manner in which critical data elements are identified and maintained to the required level of accuracy for risk aggregation and monitoring. This is in many ways a conclusion from the Financial Crisis – such information is required almost immediately in times of severe market stress to allow for timely and effective reactions. This agility to have the requisite risk data at hand in turn requires upfront defined requirements and processes to reconcile reports to risk data as well as significant automated and manual edit and reasonableness checks – including validation rules – in order to ensure the requisite accuracy of data.

Compliance with BCBS 239

One of the big challenges with BCBS 239 compliance is that it is principle-based regulation, so there are few clear predefined metrics that banks within its scope can use to monitor compliance against the regulation. It is therefore crucial that banks have an ability to accurately assess their level of compliance and actions required to improve this if needed. Regulators are viewing BCBS 239 compliance through multiple lenses – ultimately a recognition that it touches so many aspects of the regulatory reform landscape post-crisis, and therefore banks need to position it at the heart of their regulatory transformation programmes (see Figure 5.1). Many of the aspects of the failed 'living will' submissions of systemically important banks in terms of their risk data and reporting (see Chapter 10) and stress testing exercises (see Chapter 9) – such as the Firm Data Submission Framework (FDSF) in the UK, the European Banking Authority (EBA) stress tests across Europe and the Comprehensive Capital Analysis and Review (CCAR) in the USA – emphasise the capability gaps banks have to bridge. The resources required to run these exercises are not sustainable without investment in the

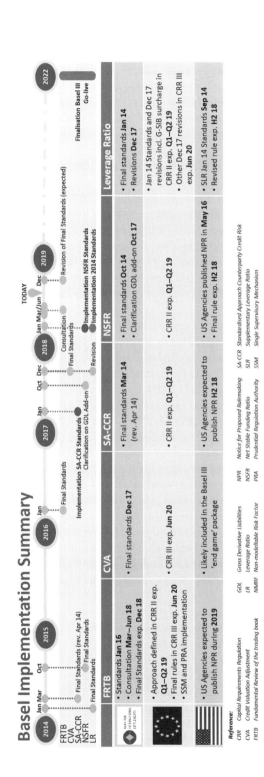

Figure 5.1 Basel implementation summary (adapted from 2018 ISDA Annual Europe Conference presentation – 'A cross-border capital framework')

infrastructure, systems and processes that ultimately assist with meeting the BCBS 239 principles. Without this, banks will be challenged by other regulations, including the Fundamental Review of the Trading Book (FRTB). A failure to demonstrate compliant solutions for data management, data governance and alignment between risk, finance and the business will result in a forced change to the way risk is modelled and valued, and ultimately a material increase in the level of capital banks need to hold.

Typical Implementation Issues to Achieve Compliance

No G-SIB has the advantage of a greenfield site on which to develop the processes, systems and architecture to achieve compliance with BCBS 239. The current IT infrastructure will of course have grown organically (including the jolts of bolting together infrastructure from various mergers and acquisitions) and is expensive to build on and operate, complex and difficult to change, with poor data quality, not timely and opaque due to large numbers of adjustments and manual workarounds. This has also been partly caused by the dramatically changing regulatory environment and associated changes to business models.

Since so much of the data for risk aggregation purposes comes from disparate systems, a major issue is that the data is often simply copied from those individual systems without enough thought as to the suitability of the data from one system to sit alongside and be used in combination with data from another system. This results in a number of operational processes to adjust the data to try and make it fit for purpose, allowing any root cause in the base data to remain uncorrected, as well as in many cases unknown. The release cycles to make changes to systems to address problems can be problematic, with a large degree of coordination required across multiple systems (e.g. coordination of changes to data feeds), causing significant issues for 'run-the-bank' work.

The most commonly cited root causes of data quality in respect of risk aggregation data tend to focus on inadequate systems validations, manual data entry errors and inadequate inter-system linkages for flow of data. Additionally, there are typically issues with the communication between producers of the data and its consumers.

Producers of data – the owners of systems (including end-user developed applications, see the EUDA discussion in Chapter 4) are often simply unaware of all of the data attributes that they hold, their meaning, intended usage and values, and the way in which the attributes are sourced or derived, as well as the full set of downstream consumers of the data.

Consumers of data – the consumers of data are often unaware of the full set of data attributes that they require, the upstream sources from which they are taken and the effect of poor data quality on their processes.

The rise of ETL technologies (see Chapter 4) has helped firms deal much better with heterogenous data sources, replacing many prior practices of tactical shell scripts and spreadsheet macros (although these still do exist, even in relation to key risk data processes) to deal with this challenge. It needs to be recognised, however, that the use of ETL technologies is no substitute for properly unified data sources. Overuse of ETL layers without such a holistic and unified approach to data can simply paper over the data issues (such as governance and accuracy) that BCBS 239 attempts to force firms to address.

Implications of Failure to Comply with BCBS 239

There are no defined penalties and/or implications for non-compliance, unlike many other financial regulations. If there is a failure to comply with the principles, and if the data infrastructure is not transformed to align with BCBS 239 expectations, the likely consequences could be:

- penalties and increased capital add-on charges;
- reputational risk; or
- loss of competitive advantage.

In many ways, BCBS 239 approaches the fundamental data required to adequately manage and run a financial institution in a defensive manner; a formally defined regulatory expectation is expressed that firms need to meet a number of sensible data principles. Adherence to the principles presents an opportunity for firms to optimise their businesses by better utilising the data and making better business decisions based on the insights provided. A failure to comply with BCBS 239 compared to peers might therefore represent a loss of competitive advantage.

The Legal Data Requirements of BCBS 239

Although BCBS 239 focuses on data for risk aggregation purposes, the purpose of the data can be viewed as being required by the institution itself for a number of different areas, each of which has a strong legal agreement data component:

- Business optimisation (e.g. capital optimisation through the use of close-out netting and collateral optimisation through details of the collateral optionality in collateral agreements in respect of the assets that may be provided to the counterparty).
- Risk management (e.g. rating downgrade triggers applicable to the parties, key collateral agreement terms and net asset value decline clauses in respect of hedge fund counterparties).
- Regulatory reporting (e.g. living wills and qualified financial contracts (QFC), liquidity and client assets and money reporting).
- Operations (e.g. details of how payments are to be made, such as whether payment netting applies).

The problems of siloed data sets are exacerbated when it comes to the legal agreement data, which has typically been poorly managed by legal departments, often leading to other departments maintaining such data (such as collateral management units), as required for their own purposes. The lack of defined ownership – responsibility and accountability – for the legal agreement data has been at the heart of the problem. When this data then needs to be aggregated across a firm, there are many issues that arise around unintended usage of data (compared to the purpose and manner in which it was captured – see e.g. Chapter 7). That is why the legal data is such an important piece of the BCBS 239 requirement.

The problems cannot, however, be solved just through the legal agreement data. This data domain relies heavily on client and product data, and firms are usually plagued by issues created relating to the legal agreement entity not lining up with client hierarchies in the firm, counterparty types for onboarding purposes not aligning with the types required for a close-out netting determination and product details in the agreement not aligning with trading system product hierarchies – to name just a few of the issues. These all raise significant critical data element problems for BCBS 239 compliance, ranging from the governance and definition of these data attributes, their actual (compared to intended) usage and veracity.

Bibliography

Bank for International Settlements (BIS) (2013) 'Principles for effective risk data aggregation and risk reporting', January 2013

Bank for International Settlements (BIS) (2017) 'Progress in adopting the principles for effective risk data aggregation and risk reporting', March 2017

Bank for International Settlements (BIS), 'History of the Basel Committee', www.bis.org/bcbs.history.htm, 14 April 2018

EY (2015) 'Global Regulatory Reform: BCBS 239 – Risk data aggregation and reporting: a practical path to compliance and delivering business value'

Haines, Peter; Choueri Hany; Pellizzari, Giancarlo; Poloni, Paolo and Redinger, Gerald (2017) *BCBS 239: Guiding Principles for Compliance*, Risk Books

Hughes, P. and Grody, A. (2016) 'Risk accounting: The risk data aggregation and risk reporting (BCBS 239) foundation of enterprise risk management (ERM) and risk governance', *Journal of Risk Management in Financial Institutions*, Part 1: 9(2), pp. 130–146; Part 2: 9(3), pp. 224–248

6

Capital and Netting

In this chapter we examine the requirement for prudentially regulated financial institutions to maintain a prescribed level of regulatory capital – first providing a definition of the term, before examining the relevant regulations themselves and the impact that this requirement will have, from both a legal data and more general commercial perspective.

The netting section begins by providing an overview of the different types of netting in use, before focusing in much greater detail on close-out netting and the legal data requirements involved in this process. It also covers the requirement to have the benefit of appropriate legal opinions on file to support close-out netting, and the different forms such legal opinions can take.

What is Regulatory Capital?

Banks are vital to the modern economy. After all, they provide major sources of credit, meaning they control the availability of money for consumers and businesses who, in turn, use that money to participate in the economy. This is a double-edged sword, as banks also pose a systemic risk to the wider economy; risks that have the potential to propagate globally and have major repercussions for economies around the world, as was evidenced by the Financial Crisis. The interconnectivity of financial institutions in the financial system means that the failure of one major bank can have a 'domino effect' causing the failure of other major financial institutions. As a means of mitigating these systemic risks, banks are heavily regulated, in particular through the imposition of regulatory capital and capital adequacy requirements. Because of the systemic nature of the banking system, such regulations protect not just the financial institutions themselves, but also the financial system and the economy as a whole.

'Regulatory capital'[1] – also known as 'capital requirement' or 'capital adequacy' – is the amount of capital a financial institution must hold against its assets as specified by its regulator, thus in effect limiting the amount of credit the institution can make available as part of its business activities. Regulatory capital improves banking stability by helping ensure banks are better able to survive market or credit collapses, as it acts as a buffer providing a first line of defence. The key proposition underpinning regulatory capital is that banks need to be able to recover their assets to repay depositors in

---

1 Please note, *capital requirements* should not be confused with *reserve requirements*, which govern the assets side of a bank's balance sheet (i.e. the proportion of its assets it must hold in cash or highly liquid assets).

the event of a catastrophe; if there is a risk that an asset cannot be recovered in full, it must be backed by capital to create a 'buffer' of regulatory capital against those assets. The required amount of regulatory capital is usually expressed as a ratio – capital to risk (weighted) assets ratio (CRAR) or capital adequacy ratio (CAR) – of equity that must be held as a percentage of risk-weighted assets (RWAs); it is essentially a ratio of a bank's capital to its risk. The original aim of RWA was to encourage capital requirements that are based on the riskiness of asset classes as opposed to being static. Because different types of assets have different risk profiles, the CAR adjusts depending on the level of risk – allowing a greater discount for lower risk assets. The specifics of the CAR will vary from jurisdiction to jurisdiction, but are broadly in line for those countries which apply the Basel Accords.

Two[2] types of capital are measured via this system:

1) Tier 1 capital consists of shareholders' equity and retained earnings. It is used by regulators as the core measure of financial strength, as this sort of capital can be most readily used to absorb losses without having to cease trading. (Note, under Basel III, as discussed below, the minimum Tier 1 capital ratio is 6%, calculated by dividing Tier 1 capital by total risk-based assets).

2) Tier 2 capital is composed of undisclosed reserves, general loss reserves, hybrid debt capital instruments and subordinated debt. It can also function as supplementary capital due to being able to absorb losses, but is considered to be less secure than its Tier 1 counterpart. This is because it is regarded as being more difficult to calculate accurately and is composed of assets that are more difficult to liquidate.

Today, under Basel III as it currently stands, the starting point for the minimum amount of regulatory capital a bank must hold is 8% of the risk-weighted value of each asset, although regulatory bodies can increase the percentage as is felt necessary (either for individual institutions or across the market). So, as a minimum requirement, making a £1 million loan with a risk weight of 100% would require a bank to hold at least £80,000 of capital (subject to a risk-weighted increase in this percentage). This minimum level can be contrasted to the position prior to the 2007–2008 Financial Crisis, where some banks had critically low unweighted capital ratios.

Types of Banks and Basel Measurement Approaches

There are three 'types of banks' with respect to approaches to measurement of capital requirements for credit risk.

Standardised Approach Bank:

Under the Standardised Approach, credit risk is measured in a standardised manner using external credit assessments. This is the least sophisticated approach to capital calculations, offering the least differentiation in required capital between safer and riskier credits. Accordingly, it is generally afforded the highest capital burdens.

---

2 Tier 3 capital was previously also a regulatory requirement under Basel II but will subsequently be eliminated under Basel III. Tier 3 capital instruments consisted of short-term subordinated debt – i.e. with a minimum maturity of 2 years that is fully paid up and cannot be repaid before maturity without prior regulatory approval.

> **Foundation and Advanced Internal Ratings Based Bank:**
>
> These two approaches measure credit risk using sophisticated formulas with internally determined input items such as probability of default and inputs fixed by regulators such as loss given default. It is subject to approval by the bank's regulator. The typically lower capital requirements incentivise banks to have robust internal risk management systems and data to be able to facilitate this approach.

The BCBS and the Basel Accords

As stated in the Chapter 5, the original aim of the BCBS was the enhancement of financial stability by improving banking supervision worldwide. Subsequently, a key role of the BCBS today is its work advising on the capital adequacy of banks in order to promote the stability of the banking system as a whole. The Basel Accords – a set of recommendations for regulations in the banking industry – were prepared and developed by the BCBS as a means of preventing the spread of capital, market and operational risk. The Basel Accords comprise three sets of recommendations (Basel I published in 1988, Basel II published in 2006 and Basel III published in 2010 and revised in 2013 and 2014). As the BCBS has only an advisory function, it does not have the authority to enforce recommendations. The Basel Accords are therefore not law but a set of internationally agreed standards – although most major financial jurisdictions implement the Committee's policies. Implementation is effected by transposing the recommendations into national (and cross-border, in the case of the EU) law, being made to fit with existing national (and EU) laws.

In respect of EU Member States, it is the Capital Requirements Directive IV (CRD IV) that, at the time of writing, implements Basel III. The CRD IV package is composed of two parts: the Capital Requirements Directive (CRD) and the Capital Requirements Regulation (CRR). EU law is imposed on Member States by necessitating compliance with enacted regulations and directives, both of which are dealt with slightly differently. Whilst a regulation becomes immediately enforceable as law in all Member States, directives must be transposed into national law. Laws are transposed by each Member State passing primary or secondary legislation, giving force to that directive within its own jurisdiction. Member States are given a period of time to transpose directives and change national laws. This is currently the case for CRD IV/Basel III, which is not expected to be fully implemented until 2023, 10 years after being approved by the European Parliament.

In the USA, the Board of Governors of the Federal Reserve System (the Federal Reserve) and other bank regulatory agencies approved final rules in July 2013, which codified regulatory capital rules implementing the Basel III capital framework into a single, comprehensive regulatory framework (including relevant provisions of the Dodd–Frank Act).

Basel II was only scheduled to be implemented in full in early 2008 in major jurisdictions. It was, therefore, not fully effective by the time Lehman Brothers collapsed. The ensuing Financial Crisis spurred regulators into increasing banking supervision and tightening regulatory requirements – including regulatory capital – even further. This is because poor risk management and overleveraging were seen as reasons for the collapse by the BCBS. Basel I and II, as a result of the crisis, were subsequently deemed insufficiently stringent. In July 2010, Basel III was released, proposing a new capital and liquidity reform package. Subject to transitional provisions, the Basel III rules were implemented in Europe from the beginning of 2014 by the CRD IV Framework and are, at the time of writing, in the process of being phased in.

Basel III applies a number of amendments to Basel II and, as such, will be more stringent than its predecessor. Ultimately, the main purpose of Basel III is to improve both the quality and level of capital. Specifically, key changes include the following:

a) **Basic capital requirements.** The basic 8% minimum ratio of capital to RWA remains under Basel III but banks must have a greater percentage of Tier 1 capital (the core measure of a bank's financial strength, see above). So, even though the minimum ratio will stay at 8%, the effective equivalent will be in the region of 14%. Tier 2 capital (supplementary capital, see above) will be simplified. Tier 3 capital (which includes a greater range of debt types than Tier 1 and 2 capitals, see above) is abolished so as to ensure market risks are met with the same quality of capital as credit and operational risks. There will thus be an increase in the capital requirement for global and domestic 'systemically important banks'.

b) **Capital buffers.** As a result of the fact that some institutions with depleted capital during the Financial Crisis were still distributing dividends to shareholders, two capital buffers will be added: a capital conservation buffer equal to 2.5% of RWA imposed if a bank is facing financial difficulties and a countercyclical buffer of an additional 0–2.5% of RWA requiring banks to build reserves during periods of high economic growth, both of which are to be raised through common equity. So, if an institution does not have the required capital buffers, Basel III will restrict the institution's ability to distribute earnings to shareholders.

c) **Leverage ratio.** 'Leverage' (or 'gearing') is the ratio of a company's debt capital to the value of its equity capital (or ordinary shares). Being highly leveraged, or having a large amount of debt in relation to the available equity capital, are a greater risk of not being able to distribute earnings to shareholders (see above) and of not being able to repay the interest on the debt. Of course, the reasons why banks prior to the Financial Crisis were so highly geared was the potential to expand quickly and make large profits via quick and cheap borrowing. One of the underlying features of the crisis was the build-up of excessive on- and off-balance-sheet leverage. During the worst of the crisis, the banking sector was forced by the market to reduce its leverage, which exacerbated the downward pressure on asset prices, causing declines in capital and a dramatic reduction in available credit. Basel III introduces a leverage ratio with the intention of constraining the build-up of leverage, which may need to be dramatically reduced in times of market stress.

d) **Liquidity ratios.** During the Financial Crisis, a number of banks suffered from liquidity problems when large amounts of deposits were withdrawn in a short space of time. Liquidity refers to the extent to which an asset or security can be quickly bought or sold within the market (without the price being affected). Two liquidity standards are introduced by Basel III. Firstly, the liquidity coverage ratio (LCR), which will ensure banks have sufficient liquidity to deal with severe market shocks by requiring banks to hold sufficient high-quality liquid assets that can be converted into cash in high-stress scenarios. Secondly, a net stable funding ratio

(NSFR), which establishes a minimum amount of stable funding based on the liquidity characteristics of an institution's assets and activities to promote more medium- and long-term funding of banks' activities (these are covered in more detail in Chapter 9).

Despite some overlap between the EU and US implementations of Basel III, there is significant divergence. This gives rise to a number of regulatory arbitrage opportunities. In particular, the Dodd–Frank Act introduced several capital-related provisions unique to US financial institutions that are stricter than the Basel III framework. For example, the so-called Collins Amendment of the Dodd–Frank Act (Section 171) prevents advanced-approach banks from having minimum capital requirements below the general risk-based capital requirements. As a result, a non-US bank employing the advanced approach of Basel III and pursuing a strategy of lower-risk loans and investment-grade assets may enjoy a competitive advantage over US institutions, as the capital floor imposed under the Collins Amendment would eliminate any ultimate capital relief large US banks may otherwise obtain under the internal models approach of Basel III.

The implementation of Basel III in the EU was delayed as a result of political disagreement between EU Member States over the ability of a Member State to impose higher capital requirements than applicable under CRD IV (i.e. by 'gold-plating'). The final position is to prohibit such super-equivalent standards being imposed by Member States. The rationale for this restriction is that there would otherwise be regulatory arbitrage, with risky activities migrating to Member States with lower capital and liquidity requirements. Member States may, however, increase their capital ratio by use of the countercyclical, systemic risk and global/systemic institution buffers (Figure 6.1).

Risks and Implications of Regulatory Capital Requirements

Ultimately, the impact of implementing higher capital adequacy requirements in the long term will be of benefit, despite some short-term aggravations. In the long term, as banks gradually build up capital reserves and reduce high RWAs, they are likely to experience a reduction in the cost of capital which would, in turn, improve credit margins. In the short term, however, in reducing the amount of high RWAs, lending volumes are of course, negatively affected.

It should be noted that the new rules require that banks have in place adequate procedures and resources (including data and systems) to comply with the range of capital, liquidity, leverage and counterparty requirements. The costs of implementation of the rules have a substantial impact on the regulatory costs of systemically important institutions and relative costs for small firms are also significant, given the infrastructure needed, despite the smaller size of such firms.

Complying with all the regulatory capital requirements is expensive and introduces certain operational risks to firms. This includes – as a subset within it – legal risk. Operational risk can be defined as the risks stemming from deficient internal processes. These internal processes might be reliant on people – or systems, but ultimately includes

Exposures to banks						
Risk weights in jurisdictions where the ratings approach is permitted						
External rating	**AAA to AA−**	**A+ to A−**	**BBB+ to BBB−**	**BB+ to B−**	**Below B−**	**Unrated**
Risk weight	20%	30%	50%	100%	150%	As for SCRA below
Short-term exposures						
Risk weight	20%	20%	20%	50%	150%	As for SCRA below

Risk weights where the ratings approach is not permitted and for unrated exposures			
Standardised Credit Risk Assessment Approach (SCRA) grades	**Grade A**	**Grade B**	**Grade C**
Risk weight	40%[1]	75%	150%
Short-term exposures	20%	50%	150%

Exposures to covered bonds			
Risk weights to <u>rated</u> covered bonds			
External issue-specific rating	**AAA to AA−**	**A+ to BBB−**	**BB+ to B−**	**Below B−**
Risk weight	10%	20%	50%	100%

Risk weights for <u>unrated</u> covered bonds						
Risk weight of issuing bank	**20%**	**30%**	**40%**	**50%**	**75%**	**100%**	**150%**
Risk weight	10%	15%	20%	25%	35%	50%	100%

Exposures to general corporates					
Risk weights in jurisdictions where the ratings approach is permitted					
External rating of counterparty	**AAA to AA−**	**A+ to A−**	**BBB+ to BBB−**	**BB+ to BB−**	**Below BB−**	**Unrated**
Risk weight	20%	50%	75%	100%	150%	100% or 85% if corporate SME

Risk weights where rating approach is not permitted		
SCRA grades	**Investment grade**	**All other**
General corporate (non-SME)	65%	100%
SME general corporate	85%	

Exposures to project finance, object finance and commodities finance		
Exposure (excluding real estate)	**Project finance**	**Object and commodity finance**
Issue-specific ratings available and permitted	Same as for general corporate (see above)	
Rating not available or not permitted	130% pre-operational phase 100% operational phase 80% operational phase (high quality)	100%

[1]A risk weight of 30% may be applied if the exposure to the bank satisfies all of the criteria for Grade A classification and in additional the counterparty bank has (i) a CET1 ratio of 14% or above and (ii) a Tier 1 leverage ratio of 5% or above.

Figure 6.1 Overview of Basel III standardised approach to credit risk (reproduced from Basel Committee on Banking Supervision and High-level Summary of Basel III Reforms (2017))

Retail exposures excluding real estate

	Regulatory retail (non-revolving)	Regulatory retail (revolving)		Other retail
		Transactors	Revolvers	
Risk weight	75%	45%	75%	100%

Residential real-estate exposures

LTV bands	Below 50%	50% to 60%	60% to 70%	70% to 80%	80% to 90%	90% to 100%	above 100%	Criteria not met
General RRE								
Whole-loan approach RW	20%	25%	30%		40%	50%	70%	RW of counterparty
Loan-splitting approach[2] RW	20%		RW of counterparty					RW of counterparty
Income-producing residential real estate (IPRRE)								
Whole-loan	30%	35%			45%	60%	75%	105%

Commercial real estate (CRE) exposures

General CRE			
Whole-loan approach	$LTV \leq 60\%$	$LTV > 60\%$	Criteria not met
	Min (60%, RW of counterparty)	RW of counterparty	RW of counterparty
Loan-splitting approach[2]	$LTV \leq 55\%$	$LTV > 55\%$	Criteria not met

Income-producing commercial real estate (IPCRE)				
Whole-loan approach	$LTV \leq 60\%$	$60\% < LTV \leq 80\%$	$LTV > 80\%$	Criteria not met
	70%	90%	110%	150%

Land acquisition, development and construction (ADC) exposures

Loan to company/SPV	150%
Residential ADC loan	100%

Subordinated debt and equity (excluding amounts deducted)

	Subordinated debt and capital other than equities	Equity exposures to certain legislated programmes	'Speculative unlisted equity'	All other equity exposures
Risk weight	150%	100%	400%	250%

Credit conversion factors for off-balance sheet exposures

	UCCs	Commitments, except UCCs	NIFs and RUFs, and certain transaction-related contingent items	ST self-liquidating trade letters of credit arising from the movement of goods	Direct credit substitutes and other off balance sheet exposures
CCF	10%	40%	50%	20%	100%

[2]Under the loan-splitting approach, a supervisory risk weight is applied to the portion of the exposure that is below 55% of the property value and the risk weight of the counterparty is applied to the remainder of the exposure. In cases where the criteria are not met, the risk weight of the counterparty is applied to the entire exposure.

Figure 6.1 *(Continued)*

legal risk. Legal risk can be broadly broken down into two categories. Firstly, there is the risk borne from inadequate documentation or a legally invalid agreement, meaning that parties are exposed to the risk of some sort of financial or reputational loss, perhaps because of a 'bad deal', failing to properly protect assets or litigation.[3] This particular type of risk is a commercial one. Secondly, there is the risk that is borne from activities which are illegal or uncompliant with regulation, meaning that parties are at risk of some sort of penalty, financial or otherwise.

Although the benefits from increased regulatory transactional controls are not disputed, there are drawbacks. Importantly, banks are now under more pressure than ever to comply with burdensome, complex and expensive regulatory requirements or face penalties. A failure to comply with the regulatory rules put in place can result in unwanted consequences for firms, their directors and managerial staff. Most firms attempt to address legal risks by establishing well-developed compliance programmes and legal documentation agreement management systems. After all, banks process a large number of transactions each day across diverse markets, exposing themselves to operational and legal risks relating to record maintenance and settlement activities. As such, banks are reliant on their employees, automated systems and other internal controls to ensure each transaction is correctly documented and recorded. Mistakes can and do occur between the point of processing a transaction and the entry and refresh of records. It goes without saying that efforts to improve procedures and controls have been prompted in part by the increased supervisory and regulatory focus on these. Regulators, in increasing requirements for capital, mandating record-keeping and reporting, are ensuring that firms adopt sound transactional controls.

Under Article 65(2) of CRD IV, there are a number of penalties that firms can face if they have failed to take the appropriate measures to deal with the regulations and the inherent operational risks they present. Such penalties are applicable to both directors and/or responsible individuals. Chosen sanctions are determined based on criteria including the gravity and duration of a breach, the degree of cooperation and any potential systemic consequences, and can include the following:

Pecuniary penalties

- Individuals face fines up to €5 million.
- Banks face fines up to 10% of consolidated turnover (calculated based on figures from the year prior to the violation).
- Individuals and/or banks also face additional fines up to double the illicit profit obtained through the violation (assuming the amount can be determined).

Non-pecuniary penalties

- Banking licence withdrawal/withdrawal of authorisations.
- Cease and desist orders – binding orders on companies and/or individuals to immediately stop the violation.
- Public censure – a declaration which publicly identifies the authors of the violation.

---

3 For example, in 1991, derivative transactions entered into by English local authorities were found to be void, since the local authorities did not have the legal power to enter into such transactions, with the result that a number of banks suffered losses as a result of the unwinding of the transactions.

- Temporary bans for management body members – removal of the author of the violation from his or her position, whether that be board, managerial body or auditing functions.
- Banning of the author of the violation from the European financial system.
- The withdrawal of the right to vote from shareholders who have performed a violation.
- A Skilled Person Review[4] under section 166 (Reports by Skilled Persons) (or section 166A, Appointment of Skilled Person to collect and update information) FSMA 2000.

Passing on the Costs of Maintaining Regulatory Capital

Often, the cost of maintaining regulatory capital in respect of a loan is handled by being passed on to the borrower as part of the margin on a transaction such as a loan – usually via an 'Increased Costs' clause. Without this sort of provision, if the regulations change and the cost of capital increases, the profits earned by a bank will be reduced. However, an 'Increased Costs' provision can be very complex – increased costs and the cost of capital are difficult to calculate, and counterparty relationships may become strained by perceived relationship and market issues as a result of such a clause. Note also that prudent borrowers would try to limit the application of such contractual clauses to 'changes which affect the banking market' as opposed to individual bank changes such as an increase in regulatory capital requirements. Many 'Increased Costs' clauses specifically excluded costs due as a result of implementing Basel II, on the basis that banks should have already factored those costs into their margins. Worse still, Basel III is technically an *amendment* to Basel II and so arguably would fall within the exclusion. Hence, if a bank wishes to claim for Basel III increased costs, the 'Increased Costs' clause should be specifically drafted to account for this.

The Legal Data Needed for Regulatory Capital Calculations

It is, however, the possible credit risk mitigation that can be used to assist in the reduction of regulatory capital requirements that places a real requirement on accurate and granular legal agreement data (as well as legal opinion data), which we will consider after a discussion of credit risk mitigation.

Credit Risk Mitigation

Credit risk mitigation reduces credit risk-weighted assets and there are broadly two forms of credit risk mitigation: 'funded' and 'unfunded' credit protection. In a capital adequacy context, such credit risk mitigation techniques must be legally robust, in order to take regulatory capital benefit from them.

Funded credit protection is where the reduction of the credit risk on the exposure of an undertaking is derived from the right of the undertaking, in the event of the default of the counterparty or on the occurrence of other specified credit events relating to the counterparty, to liquidate, or obtain transfer or appropriation of, or retain certain assets

---

4 A Skilled Person Review gives the power to obtain a view from a third party (a 'skilled person') about aspects of a regulated firm's activities if the FCA deem the firm a cause for concern.

or amounts, or reduce the amount of the exposure to, or replace it with, the difference between the amount of exposure and the amount of a claim on the undertaking.[5] Funded credit risk protection refers, therefore, to the recourse a bank has to cash (or some other asset) as security in order to recover the monies owed to it. As a result, funded credit protection is concerned with the nature of the asset and the credit standing of the issuer. As such, funded credit protection can take place via the provision of collateral or the use of 'close-out netting', which we will shortly focus on given its legal data requirements.

Unfunded credit protection is where the reduction of the credit risk on the exposure is derived from the undertaking of a third party to pay an amount in the event of the default of the borrower or on the occurrence of other specified events.[6] So, unfunded credit protection involves the unsecured obligation of a third party and it is implicit in this concept that the entity providing the credit protection is more creditworthy than the primary borrower, thus allowing a reduction in the capital which the bank must ascribe to the transaction(s) at hand. Unfunded credit protection includes uncollateralised guarantees (and, by analogy, risk participations) and credit derivatives, in each case provided by eligible protection providers and satisfying certain conditions. Eligible protection providers include sovereigns, local governments, banks, investment firms and other rated entities.

We previously touched on the process, systems and data burden that compliance with the Basel regimes brings. It is noteworthy that, at the time of writing, the European Central Bank has carried out examinations of the balance sheets of banks within its supervisory role, including reviewing the documentation and legal opinions related to the use of credit risk mitigation. In many cases, the finding is that the level of detailed documentation to support the assessment of the legal risk in respect of close-out netting (and collateral enforceability – more on this to follow) is inadequate, with possible subsequent impacts on the calculation of RWAs and the leverage ratio, with a particular need to improve the quality and retention of legal opinion data (e.g. the key limitations, assumptions and caveats within the external legal opinions on which the firm is placing reliance as part of their legal risk management). This process is prompting many such institutions to make documentary and procedural changes to ensure that their use of credit risk mitigation is robust and subject to proper due diligence from a legal perspective. However, the legal analysis is not sufficient by itself, as we will see, to ultimately give correct treatment to the regulatory capital requirements – both the legal opinion and the agreement data are key to this.

Netting

As mentioned above, one crucial method of credit risk mitigation is through the use of close-out netting. We initially begin by contrasting netting from set-off – a common area of confusion – and then considering the different types of netting that exist, before focusing on the most important type of netting from a regulatory capital perspective: close-out netting. It should be noted that sometimes the term netting is used, somewhat lazily, to refer to all forms of the below concepts, as well as collateral enforceability – this should be regarded as loose financial vernacular.

---

5 FCA Handbook, Glossary, definition 'Funded credit protection'.
6 FCA Handbook, Glossary, definition 'Unfunded credit protection'.

The Distinction Between Netting and Set-off

Set-off is the discharge of reciprocal obligations to the extent of the smaller obligation. It is a form of payment whereby, instead of the payment of money, a claim owed to a party is used to pay a claim that is owed. An obligation is used for payment.

In contrast, netting involves the contractual cancellation of rights and obligations and their replacement with a single amount (see Figure 6.2).

Types of Netting[7]

Payment Netting Payment netting (see Figure 6.3) is often referred to as settlement netting. Under this type of netting, contracting parties undertake to accept the net performance of the other(s). It generally only applies to amounts (or deliveries) due on the same date and only if the payments are in the same currency (or the deliveries are of the same asset). On a payment date, each party will aggregate the amounts of a currency to be delivered by it, and only the difference in the aggregate amounts will be delivered by the party with the larger aggregate obligation. The main advantage of this type of netting

Netting	Set-Off
One debt only	Two or more debts
Operates where there are no due and payable debts	Debts must be due and payable
Mutual dealings	Mutual obligations
Creates an original liability; operates to the exclusion of any contingent liabilities	Does not deny original liability
Value of debt determined after netting	Value of debt(s) determined before set-off
A creature of contractual agreement	May arise by operation of law
Intent: aggregation/unit	Intent: separation/segregation
Calculates amount of outstanding debt between parties	Deprives one party of property
Non-discretionary	Discretionary
Parties define a triggering event as well as their remedy	No need to define a 'triggering event'
Notice/consent not an issue	Notice/consent is an issue
Reduces systemic risk	Increases systemic failure
No need for judicial review	Subject to legal defences
Often separate statutory regime	Rarely separate statutory regime
Fundamental issue for derivative market	More limited interest (increasing) in derivatives market

Figure 6.2 The distinction between netting and set-off

---

7 It should be noted that the concepts of cross-product netting, a master–master netting agreement, and cross-affiliate netting exist and are used, however, they are excluded from the scope of this text for the purposes of simplicity.

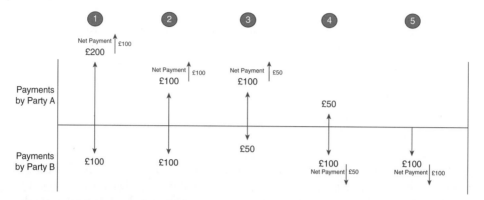

Figure 6.3 Illustration of payment netting

is that it addresses settlement risk,[8] which is the risk that a party will fail to deliver at the time of settlement. Where, for example, two payments in the same currency are due on the same day, there is the possibility that one party might make payment before the other, and that the second party becomes insolvent before such payment is ever made. Payment netting therefore addresses such a scenario. On a payment date, each party will aggregate the amounts of a currency to be delivered by it, and only the difference in the aggregate amounts will be delivered by the party with the larger aggregate obligation. Payment netting reduces settlement risk but does not achieve netting for balance sheet or regulatory capital purposes, because the transactions remain gross. Accordingly, although important, it is dwarfed in comparison with the potential benefits of close-out netting.

It should be noted that payment netting also dramatically reduces the number of payments between market participants, and therefore a reduction in operational costs of making payments, lowering the risk of insufficient liquidity and the occurrence of errors. It can, in some cases, reduce the effects of withholding taxes imposed on the payments.

The limitation of payment netting is that it does not consider future payments. One would be rather fortunate if every counterparty default happened upon the settlement of the last payment date, across all financial transactions conducted (which might be governed by a single master agreement) with them. It is much more likely that a counterparty will stop performing during the life of one or more financial transactions, and further the importance of close-out netting, which facilitates netting upon (early) termination of a financial contract.

Netting by Novation (We cover this for completeness, although, at the time of writing, there are no widely used master agreements which use novation netting. In a specific

8 Settlement risk is sometimes called 'Herstatt risk'. When the German Bankhaus Herstatt became insolvent, the German regulator withdrew its banking licence at the close of business in Germany on 26 June 1974, when banks in New York were still open and settling payments in US dollars. As a result, banks which had paid European currencies to Herstatt during the day in Europe did not receive the corresponding payment in US dollars to complete the settlement of the foreign exchange transactions.

situation where close-out netting may not be legally enforceable but netting of balances on a running current account may be, it might be possible to craft a bespoke agreement that uses novation netting, however, the increasing statutory recognition of close-out netting in most major jurisdictions has removed the rationale behind novation netting.)

Netting by novation is a contractual mechanism under which the contracting parties agree that all contracts between them shall be consolidated into a single contract as soon as each new contract is entered into. Each new contract is effectively combined with the existing contract. Netting by novation therefore offers the means of discharging mutual obligations and their replacement by a new net obligation. The obligations to be terminated do not need to be mature. As the transactions do not remain gross, it can achieve netting for regulatory capital purposes. Netting by novation may also be used at a multilateral level through a clearinghouse.

A disadvantage of novation netting is the possibility that it may be considered a sham if the parties do not reflect the novation netting in their bookkeeping; but this can be somewhat impractical, in cases where many contracts are consolidated under this technique – consider rebooking a contract involving hundreds if not thousands of cash flows each time a new contract is agreed.

Balance-Sheet Netting

Article 296 CRR

Bilateral contracts for novation between an institution and its counterparty under which mutual claims and obligations are automatically amalgamated in such a way that the novation fixes one single net amount each time it applies so as to create a single new contract that replaces all former contracts and all obligations between parties pursuant to those contracts and is binding on the parties.

Balance-Sheet Netting   This term refers to the offsetting of financial liabilities and assets in the balance sheet if the criteria for offsetting have been met. The criteria are set out in the relevant accounting standards. A detailed discussion of these criteria is beyond the scope of this book.

On-Balance-Sheet Netting   In the original Basel Capital Accord of July 1988, explicit reference was made to off-balance-sheet netting vis-à-vis the same counterparty but not to the offsetting of on-balance-sheet assets and liabilities. This was later allowed, with the restricted scope for applicability to loans and deposits only. The International Deposit Netting Agreement (IDNA) and EMA Deposit Annex are examples of industry master agreements which facilitate such balance-sheet netting. On-balance-sheet netting can also apply in relation to repo transactions and securities, or commodities lending or borrowing transactions, which are regarded as 'on-balance-sheet transactions'.

On-Balance-Sheet Netting

Article 195 CRR

An institution may use on-balance-sheet netting of mutual claims between itself and its counterparty as an eligible form of credit risk mitigation.

Without prejudice to Article 196, eligibility is limited to reciprocal cash balances between the institution and the counterparty. Institutions may amend risk-weighted exposure amounts and, as relevant, expected loss amounts only for loans and deposits that they have received themselves and that are subject to an on-balance-sheet netting agreement.

Article 219 CRR

Loans to and deposits with the lending institution subject to on-balance-sheet netting are to be treated by that institution as cash collateral for the purpose of calculating the effect of funded credit protection for those loans and deposits of the lending institution subject to on-balance-sheet netting which are denominated in the same currency.

We now return to the vitally important concept of close-out netting.

As mentioned above, close-out netting is the cancellation of a series of open executory contracts between two parties (e.g. for a sale of goods or foreign exchange or investments) on the default of one of the parties and the netting of the resulting gains and losses. Close-out netting requires two steps on a counterparty default: cancellation of the unperformed contracts and then netting out the gains and losses on each contract so as to produce a single net balance owing one way or another. Strictly, three steps are required – cancellation, calculation of losses and gains – then netting to arrive at the single net balance.

Illustrating the Importance of Close-Out Netting The main benefits of close-out netting are as follows, in no particular order:

Close-out netting, in producing a single net amount payable on default, ensures that, should one of the parties fail, the other can avoid the additional losses usually associated with an insolvency process. Netting is beneficial to the parties because it reduces credit exposure and also enables the parties to actively manage their credit risk through the posting of margin to cover the exposure remaining after netting so as to reduce the credit risk even further, or indeed to eliminate the credit risk completely. As such, close-out netting is the single biggest risk mitigant for counterparty credit risk arising from traded products.

Close-out netting permits market participants to freeze their exposures in the event of the failure of a counterparty, for example, its insolvency. Without such an ability to close out their positions, market participants would find themselves locked into contracts that fluctuate in value. Because traded positions require constant attention to maintain hedged positions, this can be extremely problematic. Through the close-out mechanism, a creditor who holds the insolvent firm's debt has a known exposure, and while the eventual recovery is uncertain, it can be estimated and is capped.

Through close-out netting a party can terminate its outstanding contracts when the other party is in default, thereby avoiding the risk that it may continue to be obligated under the contracts to make payments to the defaulting party, although it may be uncertain to what extent the defaulting party may be able to fulfil its obligations.

Close-out netting can be used to mitigate bilateral trading credit risk and thereby gain regulatory capital relief, which in turn brings an economic benefit in saving on the costs of capital.[9]

It is important to put the importance of close-out netting into perspective. In terms of systemic risk, without close-out netting, it is unlikely that the OTC derivatives market would have reached its current size and liquidity. Close-out netting has reduced OTC derivatives credit exposure by over 85% and, without it, banks worldwide might face a capital shortfall of over $500 billion. The Bank for International Settlements has published data showing that the effect of close-out netting between 1998 and 2013 has been to reduce gross exposures by 62.5–90%. This benefit has generally increased over the reporting period, reflecting the increasing importance prudentially regulated entities – and their regulators – attach to close-out netting.

The concept of close-out netting is based on the assumption that each and every financial transaction has a value which can be ascertained and brought into the calculation of the single net balance. To understand this, a discussion of the mark-to-market value of a financial contract follows, using the classical example of an OTC derivative, for necessary context.

Mark-to-Market In the OTC derivatives market, transactions are valued by a process known as 'mark-to-market'. Traditional financial contracts, bonds and loans are relatively easy to value. In derivative transactions, which typically impose obligations on both parties (one of the reasons that historically they were documented as parallel loans), the calculation is more complicated. One needs to consider the balance between the value of the rights a party has under the contract and the value of the rights of the other party.

The mark-to-market value of a contract defines the net value of all future payments and/or deliveries involved in that contract – it is therefore the amount that would have to be paid, or which would be received, if the contract were terminated and replaced with an equivalent contract, involving identical rights and obligations for the period remaining outstanding at current market rates. Put another way, it directly relates to what could potentially be lost or gained today in the event of a default. It does not constitute an immediate liability, rather it is the present value of all future liabilities of both parties under the contract. Accordingly, such future obligations will be subject to a number of market variables and might be positive or negative.

Pricing or Valuing an Interest Rate Swap The market value of a swap at the time of its entry should in theory be zero, if it is a 'fair deal' between the parties and the future payments under the swap reflect the level of swap rates at the time the swap is entered into.

---

9 Assuming that a bank's cost of capital is 10% p.a., for each £100 of RWA saved, the bank will save £0.8 per annum (£100 × 8% × 10% p.a.). The actual cost of capital for a bank will, of course, vary from bank to bank. The purpose of this example is simply to illustrate the importance of capital costs in the derivatives business. Derivatives dealers will usually factor their capital costs into the pricing for new transactions, taking into account whether the transaction will be adding to the counterparty credit risk or may be reducing the counterparty credit risk if the transaction can be netted with existing transactions.

Over time, the market value (predominantly the present value of all future cash flows) of the swap will fluctuate with changing market conditions. Two factors influence the mark-to-market exposure: the number of payments remaining and the potential value movement of (random) variables on the underlying. The mark-to-market exposure will begin to decrease as the number of future payments remaining decreases. This is called the amortisation effect. The rising replacement cost due to changing market conditions is offset by the decreasing number of payments remaining until maturity.

Coming back to the concept of the mark-to-market value of an instrument – it is therefore essentially the secondary market value of the instrument. Unlike traditional instruments like a loan, it can be negative as well as positive, to reflect the fact that a purchaser will often be undertaking obligations as well as obtaining rights.

One typically documents each derivative transaction, such as the interest rate swap described above, using a trade confirmation,[10] and the transaction is expressed as being governed by the derivatives master agreement between the parties (e.g. the ISDA Master Agreement, the framework master agreement described in detail in Chapter 3). Between two major investment banks there are likely to be hundreds of thousands of such derivative transactions, all governed by a single ISDA Master Agreement which seeks to allow the ability to net transactions upon termination (i.e., on a close-out), as well as adjust those positions through collateralisation (see Chapter 7).

It should be noted that, contractually, master agreements tend to refer to replacement costs (in this regard, the 1992 ISDA Master Agreement allowed for two methods of calculation, one of which – 'Market Quotation' – is based on replacement cost[11] while the other – 'Loss' – instead broadly allows the non-defaulting party upon a termination to calculate the loss that it has suffered as a result of termination). The mark-to-market value is closely related to the replacement cost, but practically there are a number of nuances to this, such as bid/offer spreads, which may be significant in respect of illiquid product types. Additionally, replacement costs will naturally contain XVAs (see Chapter 3).

As discussed previously, close-out netting refers to a process involving the termination of obligations under a contract with a defaulting party and the subsequent combination of positive and negative replacement values into a single net payable or receivable. For now, we will ignore the additional considerations that collateral arrangements might add to this, but essentially recourse to credit support, if any, should be taken into account (see Chapter 7 on collateral more broadly).

As an example, assume Bank A has 5,000 trades with Bank B. Some may be of positive value to Bank A ('in-the-money' – Bank A would need to pay a third party to replace Bank B on the other side), whereas the others are negative in value to Bank A ('out-of-the-money' – a third party would pay Bank A to replace Bank B on the other side).

---

10 As already discussed, derivative transactions are generally concluded on the telephone and subsequently confirmed by an exchange of written confirmations which set out the details of the terms agreed between the parties.

11 It is interesting to note the number of cases whereby the courts have examined the true meaning of 'Loss' under the 1992 ISDA Master Agreement, such as *Enasarco v Lehman Brothers Finance S.A.* [2015] EWHC 1307.

If Bank B is not performing (e.g. is failing to make payments due under the various trades), then we will usually want to replace them. Typically, we want to close out all of our transactions with them and make a claim on our counterparty's estate for what is owed. There are two contrasting situations here:

1) If we can make a single net claim for the value of the whole portfolio of trades we have with them, then the counterparty exposure is as low as possible, given the circumstances. We balance transactions with a positive value to Bank B against those with a negative value, coming to a final net value.
2) If we cannot make a net claim, if the net close-out is not permitted – then we have to:
   A) Pay them the value of each transaction where we owe them money.
   B) Make a claim against them for each transaction with credit exposure.
   As we will now see, this 'gross close-out' increases the counterparty credit risk.

So, let's illustrate the difference between the two scenarios with some figures. We simplify first, and assume we have just three transactions between Bank A and Bank B, as set out in Figure 6.4. Two of these are 'in-the-money' to Bank A, one is 'in-the-money' to Bank B.

Let's assume that we can form a net sum. If we can net the values of the transactions, you will see we add the first two (which have value to Bank A – so they are in-the-money from a Bank A perspective). We can then subtract the third transaction – the one that has value to Bank B. Overall, netting the amounts, the portfolio of the three transactions has a value of MINUS 100 to Bank A and a value of PLUS 100 to Bank B.

Note the sign, it is Bank B that has a credit exposure of 100 net to Bank A that Bank B would need to manage and, if it were prudentially regulated, set regulatory capital against. This is in relation to the £100 million Bank A would owe to Bank B's insolvent estate were Bank B to go insolvent.

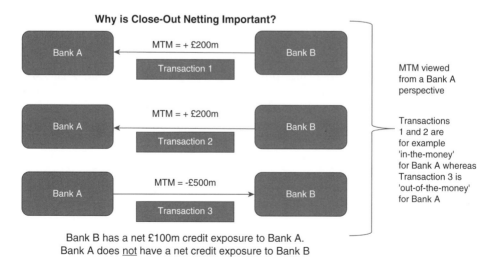

Why is Close-Out Netting Important?

Bank A ← MTM = + £200m — Bank B	
Transaction 1	MTM viewed from a Bank A perspective
Bank A ← MTM = + £200m — Bank B	
Transaction 2	Transactions 1 and 2 for example 'in-the-money' for Bank A whereas Transaction 3 is 'out-of-the-money' for Bank A
Bank A — MTM = -£500m → Bank B	
Transaction 3	

Bank B has a net £100m credit exposure to Bank A.
Bank A does not have a net credit exposure to Bank B

Figure 6.4 Why is close-out netting important?

But what if we can't make a net claim? We said that there are two steps in this scenario:

1) Bank A pays Bank B the mark-to-market value of each transaction where Bank A would owe them money. So, Bank A needs to pay £500 million for transaction 3.
2) Bank A then needs to make a claim for each transaction where the trade is in-the-money to Bank A. So now, Bank A has a credit exposure to Bank B. Unlike scenario 1, Bank A now has to set aside regulatory capital against this credit exposure of £400 million.

Assuming Bank B goes into insolvency, let's presume that the recovery is only a penny in the pound. For transactions 1 and 2, Bank A will claim 200 for each, but will only receive 200*1% for each, so £4 million in total.

From a negative exposure situation to Bank B where close-out netting applies, we have now gone to £400 million exposure on Bank B. In their insolvency, we will only recover £4 million of that. What we have described here, upon Bank B's insolvency, is the ability of a liquidator/insolvency practitioner to 'cherry-pick'; disclaiming transactions it regards as unprofitable (transaction 3) whilst enforcing the rest. Bank A would need to pay £500 million but queue up as an unsecured creditor for the £400 million, and actually only receive a small portion of that.

Clearly net close-out, as a tool that reduces counterparty credit risk and a bank's capital costs, is desirable but may be subject to legal risk, as it may be challenged, due to possible issues with its enforceability under some insolvency laws. Jurisdictions have different stances towards close-out netting arrangements – the insolvency laws in many jurisdictions now recognise it; however, other jurisdictions allow insolvency administrators to pick and choose between the contracts to be performed in insolvency, so called 'cherry-picking'.

The key to achieving this is 'legal glue'? A legal document known as a master agreement that facilitates close-out netting. A master trading agreement is 'legal glue'. It seeks to bind together all of the transactions executed between two parties and (together with various other ancillary documents) to govern their terms.

By signing a master agreement, the parties signal their intention of treating all the trades between them as aspects of a single whole. Conceptually, you could regard it as the case that if two parties have a valid signed master agreement, when they trade a swap, they are not entering into a new separate transaction, but rather varying the terms of their existing agreement to include the cash flows of this new swap. But when does this glue hold? You can write more or less whatever you want in a legal agreement, but clearly stated, intent is no guarantee of enforceability. The key issue for close-out netting is whether a court would respect the agreement, or whether they would instead seek to impose a gross close-out.

This is exactly the subject matter of a close-out netting legal opinion – opining on how a court would treat an agreement in this regard. In order to gain the benefit of netting for regulatory capital purposes, broadly speaking, there is a requirement to obtain close-out legal opinions that would provide sufficient comfort on the enforceability of the close-out netting provisions. Depending on the legal certainty in the jurisdiction, the conclusion(s) in the legal opinion may be worded with varying degrees of strength. For example: 'a court would…', 'a court should…', 'it is likely that a court would…'. The regulatory capital test is binary in nature – upon meeting the requisite robustness of opinion, the financial firm may net exposures for regulatory capital purposes. However, for pricing purposes, firms are increasingly noting the robustness of the opinion and factoring this in as a valuation adjustment when pricing transactions.

Recognition of Contractual Netting as Risk-Reducing

Article 295 CRR

Institutions may treat as risk-reducing in accordance with Article 298 only the following types of contractual netting agreements, where the netting agreement has been recognised by competent authorities in accordance with Article 296 and where the institution meets the requirements set out in Article 297:

a) bilateral contracts for novation between an institution and its counterparty under which mutual claims and obligations are automatically amalgamated in such a way that the novation fixes one single net amount each time it applies so as to create a single new contract that replaces all former contracts and all obligations between parties pursuant to those contracts and is binding on the parties;

b) other bilateral agreements between an institution and its counterparty;

c) contractual cross-product netting agreements for institutions that have received the approval to use the method set out in section 6 for transactions falling under the scope of that method. Competent authorities shall report to EBA a list of the contractual cross-product netting agreements approved.

Article 296 CRR

2. The following conditions shall be fulfilled by all contractual netting agreements used by an institution for the purposes of determining exposure value in this Part:

a) the institution has concluded a contractual netting agreement with its counterparty which creates a single legal obligation, covering all included transactions, such that, in the event of default by the counterparty it would be entitled to receive or obliged to pay only the net sum of the positive and negative mark-to-market values of included individual transactions;

b) the institution has made available to the competent authorities written and reasoned legal opinions to the effect that, in the event of a legal challenge of the netting agreement, the institution's claims and obligations would not exceed those referred to in point (a). The legal opinion shall refer to the applicable law:

   i) the jurisdiction in which the counterparty is incorporated;

   ii) if a branch of an undertaking is involved, which is located in a country other than that where the undertaking is incorporated, the jurisdiction in which the branch is located;

   iii) the jurisdiction whose law governs the individual transactions included in the netting agreement;

   iv) the jurisdiction whose law governs any contract or agreement necessary to effect the contractual netting.

There are three main variables relevant for a close-out netting opinion: the type of agreement (e.g. the particular ISDA Master Agreement or Global Master Repurchase Agreement, and its governing law),[12] the relevant jurisdictions applicable to the

---

12 Governing law is obviously a key variable in its own right, however, many preprint forms of Master Agreements indirectly subsume the 'governing law variable'.

insolvency analysis (mainly centred around the location of the counterparty and the location of the collateral) and the counterparty type (this is driven by the fact that the insolvency analysis may be different for different counterparty forms of organisation, for example an insurance company compared to a corporate, including various public policy considerations when one considers counterparty types such as local authorities (see Chapter 2 on legal relations). There are also second-order variables to consider, such as the specific transaction types covered by the agreement – for example, at the time of writing, some derivative transactions will only comply with the relevant netting legislation in Denmark if they meet certain conditions.

One will immediately see, from this, the data requirements to make this all work can be fairly demanding. Not only are the above legal opinion variables to be managed, but this also relates to other reference data in respect of specific arrangements with counterparties, such as client data (e.g. the counterparty type and location) and legal agreement data (the agreement type, the governing law – to name just two basic factors – and the legal opinion in question may specifically require certain terms to be contained in the master agreement which also need to be taken into account, such as automatic early termination in the case of Swiss counterparties under an ISDA Master Agreement, in order for a positive close-out netting determination to be provided based on the legal opinion).

Legal opinions must be obtained for all relevant jurisdictions to the derivative contract. A trade between two firms established in two different jurisdictions – where the trading branches are also established in a further unique different jurisdictions, for example – would potentially require legal opinions for not just the jurisdictions relating to the head offices of the two contracting entities, but also the jurisdictions of each branch involved. Although one might expect this to be limited to the main contracting entities and branches involved in the trading, in practice one needs to consider each branch of the contractual parties listed on the master netting agreement. There is a danger that a single branch in a jurisdiction that is not 'netting-friendly' may 'taint the netting set'.

Tainting the Netting Set

If the parties enter into a master agreement and each transaction in reliance on the fact that the master agreement and all confirmations are expressed to form a single agreement between the parties, they are assuming that, on default of one of the parties, close-out netting will apply to all transactions. If it transpires subsequently that a set of transactions with a branch in one jurisdiction cannot be included in the close-out netting calculations (e.g. of local restrictions on netting in the jurisdiction of the branch), there is a risk that this may provide grounds to call into question the validity of the close-out provisions in the master agreement relating to all of the transactions.

Given the historical (albeit declining) use of large multi-branch master netting agreements by large dealers, this can in some cases ultimately result in the need for more than a dozen legal opinions for the one single agreement.

To obtain a legal opinion (or multiple, as discussed above) for each individual master agreement that a large investment bank has (which typically runs into the tens of thousands) would clearly be a phenomenally expensive and burdensome exercise. It is for this reason that so-called 'industry opinions' are obtained. These are generic opinions which are commissioned by trade associations or banking associations on behalf of their members,[13] who then 'apply' its reasoning to the individual agreements by considering the specific terms of the relevant agreement compared to the various assumptions, qualifications and conditions the legal opinion may provide for. This, as one might imagine, again creates the need for an infrastructure to cope with the 'data' analysis effectively being performed and to avoid unsustainable manual review.

At the time of writing, there are currently ISDA close-out netting opinions from 64 jurisdictions (ISDA seeks to add approximately two or three new jurisdictional opinions each year in response to member requests, typically gathering the opinions in November and December and releasing them to members in the following January). In contrast, ICMA more rigidly updates its close-out netting opinions on an annual basis and, as of this date, covers some 65 jurisdictions in respect of the 1995,[14] 2000 and 2011 versions of the Global Master Repurchase Agreement (GMRA).

Importantly, the industry standard master agreements are intended to be amended through their various schedules and annexes. Amendment to core terms (such as the close-out netting provisions) could invalidate the legal opinion(s) relied upon if they take the underlying agreement outside the assumptions made in the generic legal opinion. If substantial amendments to a master agreement are proposed during negotiations between the parties, careful consideration should be given to whether the industry legal opinion can continue to be relied on. Any assumptions or qualifications must be specific and adequately explained in the legal opinion. Furthermore, no assumption or qualification should materially weaken or unduly restrict the scope and essential conclusions of the opinion.

Bespoke Close-Out Netting Legal Opinions

It should be noted, however, that for larger financial institutions, the coverage of the close-out netting legal opinions obtained solely by trade associations is unlikely to be sufficient (trade associations typically consider their broad trading membership and only obtain opinions where they would be of benefit to a large part of the membership). Bespoke opinions can be commissioned by individual firms to cover agreements with counterparties in jurisdictions not covered in association opinions, non-standard agreements, additional counterparties or additional products, for example. For the largest financial institutions, this can create a requirement to obtain and maintain nearly a thousand such bespoke legal opinions. The regulatory capital benefits of obtaining such opinions will, however, tend to far outweigh the actual cost of commissioning the bespoke opinions in cases where there is trading between the parties.

---

13 For example, ISDA in respect of the ISDA Master Agreement forms and the ICMA in respect of the GMRA have commissioned various generic close-out netting opinions for the use of their members (the opinions are addressed to the relevant trade association, but are capable of being relied upon by the members). The traditional ISDA close-out netting opinions, cover the following:

- The enforceability of the provisions under English and New York law (which are the two laws envisaged as being selected as a choice under the ISDA Master Agreement pre-printed form); and
- The enforceability of the provisions upon the insolvency of one of the parties organised and/or acting through a branch in various jurisdictions.

14 This is a bit of a hot topic at the time of writing. The industry opinion has recently been changed to no longer include the 1995 version, in part as a stick to move market participants to use the 2000 or 2011 version instead.

Refresh of Close-Out Netting Legal Opinions

It should also be noted that the close-out netting determination is a dynamic and not a static concept. In particular, the underlying regulations and case law for a particular jurisdiction's insolvency laws may change over time. Accordingly, there is a regulatory expectation that the close-out netting legal opinions will be refreshed with a certain periodicity (the exact period may be subject to a number of factors, such as the revamp of a jurisdiction's bankruptcy legislation). In cases where trade associations obtain opinions on behalf of their members, this can greatly assist with this operational requirement, however, firms will need to refresh any bespoke opinions applicable. Again, this creates a substantial infrastructure requirement in terms of legal opinion storage and linkage with the legal agreements (and their data) dependent on the close-out legal opinion in order to net.

Article 297 CRR

1. An institution shall establish and maintain procedures to ensure that the legal validity and enforceability of its contractual netting is reviewed in the light of changes in the law of relevant jurisdictions referred to in Article 296(2)(b).

Other Types of Legal Opinions

We have very much focused on close-out netting legal opinions, however, there are a number of other legal opinions (see Figure 6.5) that may be required, which we now touch on. Before this broader look, it is worth mentioning that the requirement for legal review under the CRR extends additionally to the issue of enforceability of collateral arrangements in all relevant jurisdictions (Article 207(3) in relation to financial collateral and gold and Article 209(2)(c) CRR in relation to receivables).[15] We consider collateral enforceability in more detail in Chapter 7.

Concluding on the Legal Data Requirements

To conclude, it is important to note the importance of legal data to manage the regulatory capital calculation and obtain the benefit of close-out netting as a credit risk mitigant. This is from a compliance perspective, as well as capital optimisation.

There is a need to store and manage the lifecycle of legal opinions, from their commissioning, analysis and key terms, in respect of conclusions, agreement requirements, assumptions and qualifications. There is a complex interaction between client, product and agreement taxonomies that might be used within the legal opinions themselves, as well as in document agreement stores and the systems of downstream consumers, such as risk and trading.

Additionally, there needs to be a fundamental ability to correctly link transactions to the correct master agreement intending to net transactions. With complexity such as umbrella agreements with multiple fund types, as well as the possibility of multiple master agreements (even of the same type) between parties, this can often incorrectly be assumed to be straightforward.

---

15 It also extends to the enforceability of guarantees and credit derivatives [Article 213(3) CRR] – all of which supplement the obligations in Article 194.

Type of Opinion	Contents	Purpose
Capacity (or due diligence)	Is a particular counterparty permitted or authorised to enter into the contracts in question?	To show that the contracts which a bank enters into with a particular counterparty are valid, binding and legally enforceable.
Close-out netting	Are the 'close-out netting' provisions in a particular master agreement enforceable pre- and post-insolvency of the counterparty?	To permit a bank to calculate its capital requirements in respect of trading transactions on a netted basis as per Article 295 CRR.
Collateral enforceability	Are collateral arrangements: (a) with respect to assets received as collateral from a particular counterparty; and/or (b) with respect to assets posted as collateral to a particular counterparty enforceable pre- and post-insolvency of the counterparty?	(a) To permit a bank to calculate its capital requirements in respect of collateralised trading transactions on a netted basis as per Article 295 CRR. (b) To satisfy the requirements relating to margin in respect of uncleared OTC trades in EMIR Article 11(3) and RTS 2016/2251.
Clearing member reliance opinion	Are the contractual 'close-out netting' provisions (typically of the ISDA/FIA Cleared Derivatives Addendum) enforceable in the insolvency of a clearing member and/or the CCP?	To permit a bank to calculate its capital requirements in respect of trading transactions with its clearing member on a netted basis as per Article 295 CRR.
Client clearing reliance opinion	In respect of client clearing, are the contractual 'close-out netting' provisions (typically of the ISDA/FIA Cleared Derivatives Addendum) enforceable in the insolvency of a 'client'?	To permit a bank acting as clearing member to calculate its capital requirements in respect of trading transactions with its client on a netted basis as per Article 295 CRR.
Article 305 opinions	In respect of client clearing, are the client's assets and positions segregated and can these assets and positions be ported to another clearing member, so that the client will not suffer any losses in the event of the insolvency of either (i) its clearing member or (ii) any other client of its clearing member under the law (A) of the client's jurisdiction, (B) of the jurisdiction of the clearing member, (C) of the jurisdiction of the central counterparty, (D) governing the transactions and (E) governing the collateral?	To allow a bank which is a client of a clearing member to apply a reduced risk weighting of 2% (4% if the requirement of bankruptcy remoteness on the case of the insolvency of another clearing member client is not met) for its central counterparty-related transactions with a clearing member as per Article 306 CRR.

Figure 6.5 Types of legal opinions

Type of Opinion	Contents	Purpose
Collateral custodian opinions	If initial margin is held by the collateral provider, is the collateral held in insolvency-remote custody accounts? Is the initial margin freely transferable to the posting counterparty in a timely manner in case of the default of the collecting counterparty? Segregation requirements w.r.t. initial margin in RTS Article 19 paragraphs 3, 4 and 5.	To enable a bank to show compliance with EMIR Article 11(3) and the requirements for initial margin in RTS Article 19.
Central counterparty opinions (for clearing members of central counterparties)	Is close-out netting of transactions with the central counterparty enforceable in the insolvency of the central counterparty? To what extent are assets posted as margin to the central counterparty bankruptcy remote in the insolvency of the central counterparty? To what extent is a clearing member liable to contribute to the central counterparty's default fund?	To enable a bank (as clearing member) to calculate: (a) the exposure from its transactions with a central counterparty on a netted basis as per CRR Articles 301 and 306; and (b) the own-funds requirement for default contributions as per CRR Article 307 or Article 310.
Securitisation opinions	CRR Article 243: Significant credit risk associated with the securitised exposures is considered to have been transferred to third parties and the securitised exposures are put beyond the reach of the originator institution and its creditors, including in bankruptcy and receivership. This shall be supported by the opinion of qualified legal counsel. CRR Article 244: Significant credit risk is considered to have been transferred to third parties either through funded or unfunded credit protection, and an opinion is obtained from qualified legal counsel confirming the enforceability of the credit protection in all relevant jurisdictions.	To enable a bank to exclude assets which have been transferred to third parties through a securitisation structure when calculating its capital requirements.

Abbreviations:
CRR EU Regulation 575/2013
EMIR EU Regulation 648/2012
RTS EU Regulation regulatory technical standards 2016/2251

Figure 6.5 *(Continued)*

In order to be able to optimise capital and successfully meet regulatory scrutiny, it is increasingly important to be able to also show the data lineage between the legal opinion, the master agreement, the transactions governed by that master agreement and the relevant netting determination used for regulatory capital calculation purposes. In fact, it is hard to see how the close-out netting determination can be excluded from the list of critical data attributes from the perspective of BCBS 239 (see Chapter 5).

Bibliography

Bank for International Settlements (BIS) (2013) 'Basel III phase-in arrangements', Basel Committee on Banking Supervision

Bank for International Settlements (BIS) (2016) 'History of the Basel Committee'

Bank for International Settlements (2017) 'High-level summary of Basel III reforms', Basel Committee on Banking Supervision, December 2017

Basel Committee on Banking Supervision (2009) 'Strengthening the resilience of the banking sector', Consultative Document

Bliss, R. and Kaufman, G. (2014) 'Derivatives and systemic risk: Netting, stays, and closeout', *Federal Reserve Bank of Chicago*, 15th October 2014

Cleary, L. (2017) LinkedIn, *12th* April 2017 (www.linkedin.com/in/lisa-cleary-ba7a8722/detail/recent-activity/shares/)

Datoo, Akber and Sime, Peter (22 July 2016) 'Netting risks create pricing and operational headaches', *Risk Magazine*

D2 Legal Technology LLP (2016) 'Industry survey – legal opinion management and netting determinations'

Enasarco v Lehman Brothers Finance S.A. [2015] *EWHC* 1307

FCA Handbook, Glossary

Götz, Martin R and Tröger, Tobias H (2017) 'Fines for misconduct in the banking sector – what is the situation in the EU?', *Research Center for Sustainable Architecture for Finance in Europe (SAFE)*

IASB (2010) '*Staff paper: Offsetting of financial assets and financial liabilities*', IASB Meeting

ICMA (2017) *Quarterly Report: Assessment of Market Practice and Regulatory Report*, 2nd Quarter, 6th April 2017, *Issue* 45

ISDA (2010) ISDA Research Notes: 'The importance of close-out netting'

Latham & Watkins (2010) 'Making increased cost claims under Basel III – working with the LMA provisions', 25th October 2010, No. 1094

Shearman & Sterling (2013) 'Basel III: US/EU comparison'

Shoenmaker, D. (2014) '*Regulatory capital: Why is it different?*, Duisenberg School of Finance, VU University

Wood, P. (2007) *Set-Off and Netting, Derivatives, Clearing Systems*, 2nd edn. Sweet & Maxwell: London

7

Collateral – Enforceability, Reform and Optimisation

This chapter seeks to focus on collateral (also known as margin), which acts as a credit risk mitigant (following from Chapter 6, it can also be critical in reducing the regulatory capital requirement for prudentially regulated institutions). We briefly detail the considerable regulation that has imposed (and will continue to, in the short-term future) significant new mandatory requirements on market participants in terms of their margining practices. We will of course draw out the legal data perspective as we journey through these items.

What is Collateral?

> *Collateral flows lie at the heart of any proper understanding of market liquidity, and hence of financial stability. The financial plumbing encompasses the biggest pipes that form the nexus between collateral and money; it can be seen as the interaction between nonbanks and banks in money markets and capital markets (the latter of which include securities lending, repos, derivatives, and prime brokerage). These activities are the nuts and bolts of financial plumbing.* (Singh 2017)

Collateral is a credit risk-reduction tool, which has been used for many centuries to provide security against a trade counterparty defaulting. Like close-out netting, it mitigates risk by reducing credit exposure. Its effect is to substitute the credit risk of the issuer of the collateral provided, for that of the counterparty to the transaction (on whom one is seeking to reduce credit risk). Although it reduces credit risk, it gives rise to other forms of risk, such as legal, operational and concentration risk – as well as credit risk on the issuer of the collateral provided.

Modern-day financial collateral management traces back to the 1980s, with firms such as Salomon Brothers and Bankers Trust using collateral to mitigate credit exposures. Initially, calculations regarding collateral required against such exposures were performed on spreadsheets, and are now typically managed through enterprise collateral management systems (such as Murex's MX.3 for Enterprise Collateral Management, Lombard Risk's Colline, SimCorp, SmartStream's TLM Collateral Management and Cloudmargin) linked to trading and other systems in the enterprise. Legal standardisation of collateralisation documentation in the derivatives context began in 1994 with the publication of the 1994 ISDA Credit Support Annex (Security Interest – New York Law) by ISDA. The effectiveness of collateral management practices was shown through the

Russian debt default and failure of Long Term Capital Management in 1998. It was, however, the recent Financial Crisis that highlighted a number of issues with the market practices regarding collateral management, leading to significant recent regulation on the pretext of financial stability that will be covered later in this chapter.

Credit Risk Mitigation

What is Credit Risk?

Credit risk refers to the risk that a counterparty will fail to meet its obligations in accordance with agreed terms. For example, the risk of non-payment of money by a borrower under a loan agreement to a lender because the borrower is unable to pay and defaults on its payment obligation. Credit risk exists whenever a firm has a relationship where a counterparty has an obligation to make payments or deliveries of assets in the future. Credit risk management seeks to maximise a firm's risk-adjusted returns whilst managing credit risk within acceptable parameters, and is critical to any banking operation.

Credit enhancement techniques range from simple transaction-specific, risk-reducing measures, such as obtaining a guarantee, to more complex techniques such as close-out netting, collateralisation and the use of credit derivatives. Credit risk can be reduced through the use of optional termination rights, also referred to as (credit) break rights, which can be exercised where a particular transaction generates a significant credit exposure to a counterparty that is outside the risk appetite of a party.

It should be noted that the various credit enhancement techniques need not be applied on a mutually exclusive basis – a guarantee might be provided in addition to collateral and/or providing a transaction-specific termination right. There will be many jurisdictional issues (such as insolvency laws and jurisdiction-specific regulation for certain counterparty types) and party preferences (such as those driven by the operational impact and cost to a party) that will be key in determining the most suitable credit risk-reduction method(s) for particular circumstances.

Collateral in the OTC Derivatives Context

The key idea is that an asset of value (most commonly cash or securities) is passed (this may or may not involve actual ownership changing – more on this later) from one party to a transaction to its counterparty, as a means of reducing the credit risk faced by that counterparty. The collateral 'supports' an exposure faced by the counterparty (and therefore credit risk) on the provider of the collateral. Through the provision of collateral, the exposure faced by the counterparty can in theory be reduced by the value of the collateral. Key to this is for the collateral provided in respect of a transaction to be available for such offset against the exposure, if the party to whom the counterparty has exposure defaults under the transaction. In order to maximise the effect of collateralisation as a credit-risk-mitigating technique, the value of the collateral should equal, or in fact exceed, that of the risk (thereby creating overcollateralisation of the exposure). There is, however, a risk that the value of the collateral may reduce due to market conditions at the same time as the party to whom the counterparty has exposure defaults. Accordingly, it is key that the collateral provided and the underlying transaction(s) should not be highly positively correlated (e.g. as collateral in the form of securities issued by the party to whom the counterparty is exposed would be). It is market practice that, in the context of a trading relationship where there are a large number of transactions between the parties documented under a master agreement – such as the ISDA Master Agreement – the collateral will be provided in respect of the overall net exposure (assuming close-out netting is deemed to be enforceable) between the parties rather than on an individual transaction basis. This is therefore also in line with the manner in which credit risk is typically assessed under such trading agreements, where close-out netting is enforceable.

The underlying exposure under a master trading agreement faced by one party in respect of the other is likely to be dynamic, increasing and decreasing over time, and even at times reversing in direction. Accordingly, to reduce the credit risk that may arise from such movements, parties periodically mark-to-market the transactions between them, calculate the net value of the portfolio of trades under the master agreement and adjust the collateral provided between them. Without such 'rebalancing', the collateral value will not match the exposure at a particular point in time, giving rise to credit risk to the extent of the difference. Rebalancing, however, comes with certain operational and transaction costs, and in order to keep these costs under control, posting of collateral typically occurs in blocks according to predefined rules in the collateral arrangement agreed between the trading parties.

This chapter mainly concentrates on collateralisation of bilateral OTC derivatives, although Figure 7.1 provides details of the main differences with exchange-traded derivatives. It will be noted from this that the effect of the margin reform regulation (specifically dealt with later in this chapter) is increasingly to align collateral management in the uncleared OTC derivatives world to that for exchange-traded derivatives.

OTC derivatives collateral arrangements are increasingly bilateral rather than unilateral (with both parties obliged to margin rather than it being required by just one party based on their respective commercial negotiating position), with daily margining (this is one of the key regulatory mandates post-crisis). Parties may agree on the application

	OTC Derivatives	Exchange-Traded Derivatives
Level of Collateralisation	Historically the choice of the trading parties, however increasingly regulated and mandated, with notable exceptions (e.g. sovereigns)	All trades are collateralised
Collateral Types Permitted	Highly customisable, subject to increasing regulatory constraints	Highly standardised
Rebalancing Frequency	Highly customisable, subject to increasing regulatory constraints	Daily

Figure 7.1 The main collateralisation differences between OTC derivatives and exchange-traded derivatives

of a 'threshold' which represents the level of unsecured exposure to the other party they are willing to accept. Whilst this is generally an internal credit decision, it should be noted that there are mandatory threshold limitations where margin regulations apply, as discussed later in this chapter. The collateral amounts to be provided are based on the difference between the aggregate mark-to-market of the portfolio governed by the master agreement that is agreed to be collateralised and the market value of the collateral already provided (if any). In the case of an increasing mark-to-market exposure, a party should receive collateral and with a decreasing mark-to-market exposure, they will need to return collateral.

Master agreements typically have collateral arrangement annexes, which mechanically deal with such rebalancing and collateral management details. A good example of this is the 1995 ISDA Credit Support Annex (Transfer – English Law) (see Figure 7.3 later), designed to be used with the 1992 and 2002 (the latter, albeit with some small technical tweaks) ISDA Master Agreement pre-print versions.

It should be noted that collateral has funding implications and is considered in the calculation of the funding valuation adjustment (FVA) (see Chapter 3), since a party may not have the right collateral to provide as the exposure its counterparty faces to it increases, and accordingly may need to obtain and fund such collateral.

Moving away from OTC derivatives briefly, it should be noted that repurchase (repo) transactions involve the exchange of securities against cash, together with the creation of obligations on the parties to reverse the exchange, providing equivalent securities for cash, at the maturity of the transaction. By maintaining, during the life of the transaction, the relative value of the parties' obligations by marking them to market and ensuring there are transfers to deal with any imbalance of the values of cash and security assets exchanged, and also by including a mechanism allowing these obligations to be netted against each other in the event of a default by either party, the repo transaction is economically a 'self-collateralising' transaction (see Figure 7.2).

Collateral vs Regulatory Capital

Both regulatory capital (see Chapter 6) and collateral, perform similar functions in terms of credit risk mitigation. Collateral is, however, a 'defaulter-pay' mechanism whereby

Collateralisation Advantages	Collateralisation Disadvantages
Offsets the exposure to the counterparty (and accordingly, can reduce regulatory capital requirements)	Funding volatility sensitivity
Creates increased business opportunities through reduction in counterparty credit risk	May create liquidity squeezes in respect of the underlying collateral
Allows rebalancing based on mark-to-market movements of the portfolio of trades	Creates operational risk and management costs
Diversification of credit risk	Legal risk
Increased liquidity	Creates a pricing impact
	Settlement and valuation risk

Figure 7.2 High-level advantages and disadvantages of collateralisation as a credit risk mitigation technique

the surviving party utilises the collateral it has been given, whereas regulatory capital functions by adding loss absorbency to the financial system, since it is a 'survivor-pay' mechanism through the use of the regulatory capital to meet such losses, which eats into the surviving entity's own financial resources.

Collateralisation forces market participants to better consider the cost of the risks being taken through their trading, since they have to post collateral as part of their entry into transactions. Also, margin is more dynamic and targeted than capital, with each trade portfolio with a counterparty having its own designated margin for absorbing the potential losses related to that specific counterparty – with rebalancing, it reflects changes in the trading portfolio's specific risk profile. In contrast, regulatory capital is shared collectively across the various activities undertaken by a prudentially regulated entity. It may accordingly come under much greater need at a time of stress. One also cannot rapidly adjust regulatory capital in response to changing risk exposures, as is possible with collateral. Capital requirements against each exposure are not designed to cover the loss on the default of the counterparty, but rather the probability-weighted loss given such default. Regulatory capital is also only required of prudentially regulated financial firms.

Types of Collateral: Pledge vs Title Transfer

There are two main types of collateral arrangement used in the OTC derivatives market: one based on the creation of a security interest in the collateral and the other based on title transfer of the collateral from one party to another. The legal form and effect of each approach vary according to the governing law of the collateral arrangement, the nature and location of the collateral and the parties. The two approaches can be distinguished as follows:

1) Under a security interest arrangement, the collateral giver creates a security interest in favour of the collateral taker (which is the party whose credit risk to the collateral giver the collateral is seeking to reduce) in the collateral. The collateral is typically delivered either directly to the collateral taker or to its custodian. The collateral giver generally continues to own the collateral, subject to the right of the collateral taker to sell the collateral to offset the exposure that the collateral seeks to mitigate for example, if the counterparty defaults.

2) Under a title transfer arrangement, the collateral giver transfers full title to the collateral to the collateral taker and grants the collateral taker the right to set-off or net, on default of the collateral giver, the collateral taker's net exposure to the collateral giver under the master agreement against the value of the collateral. Under this approach, the collateral taker owns the collateral provided and the collateral giver, if it performs in full, is only entitled to the return of fungible securities and/or repayment of cash in the same currency.

The use of a security interest arrangement will typically require greater formalities in its creation and perfection than a title transfer arrangement, possibly including (depending on the various factors mentioned above) registration, filing or some other form of notification of the security/pledge and other specific requirements as to the form and content of the document creating the security interest. The formalities are necessary to 'perfect' the security/pledge; that is, to ensure its formal validity and priority over any third party with a purported claim to the collateral assets. The formalities associated with perfection of a security/pledge vary in complexity from jurisdiction to jurisdiction, in terms of where the collateral and the relevant parties are located. This can be further complicated by multi-jurisdictional considerations – for example, in the case of collateral securities that are held in book-entry form through a chain of intermediaries located in various jurisdictions – and type of collateral (e.g. cash vs securities) or type of security (e.g. debt vs equity and bearer vs registered). Applicable insolvency and other laws will normally impose certain restrictions on the collateral taker as to the manner of holding and, possibly, as to the use of the collateral, recognising that the collateral taker does not have full interest in the collateral – rather, it is in respect of the specific exposure. Additionally, if the collateral giver defaults, there are likely to be numerous necessary steps, such as seeking court approvals and selling the collateral based on that approval, before the value of the collateral can actually be realised.

In contrast, under a title transfer arrangement, the collateral taker becomes the full owner of the collateral. They are therefore free to apply the collateral as they wish, even before any default of the collateral giver. This very much proves the old adage that 'possession is nine-tenths of the law'! The use of title transfer typically removes the need to perfect the collateral. Title transfer arrangements do, however, have a number of drawbacks:

- They may not be enforceable in jurisdictions that do not permit or recognise netting or insolvency set-off.
- They may be recharacterised as a form of security interest in certain jurisdictions, negating the advantages that would otherwise apply. Given the parties' initial intention to use a title transfer method, they may therefore have failed to take critical perfection steps, which then limit the effectiveness as a 'security interest'-based credit risk mitigation technique.

Legal Risks Introduced by Collateralisation

The process of collateralisation introduces a number of legal risks relating to the holding, seizure, pricing and liquidation of collateral assets. We have already detailed the recharacterisation legal risk that is inherent in transfer title collateralisation arrangements. More broadly, there is the legal risk regarding the enforceability of the collateral arrangement, particularly in the event of the insolvency of the collateral giver (although the insolvency of the collateral taker and any third party holding the collateral may also be of concern) and regarding the ability to offset the collateral against the underlying exposures between the parties under the master trading agreement. In order to obtain the regulatory capital relief from reducing the credit exposure due to any collateral, prudential regulation typically insists on the obtaining of a legal opinion to validate that the legal risks are not sufficiently significant to challenge the effectiveness of the collateral (see Chapter 6).

Operational Risks of Collateral

There is significant operational risk from the use of collateral as a credit-mitigant tool. The legal arrangements typically need to contain a number of very detailed operational steps, such as the forms of collateral agreed between the parties (and any conditions attached to their use), how exposures and collateral will be valued, the timing and transfer details. These collateral legal agreement terms have often not been robustly captured within financial firms, resulting in a mismatch between the legal terms and the manner in which the collateral is actually managed. Operational risk arises when the exposed party either fails to call for collateral on a timely basis, calls for an incorrect amount, calls for an ineligible type of collateral or misses a collateral call completely. It can also be caused in respect of the custody of the collateral, such as settlement fails. Such operational risks can easily result in actual losses if a party were to default.

One of the major operational risks concerns data. The collateral management process requires high data quality in terms of the trades that are collateralised, collateral held, client information (in order to be able to move collateral as required) – as well as other key terms of the legal collateral arrangement. Collateral management places incredibly high data demands upon a financial firm, because the transaction details and mark-to-market valuations are often required on a daily basis, with payments and/or deliveries of collateral needed to or from external counterparties dependent on this. Other users of this data, such as risk, treasury, credit and regulatory reporting, are generally not using the information on such an ongoing basis. Any erroneous omission of transactions (including sometimes just delays to bookings) or capture of transaction details will likely be immediately visible to clients, resulting in an incorrect margin call. In fact, historically, disputes regarding collateral, especially in respect of collateral valuations, have caused many disputes and delays.

It has been the legal agreement data in particular though that has been quite poorly managed by firms. Historically, legal teams at major financial institutions failed to adequately store and record the terms of the collateral arrangements, in many cases viewing this as outside the remit of the legal function. Accordingly, collateral management teams were forced to create databases of the key terms of these arrangements, in order to be able to operationally manage the collateral processes day-to-day. As will be seen, the collateral arrangements are quite complex in nature, and the focus on the terms from a purely operational perspective has resulted in many data quality and governance issues. This is particularly the case given that, over time, the need for collateral arrangement data has extended well beyond the collateral management function, to those such as risk, finance and treasury; crucially, it is viewed as an increasingly front-office task, given the funding and collateral optimisation implications. Regulation post-crisis has also created a need for this same data, ranging from recovery and resolution plans (which need to take collateral provided into account) (see Chapter 10) to client assets and money protection (see Chapter 8). As will have been noted from Chapter 4 (data governance), one of the key aspects of successfully managing data is to understand the context for the data and its intended usage. Financial firms have therefore been hit with a plethora of data quality issues when trying to use legal agreement data, for purposes outside of those originally intended.

Considerations for Selecting Appropriate Collateral

The importance of selecting appropriate collateral to provide and/or receive cannot be understated. This has increasingly moved from not only a back-office function responsibility, to one used by the business as an opportunity to optimise and therefore seen as part of a broader trading strategy. Selecting appropriate collateral potentially gives a firm better protection against counterparty risks and may reduce regulatory capital costs. Poorly selected collateral gives rise to unacceptable levels of pricing, liquidity and operational risk, as well as legal uncertainty. Pre-Financial Crisis, the range of eligible collateral provided was significantly expanding, although subsequent to the Financial

Crisis there are increasing numbers of restrictions on the eligible collateral that can be provided, due both to regulation adding conditions to the types of collateral permitted, as well as market realisation of the issues with sub-optimal collateral from the Financial Crisis, such as many of the collateralised debt obligations that rapidly lost value. A well-diversified collateral portfolio across counterparties is better protected against general market downturns and usually gives the party protected by collateral the confidence to agree to a wider range of collateral quality and smaller 'haircuts' to the assigned value of the collateral. Some degree of diversification of collateral is required through banking regulation itself (such as the margin for uncleared derivatives regulations).

Ideal Collateral Characteristics

It should be noted that the margin reform regulation has stipulated requirements, more recently, in respect of collateral assets that parties may exchange, given the regulatory view on the important role collateral plays in respect of market stability. In general, the following characteristics should be considered.

- **Liquidity.** It is important that collateral assets are liquid. This assists with the task of valuing the collateral adequately, market price transparency and ensuring that the exposure the collateral seeks to offset is adequate through rebalancing adjustments. Where less liquid collateral assets are agreed between the parties, it is usual to specify individual valuation mechanics, as well as possibly applying a 'haircut rate' to the valuation (to account for possible loss of value of the collateral, e.g. due to price volatility between margining dates and the cost of liquidating such assets) and specifying concentration limits for the usage of that type of collateral.
- **Low volatility.** It is crucial that, in the event of a default and close-out of a portfolio, one can apply and/or liquidate the collateral easily. There will inevitably be a time lag in the event of such a close-out, between the last collateral rebalancing and the close-out and the application of collateral. For the party utilising the collateral as a credit risk mitigant, it is important to try and avoid a reduction in value of the collateral since the last instance of valuation and rebalancing. Highly volatile collateral assets, if agreed between the parties, are also usually subject to haircut rates and concentration limits.
- **Short settlement period.** The delay between the point at which a collateral call is made and when it is actually delivered generates credit risk. During periods of market volatility, this credit risk is exacerbated. Accordingly, it is best to avoid more obscure collateral types that are subject to longer settlement periods.
- **Credit quality of collateral.** Collateral's purpose is to mitigate the credit risk of the counterparty providing the collateral, and therefore its effectiveness will be a function of the collateral credit quality itself – since its credit quality impacts the valuation of the collateral. To ensure collateral quality for securities, minimum acceptable credit ratings are often agreed between the parties. This is more straightforward in the case of securities. For equity collateral, parties often stipulate that the collateral must be listed on a major exchange, such as the FTSE 100 (this also assists with liquidity considerations).
- **Low correlation to exposure and the collateral provider.** In order to maximise the offset of the collateral to the exposure, one needs to ensure that the collateral used does not tend to decrease as the exposure increases, due to the correlation between

the collateral and the underlying portfolio. Additionally, any collateral whose value positively correlates with the collateral provider's credit (e.g. securities issued by the counterparty, or securities in which the collateral provider has a large position) is usually problematic.

Eligible Collateral and Collateral Optimisation

Market participants typically agree a range of collateral that is deemed acceptable to the parties (which may differ for each party), based mainly on the above criteria, as well as individual considerations such as the expected types of collateral that would be available to that party in the event of requiring to provide collateral on rebalancing.

The example in Figure 7.3 shows the optionality created in terms of collateral that a party may provide. There will of course be an ideal type of collateral from the collateral provider's[1] point of view. This might be viewed in the context of the 'cheapest to deliver'

Eligible Credit Support. On any date, the following items will qualify as 'Eligible Credit Support' *for* the party specified:				
	Valuation Percentage			
(A) Cash in an Eligible Currency	100%			
(B) Negotiable Debt Obligations issued by the Government of:	Residual Maturity			
	Less than 1 year	1 year or greater but less than 5 years	5 years or greater but less than 10 years	10 years or greater but not more than 30 years
France	99%	98%	96%	90%
Germany	99%	98%	96%	90%
Netherlands	99%	98%	96%	90%
(a) Negotiable Debt Obligations must (i) be denominated in the domestic currency of the issuing country, (ii) be issued on the relevant domestic market and (iii) exclude derivatives of such securities and inflation-linked securities.				
(b) Negotiable Debt Obligations must be rated by Moody's Investors Service, Inc. or its successor thereto ('Moody's') and/or Standard & Poor's, a Division of McGraw-Hill Companies, Inc., or any successor thereto ('S&P'), Aa3/ AA– or higher.				
(c) Where the ratings of the relevant agencies differ with respect to the same Negotiable Debt Obligation, the lower of the ratings shall apply.				
(d) If at any time the Negotiable Debt Obligations fail (or cease) to be rated by at least one of the above agencies then such Negotiable Debt Obligations shall not be considered Eligible Credit Support.				

Figure 7.3 An example from a 1995 ISDA Credit Support Annex (Transfer – English Law) of the language specifying the types of collateral parties are willing to accept from the other

---

1 The option is that of the collateral provider, not the collateral giver, at the point at which it needs to be provided, and hence is viewed from this perspective.

(i.e. the collateral asset that is least costly to provide as collateral), however, the better view is to consider the 'best to deliver', which factors in other considerations such as liquidity and availability. In particular, one now needs to think about liquidity coverage and net stable funding ratios (see Chapter 9).

Historically, the types of collateral allowed were viewed only through an operational and credit risk lens. In doing this, the specifications of eligible collateral in collateral arrangements created, as a by-product, an extremely complex financial option – which many firms even today struggle to adequately and correctly value. Addressing this was one of the drivers behind the 'Standard CSA' initiative by ISDA (covered later in this chapter). As market participants have woken up to the inherent value of this complex option, the collateral management process has shifted from being viewed as an operational function only to one that needs, at the very least, key front-office input into its management and optimisation. This in turn has put a lot of pressure on firms to understand the exact contractual terms of the collateral arrangements, in terms of the types of allowable collateral and any conditions placed on them (such as haircut rates, concentration limits and issuer credit ratings). The specific details of the collateral that may be provided by the parties (and also details of what is factually provided) also play a major part in the regulatory capital calculation. This is an area where legal agreement data has been found to fall short of front-office requirements at most financial firms.

The margin reform regulation has attempted to restrict the types of collateral that may be provided (as have other regulations, such as the liquidity coverage and net stable funding ratios) with an overall market trend, through both regulation and various internal dealer considerations, towards cash collateral and government securities, especially in the context of variation margin (see below).

Collateral Issues

OIS Discounting

Most OTC swap derivative transactions use LIBOR[2] as a reference rate for floating legs, and market participants use LIBOR-derived benchmark rates in order to value portfolios. Despite this, most collateral arrangements have referenced overnight index swap (OIS) rates, such as SONIA (Sterling Overnight Index Average), EONIA (Euro Overnight Index Average) and Fed Funds. The basis risk between a LIBOR and an OIS rate was traditionally viewed as insignificant, however, post-Financial Crisis, the two rates diverged such that this basis risk magnified. Swap transactions were being discounted at LIBOR, generating a mark-to-market value that was then being offset by collateral assets; however, these collateral assets would accrue interest only at the OIS rate, which was markedly lower than LIBOR, resulting in a net funding cost. This was within a backdrop of an increasing realisation that the choice of collateral from the range of assets chosen by parties as eligible collateral was a significant factor in the correct valuation of a derivatives portfolio. Accordingly, there has been a move in the industry away from discounting using LIBOR, to OIS rates, which are now viewed as a better proxy for the risk-free rate than LIBOR (Figure 7.4) (and accordingly, ideally used as the discount rate for both collateralised and non-collateralised portfolios).

---

2 Although a bedrock of the financial markets for over 30 years, IBOR (Inter-Bank Offered Rates) such as LIBOR has been under pressure ever since the Wheatley Review, and a speech by Andrew Bailey, Chief Executive of the UK's FCA on 27 July 2017, heralded its potential demise. Market participants are preparing for the likelihood that LIBOR and IBORs more generally will cease to exist over the next few years.

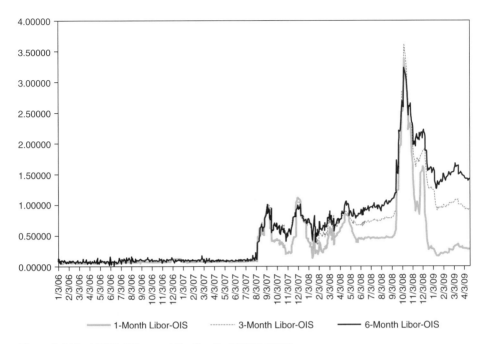

Figure 7.4 The LIBOR–OIS spread (1m/3m/6m) (2006–2009)

Accordingly, a swap collateralised with sterling cash would now typically be discounted using the SONIA rate, regardless of the underlying trade currency. Given the optionality of the collateral in many collateral arrangements, spanning a range of currencies and other asset types such as securities, this becomes hugely complex. Even once the correct discount curves have been determined for each of the eligible collateral types, one needs to work out which discount curve one should be using to calculate the net present value of trades under the collateral arrangement, typically based on the assumption that the counterparty will look to provide the cheapest-to-deliver collateral assets possible. However, this concept of cheapest-to-deliver collateral is not static and may vary in the future, meaning that one needs to compare different discount curves for each eligible collateral type, convert these into a single currency for comparison purposes and consider the cheapest collateral at each and every point in time (and this is without taking into account future changes to the market, or broader counterparty circumstances that might affect the decision-making on collateral to be delivered!). The effect is exacerbated due to the fact that many collateral arrangements also allow for a right of substitution (which may be conditional or require consent), whereby the collateral posting party can substitute the collateral assets provided for a different type of collateral.

Ultimately, the collateral arrangements to a trading master agreement have been found to not only contain operational details regarding credit risk management, but commercial- and price-sensitive terms. The sheer variance in the terms of collateral arrangements between market participants has further compounded the issues and also hindered, especially during repapering exercises in the early phases of margin reform to date, attempts to meaningfully standardise collateral arrangement terms (certainly not to the extent that would be required to create true computational and data-orientated contracts; see Chapter 11), at the time of writing. Many of these clause variants were actually never intended to be used in practice by market participants – arising in most cases as a by-product of collateral agreement negotiation dynamics where parties are often interested in providing future flexibility to deliver different types of collateral that may be operationally convenient or easy to source, counterbalanced by credit concerns about less-well-rated or liquid collateral assets. The result is a collateral arrangement that is a financial option that unintentionally too complex to value, except on a limited basis using significant computational resources.

The pricing complexity impact can sometimes mean that there is a lack of transparency for less sophisticated end-users of collateralised derivatives who are unable to compare and fully understand pricing by market dealers. There is also an impact on the novation of trades, stemming from valuation issues, as novation relies on agreement between the parties on pricing – with a counterparty having varying collateral arrangement terms with a dealer under the agreement governing the original trade, and with the transferee dealer, which will govern the novated trade.

The ISDA Standard Credit Support Annex

In 2009, ISDA board kicked off a 4-year period of research culminating in the publication of the 2013 ISDA Standard CSA – with the aim of dealing with the issues caused by the divergence of LIBOR and OIS rates; the cross-currency basis risk created from the trade exposure and collateral exposure being in different currencies; the valuation issues caused by the eligible collateral optionality and the desire to converge the manner in which trades are priced in the cleared and uncleared markets. The agreement was hoped, with such underlying aims, to drive standardisation and simplification of the collateral agreement terms.

A key feature of the published document was the removal of collateral optionality in most existing collateral arrangements, with variation margin limited to cash, although initial margin (essentially 'independent amount' in pre-margin reform collateral arrangements) could be both cash and non-cash assets, such as government bonds. Operationally, it required the grouping of transactions and the offsetting of collateral exposures into currencies or 'silos', with each currency silo being independently evaluated. This would then create the relevant collateral call as required as part of the rebalancing.

Unfortunately, the initiative fell foul of a number of regulatory, logistical and timing issues. There was a triple-whammy of regulation, across the leverage ratio (see Chapter 6), the margin for uncleared derivatives regulation and the broader Basel credit risk framework, which caused significant issues for the proposed document, where the currency of collateral does not match up to the currency of the underlying transaction exposure (e.g. attracting an 8% haircut on the collateral). A revised version of the Standard CSA was proposed in 2014, which created the concept of a 'transport currency' to address some of these issues, however, this created significant cross-currency settlement risk.

It can be extremely difficult to standardise documentation or turn it into being truly data driven without sacrifices from market participants in terms of the cost of embracing new business processes and operating systems to accommodate changes made to the documentation as part of this journey. As part of the Standard CSA project, it was intended that parties would seek to move new transactions to be governed by the Standard CSA, but that older legacy transactions would continue to be governed by the older collateral arrangements in place (as well as having the option to (a) elect certain new transactions to be governed by existing collateral arrangements and (b) move legacy transactions, where so agreed commercially between the parties, to be governed by the new Standard CSA form). As discussed previously, the ISDA documentation architecture is very flexible and modular, however, it has led to massive industry issues regarding the linkage of different parts of the documentation architecture. In many cases, this possibility for trades governed under the same ISDA Master Agreement but attached to different collateral arrangements caused too many technical issues for firms to grapple with. As a voluntary, non-mandatory regulatory initiative, there just wasn't sufficient broad industry appetite, especially considering the regulatory issues that emerged with the proposed document. As readers will note from the latter part of this chapter, the irony of course, is that the margin for uncleared derivatives regulation has indeed also forced firms to allow transactions to be governed by different collateral arrangements under the same ISDA Master Agreement.

Margin Requirements for Uncleared Derivatives

As part of the regulatory response to the Financial Crisis, the G20 initiated a significant regulatory reform programme in 2009 to reduce the systemic risk from the OTC derivatives market. This has been referred to as the 'G20 Pittsburgh Agreement'. It consists of four main elements, whereby OTC derivatives should be:

1) traded on exchanges or electronic platforms;
2) centrally cleared;
3) reported to trade repositories; and
4) where not centrally cleared, subject to higher capital charges.

Subsequent to this, in November 2011, the G20, as part of the 'Cannes Agreement', added margin requirements on non-centrally cleared derivatives to this reform programme and called upon the BCBS and IOSCO (International Organisation of Securities Commissions) to develop, for consultation, consistent global standards for these margin requirements. Based on the resulting BCBS/IOSCO framework's minimum standards, jurisdictional regulators – including the European Supervisory Authorities, Japan Financial Services Agency, US Commodity Futures Trading Commission, US Prudential Regulators, Swiss Financial Market Supervisory Authority, Monetary Authority of Singapore, Office of the Superintendent of Financial Institutions and Hong Kong Monetary Authority – have published uncleared margin rules for their respective jurisdictions.

At a high level, the proposed rules require entities to collect (and in some cases post) variation and initial margin – as well as adhere to a number of provisions and restrictions relating to collateral documentation, calculation, eligibility and rehypothecation. In relation to OTC derivatives, prior to this uncleared margin regulation, the specific distinction between types of collateral for difference purposes was relatively rare (although the concept of 'independent amounts' did exist in the ISDA collateral documentation, for example). Variation margin covers current exposure to a counterparty and is calculated using the mark-to-market value of the trades under a master agreement, whereas initial margin aims to cover the potential future exposure for the predicted time lag between the last variation margin exchange between the parties (i.e. rebalancing) and actual default of a party.

The main aims of the BCBS/IOSCO margin requirements framework were stated as:

1) reduction of systemic risk; and
2) promotion of central clearing.

Given the fact that only standardised derivatives are suitable for central clearing, there needed to be reform covering those OTC derivatives that continued to be traded bilaterally, given that they total hundreds of trillions of dollars in notional amounts and pose the same systemic risks that were viewed as being a major factor behind the Financial Crisis. This is partially due to the lack of minimum requirements and standardisation in respect of collateral terms to manage counterparty credit risks.

The framework created by BCBS/IOSCO (the most recent version, known as BCBS317, was published in March 2015) was meant to harmonise regulatory approaches, however, in practice, the jurisdictional regulations have not been entirely consistent with each other in key areas such as application timing and product scope, although subsequent phases of the regulation are gradually improving this position.

Overview of the Margin for Uncleared Derivatives Rules

The rules can be summarised through a number of different key dimensions, which are detailed at a very high level below. Note that the specifics vary per jurisdiction and/or regulator.

Phasing It was understood that the margin requirements on non-centrally cleared derivatives would represent a major change for most market participants and accordingly, the framework created a phased-in approach. The biggest change brought about by the rules is the initial margin requirements, which are not currently applied to a significant number of transactions across many market participants and need substantial operational enhancements (such as this initial margin being held with a third-party custodian) and amounts of collateral, for which liquidity planning is required (see Figure 7.5). The phased timing for initial margin therefore stretches from 2016 through to 2020, at which point the threshold, based on the aggregate average notional amount, drops to €8 billion.[3] The mandatory variation margin rules for major financial jurisdictions went live for the largest OTC trading financial groups in September 2016 and January 2017 (the EU rules were notably delayed beyond the expected September 2016 'framework' date), with a variation margin 'big bang' including a very broad range of counterparties happening in March 2017 in most major financial jurisdictions. The broad consistency across key regulators is intended to prevent market dislocations, unfair 'playing fields' and the possibility of regulatory arbitrage.

Collection/Posting of Margin The rules broadly require:

a) the collecting (and in some jurisdictions posting) of net variation margin (which is broadly similar to the situation commercially between market participants with collateralised OTC derivatives trading relationships); and

---

3 The currency of this amount does vary for different jurisdictions, but is broadly equivalent monetarily. It is also, at the time of writing, the subject of much lobbying to attempt to reduce.

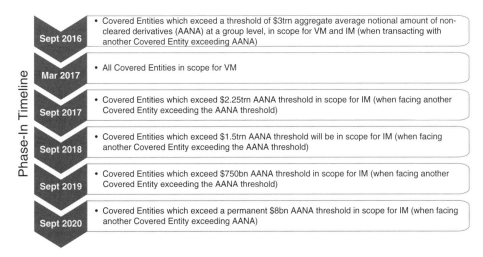

Sept 2016
- Covered Entities which exceed a threshold of $3trn aggregate average notional amount of non-cleared derivatives (AANA) at a group level, in scope for VM and IM (when transacting with another Covered Entity exceeding AANA)

Mar 2017
- All Covered Entities in scope for VM

Sept 2017
- Covered Entities which exceed $2.25trn AANA threshold in scope for IM (when facing another Covered Entity exceeding the AANA threshold)

Sept 2018
- Covered Entities which exceed $1.5trn AANA threshold will be in scope for IM (when facing another Covered Entity exceeding the AANA threshold)

Sept 2019
- Covered Entities which exceed $750bn AANA threshold in scope for IM (when facing another Covered Entity exceeding the AANA threshold)

Sept 2020
- Covered Entities which exceed a permanent $8bn AANA threshold in scope for IM (when facing another Covered Entity exceeding AANA)

Phase-In Timeline

Figure 7.5 Margin for uncleared derivatives compliance phase-in schedule. Note that this is the US regulatory timeline (the initial EU deadline was extended to February 2017)

b) the collecting (and in some jurisdictions posting) of gross initial margin. The change from a net to a gross margin amount represents a significant change to market participants in positive close-out netting jurisdictions.

Variation Margin Calculation The framework requires that the variation margin seeks to fully cover the mark-to-market of the net exposure to the counterparty (assuming it is governed by a legally enforceable netting arrangement). This involved a move to a zero threshold when calculating the variation margin (prior to the margin reform regulations, parties were free to negotiate threshold amounts based on credit risk considerations and respective negotiating power). There is the ability to apply a minimum transfer amount, however, this is set at €500,000[4] across the aggregate of initial and variation margin amounts.

Initial Margin Calculation Calculation of initial margin can be achieved either via the 'standard margin schedule' (which is regarded as punitive) or the 'model'. Fundamentally, the regulations require the initial margin amount to be calibrated to a period that includes financial stress, to ensure that sufficient margin will be available when it is most needed and to limit the extent to which the margin can be procyclical. With the latter, the period of financial stress used for calibration needs to be identified and applied separately for each broad asset class. Any such quantitative model must be approved by the relevant supervisory authority (although they can be internally developed, sourced from a counterparty or developed by a third-party vendor, but in each case, must be approved for use within each jurisdiction and by each institution seeking to use the model).

There is an initial margin threshold permitted under the BCBS/IOSCO margin requirements framework, which is a €50 million[5] threshold that operates at a group level (rather than a legal entity-specific level) and needs to be allocated across group members.

---

4 The currency of this amount does vary for different jurisdictions, but is broadly equivalent monetarily.
5 The currency of this amount does vary for different jurisdictions, but is broadly equivalent monetarily.

It should be noted that given the initial margin may not be rehypothecated (see below), the initial margin amount calculated has a significant funding cost and liquidity implication.

ISDA SIMM

Given that firms can use their own internal models to calculate initial margin as long as they meet the regulatory criteria and obtain the required regulatory approval(s), there was industry concern that these models have the potential to differ significantly, raising the possibility that counterparties will arrive at a different initial margin figure for the same trade and/or portfolio of trades. This in turn could result in a rise in the number of disputes, with no obvious way to quickly resolve them given the necessary complexity (and proprietary nature) of the underlying model methodology. Accordingly, ISDA created and launched the ISDA Standard Initial Margin Model (the 'ISDA SIMM') on 1 September 2016, and continues to update this through subsequent versions as required – with the aim of providing a standard methodology, and permitting transparent dispute resolution whilst allowing consistent regulatory governance and oversight of the initial margin model.

Eligible Collateral

A set of eligible collateral is specified, including cash and non-cash for initial and variation margin (with the exception of the US CFTC and, in certain circumstances, US PR, under which only cash is eligible for variation margin). Non-cash collateral tends to include government debt securities, certain other securities and corporate bonds and certain equities. There are some specific requirements regarding collateral wrong-way risk management and concentration limits.

Collateral Haircut Rates

Minimum haircut rates based on collateral types are specified. An additional FX haircut of 8% applies to initial margin collateral posted where the collateral currency differs from the other party's termination currency (the currency in which the close-out amount is paid on a close-out).

Segregation and Rehypothecation

Initial Margin
The initial margin is required to be segregated and held with a third-party custodian. Rehypothecation of the initial margin is not permitted and, in some cases, it must be reinvested in non-cash assets, once segregated, in order to meet segregation requirements. It should be noted that where there is no legal comfort that the initial margin posted can be effectively segregated from the counterparty's insolvency, certain rules may allow for an exception for the posting of initial margin to a counterparty based in a jurisdiction where such concerns arise.

Variation Margin
No specific segregation requirements or prohibition on rehypothecation.

Non-Netting Jurisdictions

Many jurisdictions have provided special treatment in their margin rules in respect of jurisdictions where close-out netting and/or collateral enforceability may be viewed as problematic (see Chapter 6 for a discussion of these concepts). For example, EU rules allow an EU-covered entity not to post margin to (and, in some cases, but subject to an overall cap of 2.5% of its OTC derivatives business, not to collect margin from) a counterparty in a non-netting jurisdiction (note that, under EU rules, there is a requirement to collect collateral on a gross basis if the derogation does not apply). Under US prudential regulations, the covered swap entity must treat the derivatives on a gross basis for collection of margin purposes but can net for posting purposes. Under some regulations, such as Japan, the exemption goes further, for example, providing that no compliance is required with the margin rules (both in terms of posting and collection of collateral) when facing a counterparty in a non-netting jurisdiction.

Collateral Documentation – OTC Derivatives

Initially restricting our consideration to ISDA-based forms of collateral credit support arrangements, prior to the margin reform regulation, there were five main documents (*Pre MR Collateral Documentation*) to consider:

1) 1994 ISDA Credit Support Annex under New York Law
2) 1995 ISDA Credit Support Annex (Transfer – English Law)
3) 1995 ISDA Credit Support Deed (Security Interest – English Law)
4) 1995 ISDA Credit Support Annex (Security Interest – Japanese Law)
5) 2008 ISDA Credit Support Annex (Loan/Japanese Pledge)

There were also some other documents pre-margin reform regulation that were used less frequently, such as the 2001 ISDA Margin Provisions and the ISDA Standard Credit Support Annex (the latter having been discussed briefly earlier in this chapter).

The Pre MR Collateral Documentation covers the following similar areas:

- How collateral calls are made (both for transfers and return of collateral).
- The mechanics and timing of transfers/returns.
- The method and timing of valuations made by the collateral valuation agent.
- Substitutions or exchanges of collateral.
- Resolution of disputes regarding valuation of collateral or exposure.
- Enforcement on default.
- Allocation of expenses relating to the collateral arrangement.
- Default interest.
- Rehypothecation or reuse of collateral.

The collateral documentation forms post-margin reform (*MR Collateral Documentation*), developed through an established ISDA working group, still covers these areas, but with some important distinctions driven by the regulation. These will be considered after a review of the Pre MR Collateral Documentation. Given that the Pre MR Collateral Documentation continues to exist in respect of transactions entered into prior to the regulatory compliance dates (which are phased in over a long period), the plethora of documentation terms applicable significantly increases the complexity of understanding the legal agreement data and ensuring its details are understood for business optimisation, regulatory reporting and operational management purposes.

The 1995 English Law Credit Support Annex operates by way of title transfer, whereas the 1994 New York Law Credit Support Annex creates a security interest over the collateral. The Japanese versions of the Pre MR Collateral Documentation allow the parties to elect, based on the particular collateral, whether a title transfer or security interest mechanism will be used (albeit referred to as 'loan' or 'pledge' options). Finally, the 1995 English Law Credit Support Deed uses a security interest mechanism. For the purposes of guiding through the key points of the Pre MR Collateral Documentation, we focus the next section on the 1995 ISDA Credit Support Annex (Transfer – English Law), noting that most of the changes with the other Pre MR Collateral Documentation are a natural consequence of either a security interest mechanism being used instead, or adaptation of the documentation for a different governing law. Barring these differences, there is a good degree of consistency on the structure of these documents and the manner of use of their terms (which is very helpful from a legal agreement data management perspective). ISDA, like in the case of the Master Agreement document, publishes a pre-print of the Pre MR Collateral Documentation, together with a pro-forma seeking to guide the parties into customisation of the pre-print terms in a semi-structured manner. As will be noted later in this chapter, there has unfortunately not been enough standardisation of wording. Therefore, the margin reform documentation, in seeking to address multiple jurisdictions, regulators and phase-in periods, has created a large number of 'standard' documents with inconsistent approaches in terms of wording and how matters are dealt with across the pre-print form and elections and variables section (something the industry is currently grappling with and attempting to resolve at the time of writing through ISDA's collateral infrastructure committee).

Brief Guide to the 1995 English Law Credit Support Annex (Transfer – English Law)

(Note that paragraphs of this pre-print form are referred to as 'paragraphs', with parties making their elections in the paragraph 11 pro-forma.)

The document is an annex to the ISDA Master Agreement, heavily reliant on the close-out netting provisions of the ISDA Master Agreement for its effectiveness as a credit-risk-mitigant tool. The value of collateral transferred (but not returned) to the party with exposure to the other is taken into account in the close-out calculation – effectively offset against trade exposures (see Figure 7.6). As a title transfer document, the party providing the collateral retains no proprietary interest in the collateral provided to the other party.

Preamble:
The preamble to the pre-print details that a number of the sections of the annex constitute a transaction (that is governed by the ISDA Master Agreement), for which the annex constitutes the trade confirmation. This sets up the annex to work as a counter-exposure trade to the other trades under the ISDA Master Agreement that are being collateralised.

☐ The Collateral Taker has a net contingent exposure to the Collateral Provider under the ISDA Master Agreement.
☐ If the Transactions under the ISDA Master Agreement were to be terminated, the Collateral Provider would owe a net amount equal to the Collateral Taker's exposure under Section 6(e) of the ISDA Master Agreement.
☐ To reduce/eliminate this exposure, the Collateral Provider transfers ownership rights in cash or securities (collateral) to the Collateral Taker.
☐ If the Transactions under the ISDA Master Agreement are terminated early, the net amount due by the Collateral Provider to the Collateral Taker under Section 6(e) is offset against the value of the collateral transferred under the Credit Support Annex which is included in the Section 6(e) calculation as an Unpaid Amount.

Figure 7.6 Title transfer mechanism under the 1995 English Law ISDA Credit Support Annex

Paragraph 1 – Interpretation:

This sets out the fact that the definitions are found in paragraph 10. It confirms that, in the event of inconsistency of terms, the provisions of the annex will prevail over those of the ISDA Schedule, and in the event of any inconsistency between the elections and variables provisions in paragraph 11 and the rest of the pre-print (paragraphs 1–10), that paragraph 11 of the annex shall prevail.

For the purposes of the following paragraph descriptions, these definitions are provided in paragraph 10 (but may be amended by the parties in paragraph 11):

Transferor – the party transferring collateral to the other party.

Transferee – the party receiving collateral from the other party.

Transferor's Credit Support Balance – the value assigned to the collateral transferred from the Transferor to the Transferee of collateral.

Threshold Amount – the specified amount of risk (in monetary terms) that a party is willing to tolerate without holding any collateral against it in respect of its counterparty (sometimes known as the 'permitted uncollateralised risk'). The specific amount is detailed by the parties in paragraph 11.

Independent Amount – this is an add-on to the amount of exposure a party has to the counterparty (against which collateral will be transferred). This is typically expressed to reflect the possible increase in exposure that may occur between the times/dates on which collateral is transferred due to market volatility (affecting the value of both transactions and of collateral held by the parties – i.e. rebalancing). The specific amount is detailed in paragraph 11 by the parties.

Valuation Date – the date on which exposure and the value of any collateral provided will be assessed to see if further collateral amounts need to be provided by the Transferor to the Transferee, or returned by the Transferee to the Transferor. This is therefore effectively the frequency at which collateralisation will occur (e.g. daily, weekly, monthly, etc.).

Credit Support Amount – this is the value of collateral that a party ought to receive, based on the following calculation:

$$
\begin{aligned}
\text{Credit Support Amount} = \text{Max}[0, & \text{ Exposure the Transferee has to the Transferor} \\
& + \text{Independent Amounts applicable to the Transferor} \\
& - \text{Independent Amounts applicable to the Transferee} \\
& - \text{Transferor's Threshold}]
\end{aligned}
$$

Eligible Collateral – the types of collateral that the parties agree the other may use as collateral to be provided to mitigate exposure.

Equivalent Credit Support – collateral that is of the same type, nominal value, description and amount as the collateral that forms part of the collateral held by a party. (This ensures that when collateral is returned, it matches the collateral characteristics of the collateral provided – e.g. in the case of money, the exact same notes do not however need to be returned(!), although it would need to be of the same currency.)

Paragraph 2 – Credit Support Obligations:
This is the main operative part of the annex. It firstly provides that shortly after or on a Valuation Date, a party owed collateral (a Transferee) may demand collateral equal to the 'Delivery Amount', which is the amount by which the Credit Support Amount exceeds the Transferor's Credit Support Balance, as adjusted for rounding (agreed and specified in paragraph 11) (see Figure 7.7).

It then deals with return of collateral when the exposure faced by a party holding collateral from the counterparty reduces, triggering a return of collateral. It provides that

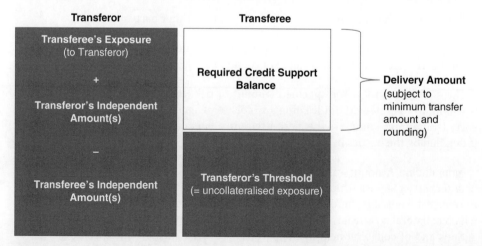

Figure 7.7 A Delivery Amount is due from the Transferor if the Transferee has Credit Exposure to the Transferor

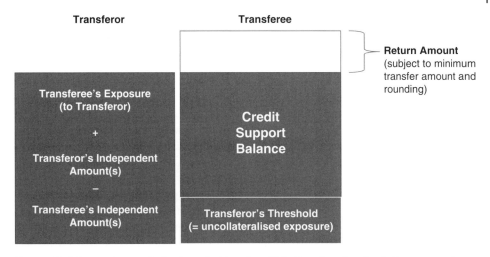

Figure 7.8 A Return Amount is due from the Transferee if the Transferor has Credit Exposure to the Transferee

shortly after or on a Valuation Date, a party owed a return of collateral (a Transferor) may demand collateral equal to the 'Return Amount', which is the amount by which the Transferor's Credit Support Balance exceeds the Credit Support Amount, as adjusted for rounding (agreed and specified in paragraph 11) (see Figure 7.8).

Paragraph 3 – Transfers, Calculations and Exchanges:

Sets out logistical details around how transfers of collateral that are in cash or securities are made. If parties wish to transfer other more exotic types of collateral (e.g. emissions allowances), the parties would need to specify the logistics of this (such as how transfers will be made) in paragraph 11.

The paragraph also details that the demands for a Delivery and/or Return Amount must be made before the 'Notification Time' (which is agreed between the parties in paragraph 11), otherwise the date on which the collateral is delivered will be delayed (to the following 'Settlement Date').

Finally, paragraph 2 provides a mechanism by which the Transferor can exchange collateral provided to the Transferee for a different type of collateral. Under the English Law Credit Support Annex, this requires the Transferee to consent/agree to such an exchange (although the parties may amend this position in paragraph 11, and should be cognisant of agreeing anything that may cause a recharacterisation risk of the title transfer nature of the arrangement to be more akin to a security interest). The operational mechanics of this clause is that the Transferee receives the substitution collateral before it is required to return the collateral to be returned.

It should be noted that the New York Law Credit Support Annex permits the parties to elect a consent requirement for substitution of collateral, however, as a standard position, the Transferor (called the 'Pledgor' in the New York Law Credit Support Annex) may require a substitution. In contrast, the English Law Credit Support Deed is built to require this consent, in order to minimise the risk that the deed might be constituted as a floating charge as a matter of English law – which has a lower ranking on insolvency than a fixed charge security interest).

Paragraph 4 – Dispute Resolution:

This paragraph provides a framework by which disputes regarding the collateral valuation agent's determination of exposure, or the valuation of collateral, can be disputed by a party to the collateral arrangement. The starting point is that the parties are required to transfer any undisputed amount of collateral and the parties will consult to resolve the dispute in relation to the remaining 'disputed' collateral.

If the dispute relates to the determination of exposure, paragraph 4 provides that the valuation agent will use market quotations in order to help with the determination of this. If relating to collateral valuation, the method of alternative determination is as agreed and set out by the parties in paragraph 11.

The Focus of Regulators

Collateral dispute resolution has been the focus of regulation, and requests by regulators, in order to improve some perceived areas of difficulty. ISDA published the 2009 Collateral Dispute Resolution Procedure in response to a request made by the Federal Reserve, Bank of New York and other financial regulators to assist in the operation of collateral disputes during periods of market volatility (which are typically accompanied by unavailability of objective prices and decreased tolerance for pricing discrepancies) when the incidence of collateral disputes increases significantly. The portfolio reconciliation and dispute resolution provisions of EMIR also deal with this area, requiring counterparties which execute uncleared OTC derivative transactions to (a) agree, prior to trading, written procedures which are 'robust, resilient and auditable' in order to reconcile key transaction terms; and (b) agree 'formalised' and 'detailed' procedures to identify, record and monitor disputes relating to the recognition or valuation of a contract and the exchange of collateral, referring to resolution mechanisms such as third-party arbitration and market polling. ISDA published the ISDA 2013 EMIR Portfolio Reconciliation, Dispute Resolution and Disclosure Protocol in order to assist market participants in compliance with these regulations.

Paragraph 5 – Transfer of Title, No Security Interest, Distributions and Interest Amount:

This paragraph sets out the fact that the Transferor will be passing title to the collateral to the Transferee upon a transfer and that the annex does not intend to create any security interest over any collateral transferred. Paragraph 5(c) provides that the Transferee shall pass to the Transferor any distribution of assets (or other rights) it receives on securities collateral it has received from the Transferor, as well as any interest on cash collateral (at the rate specified and agreed by the parties in paragraph 11).

Paragraph 6 – Default:

This is a key operative provision of the annex providing that, upon the designation or occurrence of an Early Termination Date arising from an Event of Default under the ISDA Master Agreement, the collateral transferred will be taken into account as part of the close-out. It is dealt with as an 'Unpaid Amount' under section 6(e) of the ISDA Master Agreement.

There are two common amendments that parties agree to in paragraph 11 in relation to this paragraph. The first is to disapply the effect of any haircuts on the manner in which collateral is valued upon default, as parties will typically want the full market value to be recognised in such a scenario. The second amendment is to extend the application of paragraph 6 to Termination Events (rather than just being limited to Events of Default) in relation to all transactions under the Master Agreement. This is not strictly necessary, as upon a close-out of all outstanding transactions, the exposure of each party would fall to zero under those transactions, resulting in a return of collateral under paragraph 2 as a Return Amount.

Paragraph 7 – Representation:

Under paragraph 7, the parties represent to each other that it is the sole owner of, or otherwise has the right to transfer, collateral provided under the annex, free of any security interests, liens, encumbrance or any other restrictions (other than a lien routinely imposed on securities in a clearing system).

Paragraph 8 – Expenses:

This paragraph sets out the fact that each party will pay its own costs and expenses in connection with performance under the annex and that neither party will be liable for any costs or expenses incurred by the other party.

Paragraph 9 – Miscellaneous:

This sets out a number of standard boilerplate provisions, such as in relation to default interest and acting in good faith and a commercially reasonable manner. It should be noted that given the annex forms part of the ISDA Master Agreement (as an annex to it), it is not necessary to include a governing law and jurisdiction clause.

Paragraph 10 – Definitions:

Sets out the key definitions used within the annex as detailed above.

Paragraph 11 – Elections and Variables:

The paragraph in which parties make their elections to tailor the arrangement as required commercially and operationally by the parties. The main items to be completed are as follows:

Paragraph 11(a):

Base Currency – the currency into which amounts are converted for comparison purposes and various calculations under the annex. Note that the pro-forma paragraph 11 includes US dollars here.

Eligible Currency – the currencies intended to be allowable as collateral (subject to using the formulation, or a similar formulation of the Eligible Credit Support language as per the pro-forma paragraph 11).

Paragraph 11(b):

Eligible Credit Support – the items of collateral that are acceptable to each party and the associated valuation percentages (effectively setting any haircuts).

Threshold Amounts (see above for details).

Independent Amounts (see above for details).

Minimum Transfer Amounts and Rounding levels.

Paragraph 11(c):

Valuation Agent – the party appointed by the parties to act as the valuation agent (which may be one of the parties to the agreement).

Valuation Date – when the determination of exposure and valuation of collateral balances will occur, effectively the collateralisation rebalancing frequency.

Valuation Time – the specific time at which valuations will be made.

Notification Time – the cutoff time for demands for collateral to be made (after this time, the demand is deemed to occur on the following day).

Paragraph 11(f):

Interest Rate – the interest rate applicable to each Eligible Currency.

Paragraph 11(h):

Other Provisions – other provisions required but not set out in the pro-forma that the parties may wish to add.

MR Collateral Documentation

The margin reform regulations for uncleared derivatives implemented by regulators across the globe caused the industry to have a major rethink in relation to the ISDA collateral documentation architecture. If market participants wanted to preserve pre-existing terms for pre-existing and out-of-scope transactions, they needed to document new variation margin terms and new initial margin terms (and also create new custodial relationships in order to support the segregation of the initial margin). The fastest way of dealing with this from a drafting point of view was to create a new variation margin (VM) credit support arrangement, a new initial margin (IM) credit support arrangement, as well as custodial arrangement documentation (one for each direction in which the IM would be provided).

As can be seen from Figure 7.9, this significantly complicates the collateral agreement documentation architecture.

One of the biggest obstacles for firms centres around the fact that internal collateral, risk, trading and legal agreement systems were built in a manner that only supported a single collateral arrangement to be linked to a particular master agreement (although, in practice, this idea of multiple collateral document annexes was a valid, but rare, commercial arrangement if parties wished for different collateral terms to apply to the various transactions under an ISDA Master Agreement relationship). Accordingly, not all firms had systems capable of easily supporting this.

It would of course be possible – other than for custodial documentation which includes additional parties (the custodian) – to simply amend the existing pre-margin reform collateral agreement to be regulatory compliant (and agree for these terms to apply to legacy transactions), or to include a bifurcated approach to legacy and future regulatory governed transactions within the existing document. This, however, also caused some firms significant systems issues and breaks in existing data flows.

ISDA Collateral Documentation Architecture Comparison

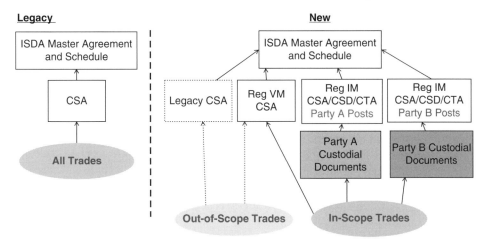

Figure 7.9 A comparison of the ISDA collateral documentation architecture before and after the margin for uncleared derivatives regulation

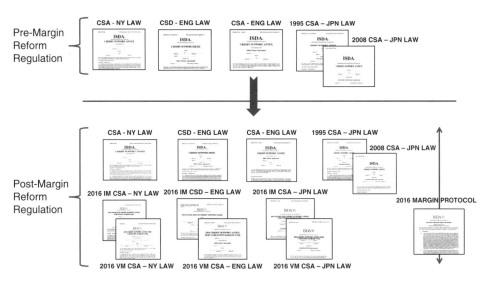

Figure 7.10 The explosion of ISDA pre-print forms post-margin reform regulation

For the purposes of simplicity, in this section we detail the approach where separate VM and IM documents have been used for future transactions in the scope of the regulation. However, we note the issues that the possible alternative approaches used by market participants cause from the perspective of documentation standardisation as an industry, which in turn create many potential pitfalls from the perspective of capital, collateral and liquidity management (especially given how crucial the terms of the collateral arrangements are). That said, the sheer proliferation of pre-print forms caused by the update of documentation for margin reform purposes has not helped either, as shown in Figure 7.10 (even ignoring the additional complexity provided by the new Phase 4 and 5 documents and custodial arrangements).

2016 ISDA Credit Support Annex for Variation Margin (VM) – English Law

We now go through the pre-print sections of the 2016 ISDA Credit Support Annex for Variation Margin, highlighting the differences with the 1995 ISDA English Law Credit Support Annex. When being created by the industry ISDA working group, it was agreed to focus on two key items:

1) The minimum changes mandated by the regulation, in order to ensure that the document was compliant with the margin reform regulation requirements (looking at the whole regulatory landscape, rather than just those in relation to the EU), were to be made from the then existing documentation.
2) Updates to the interest rate provisions given a recent issue creating uncertainty when the interest rate applicable to cash collateral is negative.

It was agreed to leave other 'nice-to-have' changes to the documentation, given the aggressive regulatory timelines, in order to agree and execute the collateral agreements in respect of variation margin in time. Below we detail the major and notable changes to the 1995 ISDA English Law CSA, but the list is by no means exhaustive.

Date and Preamble:
The preamble to the pre-print has remained the same, however, in terms of the dating of the document, the pre-print now has an area for the 'dated as of date' of the VM CSA to be inserted (rather than just referring to the 'dated as of' date of the ISDA Master Agreement to which it attaches). The rationale for this is to assist with identification, given that it is now likely that there will be more than one collateral arrangement related to a particular ISDA Master Agreement.

Paragraph 1 – Interpretation:
The main change is to insert a new paragraph 1(b), which details the scope of the VM CSA in relation to other collateral agreements related to the ISDA Master Agreement. It is expected that in most cases, the parties will already have a credit support annex to the ISDA Master Agreement, which was historically scoped to collateralise in respect of all transactions under the ISDA Master Agreement and the exposures related to them.

Paragraph 1(b) introduces a new term, 'Covered Transactions' – essentially new trades which need to be collateralised under this VM CSA in order to be regulatory compliant. There is also a consequential amendment to remove these Covered Transactions from the scope of those pre-existing collateral arrangements. Of course, the parties could amend the definition of Covered Transactions in the paragraph 11 (Elections and Variables) section if required.

The 'Covered Transactions' definition is primarily used to determine 'Exposure' under the VM CSA, thereby allowing parties to account for differences in regulations (e.g. 'swaps' vs 'non-cleared derivatives' vs 'OTC derivatives'). It is intended to capture transactions entered into on or after the date specified in paragraph 11 (e.g. the relevant compliance date). It should be noted that the pro-forma of paragraph 11 envisages and provides wording in relation to a number of options and elections:

- Defining 'Covered Transactions' by reference to the relevant regimes (with the definitions provided for inclusion in the pro-forma).
- The treatment of all transactions under the ISDA Master Agreement as Covered Transactions.
- Including existing transactions that are subject to amendment, novation or other life-cycle events which would require the collection or delivery of variation margin under laws applicable to either party.

Paragraph 1(b) provides that Covered Transactions are excluded from determinations of Exposure under any 'Other CSA' under the same ISDA Master Agreement (e.g. a legacy CSA).

Paragraph 2 – Credit Support Obligations:

Two new defined terms are created, 'Delivery Amount (VM)' and 'Return Amount (VM)'. These are identical to Delivery Amount and Return Amount respectively from the 1995 English Law CSA, except that there is now: (a) no concept of a Threshold Amount (as the margin reform regulation requires a zero threshold to be applied); and (b) no concept of Independent Amounts (the idea being that these would, to the extent required by regulation, be dealt with in the IM CSAs as initial margin). Accordingly, the 'Credit Support Amount' and 'Independent Amount' definitions are no longer required, and the paragraph simply directly refers to the 'Exposure' under the Covered Transactions. Note that ISDA subsequently published the 'Independent Amount (IA) Provisions', which set out amendments to paragraph 11 to allow the introduction of 'Independent Amount' to VM CSAs.

Paragraph 3 – Transfers, Calculations and Exchanges:

A new definition of 'Regular Settlement Date' is created, allowing transfer and settlement of collateral to be made on the same day that the demand is made (i.e. same-day settlement). This is a requirement of certain margin reform regulations. This can create issues where parties are located across different international time zones, making this logistically difficult to achieve.

Paragraph 4 – Dispute Resolution:

The Dispute Resolution provisions in paragraph 4 are largely the same as the 1995 English Law CSA as a substantive matter but contain conforming edits. The timing of the dispute resolution mechanism is adjusted to reflect the fact that transfer timing has been shortened in some cases, and the provisions also contain modifications to incorporate, where applicable, the 2002 Master Agreement (i.e. the difference between Loss/Market Quotation and Close-Out Amount). These changes are consistent with the changes made to the Credit Support Annex via the 2002 Master Agreement Protocol.

Paragraph 5 – Transfer of Title, No Security Interest, Distributions and Interest Amount:

It is only the interest on collateral provisions that are significantly amended in the VM CSA.

The first of these changes is to deal with the manner in which the parties may wish to handle negative interest rates. Negative interest rates create an area of uncertainty when they become a real prospect post-Financial Crisis, raising the question of whether interest payable on collateral, where negative, should be paid by the Transferor to the Transferee or whether the rate, for the purposes of calculation, should be floored at zero (thus the Transferor does not need to pay such amounts to the Transferee where the interest rate is negative). The 2016 VM CSA makes this change by providing a specific election in paragraph 11 as to whether negative interest rates apply or not. If they do, the change is effected through an addition to the definition of 'Interest Amount', which is floored at zero in paragraph 10 if the parties do not elect for negative interest rates to apply. Since the possible negative interest election means that interest payments may move both from the Transferee to the Transferor and from the Transferor to the Transferee, definitions are added to the annex in paragraph 10 of 'Interest Payer (VM)' and 'Interest Payee (VM)'.

The paragraph also facilitates the option for the parties to elect for collateral interest rate payments to be offset against Delivery Amount (VM) and/or Return Amount (VM) payments that are due to be made on the same day. This is subject to the conditions that the interest amounts must be less than the relevant Delivery Amount or Return Amount, and less than the cash portion of the Credit Support Balance (VM), such that the interest is only offset against cash collateral and not securities collateral.

Paragraph 6 – Default:

The main changes in this paragraph are consequently related to the acknowledgement that the ISDA Master Agreement related to the annex may be either a 1992 or 2002 pre-print form, each with different payment measures.

Paragraph 9 – Miscellaneous:

The VM CSA adds in new paragraphs 9(e)–9(h):

Paragraph 9(e) – Legally Ineligible Credit Support (VM) – this sub-paragraph introduces the concept of 'Legally Ineligible Credit Support (VM)'. This was drafted due to the fact that the different regulators each specify slightly different criteria (e.g. minimum credit ratings) and types of collateral that may be provided as variation margin (and the fact that this might change from time to time). Accordingly, this paragraph creates a mechanism for dealing with scenarios where variation margin collateral provided by one party to the other becomes ineligible after its transfer. The Transferee is required to notify the Transferor that this has happened, detailing the types of collateral impacted and the date the collateral becomes (or has become) ineffective. Once a 'Legal Ineligibility Notice' (containing information about the collateral and the relevant legal eligibility requirements) has been delivered to the Transferee, the affected collateral will be valued at zero (except in a close-out scenario) after a certain time period. It should be noted that two types of notice are envisaged; one addressing total ineligibility (i.e. the collateral no longer eligible) and the other transfer ineligibility (i.e. additional transfers of that collateral can no longer be made but existing collateral balance remains eligible).

Paragraph 9(f) – Return of Equivalent Credit Support (VM) – this sub-paragraph deals with the logistics of substitute collateral for the collateral that has become ineligible (and valued at zero) pursuant to paragraph 9(e), using the exchange of collateral mechanics from sub-paragraph 3(c) to deal with this exchange of ineligible collateral for other, eligible collateral.

Paragraph 9(g) – Reinstatement of Credit Support Eligibility – this sub-paragraph deals with collateral that has been deemed ineligible under sub-paragraph 9(e) becoming eligible again and allowing for a Legally Ineligible Credit Support notice to be withdrawn.

Paragraph 9(h) – Credit Support Offsets – this sub-paragraph introduces a new concept due to the fact that it is envisaged that parties will have multiple CSAs under the single ISDA Master Agreement. Accordingly, it is possible that collateral will move in one direction under a CSA on a particular date, but in a different direction for another CSA. This paragraph allows for, if elected to apply by the parties in paragraph 11, such transfers to be offset against each other. This can only apply if the collateral in question is fully fungible and does not need to be segregated. Like payment netting across different asset classes in the ISDA Master Agreement, this might be in theory desirable for market participants, but few have the operational systems to be able to support it.

Paragraph 10 – Definitions:
This sets out the key definitions used within the annex as detailed above.

Paragraph 11 – Elections and Variables:
This is again the paragraph in which parties make their elections to tailor the commercial arrangements. Most of the updates to paragraph 11 are a consequence of the changes already detailed above to paragraphs 1–10 of this VM CSA. It is, however, worth pointing out the addition of the 'FX Valuation Percentage'. The margin reform regulation introduces an 8% FX haircut in certain circumstances, which needs to be applied to collateral. Under the EU rules, this is in respect of non-cash collateral that is denominated in a currency other than that of eligible cash collateral currencies, whereas under the US rules it applies to collateral not in the currency of settlement, except for cash in US dollars or other major currencies. The pro-forma sub-paragraph 11(c)(v)(B) contains wording in relation to the definition of FX Haircut Percentage that caters for both of these and needs to be amended as required by the parties.

The ISDA 2016 Variation Margin Protocol (the VM Protocol)
With a single 'big-bang' deadline by which all market participants subject to the margin reform regulations had to put in place VM CSAs for transactions going forwards that would be caught by the regulations, much hope was placed by the industry in a protocol to assist with the mammoth drafting task that this presented, which would cover each of the variation margin pre-print forms published by ISDA in 2016 (i.e. English law, New York law and Japanese law), and cater for the different regulatory regimes in scope for the big-bang date. Specifically, the following regulatory regimes were catered for:

- The margin rules adopted by prudential regulators pursuant to § 4s(e)(2)(A) of the CEA and § 15F(e) of the US Securities Exchange Act of 1934, as amended ('PR Rules').
- The margin rules adopted by the CFTC pursuant to § 4s(e)(2)(B) of the CEA ('CFTC Rules').

- The margin rules adopted by the Financial Services Agency of Japan pursuant to Article 40, Item 2 of the Financial Instruments and Exchange Act (*kin'yuu shouhin torihiki hou*) (Act No. 25 of 1948, as amended) and its subordinated regulations ('Japan Rules').
- Guideline E-22, Margin Requirements for Non-Centrally Cleared Derivatives issued by the Canadian Office of the Superintendent of Financial Institutions (OSFI) in February 2016 ('OSFI Rules').
- The regulatory technical standards on risk-mitigation techniques for OTC derivative contracts not cleared by a central counterparty adopted by the European Commission on 4 October 2016 ('EMIR Rules').[6]
- Australian Prudential Standard CPS 226 Margining and Risk Mitigation for Non-centrally Cleared Derivatives published by APRA on 6 December 2016 ('Australia Rules').
- The margin rules adopted by the Swiss Federal Council pursuant to Articles 110 and 111 of the Financial Market Infrastructure Act as well as Articles 100 to 107 and Annexes 3 to 5 of the Financial Market Infrastructure Ordinance ('FMIA Rules').

Given the divergence in market participant views as to whether to use new CSAs or amend existing pre-margin reform CSAs, the VM Protocol offered four 'Methods' of documenting variation margin:

1) **Amend.** Existing CSAs are amended to be in line with the variation margin reform requirements in the relevant jurisdiction.
2) **Replicate-and-Amend.** Existing CSAs are cloned and then amended as required to be in line with the margin reform requirements in the relevant jurisdiction. The replicated and amended CSA sits under the original ISDA Master Agreement together with the 'original' CSA but is amended in accordance with variation margin reform requirements as implemented in the relevant jurisdiction.
3) **New CSA.** A new variation margin reform-compliant CSA is created that also sits under the original ISDA Master Agreement.
4) **New CSA under a deemed 2002 ISDA Master Agreement.** Creates a new CSA, as per method 3, but also creates a new deemed 2002 Master Agreement for new 'in-scope' trades. The 'original' Master Agreement and CSA apply to legacy transactions only and remain unaltered.

Questionnaires

The applicable 'Method' is determined by elections made within a standard bilateral questionnaire, which parties seeking to adhere to the VM Protocol complete and exchange. When completing these questionnaires, parties can select as many methods as they wish. A decision tree is then used to determine which 'Method' will apply in the event that multiple elections are made and the initial selections made by the parties do not match each other.

The filling out of the questionnaires captures the commercial elections by each of the parties (e.g. in relation to Base Currency, Minimum Transfer Amount, Independent Amount – which can be retained as a concept despite the IM CSA potentially covering this as 'initial margin' – and governing law). This is then used to determine the

---

6 It should be noted that the provisions for the EMIR rules were added to the text of the protocol subsequent to its original publication.

end commercial result between the parties by completing the blanks in relation to six 'exhibits' which supplement the questionnaires and set out the new contractual terms agreed by the parties depending on the method selected and the choice of governing law (New York, English or Japanese).

The issue became the complexity of the process, especially in terms of the choices made in the questionnaires, and what they actually meant by 'post-matching' when compared to a party's completed questionnaire. If the questionnaires cannot be matched (due to a disallowed combination of questionnaire selections across the two parties), the questionnaires need to be amended and re-exchanged until a match is achieved – adding further iterations to the negotiation process and adding to the overall amount of effort involved. The beauty of the initial ISDA protocols, such as the EMU and Close-out Protocol, were their sheer simplicity and ease of execution to effect mass amendments to large documentation portfolios. The VM Protocol was ultimately not used by most market participants. Even when used, it left a significant question as to the crucial end commercial terms that had been achieved through the process (and effectively did not relieve enough of the legal drafting burden). It also did not really address the question of the legal agreement data.

In many ways, it can, however, be seen as the starting point to a document negotiation platform (see Chapter 11), although the reference to the protocol more generally as a technology by some is somewhat concerning!

Initial Margin Documentation

As noted earlier in this chapter, the initial margin requirements are being phased in by the regulators over a 4-year period from 2016, through to 2020. Accordingly, at the time of writing, only the major dealers have in place with each other such initial margin collateral documentation arrangements. The forms developed for this are currently in the process of being discussed in various working groups and being standardised for broader applicability beyond the dealer group and for future IM phases (in particular, Phases 4 and 5).

One of the issues with the phased IM approach is identifying the counterparties one might have that are in scope by virtue of their level of trading activity. This may be done through the exchange of 'self-disclosure' letters, either via ISDA Amend or bilaterally, with ISDA running 'voluntary self-disclosure exercises' for its members ahead of an upcoming IM phase in order to help groups identify each other in a timely manner.

IM Documentation

Initial margin, where it is subject to margin regulation, is required to be held by a third party (i.e. not by the trading parties) and segregated from the proprietary assets on the books and records of that third-party holder or custodian or via other legally effective arrangements (Figure 7.11). It must also be available in a timely manner in the event of the collateral taker, collateral provider or custodian's insolvency. Accordingly, the documentation requirements, in particular for the collateral to be segregated and the mechanics around this IM collateral (Figure 7.12), are a lot more involved. In many ways, they should be considered as a quite distinct document from the original credit support

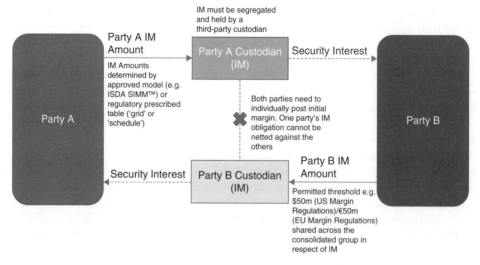

Figure 7.11 Two-way margining of initial margin

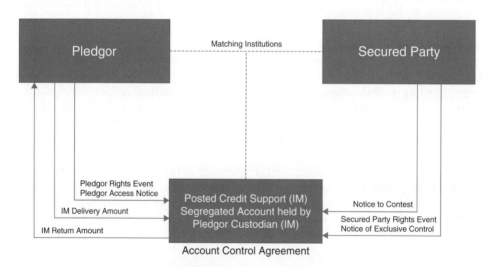

Figure 7.12 The mechanics of IM segregation

arrangements published by ISDA (such as the 1995 ISDA English Law CSA and the 2016 ISDA CSAs for Variation Margin), although the vast majority of changes are for regulatory compliance purposes.

Which regulatory IM Credit Support Documents are used, and in which combination, will depend on whether the parties are using a clearing system or bank custodian to segregate their initial margin. Parties to a relationship need to inform each other, at the outset of their discussions, of the identity of their chosen custodian/clearing system in order to establish which documents are needed for the arrangements. The following documentation was produced in respect of Phases 1, 2 and 3 of the IM regulatory requirements:

Where Euroclear or Clearstream are used to hold the collateral, the following documentation is required:

- Euroclear/Clearstream Collateral Transfer Agreement
- Euroclear/Clearstream Security Agreement
- Euroclear/Clearstream Membership Documents

In this case, the combination of the Collateral Transfer Agreement and the Security Agreement contains the provisions typically contained in an ISDA Credit Support Annex. The Collateral Transfer Agreements are each drafted as two-way margining documents, but may need to be used as one-way collateral arrangements where parties have chosen to use different custodians.[7] The various membership documents deal with a number of other items, including those that are sometimes dealt with, in respect of custody of collateral, by an account control agreement (see below).

Where a Bank Custodian is being used (e.g. JP Morgan), the following documentation is required:

- ISDA 2016 Phase 1 IM Credit Support Annex (governed by New York law) or the ISDA 2016 Phase 1 IM Credit Support Deed (governed by English law)
- An Account Control Agreement
- A Custody Agreement

The Account Control Agreement is a three-way standardised agreement between the parties to the ISDA Master Agreement and entity that acts as custodian of the initial margin collateral. It details how the custodian must treat initial margin collateral posted, generally requiring that the custodian only takes action with respect to the collateral at the request of the parties, as specified in the account control agreement. As certain parties could be required to each collect initial margin collateral from one another, a separate account control agreement (or other custodial agreement) would be required for each direction in which initial margin will be posted. The agreements typically use notices of exclusive control which are used by the non-defaulting party where there is a counterparty default under the ISDA Master Agreement to which the Account Control Agreement relates (essentially, at that point, providing that the segregated collateral is then released to the relevant party).

ISDA published a form of account control agreement in 2013, attempting to standardise provisions in a notoriously difficult area in which to align the interests of the relevant parties (namely, the collateral provider, collateral taker and custodian). The form is amended by the parties through various elections to be made in the annex to the agreement. Unfortunately, there has been little uptake of this agreement form, and none at all in the context of IM arrangements at the time of writing. The custodians each have their own form of account control agreements and regulation-compliant versions have been developed from these.

---

7 Even where both parties use Euroclear or Clearstream, there will still need to be two Security Agreements as they are one-way documents.

The increased complexity of the documentation structure (Figure 7.13) (and multiple forms of agreements that might be used, each similar but slightly different) can no doubt be immediately seen from the above. This can create a number of legal agreement data issues if the nuanced differences between the different documents are not understood, or if the relevant legal agreement data is simply shoehorned into a generic data model without enough thought.

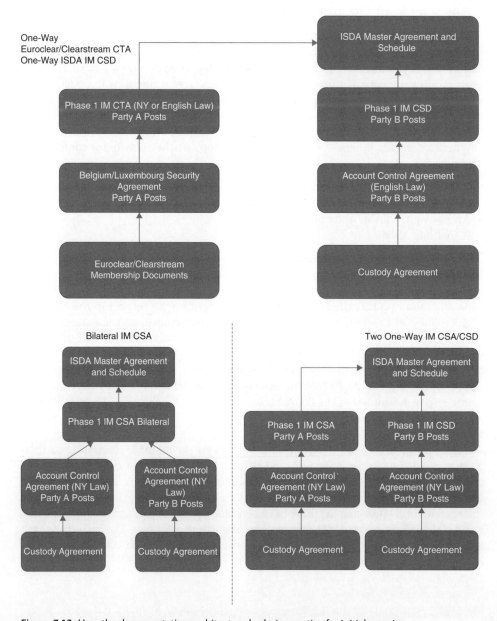

Figure 7.13 How the documentation architecture looks in practice for initial margin

The above does not illustrate the various custodian onboarding documents that may be required, such as, by way of example, in the case of Clearstream:

- KYC documents;
- RG811/RG812 (signs a party up to Euroclear Collateral Service Agreement, the Single Pledgor Pledged Account Terms and Conditions (SSPA), SSPA Amendment Agreement);
- RG147 (account opening);
- Collateral Profile;
- Confirmation of all pledging counterparties via Excel; and
- MT599 (account activation).

These may contain important provisions that the parties need to be aware of, even though they may not be negotiable (e.g. liens, voting rights, etc.), and need to be considered from the context of legal agreement data.

2016 Phase One Credit Support Annex for Initial Margin (IM) – New York Law

We now go through the pre-print sections of the 2016 ISDA Phase One Credit Support Annex for Initial Margin (IM), highlighting the differences with the 2016 ISDA Credit Support Annex for Variation Margin (VM) (English Law), ignoring the specific differences relating to the fact that this is a security interest rather than a title transfer document. We again note that this document is currently being updated for suitability for Phases 4 and 5 of the margin reform regulation, and accordingly is likely to be changed in order to allow it to be suitable for much broader use than the Phase 1 dealers.

Date and Preamble:
The preamble to the pre-print is similar, again acknowledging through the 'dated as of dates' of both the ISDA Master Agreement to which it relates and the IM CSA itself; and that there will be more than one collateral arrangement relating to a particular ISDA Master Agreement.

Paragraph 1 – Interpretation:
It is paragraph 1(c) rather than 1(b) that details the scope of the IM CSA in relation to other collateral agreements related to the ISDA Master Agreement. It is expected that in most cases, the parties will already have a 2016 ISDA Phase One to the ISDA Master Agreement, which was historically scoped to collateralise in respect of all transactions under the ISDA Master Agreement and related exposures. Paragraph 1(c) introduces a new term – 'Covered Transactions (IM)' – essentially new trades which need to be collateralised with initial margin under this IM CSA, in order to be regulatory compliant. There is also a consequential amendment to remove these Covered Transactions (IM) from the scope of independent amount calculations under those pre-existing collateral arrangements. Of course, the parties can amend the definition of Covered Transactions (IM) in the paragraph 13 (Elections and Variables) section.

Paragraph 1(d) clarifies that the annex is intended to be used in conjunction with segregated accounts maintained by third parties for the custody of initial margin posted under the annex.

Paragraph 2 – Security Interest:

The operative paragraph in relation to the security interest, whereby each party pledges to the other party initial margin under the annex.

Paragraph 3 – Credit Support Obligations:

Two newly defined terms are created: 'Delivery Amount (IM)' and 'Return Amount (IM)'.

The Delivery Amount (IM) is equal to the amount by which the Credit Support Amount (IM) exceeds the value of the Posted Credit Support (IM), taking into account the transferring party's Minimum Transfer Amount (IM). For this purpose, the Credit Support Amount (IM) is the Margin Amount (IM) less the applicable Threshold, and is floored at zero.

The Return Amount (IM) is equal to the amount by which the value of the Posted Credit Support (IM) exceeds the Credit Support Amount (IM), taking into account the recipient party's Minimum Transfer Amount (IM). For this purpose, the Credit Support Amount (IM) is the Margin Amount (IM) less the applicable Threshold, and is floored at zero.

The key definition of 'Margin Amount (IM)' is left for the parties to define in paragraph 13.

Paragraph 4 – Conditions Precedent, Transfer Timing, Calculations and Substitutions:

This paragraph is quite similar, other than some consequential changes due to other defined term changes, to the versions in the pre-margin reform security interest credit support arrangement pre-prints published by ISDA.

Paragraph 4(a) – Conditions Precedent – details that transfers (and returns) of initial margin are subject to the condition precedent that no Event of Default, Potential Event of Default or Specified Condition has occurred with respect to the other party (to the one making the transfer or return of transfer) and that no Early Termination Date has been designated or occurred for which any unsatisfied payment obligations exist (i.e. a close-out amount) in relation to all Covered Transactions (IM) or as a result of a Specified Condition. A 'Specified Condition' is an event elected by the parties as such in paragraph 13 (typically a termination event such as Illegality or an Additional Termination Event).

Paragraph 4(b) – Transfer Timing – like under the VM CSA, uses a new definition of 'Regular Settlement Date' that is created, allowing transfer and settlement of initial to be made on the same day that the demand is made (i.e. same-day settlement). This is again a requirement of the margin reform regulation.

Paragraph 4(c) – Calculations – details that the Calculation Agent (IM) may use relevant information or data – including but not limited to inputs for any applicable model specified in paragraph 13 to determine the Margin Amount (IM) – most recently available for close of business in the relevant market.

Paragraph 4(d) – Substitutions – comparable to the Exchanges mechanism in the 1994 English Law CSA, except that like the 1994 New York Law CSA, under the New York Law IM CSA, substitution does not need the consent of the secured party, unless added in by the parties in paragraph 13 specifically.

Paragraph 5 – Dispute Resolution:

Unlike the pre-margin reform CSAs and the VM CSA, any disputes of the amounts will not imply a case of resolving the exposures under transactions being collateralised, but are specifically related to initial margin amount calculation or the value of the initial margin provided. Accordingly, this paragraph removes the market quotation step and replaces it with the Calculation Agent (IM), having to recalculate the Credit Support Amount (IM) and value of Posted Credit Support (IM), as required.

Paragraph 6 – Custody Arrangements and the Control Agreement:

This is a substantially new provision. Initially, in paragraph 6(a), it sets the position that the party providing the IM collateral is liable for the acts or omissions of the custodian of that initial margin that has been provided to it (subject to any alteration of this position by the parties in paragraph 13), and that the secured party is not liable for such acts or omissions.

Paragraph 6(b) – Use of Posted Collateral (IM) – restricts the rights of the secured party to use or rehypothecate IM collateral held in the segregated account, in line with the regulatory restriction in this regard.

Paragraph 6(c) – No Offset – restricts the offsetting election detailed in the VM CSA to applying to the IM CSA (this would be contrary to the segregation and regulatory prohibition on netting initial margin amounts between the parties).

Paragraph 6(d) – Distributions and Interest Amount – details that the secured party, unlike the pre-margin reform CSAs and the VM CSA, is not obliged to transfer interest or distribution amounts to the pledgor.

The following paragraphs, although amended in some ways, do not substantially alter the pre-margin reform security interest credit support documents:

Paragraph 7 – Events of Default
Paragraph 8– Certain Rights and Remedies
Paragraph 9 – Representations
Paragraph 10 – Expenses
Paragraph 11 – Miscellaneous

Paragraph 12 – Definitions:

This adds in a number of new definitions required for this annex, as detailed above.

Paragraph 13 – Elections and Variables:

Unlike other ISDA pre-print documents, the elections and variables section in paragraph 13 of the Phase 1 IM CSA contains a fairly lengthy 'General Principles' section. Although this contains some elections, this is mostly accepted text by the Phase 1 (dealer) group.

Regime Table – this is a table setting out the regimes (EMIR, Prudential, CFTC, SEC, Canada, Switzerland and Japan) that the documentation seeks to assist with compliance, based on the affected dealers. The scope of entities under a particular regime varies, as does the OTC transactions for margin reform regulations. Accordingly, within this table, each party to the IM CSA sets out which regimes are applicable to it as secured party and which regimes are applicable to it as pledgor. This then provides the basis of applying the strictest requirements of the applicable regime to the CSA based on the parties' view of applicable regimes. This is in respect of the amount of initial margin, as well as the valuation of initial margin provided.

Under Phase 1, dealers sought to use the ISDA SIMM as the methodology to calculate the initial margin amounts for all regimes and asset types, although it was acknowledged, through the Exhibit to paragraph 13, that for a particular (additional) regime, and possibly for particular asset classes, some parties might choose instead for another IM model or seek to use the IM Schedule approach.

Collateral and Legal Agreement Data

This chapter has detailed the manner in which collateral is used as a credit risk mitigation tool, the agreement terms by which collateral is provided for OTC derivatives, as well as a number of the regulatory changes post-Financial Crisis in respect of collateral.

It is worth considering the huge importance the collateral agreement data plays for various purposes. It is required for day-to-day collateral management, without which daily operations would not be able to operate successfully. This importance is only increasing due to the mandatory collateralisation requirements for uncleared derivatives that have started to be phased in from 2016. It is fair to say that legal teams, despite negotiating and being key to putting this documentation in place, have for the most part left it to their collateral management colleagues to create suitable databases of the collateral agreement terms, such as the eligible collateral, thresholds, minimum transfer amounts, independent amounts and transfer/settlement timing details – in order for collateral to be successfully managed.

As the impact of the collateral optionality and collateral more broadly on pricing has become understood (see Chapter 3 on XVAs), collateral management has morphed at larger financial institutions into a front-office business optimisation rather than simply an operational management function. This has, in order to be able to calculate the specific valuation adjustment required (e.g. from an FVA perspective), required far more granular collateral agreement data.

In addition to this, it will be noted from Chapter 10 that collateral data plays a huge part in the recovery and resolution plans, and record-keeping requirements, for systemically important financial institutions.

Post-crisis, there has been intense scrutiny on the management of client money and assets, where the details of the manner in which collateral is provided (e.g. title transfer vs security interest) is very important, as well as rights of use and segregation of collateral details, both operationally and as specified in the underlying documentation (see Chapter 8 on CASS).

Furthermore, the collateral agreement data is critical to the liquidity management and reporting firms are required to manage (see Chapter 9), given the substantial liquidity outflows these can cause. Interestingly, the collateral outflow requirements in this regard will tend to increase as the exposure the counterparty has on a firm increases (due to the underlying trading), as well as in circumstances where the credit of the firm decreases due to the operation of rating-based collateral agreement clauses (e.g. threshold amounts, minimum transfer amounts and independent amounts) – in some cases, such as structured finance transactions, punitively so ('super-collateralisation clauses'). In many ways, this increasing liquidity demand is 'relieved' through the operation of any termination rights that may ultimately be utilised based on the credit rating of the firm (i.e. a rating downgrade termination event and, less common, event of default).

Despite these growing requirements from many areas for collateral agreement data, there have continued to be multiple silos of this data for specific purposes. This has led to unnecessary duplicative infrastructure and maintenance of such data. In other cases, collateral agreement data captured for one purpose (e.g. operationally for collateral calls to be made) has been used for a different purpose (e.g. regulatory capital purposes), which has led to issues in the data not being fit for purpose. This is because the legal agreement data required across these different consumers is subtly different but has not been picked up or appreciated from a data governance perspective.

There continues to be fierce debate within financial firms as to who is best placed to be the 'golden source' of the collateral agreement data, particularly between legal and collateral management teams. Data governance regulation such as BCBS 239 (see Chapter 5) is forcing discussion around the accountability and stewardship of such data to be forefront of a Chief Data Officer's discussions within financial firms.

It should of course be recognised that, through the multiple document types, protocols and potentially multiple (sometimes inconsistent) and overriding regulations, this has become a very complex area indeed! There are also collaborative platforms (e.g. ISDA Create (launched by ISDA and Linklaters, as well as MarginXchange, which is built in partnership between Allen & Overy, SmartDX and IHS Markit)) being developed to try and automate the generation of the collateral documentation, and capture some of the required agreement at the point of documentation. The success of such initiatives will be crucial to the industry's ability to cope with businesses' operational and regulatory requirements on collateral agreement data going forwards.

Bibliography

Banking Committee on Banking Supervision (2013) 'Margin requirements for non-centrally cleared derivatives', September 2013

Clifford Chance (2013) 'BCBS–IOSCO minimum standards for margin requirements for uncleared derivatives', *Clifford Chance*, 4th March 2013

Clifford Chance (2017) 'LIBOR – the beginning of the end?', *Clifford Chance, 28th* July 2017

FSB (2017) 'Transforming shadow banking into resilient market-based finance – re-hypothecation and collateral re-use: Potential financial stability issues, market evolution and regulatory approaches', 25th January 2017

Harding, P. and Harding, A. (2018) *A Practical Guide to the 2016 ISDA Credit Support Annexes for Variation Margin Under English and New York Law.* Harriman House: Petersfield

ISDA (1995) 'Credit Support Annex' (www.isda.org/a/JnMDE/1995-ISDA-Credit-Support-Annex-English-Law.pdf)

ISDA (2016) ISDA 2016 Variation Margin Protocol, 16th August 2016

ISDA (2017) ISDA SIMM, Crowdsourcing Utility User Guidelines – Data Submission, Determination, and Output of Results, Version 13.3, 16th February 2017

ISDA (2018) 'ISDA partners with Linklaters on online margin documentation negotiation tool', ISDA Press Release, 25th April 2018

ISDA, MFA & SIFMA (2010) 'Independent amounts: Release 2.0', White Paper, 1st March 2010

Ivey, E., Ashall, P., Fujita, M. and Soong, I. (2016) 'Global margin requirements for non-cleared derivatives: Important differences in the margins', *Journal on Law of Investment & Risk Management Products' Futures & Derivatives Law*, 36(6)

Maizar, M., Jacquet, M. and Spillmann, T. (2010) 'Credit and counterparty risk: Why trade under an ISDA with a CSA', GesKR

Singh, M. (2017) 'Collateral reuse and balance sheet space', IMF Working Paper WP/17/113

Thornton, D. (2009) 'What the Libor–OIS spread says', Federal Reserve Bank of St Louis, No. 24

8

CASS – Client Assets and Client Money

In this chapter, we begin by examining the link between the Financial Crisis – in particular, the Lehman Brothers' collapse – and the introduction of the updated UK Clients Assets Sourcebook (CASS) rules, as well as subsequent FCA enforcement. We then go on to cover the content of the CASS rules themselves as well as the interconnectivity between CASS and other regulatory requirements. The legal data requirements involved with CASS compliance are, of course, also considered.

The Collapse of Lehman Brothers

In the aftermath of the collapse of Lehman Brothers, the shortcomings that client protections afforded to investors in the UK prompted a group of the largest US hedge funds to call on the Bank of England to intervene to free an estimated £38 billion in assets frozen in London during the collapse, warning that delays 'could be disastrous for UK plc'. The warnings came as hedge funds were starting to shift billions of dollars of assets out of London to the USA, claiming that the US legal system provided greater client protection, with Richard Baker, a former Congressman and Chief Executive of the Managed Funds Association, writing a letter in the second half of 2008 to the then Governor of the Bank of England, stating:

> Prime brokerage clients are already withdrawing their assets from the UK prime brokers/UK branches of overseas prime brokers … calling into question the future of the UK prime brokerage market.

The collapse of Lehman Brothers had exposed a multi-billion-dollar shortfall in segregated client accounts, forcing the FCA to create much stricter rules on how a firm should separate client money from its own cash. The UK's client money rules in place were simply not fit for purpose, in particular the distribution and insolvency rules. Before any money could be returned to clients of Lehman Brothers, a whole series of tortuous legal questions had to be answered, which meant the rules ultimately failed to protect clients as they had intended to.

In particular, the drafting of the UK's client money regulatory regime had failed to consider that an entity might not be compliant with the rules and how client funds should be distributed in such a scenario. This was immediately apparent when Lehman Brothers International (Europe)'s (LBIE's) failure to observe the rules was exposed, leaving the administrators with an impossible task in deciding how to distribute client funds. In practice, if this scenario had been better contemplated by the regulatory regime, the matter should have been reasonably straightforward. In the words of the Supreme Court, which ended up looking at a number of the resultant issues, there had been 'regulatory non-compliance on a truly spectacular scale' amounting to a 'shocking underperformance'.

It did not, however, end the issues with the Lehman Brothers insolvency, and similar shortcomings in terms of compliance with the regulatory regime were also uncovered during the administration of MF Global UK Ltd, the UK entity company of MF Global which entered into insolvency proceedings in 2011.

In 2014, the FCA made material changes to the rules with the aim of offering better protection and speeding up the recovery of client assets, through a significant update of the CASS. The new CASS rules require significant controls, operational, legal, contractual documentation and data processes, systems, management and oversight – with both firms and individuals facing the potential of regulatory action for breaches of the regulation – even where no actual client losses have occurred (Figure 8.1).

Specific Client Money and Assets Issues in the Lehman Brothers Collapse

When Lehman Brothers collapsed in September 2008, claims on its UK investment bank, LBIE, by clients who alleged that their money should have been held by the firm as client money exceeded by a huge margin (several billion dollars) the money actually held in the segregated client money account.

Those claiming a right to client money fell into three main categories:

1) Those whose money was held in segregated client accounts;
2) Those whose money would have been segregated but at the time the firm entered into administration the money was held in its general account; and
3) Those whose money should have been recognised and segregated as client money in accordance with CASS rules but was not treated as such.

This led to a series of litigated cases, ultimately leading to the UK Supreme Court needing to establish principles for the designation and distribution of client money held by LBIE, and how money should be distributed and applied.

Under CASS, there is a requirement to segregate money received from clients in special accounts designed for that purpose. Adequate arrangements must be made to safeguard clients' rights over that money and not to use client money for a firm's own purposes – a key client protection in the event of insolvency of the firm.

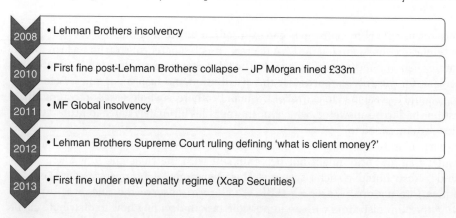

2008 • Lehman Brothers insolvency

2010 • First fine post-Lehman Brothers collapse – JP Morgan fined £33m

2011 • MF Global insolvency

2012 • Lehman Brothers Supreme Court ruling defining 'what is client money?'

2013 • First fine under new penalty regime (Xcap Securities)

Figure 8.1 Defining moments resulting in the CASS regulatory focus

A statutory trust is used to result in the client money not forming part of the firm's property; rather it is held in a fiduciary capacity or by the firm as an agent – on behalf of the client. There are then two permitted ways of dealing with incoming client money. Under the 'normal approach', firms must pay client money into 'trust-status' client bank accounts by the following business day. Under the 'alternative approach', client money may be paid into a firm's own accounts, providing that a daily reconciliation of records and accounts is performed and an equivalent amount of money is deposited into segregated client bank accounts. LBIE purported, but demonstrably failed, to be following the alternative approach.

The general purpose of CASS was to protect client money from both misuse and the failure of a firm holding that client money. If a firm does enter into insolvency whilst holding client money, the main purpose of CASS is to facilitate timely repayment, by triggering a pooling of client money, which is then repaid to clients.

There was an undisclosed amount of unsegregated client money belonging to independent clients, and nearly $3 billion of client money owing to other Lehman entities, which, according to CASS, was to be treated as if it had come from any other client of the firm. Altogether, client money claims exceeded the money actually held in the segregated client money accounts by a very big margin. The drafters of CASS had entirely failed to contemplate the possibility that their rules would simply not be followed, and that a substantial difference between the amount of client money which should have been segregated and the amount which was actually segregated would arise. This lack of provision for such a circumstance meant that the UK courts were asked to fill in the gaps and legal questions, with the following reaching all the way to the Supreme Court (adding to the unfortunate delay in dealing with the urgent client monies under question):

a) Does a statutory trust arise when money has been placed in a segregated client account or as soon as it is received by a firm?
b) Should client money that was incorrectly omitted from segregated client accounts be included in the client money pool for redistribution to clients?

The UK Supreme Court found, unanimously, that a statutory trust arises immediately on receipt of client money by a firm. Following 20 days of argument in the courts over the nature of the statutory trust, client money pooling and the precise wording of individual sections of CASS (which unfortunately did not stand up well to such close scrutiny as many drafting inconsistencies were revealed), a sharp division of opinion arose between the UK Supreme Court justices. The final ruling was made on a majority of only 3:2 that unsegregated client money should be included in the client money pool. This was somewhat in contradiction to English trust law, which states that those with a proprietary interest in money will be protected only if both a trust is declared and the money is in fact properly segregated. Here, the majority justices insisted that it was the CASS rules, not English trust law, that was at issue.

The insolvency of both Lehman Brothers and MF Global showed the issues of non-harmonised regulation of rehypothecation – the practice by banks and brokers of using, for their own purposes, assets that had been given to them as collateral, resulting in arbitrage strategies between the USA and the UK to bypass regulatory rehypothecation limits on the reuse of clients' assets in the USA. In particular, there was insufficient transparency regarding the ability of LBIE to use US clients' assets deposited with Lehman Brothers US through prime brokerage agreements. (At a high

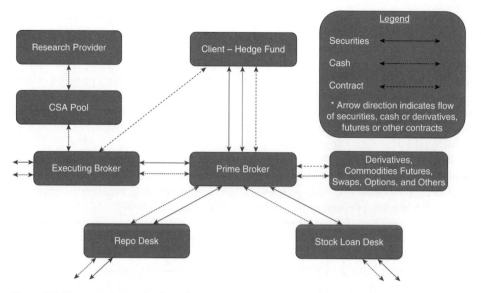

Figure 8.2 The typical prime broker relationships

level, prime brokers provide full-service trading, securities lending, additional leverage and other services to hedge funds.) Figure 8.2 illustrates the typical relationships.

FCA Enforcement of CASS

The LBIE client money and broader custody issues have also brought FCA focus onto the enforcement of CASS regulation. This has been highlighted by a series of large regulatory fines, such as the £33 million fine in 2010 to JP Morgan Securities for failure to segregate and adequately protect billions of pounds of client money held by its futures and options business with JP Morgan Chase Bank for a period of 7 years following the merger of JP Morgan and Chase. It is important to note the level of penalty, despite the misconduct not being deliberate and the fact that the firm self-reported on discovering the issue and immediately remedied the situation. The fine amount actually included a 30% reduction for working constructively with the (then) FSA (Financial Services Authority), however, it still amounted to 1% of the average amount of unsegregated money held during the relevant period.

In 2015, the FCA fined Barclays £38 million for putting some £16.5 billion of clients' custody assets at risk, meaning that their clients risked incurring extra costs, lengthy delays or losing their assets had Barclays become insolvent during the relevant period. The FCA issued a statement in relation to the Barclays fine, stating:

> *The FCA's Rules are there to protect client assets if a firm becomes insolvent. Barclays failed to properly apply these rules when opening 95 custody accounts in 21 countries. As a result, Barclays' records did not correctly reflect which company within its Investment Banking Division was responsible for the assets in the accounts. Barclays also failed to set up appropriate legal arrangements with these companies.*

These failings were compounded by flaws in account naming or incorrect data that suggested assets belonged to Barclays instead of its clients.

This breached the FCA's Client Asset Rules and requirements that firms should have adequate management, systems and controls (Principle 3) and properly safeguard clients' assets (Principle 10).

Also, in 2015, the Bank of New York (BNY) Mellon Group, at the time the world's largest global custody bank by safe custody assets, was fined £126 million for failing to adequately keep entity-specific records and accounts, which would be needed by an insolvency practitioner were the firm to go insolvent, in order to identify those client assets that are safeguarded and due to be returned (instead, global platforms were used which did not record which BNY Mellon Group entity clients had contracted). Additionally, the firm had failed to prevent the co-mingling of safe custody assets with firm assets from various proprietary accounts and on occasion, used safe custody assets held in omnibus accounts to settle other clients' transactions without the express prior consent of all clients whose assets were held in such accounts.

The fine to Aviva in 2016 of just over £8 million showed that regulated activities, and compliance with CASS, can be delegated, but not abdicated. Aviva had outsourced the administration of client money and external reconciliations in relation to custody assets, but notably failed to ensure that it had adequate controls and oversight arrangements to effectively control these outsourced activities.

The Current CASS Rules

The FCA's regulatory regime is based on 11 principles which firms must follow, with Principle 10 in particular stating that *'a firm must arrange adequate protection for clients' assets when responsible for them'*. The main objective of the CASS regime is to maximise both the amount and speed of return of client money and assets in the event of insolvency of a regulated firm. In the event that a firm goes into administration, the CASS regime seeks to ensure that it can identify exactly what assets are owed to each of its clients, as well as ensuring that those assets are held in a way that makes them legally distinct from the firm's own assets, so as not to be lost to creditors due to a lack of distinction from other assets (Figure 8.3).

Client Money

There is a clear distinction between cash and non-cash assets under CASS. Because cash is fungible, it is treated differently to non-cash assets in both general regulatory terms as well as in the event of insolvency. The client money provisions, covered in chapter 7 of CASS, apply to investment firms when they carry out regulated activities that could give rise to them holding cash for clients. Examples of client money include money that is:

- Held pending investment (e.g. cash collateral).
- Held in the course of settlement (including settlement failures where one is not intending to hold client money but settlement fails such that the firm ends up holding funds overnight).

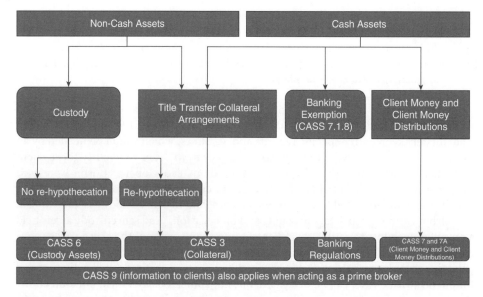

Figure 8.3 Application of CASS and banking regulation to cash and securities

- Derived from client assets that are being held in custody (e.g. dividends).
- Treated as client money in accordance with client money rules (e.g. by opting into the client money rules).

It should be noted that client money rules apply to all categories of client (i.e. retail or professional) and also apply where a firm holds money on behalf of an affiliate in respect of investment business. In terms of jurisdiction, the rules apply to all regulated firms in relation to activities conducted from an establishment in the UK and from their branches in European Economic Area (EEA) jurisdictions.

There are a number of exclusions, such that the following types of money would not be client money:

- Money to which the banking exemption applies (CASS 7.1.8). This is where money is held on deposit by a bank, provided that the bank notifies its client that it is holding their money as banker and that as a result it will not be held in accordance with the client money rules.
- Money that is due and payable to a firm.
- Title Transfer Collateral Arrangements (to which CASS 3 applies instead). (It should be noted that rehypothecation does not apply to cash.)

Money can cease to be client money (and therefore the client money rules cease to be applicable to it) when it is paid:

- To the client (or an authorised representative of the client).
- To a third party on the instructions of the client (unless it is being transferred to an exchange, clearinghouse or intermediate broker in the course of effecting a transaction). Note also that in terms of retail clients, the client must be notified that the firm may transfer the client money to the third party.

- To a bank account in the name of the client (which is not also in the name of the firm).
- To the firm when due and payable.
- In certain circumstances in relation to clearing.

Firms are restricted in where they may place client money – limited to central banks, Banking Consolidation Directive credit institutions and third-country authorised banks. Note that OTC derivative counterparties, intermediate brokers, exchanges and clearinghouses are permitted for the settlement of transactions. There is a requirement for the exercise of due skill, care and diligence when selecting where to place the client money, and a need to consider diversification, the capital of the credit institution/bank and its credit rating, as well as the level of risk undertaken by the institution. The reasons for the selection of where to place client money must be retained as records for 5 years after ceasing to use the relevant third party.

The client money rules operate to substantially reduce the risks of insolvency for clients by holding funds on trust. Accordingly, firms are required to obtain written confirmation of the trust status of client bank accounts opened within 20 business days, else withdraw all cash balances from the relevant bank. There are also requirements on the naming of accounts – the account used for deposit of client funds must be separately identified from any accounts used to hold firm money.

Client Assets

The custody provisions for non-cash assets belonging to clients are dealt with in chapter 6 of CASS. CASS 6 applies to all FCA-regulated firms in relation to activities conducted in the UK and in other EEA jurisdictions when holding financial instruments belonging to a client in the course of its Markets in Financial Instruments Directive (MiFID) business and safeguards and administers investments in the course of non-MiFID business.

Client custody can arise intentionally, such as through prime brokerage and derivatives transactions – if no right of rehypothecation is exercised, or if custody services are offered. It can also arise unintentionally, for example, in the case of settlement failures, where there is no intention to hold assets but there is a failure such that the firm ends up holding excess assets. There are, however, a number of exclusions from custody of client assets, such as:

- Title Transfer Collateral Arrangements (see Chapter 7). An example of this is the 1995 ISDA Credit Support Annex (Transfer – English Law). Note, in this case, that CASS 3 applies instead.
- Where the assets are subject to rehypothecation (note, however, that express consent is required within the agreement itself and that the exclusion only applies once the right of rehypothecation has in fact been exercised). CASS 3 applies to rehypothecated assets, rather than CASS 6.

There are a number of ways in which the client custody assets can be registered. This can be:

a) in the client's name itself;
b) in the name of a nominee company of the firm, an affiliate, exchange or sub-custodian; or

c) in the name of a third party or the firm itself if the safe custody asset is subject to law or market practice outside the UK and it is either in the client's best interests to do so or it is not feasible to do otherwise, and the firm has notified the client in writing.

A firm is required to conduct due diligence on a custodian prior to placing a client's assets with that custodian and must ensure that it only deposits safe custody assets with a third-party custodian in a jurisdiction which specifically regulates and supervises such activities. Records must be kept containing evidence of the suitability of the appointment of a third-party custodian and several factors need to be taken into account to ensure a client's assets are protected in contractual arrangements with third-party custodians, including:

- that the third party segregates the record of safe custody asset of its client from any applicable asset of the firm or third party;
- that contractual arrangements for registering or recording safe custody assets are not in the client's name;
- that the title of the account shows that safe custody investments credited to it do not belong to the firm;
- the requirements to control the way in which the third party can withdraw assets from the account;
- the procedures and conditions in place for giving instructions over the account;
- procedures relating to the claim and receipt of entitlements (e.g. dividends) accruing to the client; and
- provisions on the liability of the third-party custodian or its agent in case of loss of assets due to fraud, negligence or wilful default.

CASS and Collateral

As discussed earlier, if the firm exercises a right of rehypothecation over collateral provided by a client, which will usually be the case as prime broker under prime brokerage agreements and also in the context of trading OTC derivatives, then CASS 3 will apply rather than CASS 6. Under CASS 3, the firm is required to '*maintain adequate records to enable it to meet any future obligations, including the return of equivalent assets*'. Such 'collateral assets' do not need to be segregated, nor held in a client account, since the firm is permitted to treat the assets as its own. The same is true for collateral that is transferred by way of title, such as under an English Law CSA, since the very nature of a title transfer of the collateral assets means that these are no longer client assets!

CASS and Prime Brokerage

CASS 9 was introduced in March 2011, following the collapse of LBIE, as the (then) FSA felt that the consequences of a prime broker failing were not fully appreciated by clients, in particular, the effect of the rehypothecation rights of a prime broker on an insolvency and failings in relation to client money and custody assets. The aim of CASS 9 was to increase the quality and timing of information provided to clients of prime brokerage firms. It applies, *inter alia*, when a firm acts as principal in providing a package of services (including custody, clearing and financing) to a client under a prime brokerage agreement, where such agreement gives the firm a right to use safe custody assets for its own account.

The daily reporting obligations on firms under CASS 9 require the following details to be provided to clients:

- The total value of safe custody assets and client money.
- The cash value of loans and accrued interest, securities to be redelivered by the client under open short positions, short-sale cash proceeds held by the firm, the current settlement amount to be paid by the client under futures contracts, cash margin in respect of futures contracts, the mark-to-market (see Chapter 6) close-out exposure of OTC trades secured by safe custody assets or client money, the total secured obligations of the client against the firm and all other safe custody assets held for the client.
- The total collateral held by the firm in respect of secured transactions entered under a prime brokerage agreement, showing where the firm has exercised a right of use in respect of such assets.
- The location of all the client's safe custody assets (including with a sub-custodian).
- The list of institutions at which the firm holds or may hold client money.

Additionally, every prime brokerage agreement that includes a firm rehypothecation right is required to provide a disclosure annex, summarising the key provisions within the agreement permitting such use of safe custody assets, including any contractual limit on the use of such assets, any related contractual definitions, a list of the provisions providing for the firm to use the safe custody assets and a statement of the key risks to the client if the firm does use the assets. Updates need to be provided in the event that the disclosure annex is not an accurate reflection of the key provisions of the agreement.

It is worth reflecting on some of the key differences in terms of client asset protection at prime brokers under US and UK rules – at the time of the Lehman Brothers insolvency, the gap between the regimes was significant, although much of this has now been addressed. Most prime brokerage regulation is based on where assets are located. The transfer of assets under title transfer arrangements, and the lack of a statutory cap on rehypothecation under UK prime brokerage arrangements, are somewhat less protective to customers than the US framework is (Rule 15c3-1 of the Exchange Act requires a US firm to retain control of any fully paid and excess margin securities in excess of 140% of a customer's debit balance – there is no such limitation under the UK CASS rules). Accordingly, if the firm is allowed to freely transfer assets to an offshore account, such restrictions may not apply.

CASS Resolution Packs

A CASS resolution pack is required under CASS 10 if a firm holds client money or client assets. The purpose of this is to ensure that a firm maintains and is able to retrieve information that would, in the event of insolvency, assist an insolvency practitioner in achieving a timely return of client money and safe custody assets held by the firm to that firm's clients. CASS 10 provides that the insolvency practitioner should be able to retrieve the documents in the pack within a 48-hour timeframe. The link with recovery and resolution should be noted (including the timeframe for provision of information and overlap of information) and, in fact, CASS 10.1.2 states that one of the purposes of the CASS resolution, is *'in the event of its or another firm's resolution, assist the Bank of England in its capacity as resolution authority under the [Recovery and Resolution Directive]'*.

CASS and Legal Data

It is clear from the details of the CASS regulation that in order to operationally give effect to its requirements, it is imperative to manage legal agreement data and its interaction with transactional and collateral data.

The starting point is ensuring correct documentation is put in place to reflect terms that are CASS compliant and that the correct documents, notices and acknowledgements are in fact in place (e.g. securing acknowledgement letters from any institution with which client cash is deposited, to confirm that this cash does not belong to the firm and that it will be held in a way that enables it to be identified as such, and that any charges, liens, set-off or retention over the cash are waived), together with record-keeping of this. Standard terms are invariably negotiated by clients from time to time, and it is in these cases in particular that it is important to consider changes to wording and the impact on the requirements under CASS (e.g. a change to the right of use wording can be particularly problematic – some firms have historically agreed clauses, 'Specified Conditions' in a New York Law CSA, which remove the rights of rehypothecation in the event of a rating downgrade of the firm, which they are then unable to monitor and give effect to operationally upon a downgrade, almost invariably resulting in a CASS breach). Contract lifecycle management tools can assist (see Chapter 11) in this area, and it is important that the correct approval chains and exception processes are triggered for any terms that may have CASS implications.

Many of the CASS requirements are dependent not only on the correct documentation being in place, but its application to particular payments and asset deliveries. This operationally requires transactions to be linked to agreements and their terms, which can be pretty complex and problematic for firms. In one instance, a major investment bank operated on the basis that in the event of there being more than one master agreement (of a particular type, e.g. ISDA Master Agreement) between it and a client, an assumption could be made that the master agreement with the latter date governed the relevant trading transactions. Whereas this assumption is *likely* to be true, it is not *necessarily* true. This can very quickly lead to CASS breaches. The same is true for trade linkage to collateral agreement terms, in particular, CASS requiring determination of whether the collateral is being given on a title transfer basis (e.g. under a GMRA or English Law CSA) or a security interest basis (e.g. under a New York Law CSA), as this will determine the manner in which the (client) money and/or assets need to be handled. This is now of course further complicated by the multiple collateral arrangements that may exist with a particular counterparty, as a result of the margin reform regulation and subsequent documentation.

An additional complication can be the interrelation between principal trading agreements such as the ISDA Master Agreement (and its collateral annex, if any) and/or GMRA, and terms of business. The terms of business are often used as a fallback set of terms to the trading documentation, but where the terms relevant to CASS (e.g. client money protection statements or rights of use clauses) are inconsistent between the principal master agreement and terms of business, it is imperative to be able to manage that hierarchy of terms created, both from the perspective of determination of the terms relevant to particular payments and/or delivery of assets, as well as clarity and transparency to the client in terms of the position (there is a general regulatory requirement to be fair, clear and not misleading with client communications).

The CASS requirements for a Prime Brokerage Disclosure Annex can be seen as a good test of legal agreement data, and many firms have seen the significant benefit of generating the prime brokerage agreement itself through structured data, with the result that the Disclosure Annex can be automatically generated (see Chapter 11 for a discussion on data-orientated contracts), and there is a reduction in the risk that the disclosure in the Disclosure Annex does not match up to the terms of the underlying Prime Brokerage Agreement itself.

The importance of integration between the legal agreement data and CASS can be summarised in three points:

1) Alignment of client contractual arrangements and treatment of client money and client assets – the basis on which client money and client assets received are held for clients and the agreements under which such client money and client assets may be used by a firm, together with the level of client protection afforded, are clear and documented between the firm and its clients (and reported to them as required), and aligned with operational processes.
2) Identification and segregation of client money and assets – client money and assets are clearly identifiable and segregated from the firm's own assets (therefore meeting requirements such as identification, segregation, calculation and diversification), for which the firm is responsible or has the ability to control, based on the linkage of transactions and services to the legal agreements under which such trading and services are provided, ensuring that sufficient funds and assets are in client accounts/safe custody locations to cover client obligations.
3) The contractual arrangements in place with clients, including general terms of business, are a golden source of the data required for client money calculation and segregation.

Bibliography

Aikman, J. (2010) *When Prime Brokers Fail: The Unheeded Risk to Hedge Funds, Banks, and the Financial Industry*. Wiley: New York

Carruzo, F. and King, D. (2017) 'Client asset protection at prime brokers under US and UK rules: Comparison chart', *Kramer Levin*, 3rd April 2017

FCA (2015) 'Barclays fined £38 million for putting £16.5 billion of client assets at risk', *FCA Press Release*, 30th August 2015

FCA (2015) 'FCA fines the Bank of New York Mellon London branch and the Bank of New York International Limited £126 million for failure to comply with custody rules', *FCA Press Release*, 15th April 2015

FCA (2016) 'FCA fines Aviva Pension Trustees UK Limited and Aviva Wrap UK Limited £8.2m for client money and assets failings', FCA Press Release, 3rd November 2016

Financial Conduct Authority Handbook: Business Standards

Lehman Brothers International [Europe] v CRC [2012] UKSC 6, [202] Bus LR 667

Mackintosh, J. (2008) 'Hedge funds call for intervention on Lehman', *The Financial Times*, 15th October 2008

Phillips, S. and Morrison, S. (2014) 'The Lehman client money litigation', *Orrick*, 6th October 2014

9

Liquidity Risk Management and Reporting

The Financial Crisis raised fundamental questions regarding liquidity risk, with financial firms across the global financial system experiencing an urgent demand for cash from counterparties, short-term creditors and borrowers. It was the banks' credit that was hit hardest by liquidity pressures. Many solvent banks were denied access to short-term interbank lending (which many had in fact built their business models on). Emergency central bank lending programmes assisted some banks, although others went into liquidation. It is against this backdrop that the Bank of International Settlements enhanced the Basel II framework, in particular putting liquidity management front and centre of the Basel III framework, which this chapter details. In particular, the chapter explains the impact of credit rating downgrade clauses (for example, see Appendix A) that had been in many trading agreements, causing somewhat unexpected outflows of cash during the Financial Crisis due to the manner in which it unfolded.

Bank Liquidity

Given the central role banks play in financial markets, their stability and perception of being 'safe' is critical. This is mainly derived from solvency, whereby assets are worth significantly more than liabilities (i.e. having a 'capital buffer'). However, having a liquidity buffer is also key in order to be able to cover 'unexpected outflows' (such as a 'bank run') or a sudden inability to access the debt markets for funding. A bank may be solvent in terms of its assets exceeding its liabilities, however, they can still fail if the timing of outflows means that there isn't sufficient funding to meet the required obligations, perhaps because the assets are illiquid whereas the liabilities have short-term maturities. Liquidity reflects a financial institution's ability to fund assets and meet financial obligations, without incurring unacceptable losses. Liquidity is essential in all financial firms for investor customer withdrawals, to compensate for balance sheet fluctuations and provide funds for growth. Banks fundamentally transform the maturity of short-term deposits into long-term loans, which makes them particularly vulnerable to funding risk. Funding risk is the risk that the firm will not be able to meet current and future cash flow and collateral needs without affecting daily operations or financial conditions. In contrast, market liquidity risk is the risk that the firm will not be able to eliminate or exit a position at the market price because of market disruption or inadequate market depth.

Bank liquidity can come from a number of sources, at its simplest, cash it holds directly, or on account at central banks. It can also be liquid securities, which can be sold quickly with minimal loss (e.g. transaction costs, such as government securities). One also needs to consider the maturity of less liquid assets, since some of those might be required in a stress situation before the stress passes – since they may either mature or be required to be sold. On the liabilities side, banks have a number of contingent commitments which ultimately may result in an outflow of liquid assets, such as lines of credit offered to customers and client deposits (which will typically be 'on-demand').

Both funding and market liquidity became a significant issue in 2007 upon the collapse of Lehman Brothers. Prior to the crisis, the asset markets were buoyant, and funding was easily and readily available. The sudden lack of market and funding liquidity meant that, despite broadly adequate capital levels, the banking system came under severe stress and a number of central banks needed to take drastic action to support the stability of the financial markets. The sudden market conditions illustrated just how quickly liquidity can dry up and the time that may pass before it returns. As a result of this, the Basel Committee on Banking Supervision published a paper in February 2008 entitled 'Liquidity risk management and supervisory challenges', which highlighted that a number of financial firms had failed to follow sound liquidity risk management principles prior to the crisis.

In particular, the following shortcomings existed in respect of banks' liquidity risk management practices:

- The conditions pre-Financial Crisis, in particular regarding the deep market liquidity through the money markets, low volatility and low interest rates, were taken for granted and too much reliance placed on these conditions continuing to support business models.
- The contagion effects of a stressed market, and the impact this might have on liquidity needs (in particular, through drawdowns on backstop facilities to conduits, contingent liabilities arising from collateralisation of OTC derivatives and 'liquidity hoarding'), were largely underestimated and therefore ignored in liquidity contingency planning.
- Incorrect pricing of liquidity risk, especially for off-balance-sheet positions and contingent liquidity risk.
- Deep reliance by banks on purely quantitative models without sufficient qualitative judgment.
- A lack of regulatory scrutiny of liquidity risk and its management (as it was not sufficiently addressed in the Basel II framework).

This paper was followed by a fundamental review of the previous guidance (published in 2000) and principles on liquidity risk management, published in September 2008 (Figure 9.1), providing some 17 principles for managing and supervising liquidity risk. This recognised the increased complexity of liquidity management for banks with investment banking and capital markets businesses, in order to support activities such as derivatives, repo and prime brokerage businesses.

Fundamental Principle for the Management and Supervision of Liquidity Risk:

Principle 1 – a bank is responsible for the sound management of liquidity risk. A bank should establish a robust liquidity risk management framework that ensures it maintains sufficient liquidity, including a cushion of unencumbered, high-quality liquid assets, to withstand a range of stress events, including those involving the loss or impairment of both unsecured and secured funding sources. Supervisors should assess the adequacy of both a bank's liquidity risk management framework and its liquidity position, and should

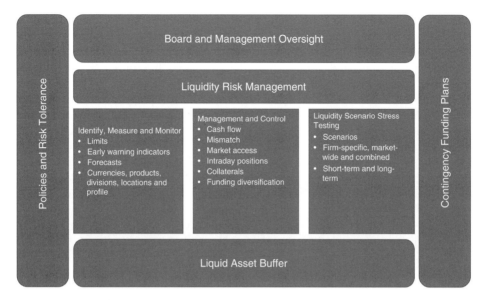

Figure 9.1 A simplified view of the 'Sound Principles' guidelines published by the Basel Committee

take prompt action if a bank is deficient in either area in order to protect depositors and limit potential damage to the financial system.

Governance of Liquidity Risk Management:

Principle 2 – a bank should clearly articulate a liquidity risk tolerance that is appropriate for its business strategy and its role in the financial system.

Principle 3 – senior management should develop a strategy, policies and practices to manage liquidity risk in accordance with the risk tolerance and to ensure that the bank maintains sufficient liquidity. Senior management should continuously review information on the bank's liquidity developments and report to the board of directors on a regular basis. A bank's board of directors should review and approve the strategy, policies and practices related to the management of liquidity at least annually and ensure that senior management manages liquidity risk effectively.

Principle 4 – a bank should incorporate liquidity costs, benefits and risks in the internal pricing, performance measurement and new product approval process for all significant business activities (both on- and off-balance sheet), thereby aligning the risk-taking incentives of individual business lines with the liquidity risk exposures their activities create for the bank as a whole.

Measurement and Management of Liquidity Risk:

Principle 5 – a bank should have a sound process for identifying, measuring, monitoring and controlling liquidity risk. This process should include a robust framework for comprehensively projecting cash flows arising from assets, liabilities and off-balance-sheet items over an appropriate set of time horizons.

Principle 6 – a bank should actively monitor and control liquidity risk exposures and funding needs within and across legal entities, business lines and currencies, taking into account legal, regulatory and operational limitations to the transferability of liquidity.

Principle 7 – a bank should establish a funding strategy that provides effective diversification in the sources and tenor of funding. It should maintain an ongoing presence in its chosen funding markets and strong relationships with funds providers to promote effective diversification of funding sources. A bank should regularly gauge its capacity to raise funds quickly from each source. It should identify the main factors that affect its ability to raise funds and monitor those factors closely to ensure that estimates of fundraising capacity remain valid.

Principle 8 – a bank should actively manage its intra-day liquidity positions and risks to meet payment and settlement obligations on a timely basis under both normal and stressed conditions and thus contribute to the smooth functioning of payment and settlement systems.

Principle 9 – a bank should actively manage its collateral positions, differentiating between encumbered and unencumbered assets. A bank should monitor the legal entity and physical location where collateral is held and how it may be mobilised in a timely manner.

Principle 10 – a bank should conduct stress tests on a regular basis for a variety of short-term and protracted institution-specific and market-wide stress scenarios (individually and in combination) to identify sources of potential liquidity strain and to ensure that current exposures remain in accordance with a bank's established liquidity risk tolerance. A bank should use stress-test outcomes to adjust its liquidity risk management strategies, policies and positions, and to develop effective contingency plans.

Principle 11 – a bank should have a formal contingency funding plan (CFP) that clearly sets out the strategies for addressing liquidity shortfalls in emergency situations. A CFP should outline policies to manage a range of stress environments, establish clear lines of responsibility, include clear invocation and escalation procedures and be regularly tested and updated to ensure that it is operationally robust.

Principle 12 – a bank should maintain a cushion of unencumbered, high-quality liquid assets to be held as insurance against a range of liquidity stress scenarios, including those that involve the loss or impairment of unsecured and typically available secured funding sources. There should be no legal, regulatory or operational impediment to using these assets to obtain funding.

Public Disclosure:
Principle 13 – a bank should publicly disclose information on a regular basis that enables market participants to make an informed judgment about the soundness of its liquidity risk management framework and liquidity position.

The Role of Supervisors:
Principles 14–17 relate to the role of supervisors – omitted for the purposes of this text.

How Much Liquidity Should be Required?

In 2007, Northern Rock became the first UK bank since 1866 to suffer a bank run, requiring the Bank of England to step in to replace rapidly evaporating short-term money-market funding with emergency liquidity support. Even this could not ultimately prevent the bank from becoming nationalised in 2008. Coupled with the lessons from the Lehman Brothers' collapse, liquidity was placed as a key pillar alongside capital, leverage and funding within the Basel III framework.

To work with the published principles, the Basel Committee further strengthened its liquidity framework, creating two minimum standards in relation to funding liquidity, addressing two separate, but complementary, objectives:

1) Promoting short-term resilience of a bank's liquidity risk profile – by requiring banks to hold sufficient high-quality liquid assets (HQLAs) to survive a 'significant stress event' for a 30-calendar-day period (note this objective is met through the liquidity coverage ratio (LCR)).
2) Promoting resilience over a longer-term horizon of 1 year through the creation of incentives for banks to fund their activities through stable sources of funding, and disincentivising excessive maturity transformations (or doing this in too risky a manner). (Note this objective is met through the net stable funding ratio (NSFR).)

Both of these standards are parameterised, with the Basel Committee prescribing values to achieve international harmonisation. However, where specifics for particular regions and jurisdictions apply, then national regulators have the ability to use their discretion in adjusting some parameters. In particular, the national regulators may exercise their supervisory powers to impose additional requirements if they feel that financial firms face greater liquidity risk than reflected under the minimum standards, or if there is a shortcoming in the way in which the standards capture certain market conditions and/or periods of stress.

Both the LCR and NSFR strongly incentivise banks to hold assets in the form of cash and government securities, changing the way firms operate, in particular, reducing the use of wholesale funding. It should be noted that neither of these ratios are particularly favourable towards derivatives or repos (although little of the post-Financial Crisis regulation is(!), indicating the role the regulators' view of such trading activity played in the Financial Crisis).

Liquidity Coverage Ratio

The stress scenario for the LCR involves a shock that would result in, *inter alia*, the run-off of a proportion of retail deposits, partial loss of unsecured funding capacity and secured short-term financing, contractual outflows that would arise from a credit rating downgrade (see later in this chapter) of up to three notches (including collateral implications of such a downgrade), increases in market volatilities, unscheduled drawdowns on committed but unused credit and liquidity facilities that have been provided to clients and any buyback of debt or non-contractual obligations that would be honoured in order to mitigate reputational risk. It should be noted that the characteristics of this stress scenario are unsurprisingly similar in many regards to the Financial Crisis. It is the contractual outflows from a credit rating downgrade of a firm that will be considered in most detail within this chapter, this being the stress scenario most heavily reliant on legal agreement data. Often, master trading agreements have clauses that require the posting of additional collateral, drawdown of contingent facilities, or early repayment of existing liabilities – upon the bank's downgrade by a recognised credit rating organisation. The stressed LCR scenario therefore requires that for each contract in which 'credit rating downgrade triggers' exist, the firm assumes that 100% of this additional collateral or cash outflow will have to be posted for any downgrade up to and including a three-notch downgrade of the bank's long-term credit rating (triggers linked to a firm's short-term rating are assumed to be triggered at the corresponding long-term rating).

The LCR is then calculated as the value of held stock of HQLAs in the stressed conditions divided by the total net cash outflows over the next 30 calendar days – a ratio that must be equal to or greater than 100%. In order to qualify as HQLAs, assets must be liquid in times of market stress and ideally be central bank eligible. The total net outflows over the subsequent 30 calendar days are calculated by multiplying the outstanding balances of certain types of liabilities and off-balance-sheet commitments by the rate at which they are expected to be run off or drawn down. This can be offset (up to a maximum of 75% of the calculated outflows) by the outstanding balances of certain types of contractual receivables multiplied by the rates at which they are expected to flow in. The 75% cap set on the offset of inflows against outflows ensures a conservative approach by not exclusively relying on expected inflows to meet outgoing cashflow demands.

It should be noted that derivatives cash outflows may be calculated on a net basis (i.e. inflows can offset outflows) by counterparty only where a valid master netting agreement exists, and close-out netting is enforceable (see Chapter 6). Where derivative payments are collateralised by HQLAs, cash outflows are to be calculated net of any corresponding cash or collateral inflows that would result, all other things being equal, provided to the bank as part of the contractual obligations of a counterparty if the bank is legally entitled (note the questions this raises in respect of collateral enforceability – see Chapter 7) and the collateral is operationally capable of reuse once received (this is to prevent double-counting of liquidity inflows and outflows).

Contractual Outflows and Collateral

Counterparties to transactions are increasingly collateralised to secure the mark-to-market valuation of the underlying positions. This is typically done using assets that have a 0% risk weighting under the Basel II standardised approach. In such cases, firms are not required to consider valuation changes of the posted collateral during a stressed period. If, however, other non-'Level 1 Liquid Asset Securities' are used as forms of collateral, firms are required to incorporate 20% of the value of such collateral into the expected cash flows, provided that the collateral received is not subject to restrictions on reuse or rehypothecation to cover the potential loss of market value on that collateral. Any collateral that is in a segregated margin account can only be used to offset outflows that are associated with payments that are eligible to be offset from that same account. Where a firm holds excess non-segregated collateral that could contractually be called at any time by the counterparty, or where the counterparty has a right to collateral which has not yet been demanded, all of this needs to be incorporated into the calculation. Where collateral may be contractually substituted from HQLA to non-HQLA assets, the entire amount of HQLA collateral that can be substituted for non-HQLA assets without the consent of the bank (received to secure unsegregated transactions) needs to be incorporated into the calculation. Any outflow generated by the increased needs related to market valuation changes under derivatives or other transactions is required to be included in the LCR, calculated by identifying the largest absolute net 30-day collateral flow realised during the preceding 24 months.

High-Quality Liquid Assets

HQLAs are calculated by reference to those assets that the firm is holding on the first day of the stress period, irrespective of their residual maturity. There are two categories of assets included in the definition of HQLA. 'Level 1' assets can be included without limit, while 'Level 2' assets can only comprise up to 40% of the asset stocks (although in certain circumstances regulators may allow for additional asset classes in this Level 2, referred to as 'Level 2B'; if such assets are included, they can only make up 15% of the total HQLA stock). Level 1 assets can comprise an unlimited share of the pool and are not subject to a haircut under the LCR, however, national supervisors can require haircuts for Level 1 securities based on, amongst other factors, their duration, credit and liquidity risk, and typical repo haircuts. There are various haircuts applicable to Level 2 assets.

Level 1 assets are limited to:

a) Coins and banknotes;
b) Central bank reserves (including required reserves), to the extent that the central bank policies allow them to be drawn down in times of stress; and
c) Marketable securities representing claims on or guaranteed by sovereigns,[1] central banks, public-sector entities, the Bank for International Settlements, the International Monetary Fund, the European Central Bank and European Community, or multilateral development banks, and satisfying all of the following conditions:
   • Assigned a 0% risk weight under the Basel II standardised approach for credit risk;
   • Traded in large, deep and active repo or cash markets characterised by a low level of concentration;
   • Proven record as a reliable source of liquidity in the markets (repo or sale) even during stressed market conditions; and
   • Not an obligation of a financial institution or any of its affiliated entities.

Level 2 assets consist of:

a) Marketable securities guaranteed by central banks, sovereigns, public-sector entities, the Bank for International Settlements, the International Monetary Fund, the European Central Bank and European Community and multilateral development banks, where they have been assigned a 20% risk weight under the Basel II standardised approach for credit risk.

---

1 Where the sovereign has a non-0% risk weight, sovereign or central bank debt securities issued in domestic currencies by the sovereign or central bank in the country in which the liquidity risk is being taken or in the bank's home country and where the sovereign has a non-0% risk weight, domestic sovereign or central bank debt securities issued in foreign currencies are eligible up to the amount of the bank's stressed net cash outflows in that specific foreign currency stemming from the bank's operations in the jurisdiction where the bank's liquidity risk is being taken.

b) Corporate debt securities, including commercial paper and certain covered bonds not issued by the bank or its affiliated entities, rated at least AA.[2]

Level 2B assets consist of:

a) Residential mortgage-backed securities (RMBSs).
b) Corporate debt securities, including commercial paper and certain covered bonds not issued by the bank or its affiliated entities, rated between A+ and BBB.[3]
c) Common equity shares.

It should be noted that the LCR started to be phased in from 2015, when the minimum standard was 60%. This will increase over time, by 10% every year, until it reaches 100% in 2019 (Figure 9.2), by which time firms need to ensure that their HQLA stock is at least equal to their net cash outflows over the 30-day time period.

The LCR requires banks to make quantitative and qualitative disclosures related to their LCR calculations and liquidity management practices. An example of such a disclosure can be seen in Appendix B, in relation to Morgan Stanley for the quarterly period ending 31 March 2018.

Net Stable Funding Ratio

The NSFR is intended to prevent and deter firms from excessive maturity transformation by making a large number of illiquid long-term commitments backed with only short-term funding. It is defined as the amount of 'Available Stable Funding' (ASF) relative to the amount of 'Required Stable Funding' (RSF). The requirement is for this ratio to be equal to at least 100% on an ongoing basis. It should be noted that, at the time of writing, the NSFR is only expected to become a binding standard in the EU in 2019.

For this purpose, ASF is a factor between 0 and 100, reflecting the portion of capital and liabilities expected to be reliable over a 1-year NSFR time horizon. A firm's RSF is a factor between 0 and 100, operating as a function of the liquidity characteristics and residual maturities of the various assets held by that firm as well as those of its off-balance-sheet exposures. The NSFR thereby promotes long-term structural funding of a bank's balance sheet. For example, it forces securitisation pipelines and similar activities to be funded with at least a minimum amount of stable liabilities in relation to their risk profiles (see Figure 9.3).

	1 Jan 2015	1 Jan 2016	1 Jan 2017	1 Jan 2018	1 Jan 2019
Minimum LCR	60%	70%	80%	90%	100%

Figure 9.2 The phased-in increase to the minimum Liquidity Coverage Ratio (LCR) from 2015 to 2019

---

2 Standard & Poor's long-term credit rating.
3 Standard & Poor's long-term credit rating.

	Available Stable Funding	Required Stable Funding
100%	Capital borrowing ≥ 12m	Assets encumbered for ≥12m Net Derivatives Receivable Other assets
95%	Stable retail/SME deposits >12m	
90%	Less stable retail/SME deposits < 12m	
85%		Loans to non-financials ≥ 12m & RW ≤35% Non-HQLA securities Physical traded commodities (including gold)
65%		Residential mortgages ≥12m & RW <35% Other loans not to financials ≥12m
50%	Corporate deposits < 12m Public-sector lending < 12m Other lending 6–12m	LCR Level 2B assets HQLA encumbered for 6–12m Loans to supervised banks 6–12m Operational deposits Non-HQLA assets < 12m Loans to non-bank financials < 12m Loans to non-financial corporates < 12m Retail loans < 12m SME loans < 12m
15%		LCR Level 2A assets
5%		LCR Level 1 assets Irrevocable/conditionally revocable credit and liquidity facilities
0%	Net Derivatives Payable	Cash Central bank reserves Interbank lending < 6m

Figure 9.3 A comparison of Available Stable Funding (ASF) and Required Stable Funding (RSF)

ASF is calculated by assigning a weighting to the category of borrowing, reflecting the stability of the category of funding to which it applies. This is a function of term to maturity, lender type, as well as the type of asset itself. The higher the ASF factor, the higher the level of stability attached to the relevant liability item. Accordingly, regulatory capital is assigned an ASF factor of 100%, whereas funding from a financial institution with residual maturity of less than 6 months is assigned an ASF factor of 0% (see Figure 9.4).

RSF is calculated by assigning a weight to the category of lending, reflecting the assumed liquidity of the category of lending to which it applies. This is a function of the

Liability Type	Residual Maturity	ASF Factor
Regulatory capital	< 1 year (if Tier 2)	100%
Other Capital Instruments	> 1 year	100%
	6–12m	50%
	< 6m	0%
Retail and SME Deposits	Stable under LCR < 1 year	95%
	Less stable under LCR < 1 year	90%
Funding from non-financial customers (includes sovereigns and public-sector entities)	> 1 year	100%
	6–12m	50%
	< 6m	50%
Funding from financial customers	> 1 year	100%
	6–12m	50%
	< 6m	0%
Operational Deposits		50%
Liabilities without a stated maturity		0%
Derivative liabilities		0%
Trade Date Payables		0%
Other Liabilities		0%

Figure 9.4 Factors for bank assets and liabilities – ASF Factors (assets)

term to maturity and lending quality. Liquid assets receive low RSF factors while illiquid assets receive high RSF factors. As such, cash and central bank reserves are assigned an RSF factor of 0% due to their high liquidity. In contrast, undrawn commitments that are conditionally revocable and liquidity facilities are assigned a 5% RSF factor (see Figure 9.5).

To determine the NSFR, the ASF numerator is first calculated by assigning the carrying value of the bank's capital and liability items to the appropriate ASF categories. This is done prior to any regulatory deductions, filters or other adjustments. These ASF factors are then multiplied by the value of the relevant corresponding liability. Finally, these weighted values are added together across ASF categories to get the value of a bank's available stable funding according to the NSFR framework. The determination of the RSF value follows a similar method. First, a firm's assets are assigned to the appropriate RSF factor category and then the amounts assigned to each RSF category are multiplied by their corresponding RSF factor. Finally, the weighted values are added together to give the combined sum across the different RSF categories.

If a firm funds itself from categories in the same weighting category as its lending, then the NSFR will be 100%. If, however, the firm funds itself from borrowing in an ASF category that has a higher weighting than its lending, the NSFR will be less than

Asset Type	Residual Maturity	RSF Factor
Cash and Central Bank Exposures	<6m	0%
Level 1 Assets	Unencumbered	5%
	Encumbered < 6m	5%
	Encumbered 6–12m	50%
	Encumbered > 12m	100%
Level 2A Assets	Unencumbered	15%
	Encumbered < 6m	15%
	Encumbered 6–12m	50%
	Encumbered > 12m	100%
Level 2B Assets	Unencumbered	50%
	Encumbered < 6m	50%
	Encumbered 6–12m	50%
	Encumbered > 12m	100%
Non-HQLA Securities (including physically traded commodities)	Unencumbered	85%
	Encumbered < 6m	85%
	Encumbered 6–12m	85%
	Encumbered > 12m	100%
Loans to Financial Institutions	Secured against a Level 1 Asset < 6m	10%
	Unsecured or secured against a non-Level 1 Asset < 6m	15%
	6–12m	50%
	>12m	100%
Loans to non-Financial Institutions (includes loans to retail and SMEs)	<12m	50%
	>12m	85%
Residential Mortgages	>12m	65%
Initial Margin posted		85%
Derivative assets		100%
Derivative Liabilities		20%
Undrawn commitments (irrevocable and conditionally revocable credit and liquidity facilities)		5%

Figure 9.5 Factors for bank assets and liabilities – RSF Factors (Liabilities)

100%, resulting in the firm needing to cover a shortfall in the net stable funding ratio requirement by borrowing from a higher-risk-weighted category (Figure 9.6).

The NSFR standard requires the stable funding to cover an extended 1-year stress period, where a firm encounters, and investors and customers become aware, of:

a) A significant decline in profitability or solvency arising from heightened credit, market and/or operational risk.
b) A (potential) credit rating downgrade.
c) A material event calling into question the credit quality or reputation of the bank.

Available Stable Funding (Sources)		Required Stable Funding (Uses)	
Item	Availability	Item	Required Factor
• Tier 1 and 2 Capital Instruments • Other preferred shares and capital instruments in excess of Tier 2 allowable amount having an effective maturity of one year or greater • Other liabilities with an effective maturity of 1 year of greater	100%	• Cash • Short-term unsecured actively-traded instruments (< 1 yr) • Securities with exactly offsetting reverse repo • Securities with remaining maturity < 1 yr • Non-renewable loans to financials with remaining maturity < 1 yr	0%
• Stable deposits of retail and small business customers (non-maturity or residual maturity < 1yr)	85%	• Debt issued or guaranteed by sovereigns, central banks, BIS, IMF, EC, non-central government, multilateral development banks	5%
• Less stable deposits of retail and small business customers (non-maturity or residual maturity < 1 yr)	70%	• Unencumbered non-financial senior unsecured corporate bonds (or covered bonds) rated at least AA, maturity ≥1yr	20%

Figure 9.6 Summary of the non-stable funding requirements (adapted from the Basel Committee on Banking Supervision paper (2010))

OTC Derivatives and the NSFR

Derivatives can be either assets or liabilities, depending on whether they are in-or out-of-the-money. Accordingly, the NSFR treats these contracts in a special manner to take this into account. Derivatives transaction values are first calculated based on their replacement cost (i.e. the hypothetical amount a third party would pay to enter into the derivative contract). Those with negative replacement costs are treated as derivative liabilities; those with positive replacement costs are treated as derivative assets. Where there are multiple transactions between two parties under a master netting agreement, they have their replacement cost calculated on a net, rather than a gross, basis (subject to, as would be expected, requirements regarding the enforceability of close-out netting).

A financial firm with a greater amount of derivative assets than derivative liabilities will attract an RSF quota equivalent to this excess. In contrast, where the derivative liabilities exceed the derivative assets, a firm is required to apply a 0% ASF weighting to these, and 20% of this, before deduction of any variation margin posted, requires funding as an RSF.[4] This derivatives funding asymmetry under the NSFR means that derivatives that provide a funding benefit are penalised even if they might economically offset the funding costs of other derivatives, or even other assets on the balance sheet.

In calculating NSFR derivative liabilities, collateral posted in the form of variation margin is deducted from the negative replacement cost amount. Received collateral may not offset the positive replacement cost amount unless it is received in the form of (in the case of the EU proposals, cash[5]) variation margin and meets the conditions specified in the Basel III leverage ratio framework and disclosure requirements, such as it being exchanged daily and being in the same currency as that specified as the currency in which a close-out amount is to be paid (see Chapter 6; known as the 'Termination Currency' in respect of the ISDA Master Agreement). Any initial margin collateral received may not offset the derivative assets and be assigned a 0% ASF factor.

Looking at (2) in Figure 9.7, the net derivative asset position is assigned a 100% RSF factor, as a result of which, banks need to hold long-term funding that corresponds to the value of the net derivative assets. This is calculated as the NSFR derivative assets less NSFR derivative liabilities. Note that this is only assigned an RSF Factor is positive.

Derivative liabilities that are not netting with derivative assets do not receive any available funding recognition. A 20% RSF factor is assigned to the derivative liabilities (see (3) in Figure 9.7). Accordingly, much of the collateral under derivatives trading agreements will need to be funded long-term. Additionally, initial margin posted will

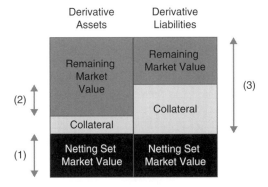

Figure 9.7 Illustration of the NSFR treatment of derivatives

---

4 This 20% add-on for gross derivative liabilities was regarded as punitive. The position as of January 2018 is that the Basel Committee has given national jurisdictions the ability to lower this 20% to 5%.

5 Note that the divergence in this regard between the EC proposals and the BCBS standard has been, at the time of writing, a point of industry lobbying, through trade associations such as ISDA and SIFMA (see Figure 9.8).

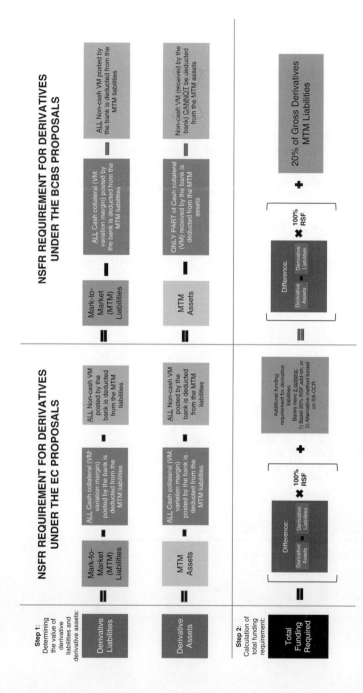

Figure 9.8 A comparison of the NSFR requirements for derivatives under the EC proposals and the NSFR requirements for derivatives under the BCBS proposals

not receive available funding recognition.[6] However, the initial margin that is posted by the bank is required to be backed up by long-term funding equal to 85% of the value of the initial margin.

Secured Financing Transactions and the NSFR

It is worth considering for a moment the substantial impact the NSFR has in respect of securities financial transactions, such as repos. The NSFR treatment of collateral received under securities financing transactions is determined by the collateral's balance sheet and accounting treatments, which generally result in exclusion from assets and securities that have been borrowed under such transactions (e.g. reverse repos and collateral swaps) which are kept off-balance-sheet – so there is no NSFR treatment for the collateral.

Standalone repos are treated as leveraged purchases of securities because of the fact that the collateral remains on the balance sheet of the seller (and the collateral therefore requires an RSF factor). Therefore, an ASF factor is applied to the cash side of a repo and an RSF factor to the collateral. The RSF factor is determined by the type of collateral (in contrast to unsecured lending, where the RSF factor depends on the counterparty and term of lending). Securities which have been borrowed under securities financing transactions, where the firm does not have beneficial ownership of the securities (such as reverse repos and collateral swaps), are excluded from the available stable funding calculation.

As can be seen from Figure 9.9, there is a certain amount of asymmetry between repos and reverse repos, depending on the type of counterparty and the residual maturity of the transaction.

Unencumbered assets, such as cash trading desk positions, are subject to RSF. The scale for these assets is related to the HQLA scale used for the LCR, with the applicable RSF proportions being:

- 5% RSF for Level 1;
- 15% RSF for Level 2A;

Residual Maturity	< 6 m		≥ 6 m and > 1 year		≥ 1 year	
	Repo ASF	Reverse RSF	Repo ASF	Reverse RSF	Repo ASF	Reverse RSF
Non-financial Institution	50%	50%	50%	50%	100%	65%/85%
Central Bank	0%	0%	50%	50%	100%	100%
Bank/Financial Institution	0%	10%/15%	50%	50%	100%	100%
Retail and SME	0%	50%	50%	50%	100%	65%/85%

Figure 9.9 Analysis of BCBS NSFR in the context of repos

---

6 Note however, that initial margin posted by the back will need to be backed by 85% of its value as long-term funding.

- 50% RSF for Level 2B;
- 85% RSF for non-HQLA (where not in default and with a residual maturity greater than 1 year); and
- 100% RSF for other assets.

Where such assets are funded through the proceeds of repo financing transactions, the minimum NSFR requirement will create a need to manage gaps between the ASF generated by such financing transactions and the RSF for the applicable funded asset.

The differences in treatment linked to type of counterparty and residual maturity mean that firms all face the same incentive structure regarding how they structure their repo and reverse repo activity. For example, for residual maturities of less than 6 months (which are the most common), there is a strong incentive to transact repos with sovereigns and non-financial corporates (which all attract 50% ASF), as opposed to with central banks, banks, other financials, and retail and small business customers (which all attract 0% ASF). A perverse incentive of this is the incentivisation it creates for firms to repo their lower-quality collateral to corporates (who are not as well placed to manage the risks associated with such lower-quality collateral).

Data and Systems Requirements

The LCR and NSFR require significant enhancements to the data and technology integration capabilities over and above what is currently being used for liquidity risk measurement and management purposes by firms. There needs to be an ability to produce detailed contractual cash flows over the entire lifetime of the transactions according to various dimensions such as currency, legal entity and line of business, as well as aligning contractual and behavioural cash flows to books and records.

There is a need for integration between legal agreement, trade, risk, finance, exposure measurement and collateral management systems. Examples of the legal agreement data needed as part of this include:

- Close-out netting determinations;
- Master Agreement 'Termination Currencies';
- Rating downgrade termination events;
- Contractual contingent liability clauses (including rating downgrade clauses) that might result in an outflow of cash upon the occurrence of certain events;
- Rehypothecation rights;
- Whether collateral is held on a title transfer or security interest basis; and
- Collateral eligibility details.

However, this cannot just be viewed as a legacy documentation management issue by firms. It is imperative that firms seek to understand the implication of the contractual terms at the point of negotiation of the documentation, and factor in any liquidity or other implications of wording when assessing the acceptance of terms with counterparties.

Ratings-Event-Driven Clauses

It is clear from the LCR, and to a lesser extent the NSFR, that ratings-event-driven clauses have been recognised by the regulators as a vital component of liquidity management of systemically important financial institutions and, ultimately, are key to ensuring financial system stability. Such clauses are typically incorporated into financial contracts such as master trading agreements and bond indentures, and require a contractual party, or in some cases a related third party, to maintain credit rating above a particular rating threshold, with certain consequences applicable should this fail to occur, typically to protect the other contractual party from deteriorating credit rating (and therefore credit risk). When incorporated into financial contracts, they have the effect of lowering the cost of borrowing capital and trading, but in the event that they are triggered, they heighten the affected party's need for liquidity at the precise moment when the party's credit risk is heightened, therefore increasing the overall probability of default.

Ratings-event-driven clauses can be broadly classified into five types:

1) **Increased pricing clauses.** The change in rating triggers an increase in the pricing of trades or borrowing, such as an increased interest rate on a payment.
2) **Increased credit-risk mitigation clauses.** These are typically included in master trading agreements and bank loan agreements, and once activated, require the affected party to either post more collateral or further security, provide a guarantee of its obligations to a party with lower credit risk, or potentially even transfer its obligations to a more creditworthy party. In some cases, these clauses also seek to remove the rights of rehypothecation that the affected party may have on the collateral it holds (see Chapter 7 and also consider the client assets – Chapter 8 – impact of such clauses).
3) **Acceleration triggers.** These accelerate the payments of the counterparty to effectively accelerate the payments under the financial contract.
4) **Default triggers.** A termination right is triggered by the change in credit rating, allowing the party exposed to the affected party to consider its increase in counterparty risk as a failure of the affected party to fulfil obligations as set out in the financial contract.
5) **Put provisions.** In the case of lending arrangements, these require a borrower whose credit rating has been downgraded to buy back the issued debt from the lenders.

The use of these clauses has increased over the last 30 years from a harmless means of resetting pricing to more extreme default and acceleration-related triggers. They now have a significant impact on firms, as shown by the LCR and NSFR requirements. An example ratings downgrade clause can be seen in Appendix A.

Credit Ratings

A credit rating is an assessment of the credit risk of an entity, predicting the ability of that entity to pay back debt (and therefore the likelihood of defaulting on such an obligation to repay the debt). They can address an entity's financial instruments (i.e. debt securities such as bonds, certificates of deposit or collateralised securities), but can also be the entity itself. The riskiness of investing is determined by the likelihood that the rated entity – be it, for example, a company, financial institution or sovereign – will fail to make timely interest payments on the debt.

Credit ratings represent the evaluation of a credit rating agency, the main such agencies being Moody's, Fitch and Standard and Poor's (S&P), of the qualitative and quantitative information it obtains for the entity (which may also include non-publicly available information as well as, of course, publicly available information). The information provided by the credit rating agencies can be seen as an integral part of the way in which investors and financial instruments gather information to overcome the otherwise asymmetric information between it and the entity whose credit underlies the potential investment, allowing it to determine the investment to make (i.e. which financial instrument to purchase) and on what terms, as well as part of the efforts by the issuer of such instruments to justify why they are worthy recipients of the investment. The ratings typically use letter designations such as A, B, C – higher grades representing a lower evaluated probability of default, with numbers and +/– to fine-tune the rating.

Ratings are typically broken down into two time horizons over which the credit risk is assessed: short-term (less than 1 year) and long-term (greater than 1 year). See Figure 9.10 for details of Rating Agency Credit Ratings.

Credit ratings have been coupled with regulation in a number of cases, for example pension fund regulation in the US requires that the funds invest only in 'investment-grade' securities and tie the definition of 'investment grade' to certain credit ratings. In the EU, there are restrictions on the investments that Undertakings for Collective Investment in Transferable Securities (UCITS) can make linked to credit ratings. As a result of this, it is perhaps too easy to regard the assigned credit rating from the major credit rating agencies as a proxy for traditional disclosure required by regulation, and ultimately a substitute for investor due diligence, noting that conducting such due diligence can be costly and laborious. In fact, the credit ratings of securities and entities form an inherent part of the Basel III regulation, as seen from the definitions covered in this chapter.

There is much criticism of the 'issuer pays' model used by the common credit rating agencies, where the issuer of debt pays the rating agencies for the initial rating of a debt security, as well as ongoing ratings, and the investors and general public can then access these ratings without charge. This can create incentives to assign higher credit ratings to attract further work and fees, and a share of the market at a rating agency. During the Financial Crisis, rating agencies were accused of having significantly misjudged the risks associated with mortgage-related securities. An 'AAA' credit rating was awarded for numerous complex-structured finance products, with downgrades of these occurring during the crisis, with accusations that the rating agencies had created complex but unreliable models to calculate the probability of default for individual mortgages as well as for the securitised products created by bundling such mortgages, and ignored broader systemic risks associated with these structured products. This can be seen as inexperience and errors of judgment when analysing highly complex and innovative products, with a real information (and often expertise) asymmetry between the issuing banks and the rating agencies, making it hard to truly test and validate the products the rating agencies were seeking to review.

Fitch Long-Term	Fitch Short-Term	Moody's Long-Term	Moody's Short-Term	S&P Long-Term	S&P Short-Term	Investment Status	Rating Description
AAA		Aaa		AAA		Investment Grade	Prime Grade
AA+	F1+	Aa1		AA+	A-1+		High Grade
AA		Aa2	P-1	AA			
AA−		Aa3		AA−			
A+	F1	A1		A+	A-1		Upper Medium Grade
A		A2		A			
A−		A3		A−			Lower Medium Grade
BBB+	F2	Baa1	P-2	BBB+	A-2		
BBB	F3	Baa2	P-3	BBB			
BBB−		Baa3		BBB−	A-3		
BB+		Ba1		BB+		Non-Investment Grade	Non-Investment Grade/ Speculative
BB		Ba2		BB			
BB−	B	Ba3		BB−	B		
B+		B1		B+			Highly Speculative
B		B2	Not Prime Grade	B			
B−		B3		B−			
CCC+		Caa1		CCC+		Junk	Substantial Risks
CCC		Caa2		CCC			
CCC−	C	Caa3		CCC−	C		
CC		Ca		CC			Extremely Speculative
C				C			Default is Imminent
DDD		C		RD			In Default
DD	D	/		SD	D		
D		/		D			

Figure 9.10 Credit Rating Agency Scales Compared

Bibliography

Abraham, A. (2011) 'BCBS – liquidity summary', Katalysys Ltd

Acharya, V. (2011) 'A transparency standard for derivatives', NBER Working Paper No. 17558, November 2011

Bank for International Settlements (BIS) (2000) 'Sound practices for managing liquidity in banking organisations', Basel Committee on Banking Supervision, February 2000

Bank for International Settlements (BIS) (2008) 'Liquidity risk: Management and supervisory challenges', Basel Committee on Banking Supervision, February 2008

Bank for International Settlements (BIS) (2008) 'Principles for sound liquidity risk management and supervision', Basel Committee on Banking Supervision, September 2008

Bank for International Settlements (BIS) (2012) 'Core principles for effective banking supervision', Basel Committee on Banking Supervision, September 2012

Bank for International Settlements (BIS) (2013) 'Basel III: The liquidity coverage ratio and liquidity risk monitoring tools', Basel Committee on Banking Supervision, January 2013

Bank for International Settlements (BIS) (2014) 'Basel III: The net stable funding ratio', Basel Committee on Banking Supervision, October 2014

Bank for International Settlements (BIS) (2017) 'Basel III: Finalising post-crisis reforms', Basel Committee on Banking Supervision, December 2017

Berrospide, J. (2012) 'Bank liquidity hoarding and the financial crisis: An empirical evaluation', FEDS Working Paper No. 2013-03

ICMA (2016) 'Impact of the net stable funding ratio on repo and collateral markets', ICMA European Repo and Collateral Council, 23rd March 2016

Mehta, D. and Fung, H. (2008) 'Globalization of global banking', in *International Bank Management*. Blackwell: Oxford

Neu, P. and Vogt, P. (2012) 'Liquidity risk management: Managing liquidity risk in a new funding environment', in M. Ong (ed.), *Managing and Measuring Capital for Banks and Financial Institutions*. Risk Books: London

Nielson, R. and Nyrup, M. (2015) 'How banks can amend their balance sheets in order to comply with the net stable funding ratio – an investigation of the balance sheet drivers of the net stable funding ratio', Copenhagen Business School, Spring 2015

Parmeggiani, F. (2012) 'Rating triggers, market risk and the need for more regulation', NYU Hauser Global Law School Research Paper

Pernot, X. (2011) 'Liquidity management under Basel III: A briefing note', *Moody's Analytics*, November 2011

Schmitz, S. (2014) 'Liquidity stress testing', Oesterreichische NationalBank, STI course on macro stress testing, Singapore, 29th September–3rd October 2014

The Economist (2007) 'The bank that failed', *The Economist*, 20th September 2007

Siadat, M. and Hammarlid, O. (2017) 'Net stable funding ratio: Impact on funding value adjustment'

York, J. (2008) 'Enterprise-wide liquidity risk management: Still slipping through our fingers?', *The RMA Journal*, September 2008

10

Contractual Impediments – Recovery and Resolution Planning

In this chapter, we explore the impact of the Financial Crisis on the growing regulatory requirements in respect of recovery and resolution planning, seeking to address financial stability concerns that came to the fore during the Financial Crisis due to some major financial firms turning out to be 'too big to fail'. After examining broader considerations of recovery and resolution, the chapter analyses the recovery and resolution approaches under the US and EU frameworks, with particular consideration given to the initiatives created to assist in complying with the new requirements.

The Context Behind Recovery and Resolution Planning

The crisis exposed severe systemic weaknesses in the global financial systems – in particular, the problems of 'too big to fail', 'too interconnected to fail' and 'too many to fail'. This refers to the threat to financial stability posed by banks, such as Citigroup and The Royal Bank of Scotland during the Financial Crisis, that were rescued using taxpayer monies, allowing for a somewhat uninterrupted provision of their services, but effectively shifting (most) of their losses to taxpayers instead of the banks' owners or investors. In the words of Harald Waiglein, Director General, Economic Policy and Financial Markets, Federal Ministry of Finance of the Republic of Austria, *'failing financial institutions were kept on life support, and the hospital bills were sent to the taxpayer'*. The US government attempted to preserve some of the US institutions, with over $1.7 trillion in bailouts to companies such as Bear Stearns, Fannie Mae/Freddie Mac, AIG, the Troubled Asset Relief Program, Citigroup and Bank of America.

The capital structure of a bank is characterised by a 'maturity mismatch', whereby assets with long maturities (such as residential mortgages and commercial loans) fund assets with shorter maturities (deposits and repo loans), rendering banks vulnerable to 'runs' from a loss in confidence in the financial system (as seen with the queues of depositors rushing to withdraw their funds from Northern Rock in 2007). National state-required depositor protection schemes attempt to limit concerns resulting in mass withdrawals from a bank in the event of a banking crisis. Even these, however, may not be enough, particularly if:

a) The failing institution is very large compared to the relevant country's GDP ('too big to fail');

b) The failing institution is so interconnected to other firms in the financial system that its failure would result in a massive domino effect, with the relevant country struggling to support and/or rescue the various affected institutions ('too interconnected to fail'); or

c) There is a concentration of banks vulnerable to the same similar shock ('too many to fail').

In such cases, the taxpayer is ultimately left on the hook, through forced state action, to rescue – in many cases – financial firms with massive balance sheets and complex subsidiary and branch structures across many countries globally. In fact, it is argued that the implicit state guarantee, with its effective subsidy to funding costs (as they can trade in riskier assets in the knowledge of implicit government backing in the event of needing a rescue), means that pre-Financial Crisis, there was an incentivisation to grow larger balance sheets, ever more complex and vital to stability, in order to receive this benefit.

Consequently, post-Financial Crisis, there has been a major drive to develop a structure whereby financial firms can be allowed to fail without putting broader financial stability at risk – removing this governmental guarantee – through the creation of a 'resolution regime'. At the Pittsburgh Summit in September 2009, the G20 declared that all '*systemically important financial firms should develop internationally-consistent firm-specific contingency and resolution plans … to help mitigate the disruption of financial institution failures and reduce moral hazard*'.

The Financial Stability Board's 'Key Attributes of Effective Resolution Regimes for Financial Institutions', endorsed by the G20 in 2011, provides a harmonised international standard for the resolution regimes of financial institutions. It focuses primarily on global systemically important banks (G-SIBS), but also serves as a guide for national resolution regimes.

Recovery vs Resolution

Successful recovery or resolution, as the case may be, of a systemically important financial institution (SIFI) requires prior planning given the size, complexity and interconnectedness of the entity groups typically in question. Such planning needs to consider management measures in the event of significant deterioration of financial condition. Recovery and resolution regimes are situated at the intersection of prudential regulation and supervision, and both insolvency law and reorganisation (see Figures 10.1–10.3).

In the context of Europe, it is the Bank Recovery and Resolution Directive (BRRD), which came into force on 1 January 2015, that details the regime for how authorities will intervene to support troubled banks. The Single Resolution Board (SRB) is the resolution authority for significant banks and other cross-border groups within the European Banking Union. Together with national resolution authorities, it forms the Single Resolution Mechanism (SRM). The mission of the SRB is to ensure the orderly resolution of failing banks with minimum impact on the real economy and public finances of the participating Member States of the European Banking Union.

A Recovery and Resolution Plan (RRP) is essentially a blueprint for saving or winding down a troubled bank without causing harm to retail depositors or the financial system, and without relying on public funds

Recovery Plan

A guide to recovery of a distressed firm wherein the firm remains principally under the control of its management and includes measures to decrease risk profile or conserve capital. This also documents strategic recovery options, i.e. divestitures, and recapitalisation

Save the Institution

Resolution Plan

Information to be used by resolution authorities to allow for an orderly, least-cost and timely wind-down of systemically important functions without impacting taxpayers if recovery measures taken were not successful or became ineffective, i.e. the firm reached or is likely to reach the point of non-viability

Enable the Authorities to resolve the Institution

Figure 10.1 What is a Recovery and Resolution Plan (RPP)?

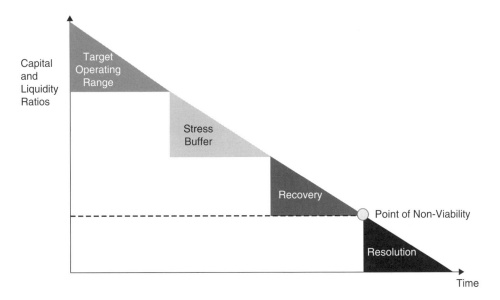

Figure 10.2 Recovery and resolution stages as capital and liquidity ratios decrease

In the USA, the resolution regime under the Dodd–Frank Wall Street Reform and Consumer Protection Act signed on 21 July 2010 seeks to mimic the insolvency regime for deposit-taking institutions for financial companies. The Lehman Brothers failure demonstrated the issues caused by the omission of investment banks that were non-deposit-taking from a special resolution regime, as is the case for insured deposit-taking institutions (such as commercial banks and savings institutions) that

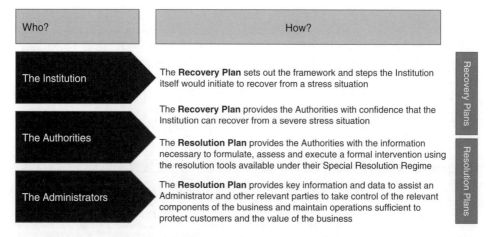

Figure 10.3 Usage of recovery and resolution plans

are exempt from the Bankruptcy Code [11 USC §109(b)(2)]. Consequently, Title II, the Orderly Liquidation provision of the Dodd–Frank Act, provides for a special resolution regime for SIFIs as an alternative to the process under the Bankruptcy Code to be used in exceptional situations only, with the liquidation of such SIFIs through the Orderly Liquidation Authority (OLA).

Normal Insolvency vs Resolution

Regular insolvency proceedings are mainly focused on the interests of creditors and maximising the value of the insolvent estate. In comparison, resolution objectives are much broader, as they aim to ensure overall financial stability; breaking the problematic nexus between bank and sovereign risk. Resolution objectives are broadly concerned with:

- ensuring the continuity of critical functions (and understanding which functions for which continuity is critical to the financial system, against those that could instead be wound up in an orderly fashion);
- avoiding significant adverse effects on the financial system;
- protecting public funds by minimising reliance on extraordinary public financial support for failing banks;
- protecting insured depositors;
- protecting client funds and client assets;
- creating a position whereby decisions and actions to be taken and executed in the event of a failing bank are undertaken in a short space of time (e.g. over a 'resolution weekend'), based on information collated prior to such an event; and
- identifying and considering the ways in which barriers that would prevent critical functions being resolved can successfully be removed.

The key advantage of a resolution is that it allows for some continuity and the maintenance of a bank's critical functions. If a bank goes into liquidation, all liabilities (except those exempted from the insolvency estate) fall due and the insolvency estate

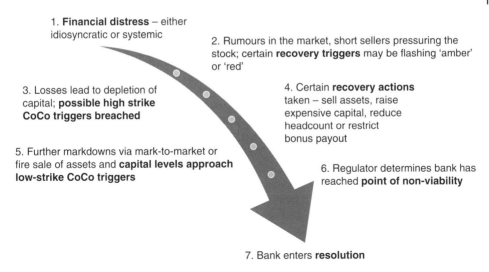

1. **Financial distress** – either idiosyncratic or systemic

2. Rumours in the market, short sellers pressuring the stock; certain **recovery triggers** may be flashing 'amber' or 'red'

3. Losses lead to depletion of capital; **possible high strike CoCo triggers breached**

4. Certain **recovery actions** taken – sell assets, raise expensive capital, reduce headcount or restrict bonus payout

5. Further markdowns via mark-to-market or fire sale of assets and **capital levels approach low-strike CoCo triggers**

6. Regulator determines bank has reached **point of non-viability**

7. Bank enters **resolution**

Figure 10.4 Timeline of events leading up to a bank entering resolution
Note: CoCos are contingent convertible bonds which can be converted to equity or written off entirely if the issuing bank's capital levels fall too far.

are protected by the imposition of a collective stay of creditor action (i.e. no further enforcement by individual creditors).

A trustee is appointed to dispose of the assets and distribute the proceeds among the creditors. The rationale in insolvency is that all creditors (with some exceptions such as secured creditors) should be treated the same and receive their pro-rata share of the estate. However, this can result in stress, interruptions and contagion risks for financial systems. The 'fire sale' that liquidation entails may also be detrimental to the interests of creditors (Figure 10.4).

For our purposes, we are concerned with the general approach of the recovery and resolution frameworks, however, we now briefly consider the differences under the EU and US recovery and resolution regimes.

Main Differences Between EU and Recovery and Resolution Regimes

In terms of objectives, both frameworks are similar, however, there is no explicit objective in the EU framework, as is the case in the US, to minimise moral hazard. In the EU, the aim is to minimise reliance on extraordinary public funds subject to state aid rules, however, in the US, the OLA explicitly prohibits any losses to taxpayers, and requires all losses to be borne by the failed company's creditors (or, if needed, other SIFIs). Both frameworks provide similar tools to facilitate continuity and avoid a destabilising collapse of operations. One of the most significant distinctions between the frameworks is that the EU allows action to prevent the failure of an institution, whereas the OLA requires that all SIFIs subject to resolution must be closed and resolved. This is a significant divergence of approach and leads to a likely divergence of outcomes across the two frameworks in practice.

Single and Multiple Point of Entry Strategies

SIFIs can be set up in a number of different ways: from a holding company model – where the holding company conducts investment banking and commercial banking from separate subsidiaries (or subsidiaries of them) – to a 'big bank' model (where activities, be they investment banking or commercial banking, are conducted out of a single legal entity with a large balance sheet) to a global multi-bank model (where there is a holding company owning a number of separate banks, typically incorporated in different jurisdictions, and which may have subsidiaries of their own separating out investment banking and commercial banking).

There are two broad strategies in respect of resolution: single and multiple points of entry. In the case of the single point of entry strategy, the losses are upstreamed to the topmost/holding entity in the group, which is the 'resolution entity'. It is the shareholders and creditors of this entity that bear the losses of the entire group. The remainder of the group operations are treated as an ongoing concern during the resolution to ensure the continuity of critical functions. Resolution tools and powers are applied at the topmost entity of the group. There is typically a single resolution authority, related to the jurisdiction responsible for the consolidated supervision of the group. In the case of the multiple point of entry strategy, the resolution tools and powers are applied to multiple parts of the group, meaning there is likely to be more than one resolution authority involved.

A number of regulators, such as the Financial Deposit Insurance Corporation (FDIC) in the USA and the Bank of England in the UK, have expressed a preference for the single point of entry resolution strategy. That said, the appropriate resolution strategy will very much depend on the group's capital and organisational structure, including questions around the location of loss-absorbing capacity within the group and also whether subsidiaries and business units can easily be separated from other parts of the group.

What Does a Recovery and Resolution Plan, a Living Will, Need to Contain?

> *The ability to plan in advance for the orderly resolution of a systemic entity is key to ending Too Big To Fail. Viable resolution plans will require systemic institutions to conduct a strategic analysis on how they could be resolved under the Bankruptcy Code as well as evaluate significant credit exposures and other key information across the entities and their affiliates. These plans will be instructive to institutions as a way for them to better understand how their business lines interact and how to mitigate the effects of failure risk. The plans also will help inform the FDIC on how to lessen the systemic ripple effects in the event one of these companies must be resolved under the new Orderly Liquidation Authority.*
>
> (Sheila Bair, FDIC Chairman, when proposing the initial living wills rules)

The resolution of a SIFI is a very complex exercise. To be conducted successfully, it requires a tremendous amount of detailed, and quite confidential, information about the relevant entity group. The following needs to be considered as the backdrop to the informational and data requirements to create effective recovery and resolution plans:

- Multiple insolvency and regulatory regimes that may apply to different entities in the relevant financial group.
- Qualified financial contracts entered into by the entity (these typically represent a significant risk to financial stability if not managed correctly in a resolution scenario (including their immediate termination at the bottom of a financial market during a crisis)).
- Pre-emptive actions that may be necessary to preserve critical functions of the failing entity (however, they may accelerate failure by starting a public crisis of confidence in the entity).
- The presence of cross-default clauses and inter-company guarantees and service arrangements (or lack of!).

US Recovery Plans

Unlike in the EU, there is no specific requirement for a recovery plan in the USA under the Dodd–Frank Act, although there is a need for undercapitalised entities to provide a capital restoration plan if their capital erodes beyond certain levels.

US Resolution and Recovery Plans

There is both a resolution plan requirement under the Dodd–Frank Act for non-bank financial companies designated as systemically important, as well as for bank holding companies with a certain level of consolidated assets to maintain enhanced supervision and prudential standards.[1] There is also a requirement for covered insured depository institutions (CIDIs) to submit resolution plans to the FDIC,[2] which complements the Dodd–Frank Act resolution plan requirements in that most holding companies of CIDIs would be expected to file Dodd–Frank resolution plans as well. We concentrate on the Dodd–Frank Act resolution plan requirements for the purposes of this section.

There are three objectives of the Dodd–Frank Act resolution plan requirement:

- Facilitate planning of resolution authorities by highlighting the structure and complexities, as well as the resolution processes and strategies, of covered companies.
- Assist the Federal Reserve Board in its supervisory responsibilities to ensure that covered companies operate safely and soundly without posing risks to financial stability.
- Enhance the authorities' understanding of foreign firms' US operations, allowing for a more comprehensive and coordinated resolution strategy for cross-border firms.

The resolution plan must contain a public section, as some of these details are useful in the public domain to assist with broader financial stability planning. This is posted on the Federal Reserve and FDIC websites. There is also a confidential section (and it is important that the covered entity specifically requests confidential treatment, which should be excluded from disclosure to the public).

---

1 Dodd–Frank Act, s165(d), codified as 12 U.S.C. § 5365(d).
2 12 U.S.C. § 1819(a).

The key sections are:[3]

- **Executive Summary.** A summary of the key elements of the strategic plan for rapid and orderly resolution in the event of failure of the entity.
- **Strategic Analysis.** The details of the plan for orderly resolution, including key assumptions and supporting analysis (such as the financial and economic conditions in which it would be executed) and specific actions to facilitate resolution. There is a requirement to detail funding, liquidity, support functions and other resources such as capital, mapping these to:
  - material entities;
  - core business lines; and
  - critical operations.

  The strategic analysis needs to provide timings for the execution of the proposed plan, identify potential material weaknesses in the plan and mitigating actions thereto, demonstrate how core assets and critical operations could be resolved and transferred to potential acquirors, and how critical elements of business operations would continue during failures of key entities in the group.
- **Corporate Governance Related to Resolution Planning.** In the context of this text, it is worth highlighting the need to describe the process by which data forming the basis of the resolution plan is collected and reported (note the relevance in relation to contractual impediment reporting described below).
- **Organisational Structure and Related Information.** This needs to provide an organisational chart of all material legal entities and a mapping of the critical operations and business lines to this. There is a requirement to identify pledged collateral – including the jurisdiction in which it is held and details regarding its enforceability. This places a significant demand on items such as collateral agreement data (see Chapter 6) and determinations made regarding collateral enforceability (see Chapters 6 and 7). Material off-balance-sheet exposures need to be identified, including contractual obligations and guarantees (which have traditionally been – if at all – poorly stored, tracked and detailed in legal agreement data systems at large financial institutions), material hedges, major counterparties and whether failure of those major counterparties would have an adverse impact on the group and each payment, the clearing and settlement system of which there is direct or indirect membership, and how that maps to material entities, core business lines and critical operations.
- **Management Information Systems.** This includes details of systems for risk management, accounting, financial and regulatory reporting. The legal owner of key management information systems needs to be identified, as well as the process by which regulatory bodies would be able to access the systems.
- **Interconnections and Interdependencies.** This section needs to detail critical relationships, highlighting interconnections and interconnectedness within the group,

---

3 Regulation QQ for the FRB (12 C.F.R. pt. 243). On 13 September 2011 and 17 October 2011, the FDIC and FRB, respectively, approved a joint rule that implements the resolution plan requirements of section 165(d) of the Dodd–Frank Act. The joint rule is codified as Regulation QQ for the FRB (12 C.F.R. pt. 243) (the 'FRB Rule') and Part 381 for the FDIC (12 C.F.R. pt. 381) (the 'FDIC Rule'), together with the FRB Rule: the 'Resolution Plan Rule').

such as common resources and systems, capital funding liquidity arrangements, existing and contingent credit exposures and cross-default provisions, cross-guarantee arrangements, cross-collateral arrangements and cross-affiliate netting agreements. There can be great difficulty in understanding and detailing cross-default provisions (see Chapter 3) in a group's large trading documentation portfolio (typically in the high tens of thousands) even when restricted to dormant agreements only (many financial institutions struggle to apply an appropriate dormancy filter on such agreements, meaning that this identification task is significantly magnified). One of the issues in this context is that the language of the contracts is somewhat divorced from key client data systems, and it can be very challenging to accordingly piece together how these default provisions relate both within the group and with other market participants.

- **Supervisory and Regulatory Information.**
- **Miscellaneous.**

There are a number of regulator-provided assumptions to be used for the resolution plans, such as the fact pattern being that all material entities fail (although they do not need to be assumed to fail simultaneously, provided the rationale and timing is explained as part of the plan).

If a particular resolution plan is viewed as not being credible or would not facilitate an orderly resolution, the entity is given a reasonable opportunity to cure the deficiency.

EU Recovery Plans

Under Article 5(1) of the BRRD, institutions that are systemically important must draw up and maintain recovery plans in the event of a 'significant deterioration' in order to restore financial soundness. Section A of the Annex to the BRRD provides a list of information to be provided in such recovery plans. It is the resolution authorities, in consultation with the component supervisory and resolution authorities of the jurisdiction in which branches of the relevant group are located, that have to prepare for each institution – setting out the resolution actions that would be taken where the institution meets the conditions for resolution (Article 10(1) BRRD). Section B of the Annex to the BRRD provides a list of information that may be requested from institutions for the purpose of drawing up and maintaining these resolution plans. There is substantial overlap between the information requirements across the Dodd–Frank Act and the section A/section B requirements of the Annex to the BRRD.

Data Requirements of Living Wills

The rich array of data required as part of the recovery and resolution plans cannot be underestimated. It is key that firms develop a well-defined top-down resolution strategy, to avoid expensive recapture/gathering of data that is ultimately not relevant or useful. The data-gathering plan initially should very much create processes that are repeatable and can become systems-driven in later years.

Resolution After Failure of Preventative Tools

Despite the recovery plans and increased supervision to try and prevent the failure of a systemically important group, it is inevitable that some financial firms will fail. The following resolution tools are available:

- **Sale of business tool.** This is a transfer of the failing group, or part of it, to a private-sector purchaser, for a consideration.
- **Bridge institution tool.** This would typically be looked at if there were no private-sector purchaser forthcoming for the sale of the business tool. Accordingly, the resolution authorities transfer all, or some of, the assets, rights and liabilities of the failing group to a bridge institution. This bridge institution is a legal entity owned by the resolution authority/resolution financing arrangements, but shareholders or creditors 'left behind' do not have any claims against the bridge institution. This effectively recapitalises the viable parts of the group. This method was used for the resolution of the Portuguese bank Banco Espirito Santo in 2014.
- **Bail-in tool.** This is the recapitalisation of the failing group through a write-down and conversion of liabilities into equity. In practical terms, this shifts losses to shareholders and creditors such as bondholders, thereby avoiding either liquidation or bail-out by the taxpayer.
- **Asset separation tool.** The failing banking group's balance sheet is cleansed of toxic assets and placed into a separate entity (the 'bad bank'). This idea of removing toxic assets from the troubled group's balance sheet raises concerns that it might encourage a riskier business strategy – accordingly, under the BRRD, it may only be applied with one of the other resolution tools.

The BRRD A55 Contractual Recognition Requirement

Resolution plans in respect of systemically important banking groups hit a number of cross-border scenarios in practice, due to the global footprint of these firms. Accordingly, due to the different regulatory regimes and governing laws, a key challenge exists in ensuring the effectiveness of any special resolution powers, such as suspension of termination rights, asset transfers and bail-in, outside the group's home jurisdiction. For example, in respect of BRRD powers, there is a risk that a non-EU court may not give effect to the bail-in, especially where the contract is governed by the law of a non-EU country – thus potentially frustrating efforts to restore the failing firm and preserve financial stability.

A55 of the BRRD requires financial institutions subject to the BRRD to include a contractual term in contracts (often referred to as an 'Article 55 Clause'), where such contracts are governed by the laws of a non-EU country. Article 55 Clauses must include:

- A description of the relevant bail-in powers.
- An acknowledgement and acceptance by the counterparty that the liabilities in the contract may be subject to the bail-in powers of the BRRD (i.e. they may be written down and converted into equity as part of the bail-in, with the terms of the agreement varied as necessary for this, and ordinary shares or other ownership instruments issued to the counterparty as a result of such exercise).

- The counterparty's agreement to be bound by the effect of an application of these bail-in powers.

Documents meeting the following requirements must contain a contractual recognition of the bail-in clause:

- those entered into (or materially amended) after 1 January 2016;
- those governed by the law of a non-EEA jurisdiction;
- not related to a covered bond or protected deposit; and
- not capable of otherwise being excluded from the requirement.

This effectively covers a very wide range of agreements, including master trading agreements, commitment letters, facility agreements, underwriting agreements, inter-creditor agreements and security agreements.

It should be noted, however, that there are no specific sanctions set within the BRRD for a breach of the contractual recognition of bail-in requirements, leaving this to individual Member State implementations. They may, subject to specific implementations, include pecuniary fines and/or disciplinary sanctions (such as licence withdrawal) – although the contract itself should not be affected.

As a practical matter, the following must be considered:

- In-scope entities need to be able to determine the range of contracts affected by the A55 requirement. Given the very broad types of agreements (see above) that will contain relevant liabilities, they are typically not stored within one agreement system, and some contract types will not be adequately stored (e.g. in filing cabinets and/or email folders only, to facilitate easy retrieval).
- Identifying the relevant agreements, assuming they are in a legal agreement system, relies on being able to query the governing law of a contract, as well as being able to identify the relevant liabilities. The governing law of contracts historically was not stored in detail in legal agreement systems of major financial institutions, on the basis that this had not previously been a regulatory requirement and the lack of a business consumer need for such legal agreement data. This has changed through a number of regulatory requirements, such as recovery and resolution and margin reform. The governing law, however, is such a seemingly crucial aspect of the representation of a contract in a legal agreement data model that this perhaps serves as a reminder that the legal agreement data domain needs to be considered as a whole and with forward flexibility in mind.
- Firms need a process for ensuring that (i) all affected contracts entered into after the implementation of A55 (1 January 2016); and (ii) existing contracts with material amendments after this date (or if the liability is created after this date) have the relevant Article 55 Clause.
- Firms need to update templates, negotiation guidelines and systems to track the Article 55 Clause where relevant, as well as considering whether industry protocols may assist – e.g. the ISDA Article 55 BRRD Protocol (see below) – and/or unilateral notices to clients for practicality reasons, if they might be effective under local law.
- The possible utility of a digitised contract portfolio (i.e. one that is machine searchable – see Chapter 11) to assist with locating agreements requiring amendment for regulatory requirements, such as Article 55, as well as the use of document generation tools.

Initiatives to Assist with Article 55 BRRD Compliance

There are a number of ISDA protocols (see Chapter 3 for details of the operation of protocols) that seek to assist with the documentation challenge firms within scope face in respect of the A55 requirement.

ISDA 2016 Bail-in Article 55 BRRD Protocol (Dutch/French/German/Irish/Italian/Luxembourg/Spanish/UK entity-in-resolution version):

This amends existing ISDA Master Agreements (including any outstanding transactions under them and any related credit support arrangements) and other master framework, netting or set-off agreements between two adhering parties governed by a non-EU member law that are entered into on or prior to the date on which the latter party adheres, except in situations where:

- the parties agree bilaterally that the protocol does not apply;
- there are already written agreements existing between the parties covering the same issues and substance of this protocol;
- the relevant resolution authority determines that the relevant liabilities may be subject to bail-in pursuant to the laws of the third-country governing, such as liabilities or a binding agreement, concluding that such third-country laws – together with the relevant implementation legislation – has been amended to reflect such determination; or
- the relevant implementation legislation has been repealed or amended in such a manner that the requirement for the contractual recognition of bail-in is removed.

The substantive operational text of this protocol cannot be amended, so therefore – where an adhering party wishes to amend it – the parties must revert to bilaterally negotiating and amending their relevant agreements. It should be noted that ISDA carried out due diligence on the amendments made by the protocol on ISDA Master Agreements, but not to the same extent with non-ISDA-sponsored agreements, so adhering parties seeking to use it to amend non-ISDA agreements would ideally carry out their own due diligence on such agreements to ensure compatibility. The national laws covered by the protocol include those in respect of which final implementing rules were available at the time the protocol was drafted, and that were agreed as priority jurisdictions with the ISDA working group.

ISDA 2017 Bail-in Article 55 BRRD Protocol (Austrian/Belgian/Danish/Swedish entity-in-resolution version):

This protocol is very similar to the ISDA 2016 Bail-in Article 55 Protocol, except it covers countries for which the final implementing rules were not available at the time of that protocol, but were subsequently finalised, namely Austria, Belgium, Denmark and Sweden. To the extent that the implementing rules in any other member state jurisdiction(s) require parties to contractually recognise bail-in, then in-scope entities could consider the ISDA 2016 Bail-in Article 55 BRRD Protocol (covering Dutch, French, German, Irish, Italian, Luxembourg, Spanish and UK), or need to comply with the relevant rules in some other way.

Model Clauses:

On 1 August 2016 the Association for Financial Markets in Europe (AFME) published Article 55 BRRD Bail-in model clauses, covering entities organised in the UK, France, Italy, Belgium and Germany, respectively. This is intended for use in debt and equity instruments.

Stay Termination Rights

The exercise of termination rights, including that of OTC derivatives, by counterparties of Lehman Brothers was a key factor in the destabilisation that resulted from its failure. Prior to its bankruptcy, Lehman's global derivatives position was estimated at some $35 trillion in notional value, accounting for some 5% of derivatives transactions globally. The termination of such contracts, when 'in-the-money' to the counterparty, caused essentially a fire sale of financial assets, including that of the collateral related to them – and a significant outflow of liquidity. In contrast, many counterparties, which owed Lehman Brothers money in 'out-of-the-money' contracts, chose not to exercise their termination rights, instead suspending payment and reducing the funds available to the bankruptcy estate.

This resulted in substantial losses on Lehman Brothers' derivatives book and a significant outflow of cash from Lehman Brothers' material operating subsidiaries to counterparties, as subsidiaries attempted to satisfy their obligations under terminated contracts and respond to increased collateral demands under open contracts, impairing the continued viability of the operating subsidiaries.

Subsequently, other counterparties exercised direct default rights against the material operating subsidiaries, including when the subsidiaries commenced their own bankruptcy or similar proceedings.

Global regulators felt that this disorderly exercise of default termination rights under financial contracts undermined the resolution. Accordingly, the regulators sought to address this concern by granting resolution authorities the power to temporarily stay the ability of a counterparty to exercise such default rights (based on the entry into resolution proceedings). Furthermore, if certain creditor protections are satisfied, those default termination rights might be permanently overridden.

A further concern relating to indirect default rights can be shown by way of example. Under an ISDA Master Agreement, the counterparty will, under the standard pre-print termination rights, have the ability to terminate and close out the counterparty if the institution enters into insolvency proceedings (including resolution proceedings). In many cases, the counterparty would also be able to terminate and close out if the insolvency or resolution affected an affiliate or related entity to that being resolved under cross-default provisions (or similar terms). This would undermine the efforts to allow the banking group to continue operations through resolution. When the Lehman Brothers' parent holding company filed for bankruptcy, counterparties exercised their cross-default rights under financial contracts with Lehman's material operating subsidiaries based on the bankruptcy of the Lehman parent, which had acted as guarantor to the subsidiaries (see Figures 10.5 and 10.6).

G-SIB

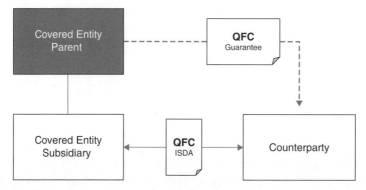

Figure 10.5 The Lehman Brothers failure problem: sudden termination of Lehman's financial contracts arising initially from the counterparties' exercise of cross-defaults based on the bankruptcy of the Lehman parent and subsequently on the counterparties' exercise of direct defaults against Lehman's material operating subsidies when they commenced their own bankruptcy proceedings

US G-SIB

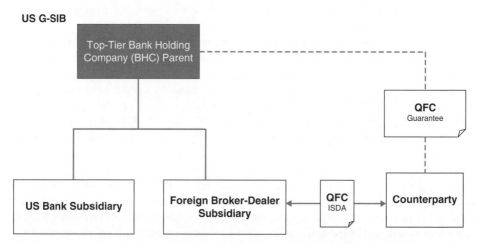

Figure 10.6 An example of a counterparty exercising their cross-default rights under financial contracts against a Bank Holding Company (BHC) under the US Bankruptcy Code with the inclusion of a foreign broker–dealer subsidiary in the insolvency proceedings

A concern also exists with respect to whether such stay powers would be enforced in cross-border cases, where contracts are governed by a law other than that of the special resolution regime. Accordingly, the following protocols were created by ISDA in order to assist, in each case, in consultation with the regulators:

ISDA 2014 Resolution Stay Protocol:
This amends ISDA Master Agreements and related collateral support arrangements between adherents to the protocol. Under section 1 of the substantive protocol text, it clarifies that if an adhering party becomes subject to a resolution, the adhering counterparty can only do so to the extent that this is permitted under the resolution regime, regardless of the governing law of the agreement. Additionally, any transfers of the agreements would be enforceable to the same extent as provided under the resolution regime (again, regardless of the governing law of the agreement).

The US Bankruptcy Code and the FDIA do not provide for a stay on the exercise of cross-default rights. Under the subsequent sections of the protocol, adhering parties agree not to exercise certain cross-default and direct-default rights if an affiliate (including a parent) of their counterparty becomes subject to certain insolvency regimes, including the US Bankruptcy Code and the FDIA.

The adherents to this protocol were limited to sell-side dealers. Buy-side institutions (such as asset managers) felt that they were unable to voluntarily adopt the protocol due to fiduciary responsibilities to their clients. By voluntarily giving up advantageous contractual rights, they could have potentially left themselves open to lawsuits for breach of these fiduciary responsibilities.

ISDA 2015 Universal Resolution Stay Protocol:

The ISDA 2015 Universal Protocol replaced the ISDA 2014 Protocol in its entirety (for those parties that adhere to it) and adherence to the ISDA 2014 Protocol is accordingly closed. The operative provisions of the ISDA 2015 Universal Protocol are nearly identical to the ISDA 2014 Protocol. Substantive additions are that the annex expands the protocol to cover certain securities finance master agreements (such as the GESLA, GMRA, GMSLA, MEFISLA, MRA, MSLA and OSLA).

ISDA Resolution Stay Jurisdictional Modular Protocol:

The ISDA Jurisdictional Modular Protocol is a standalone protocol with its own operative provisions, separate from those of the ISDA 2014 Protocol and the ISDA 2015 Universal Protocol. It is composed of boilerplate provisions and jurisdictional modules with respect to particular stay regulations in particular jurisdictions (each a 'Jurisdictional Module'). Parties may choose to adhere to one or more Jurisdictional Modules to the protocol.

The specific provisions of the ISDA 2015 Universal Protocol (and the ISDA 2014 Protocol on which it was based) differ from the requirements of stay regulations as they were in practice enacted (which occurred after their publication), effectively 'overcomplying', creating issues for the buy-side in particular to adhere to them. The ISDA Resolution Stay Jurisdictional Modular Protocol addresses this issue by amending agreements only to the extent required by stay regulations (which is likely the approach that parties would take were they to choose not to adhere to any of the protocols and instead amend their agreements bilaterally).

ISDA 2018 US Resolution Stay Protocol:

The Board of Governors of the Federal Reserve System adopted final Qualified Financial Contract (QFC) Stay Rules in late 2017. These provide for a phased-in compliance period based on counterparty type for qualified financial contracts (including those documenting derivatives, repos, securities lending and many other types of commonly used financial instruments), to be amended to ensure that each such contract includes contractual terms restricting the counterparty's right (when facing a SIFI) to terminate such contracts in the event such an entity enters into bankruptcy or resolution proceedings.

The phase-in timing detailed in the rule is:

Phase 1. Covered entities will have to conform to covered QFCs with other covered entities by 1 January 2019.

Phase 2. Covered entities will have to conform to covered QFCs with financial counterparties other than small financial institutions as defined in the rules by 1 July 2019.

Phase 3. Covered entities will have to conform to covered QFCs with all other counterparties, including general corporate counterparties, small financial institutions, central banks and sovereign entities, by 1 January 2020.

The rule outlines the requirements of a US specific protocol which may be used to assist with the amendment of agreements to comply with the US QFC Stay Rules. It is this requirement that the ISDA 2018 US Resolution Stay Protocol addresses.

Financial Contract Record-Keeping Requirements

A further part of the recovery and resolution regulatory agenda has been the requirement for financial institutions to maintain certain records and information in respect of key financial contracts. The main regulations in this regard have been the Qualified Financial Contracts (QFC) record-keeping requirements of Dodd–Frank (the QFC Record-Keeping Rule) and Article 71(7) of the BRRD.

The QFC Record-Keeping Rule

The final rule in respect of QFC record-keeping was adopted in October 2016, implementing record-keeping requirements for qualified financial contracts in connection with Title II of the Dodd–Frank Act. This broadly requires in-scope entities to maintain specific information electronically on QFC positions, counterparties, legal agreements and collateral, and be in a position to report this information to regulators within 24 hours of request. The purpose is to assist the FDIC make an informed determination on whether to transfer, disaffirm or terminate QFCs entered into with counterparties upon a distressed scenario and conclude whether any financial systemic risks would be posed by such a decision.

The QFC Record-Keeping Rule applies to certain financial companies organised under US state or federal laws that are party to a QFC. A financial company is defined as any of:

- a bank holding company;
- a non-bank financial company designated as a non-bank SIFI;
- a company that is predominantly engaged in financial activities; or
- a company that is a subsidiary of one of the above and is predominantly engaged in financial activities.

The QFC record-keeping requirements apply only if one of the following conditions are met by the particular entity:

- it has been designated as a non-bank SIFI;
- it has been designated by the Financial Stability Oversight Council (FSOC) as a financial market utility that is systemically important for the financial stability of the USA;
- it has total assets equal to or greater than $50 billion (excluding those that have, on a consolidated basis, total gross notional derivatives outstanding of less than $250 billion and derivative liabilities of less than $3.5 billion); or
- it is a member of a group in which at least one entity meets one of the above conditions.

It should be noted as well that there is an exemption for entities that are party to 50 or fewer open QFC positions (such entities are only required to maintain copies of the documents that govern the QFC transactions).

The definition of 'QFC' comprises five contract types: securities contracts, commodity contracts, forward contracts, repurchase agreements and swap agreements. The file structure for the US QFC record-keeping requirements is organised into an appendix of four tables and reports:

1. Table A-1 (Position-Level Data). This requires each in-scope entity to maintain detailed position-level data to enable the FDIC as receiver to evaluate a records entity's QFC exposure to each of its counterparties on a position-by-position basis. The records required by the table include critical information about the type, terms and value of each of the records entity's QFCs. Position-level information must be available for each counterparty, affiliate and governing netting agreement to allow the FDIC as receiver to model the potential impacts of its decisions relating to the transfer or retention of positions. This information is envisaged to enable the FDIC to confirm that the netting-set-level data provided in Table A-2, such as the market value of all positions in the netting set, based on the aggregated data from Table A-1, is accurate and can be validated across different tables. In addition, position-level information is expected to assist the receiver or any transferee in complying with the terms of the records entity's QFCs and thereby reduce the likelihood of inadvertent defaults.

2. Table A-2 (Counterparty Collateral Data). This requires each in-scope entity to maintain records of the aggregated QFC exposures under each netting agreement between the records entity and its counterparty. It also requires comprehensive information on the collateral exchanged to secure net exposures under each netting agreement. Information on collateral required by the table includes the market value of collateral, any collateral excess or deficiency positions, the identification of the collateral safekeeping agent, a notation as to whether the collateral posted by a counterparty or a records entity is subject to rehypothecation and the market value of any collateral subject to rehypothecation. The information required by Table A-2 must be maintained at each level of netting under the relevant governing agreement. For example, if a master agreement includes an annex for repurchase agreements and an annex for forward exchange transactions and requires separate netting under each annex, then the information required by Table A-2 with respect to the net exposures under each annex would need to be maintained separately. In evaluating whether to transfer or retain QFCs between a records entity and a counterparty, the receiver must be able to assess the records entity's net exposure to the counterparty (and the counterparty's affiliates), the counterparty's net exposure to the records entity and the amount of collateral securing those exposures. Net QFC exposure data is expected to assist the receiver in aggregating exposures under netting agreements with a counterparty and its affiliates based on the netting rights of the entire group, in order to determine relative concentrations of risk under each applicable netting agreement. Additionally, the information enables the modelling of various transfer or termination scenarios and evaluating the effects and potential impact of the FDIC's decision to transfer the covered financial company's QFCs, retain and disaffirm or repudiate them, or retain them and allow the counterparty to terminate them. Information on collateral also ensures that the

FDIC, as receiver, is able to comply with its statutory obligation to transfer all collateral securing the QFC obligations that it elects to transfer. It is also expected to assist the receiver in identifying any excess collateral posted by a counterparty for possible return to the counterparty should the contracts be terminated after the stay period.

3. Table A-3 (Legal Agreements). This is intended to ensure that the FDIC as receiver has available to it the legal agreements governing and setting forth the terms and conditions of each of the QFCs subject to the rules. It requires each legal agreement to be identified by name and unique identifier, and requires the maintenance of records on key legal terms of the agreement, such as relevant governing law, events of default, termination events and specified financial conditions and information about any third-party credit enhancement agreement. It should be noted that in response to comments received on the proposed rules, the final QFC Record-Keeping Rule included several changes to reduce the record-keeping burden, including the requirements to provide any information on transfer restrictions and a substantial reduction in the amount of information required as to default provisions. The draft rule had also included a requirement for the legal agreement data to be maintained for each QFC agreement/master agreement (including credit support and assignment documents) in electronic form, which is readily accessible and in a searchable format for the following documents, however, this was removed from the final rule on the basis of the burden and cost of compliance to firms. This is somewhat of a missed opportunity, as this data is clearly crucial in a resolution scenario, and also forms key terms for day-to-day trading and risk management. As noted elsewhere, these legal agreement terms are crucial to operational management, business optimisation and risk management, and the digitisation of contract portfolios to enable searches for and extraction of key terms is very much required by firms outside their resolution (see Chapter 11)!

4. Table A-4 (Collateral Detail Data). This builds on the details set out in Table A-2. It requires detailed information, on a counterparty-by-counterparty basis, relating to the collateral received by and the collateral posted by the records entity as reported in Table A-2. This information includes, for each collateral item, the unique collateral identifier, information about the value of the collateral, a description of the collateral, the fair value asset classification, the collateral segregation status, the collateral location and jurisdiction, and whether the collateral is subject to rehypothecation. This collateral detail data, together with the netting-set-level collateral data in Table A-2, is intended to enable the receiver to more fully assess the type, nature, value and location of the collateral and to model various QFC transfer or termination scenarios. Collateral detail information enables the receiver to ensure that collateral is transferred together with any QFCs that it secures. For cross-border transactions, the comprehensive information on collateral is intended to assist the receiver in determining the sufficiency and availability of collateral posted outside the USA, as well as any close-out risk if the receiver does not arrange for the transfer of QFC positions.

The data elements in each of these reports must be readily available and in a standardised format, with identifiers used to segment or link the data for certain counterparties, trade confirmations, booking units and between tables. Overall, these records allow the FDIC to better comprehend QFC portfolio risk and systemic or practical implications when evaluating and modelling various QFC transfer or termination scenarios to expeditiously effectuate an orderly resolution.

Article 71(7) BRRD

As part of the implementation of the BRRD, the European Banking Authority (EBA) published final draft Regulatory Technical Standards (RTS) in December 2015 on a minimum set of information on financial contracts that should be contained in the detailed records, including the circumstances in which the requirement should be imposed. Subsequently, this was then detailed as part of delegated regulation (EU) 2016/1712. The purpose of these standards was to achieve a consistent and systemic approach to ensure that resolution authorities are able to promptly attain relevant information on financial contracts directly from relevant institutions to support the application of resolution powers or tools. The RTS does not itself introduce additional reporting obligations, but instead requires institutions to maintain detailed records on a continual basis and make them accessible to the relevant authorities upon request. It should also be noted that it specifies the minimum list of information which should be maintained, however, authorities can impose additional requirements where considered appropriate.

This Article 71(7) requirement to maintain detailed records of financial contracts applies to institutions which are subject to the BRRD, where its resolution plan contemplates that it would be subject to resolution rather than standard insolvency proceedings. The 'financial contracts' covered include: (a) securities contracts; (b) commodities contracts; (c) futures and forwards contracts; (d) swap agreements; (e) inter-bank borrowing agreements where the term of the borrowing is 3 months or less; and (f) master agreements in relation to (a)–(e) above.[4]

The requirement to store this information is based on the need to support the effective and efficient application of resolution powers and resolution tools, particularly the power to temporarily suspend termination rights, by understanding the underlying financial contracts to which they apply.

The Annex to Regulation 2016/1712 (see Figure 10.7) contains a full list of the data points that are required to be maintained, together with an indication of where these would typically be obtained from.

It should be noted that the prior proposal from the EBA contained a requirement that information be kept in a *'central location on a relational database capable of being accessed by the competent and resolution authorities from which information can be extracted readily and transmitted to the relevant authority'*. Such a database would be challenging in light of cross-border privacy, banking secrecy and data protection laws. The EBA accepted the strong negative feedback in respect of this provision and the requirement is now just that the information is collected in advance and made available to the authorities on request within the timescale specified within the request (A2(2)).

There are significant data challenges with the collation of this data for in-scope firms, coupled with the lack of guidance on data format, presenting a challenge of usefulness for the authorities on being presented with the information (e.g. in respect of termination rights).

---

4 Article 2(1)(100), BRRD.

Field	Description of information in detailed records of financial contracts	Type of data
Section 1: Parties to the financial contract		
1 Record-Keeping Timestamp	Date and time of record entry	Record-keeping metadata
2 Type of ID of the Reporting Counterparty	Type of code used to identify the reporting counterparty	Client data
3 Reporting Counterparty ID	Unique code [Legal Entity Identifier (LEI), where available] identifying the reporting counterparty	Client data
4 Type of ID of the Other Counterparty	Type of code used to identify the other counterparty	Client data
5 ID of the Other Counterparty	Unique code (LEI, where available) identifying the other counterparty of the financial contract. This field shall be filled from the perspective of the reporting counterparty. In the case of an individual, a client code shall be used in a consistent manner	Client data
6 Name of the Reporting Counterparty	Corporate name of the reporting counterparty. This field can be left blank where the LEI is used to identify the reporting counterparty	Client data
7 Domicile of the Reporting Counterparty	Information on the registered office, consisting of full address, city and country of the reporting counterparty. This field can be left blank where the LEI is used to identify the reporting counterparty	Client data
8 Country of the Other Counterparty	The code of the country where the registered office of the other counterparty is located or the country of residence in case the other counterparty is a natural person	Client data
9 Governing Law	The law governing the financial contract	Legal agreement data
10 Contractual Recognition – Write-Down and Conversion Powers (only for contracts governed by third-country law subject to the requirement of the contractual term under the first sub-paragraph of Article 55(1) of Directive 2014/59/EU)	The contractual term required under Article 55(1) of the Directive 2014/59/EU. When such a contractual term is included in a master agreement and applies to all trades governed by that master agreement, it can be recorded at the master agreement level	Legal agreement data (including protocol data)

Figure 10.7 Adapted version of the annex to the minimum set of information on financial contracts to be included in the detailed records in Regulation 2016/1712

11	Contractual Recognition – Suspension of Termination Rights (only for contracts governed by third-country law)	The contractual term by which the creditor or party to the agreement creating the liability recognises the power of the resolution authority of a Member State to suspend termination rights. When such a contractual term is included in a master agreement and applies to all trades governed by that master agreement, it can be recorded at the master agreement level	Legal agreement data (including protocol data)
12	Contractual Recognition –Resolution Powers (only for contracts governed by third-country law)	The contractual term, if any, by which the creditor or party to the agreement creating the liability recognises the power of a Member State resolution authority to apply resolution powers other than those identified in fields 10 and 11. When such a contractual term, if any, is included in a master agreement and applies to all trades governed by that master agreement, it can be recorded at the master agreement level	Legal agreement data (including protocol data)
13	Core Business Lines	The core business line(s) the financial contract relates to, if any	Trade data
14	Value of Contract	Mark-to-market valuation of the financial contract, or mark-to-model valuation reported in application of Article 3(5) and 3(6) of the Delegated Regulation on Article 9 of Regulation (EU) No. 648/2012.	Trade data
15	Currency of the Valuation	The currency used for the valuation of the financial contract	Trade data
16	Valuation Timestamp	Date and time of the last valuation. For mark-to-market valuation the date and time of publishing of reference prices shall be reported	Trade data
17	Valuation Type	Whether valuation was performed mark-to-market or mark-to-model or provided by a CCP	Trade data
18	Collateralisation	Whether a collateral agreement between the counterparties exists. Where a financial contract is covered by the reporting requirement under Delegated Regulation on Article 9 of Regulation (EU) No. 648/2012, collateralisation as required by these requirements	Legal agreement data and collateral data

Figure 10.7 *(Continued)*

	Field	Description of information in detailed records of financial contracts	Type of data
19	Collateral Portfolio	Indicates whether the collateralisation was performed on a portfolio basis. Portfolio means the collateral calculated on the basis of net positions resulting from a set of contracts, rather than per trade	Collateral data
20	Collateral Portfolio Code	If collateral is reported on a portfolio basis, the portfolio should be identified by a unique code determined by the reporting counterparty	Collateral data
21	Initial Margin Posted	The value of the initial margin posted by the reporting counterparty to the other counterparty. Where the initial margin is posted on a portfolio basis, this field includes the overall values of the initial margin posted for the portfolio	Collateral data
22	Currency of the Initial Margin Posted	The currency of the initial margin posted	Collateral data
23	Variation Margin Posted	The value of the variation margin posted, including cash settled, by the reporting counterparty to the other counterparty. Where the variation margin is posted on a portfolio basis, this field includes the overall value of the variation margin posted for the portfolio	Collateral data
24	Currency of the Variation Margin Posted	The currency of the variation margin posted	Collateral data
25	Initial Margin Received	The value of the initial margin received by the reporting counterparty from the other counterparty. Where the initial margin is received on a portfolio basis, this field includes the overall value of the initial margin received for the portfolio	Collateral data
26	Currency of the Initial Margin Received	The currency of the initial margin received	Collateral data
27	Variation Margin Received	The value of the variation margin received, including cash settled, by the reporting counterparty from the other counterparty. Where the variation margin is received on a portfolio basis, this field includes the overall value of the variation margin received for the portfolio	Collateral data

Figure 10.7 *(Continued)*

28	Currency of the Variation Margin Received	The currency of the variation margin received	Collateral data

Section 2a: Financial contract type

29	Type of Financial Contract	Classification of the financial contract according to Article 2(100) of Directive 2014/59/EU	Legal agreement data
30	Financial Contract ID	Unique trade ID where the financial contract is covered by the reporting requirements under [Delegated Regulation on Article 9 of Regulation (EU) No. 648/2012]. For any other financial contract, ID assigned by the reporting counterparty	Trade data

Section 2b: Details on the transaction

31	Effective Date	Date when obligations under the financial contract come into effect	Trade data
32	Maturity Date	Original date of expiry of the reported financial contract. An early termination shall not be recorded in this field	Trade data
33	Termination Date	Termination date in the case of an early termination of the reported financial contract (blank if not different from the maturity date)	Trade data
34	Termination Rights	Whether the counterparty's termination rights under the reported financial contract are based on the insolvency or financial condition of the institution under resolution. When such a contractual term is included in a master agreement and applies to all trades governed by that master agreement, it can be recorded at the master agreement level	Legal agreement data
35	Master Agreement Type	Reference to the name of the relevant master agreement, if used for the reported financial contract (e.g. ISDA Master Agreement, Master Power Purchase and Sale Agreement, International ForEx Master Agreement, European Master Agreement, or any local master agreements)	Legal agreement data

Figure 10.7 *(Continued)*

	Field	Description of information in detailed records of financial contracts	Type of data
36	Master Agreement Version	Reference to the year of the master agreement version used for the reported trade, if applicable (e.g. 1992, 2002, etc.)	Legal agreement data
37	Netting Agreement	If the financial contract is part of a netting arrangement as defined in Article 2(1)(98) of Directive 2014/59/EU, a unique reference for the netting arrangement	Legal agreement data
38	Type of Liability/Claim	Indicates whether liabilities arising from the financial contract are: • entirely excluded from bail-in pursuant to Article 44(2) of Directive 2014/59/EU; • partially excluded from bail-in pursuant to Article 44(2) of Directive 2014/59/EU; • not excluded from bail-in pursuant to Article 44(2) of Directive 2014/59/EU	Regulatory and legal agreement data
Section 2c: Clearing			
39	Clearing Obligation	Indicates whether the reported financial contract belongs to a class of OTC derivatives that have been declared subject to the clearing obligation and both counterparties to the contract are subject to the clearing obligation under Regulation (EU) No. 648/2012, as of the time of execution of the financial contract	Trade data
40	Cleared	Indicates whether clearing has taken place	Trade data
41	Clearing Timestamp	Time and date when clearing took place	Trade data
42	CCP	In the case of a financial contract that has been cleared, the unique code for the CCP that has cleared the financial contract	Trade data
43	Intragroup	Indicates whether the financial contract was entered into as an intragroup transaction, defined in Article 3 of Regulation (EU) No. 648/2012.	Trade data

Figure 10.7 *(Continued)*

Bibliography

Alloway, T. (2013) 'Lehman "zombie company" nears its end', *The Financial Times*, 12th September 2013

Beaton, M. (2012) 'Educational insights: An introduction to recovery and resolution planning in the UK', *DerivSource*, 18th June 2012

Cadwalader, Wickersham & Taft LLP (2011) 'Living wills: A user's guide to Dodd–Frank's bequests to banks', *Client & Friends Memo*, 13th June 2011

European Banking Authority (2015) 'EBA FINAL Draft Regulatory Technical Standards on criteria for determining the minimum requirement for own funds and eligible liabilities under Directive 2013/59/EU', 3rd July 2015

FDIC (2017) 'Single Resolution Board and Federal Deposit Insurance Corporation sign cooperation agreement', FDIC Press Release, 14th December 2017

Federal Register (2011) 'Resolution Plans Required', 76 FR 67323

Federal Register (2018) 'Qualified Financial Contracts Record Keeping Related to Orderly Liquidation Authority', 83 FR 17619

Financial Sector Advisory Centre (2017) 'Understanding bank recovery and resolution in the EU: A guide to the BRRD', World Bank Group, April 2017

Financial Stability Board (2010) 'Overview of progress in the implementation of the G20 recommendations for strengthening financial stability: Report of the Financial Stability Board to G20 leaders', 18th March 2010

Financial Stability Board (2011) 'Key attributes of effective resolution regimes for financial institutions', October 2011

Fleming, M. and Sarkar, A. (2014) 'The failure resolution of Lehman Brothers', *FRBNY Economic Policy Review*, 20 pp. 175–206

Gilani, S. (2011) '"Living wills" for banks won't kill systemic risk or greed', *Forbes*, 27th June 2011

ISDA (2016) 'ISDA Bail-in Art 55 BRRD Protocol (Dutch/French/German/Irish/Italian/Luxembourg/Spanish/UK entity-in-resolution version)', 14th July 2016

ISDA (2016) 'ISDA Resolution Stay Jurisdictional Modular Protocol', 3rd May 2016

Lastra, R. and Wood, G. (2010) 'The crisis of 2007–09: Nature, causes and reactions', *Journal of International Economic Law*, 13, pp. 531, 539

Legal Information Institute, 'Dodd–Frank: Title II – Orderly Liquidation Authority', Cornell Law School

'Resolving globally active, systemically important financial institutions: A joint paper by the Federal Deposit Insurance Corporation and the Bank of England', 10th December 2012

Schilling, M. (2015) *Resolution and Insolvency of Banks and Financial Institutions*. Oxford University Press: Oxford

Scott, H. (2012) 'Interconnectedness and contagion', *Committee on Capital Markets Regulation*, 20th November 2012

SIPC (2008) 'Case information – Lehman Brother Inc.', *Securities Investor Protection Corporation*, 19th September 2008

Summe, K. (2012) 'An examination of Lehman Brothers' derivatives portfolio post bankruptcy: Would Dodd Frank have made a difference?', in K. Scott and J. Taylor (eds), *Bankruptcy Not Bailout: A Special Chapter* 14. Hoover Institution Press: Stanford, CA

Thomson Reuters (2010) 'Lehman creditors file competing reorganization plan', *Thomson Reuters*, 15th December 2010

11

Document Generation/Data-Driven Contracts

This chapter moves away from the various financial regulations that we have discussed in the past few chapters and considers contract management, which seeks to document financial instruments and trading whilst meeting business objectives and complying with financial regulation. The benefits of legal technology being used with regards to the creation, negotiation and monitoring of financial contracts are also debated, followed by a consideration of whether legal agreement data should in fact be considered earlier in this contract lifecycle management process (rather than the typical creation of most contract metadata as a post-execution process). This, of course, leads to the question of whether contracts should be 'data-driven' in their creation, rather than the legal agreement data only being truly focused on once the agreement exists as unstructured data, in the form of characters in a hardcopy executed document (or scan of this).

Contract Lifecycle Management

We have seen the importance of legal agreement data throughout the course of this text. Financial firms are increasingly looking to address this through the use of contract lifecycle management solutions (Figure 11.1), assisting with the initial request for an agreement to be put in place, the drafting of the initial contract, its negotiation (including stakeholder approvals and tracking of changes during this process), execution, tracking and reporting of contract status, management of contractual obligations, amendments and, where it arises, dispute management. Such solutions have spanned various industry verticals and their multiple document types, such as procurement, sales, confidentiality, employment, insurance, banking and trading agreements.

The merits of a contract lifecycle management solution go beyond that of legal agreement data management, however, the potential advantages from a data perspective are significant. In particular, financial firms face a lethal portfolio of legacy contracts, often struggling to convert the words and legalese (essentially unstructured data) into understandable data, in order to make the optimal business decisions based on the contractual agreements and key commercial and operational variables contained therein, as well as to manage risks and tracking of contractual terms required for regulatory and compliance purposes. The contracts in the capital markets space are incredibly complex, however, they contain a wealth of important information to financial firms, that have not historically been tracked. As the scale of the business has grown, this

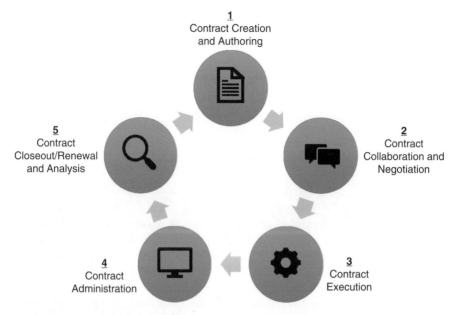

Figure 11.1 The lifecycle of a contract

neglect of the legal agreement terms has become unsustainable, prompting a need to revisit the hardcopy documents (or their scans), and an attempt to convert these into the structured, from which the required business intelligence can be derived.

This conversion process from unstructured data – the raw contract text – to structured data can be extremely difficult and costly, especially for complex contract types (the process of digitisation, through optical character recognition and legacy legal agreement data capture, will be detailed later in this chapter). This is also a reflection in the current limitations of natural language processing. Most successful natural language processing techniques are based on statistical approaches. They have been used in some areas, such as electronic discovery for litigation purposes, with some success – however, they have been found wanting for the task of understanding the meaning of natural language-based contracts. Tasks such as the identification of names that are seemingly trivial for human reviewers, pose significant difficulties for computer algorithms.

It is therefore no surprise that many seek to remove this need to convert unstructured data into structured data, and rather provide that the agreements are themselves drafted on the basis of structured data – and perhaps even negotiated with counterparties based on that structured data.

Lifecycle of a Contract and Associated Processes

In order to understand the benefits of a contract management solution from a legal agreement data management perspective, we must first understand the current processes involved in the lifecycle of an agreement (Figure 11.1), which we detail at a high and generic level in respect of master trading documentation, such as the ISDA Master Agreement.

1. **Matter initiation.** A request for documentation to 'onboard' a new client is generated by the front office containing basic commercial terms. This is sent to the credit department, who provide the basic credit terms appropriate to the commercial request, which is then forwarded through to the legal department to produce a first draft of the documentation. There may be iterations of this process to deal with queries from any of the parties in the process.

2. **Document generation.** The legal department create a first draft of the contract based on standard approved templates (typically non-transaction specific, but with different templates based on the products being traded, the counterparty type and jurisdiction) and various transaction precedents. In the event the counterparty is producing the first draft of the documentation, this step is skipped, although it is common to compare any counterparty-provided initial draft against the form of an equivalent internal template. Any non-standard wording typically requires approval from the appropriate departments such non-standard wording might affect (e.g. legal, credit, front office, collateral management, etc.). Approvals or rejections are stored and kept for audit trail purposes.

Knowledge management of legal documentation 'know-how' facilitates the document generation process. This relies on the filing of standard templates, transaction precedents, clause libraries and other 'know-how' documents (internal emails, law firm bulletins, etc.).

3. **Document negotiation/finalisation.** The parties negotiate the document into an agreed form, typically through emails as the primary mode of communication. These communications are usually stored under a client/transaction-specific file, as well as any revised drafts of the documentation. Historically, this would have been through hardcopy documents and files, which transitioned into email inboxes and content management systems. Certain counterparty amendments/comments require internal approval before being 'acceptable' to be treated as 'agreed' with the counterparty. Approvals or rejections of proposed wording are typically carefully stored to be auditable in the future.

The status of negotiations hence goes back and forth through the following steps:

- Awaiting initial credit terms.
- Nth draft with legal/documentation teams.
- Nth draft with counterparty.
- Awaiting internal approvals.

It should be noted that during the above back and forth of the negotiations between documentation and legal teams, the business imperative to put the documents in place (e.g. for a particular trade that had been urgent) may change, possibly resulting in the suspension or cancellation of the document negotiation.

Various stakeholders will want updates on the status of the documentation being put in place, for example, the front office to be able to commence trading under the documentation, or in order to meet a regulatory deadline for certain provisions to be inserted into the documentation (e.g. the margin reform for uncleared derivatives requirements discussed in Chapter 7).

It can be helpful to consider the storage of key data terms with respect to each document version (to enable searching of the negotiation history for the purposes of current negotiations as well as for comparison/precedent purposes with respect to future negotiations – these might be with a different counterparty).

4. **Document execution.** Finally, once the documentation is in an agreed form, the parties will move to execution of the documents. This can be done with the relevant approved signatories of the parties signing in person, or by counterpart with a subsequent exchange of the counterparts of the document (as we will see in Chapter 13, the document execution phase can be streamlined through the use of e-signature software). In either event, care must be taken regarding the formalities of execution and ensuring signatories are authorised and able to bind the contractual parties to the agreement terms.

5. **Post-documentation processes.** The post-documentation process deals with the storage of the executed versions of the documents, typically considering both image-based documents and physical copies, and the maintenance of any legal agreement data required for business, regulatory and operational purposes.

Subsequently, there may be a need for notification of document stakeholders regarding the execution of documentation, allowing them to start the post-documentation processes (e.g. to trade!). There may also be a requirement for certain key terms to be provided to such stakeholders (ideally through the medium of structured legal agreement data that has been captured either during the preceding steps, or as a post-execution step – e.g. whether close-out netting applies to trades governed by the agreement or whether there is a right for any collateral provided by the counterparty to be rehypothecated).

Amendments

Amendments can be considered through the same steps as above, except that the existing contractual obligations are being amended. Amendments will have a 'matter initiation' step whereby the amendment is raised for a particular reason (e.g. a change in commercial terms or a regulatory requirement).

ECM Solutions Overview

'Enterprise Contract Management' (ECM) is a term used to refer to the end-to-end lifecycle of contract management, from initiation and creation, negotiation (including internal approval processes), execution (see Chapter 13 for more on the execution of contracts through e-signature software), administration, amendments, termination and analytics – with the goal of minimising costs, management of legal and operational risks, optimising business decisions – as well as compliance with policies, procedures and regulations.

Over the last 20 years there has been a huge increase in the development and use of technology solutions, known as ECM solutions, in order to address the challenges in this contract lifecycle, in particular:

- Contract template management.
- Contractual clause libraries.
- The ability to create draft contracts based on a user's responses to questions (or input from other systems).

- Collaboration tools (allowing approvals for commercial positions/wording and negotiation of commercial terms).
- Document management (including control and access to workflow, change management, audit trails and versioning).
- Electronic signature software to provide the bridge between a traditional paper contract to a more data-orientated contract that can be executed without the need for a 'wet-ink' signature (see Chapter 13).
- Resource management (planning and scheduling various tasks in the contract lifecycle).
- Integration with other systems (e.g. client and trading/sales data systems).
- Contract data management (both metadata of the document and information about the subject matter of the contract) and analytics.

There are a number of established vendors, such as Apttus, Contract Express, Determine Inc., Exari, Hotdocs, SAP (Ariba)[1] and Smart Communications in this area. Likewise, in the e-signature vendor environment, the more established vendors in the markets are DocuSign and Adobe Sign.

We now discuss the concept of data-orientated contracts, in order to understand the potential evolution to a strategic state where the document is driven by structured commercial and operational data, rather than this data being created only as part of the post-execution process for those impacted by the terms of the contracts (at which point its terms cannot easily be altered, despite any potential impact of those terms).

Data-Orientated Contracts

By data-orientated contracts, we mean a representation of the contractual terms in a manner that follows a consistent and predictable format and is defined to have particular meaning in the natural language. The expression used in this structured data format is necessarily constrained, in contrast to natural language (in fact, it would minimise the ability to vary the structured data representation for a particular 'meaning'). This rigid defined structure allows it to be 'machine-readable', whilst maintaining a link between the structured data and the intended human meaning.

XML and FpML®

XML (see Chapter 4) offers the ability – given its extensible and flexible nature – to turn narrative contract text into structured data in a modular form defined by XML standards and schemas. FpML® (Financial products Markup Language) is a good example of this (see Figure 11.2), as an open-source XML standard for electronic dealing and processing of OTC derivatives. It establishes an industry protocol for sharing information on, and dealing in, financial derivatives and structured products.

(Continued)

---

1 Who are now in partnership with IBM.

(Continued)

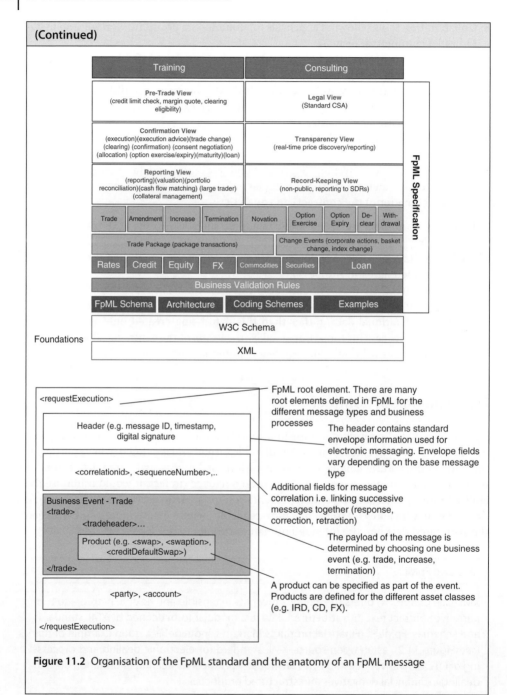

Figure 11.2 Organisation of the FpML standard and the anatomy of an FpML message

Example FpML:

```
1   <?xml version="1.0" encoding="utf-8"?>
2   <!--View is confirmation-->
3   <!--Version is 5-4-->
4   <!--NS is http://www.fpml.org/FpML-5/confirmation-->
5   <!--
6           == Copyright (c) 2002-2012 All rights reserved.
7           == Financial Products Markup Language is subject to the FpML public license.
8           == A copy of this license is available at http://www.fpml.org/license/license.html
9   -->
10  <!--With forward starting, the deal needs to be updated on/after the strike date to add (Initial Price) and replace with (Equity Notional)
11  <!--5.0:Message type is a Root of the message-->
12  <!--5.0 Messaging: changed <requestTradeConfirmation> -><requestConfirmation>-->
13  <requestConfirmation xmlns="http://www.fpml.org/FpML-5/confirmation" xmlns:xsi="http://www.w3.org/2001/XMLSchema-instance" fpmlVersion="5-4
14    <header>
15      <messageId messageIdScheme="http://www.partyA.com/coding-scheme/messageId">FX098765</messageId>
16      <sentBy messageAddressScheme="http://www.partyA.com/partyId">DEUTDEFF</sentBy>
17      <sendTo messageAddressScheme="http://www.partyA.com/partyId">PARTYAUS33</sendTo>
18      <creationTimestamp>2007-01-05T15:38:00-05:00</creationTimestamp>
19    </header>
20    <isCorrection>false</isCorrection>
21    <correlationId correlationIdScheme="http://www.partyA.com/coding-scheme/correlationId">FX12345</correlationId>
22    <sequenceNumber>1</sequenceNumber>
23    <trade>
24      <tradeHeader>
25        <partyTradeIdentifier id="nearLegId">
26          <issuer issuerIdScheme="http://www.fpml.org/coding-scheme/external/cftc/issuer-identifier">1031234567</issuer>
27          <tradeId tradeIdScheme="http://www.fpml.org/coding-scheme/external/unique-transaction-identifier">71234567890123456789012
28        </partyTradeIdentifier>
29        <partyTradeIdentifier id="farLegId">
30          <issuer issuerIdScheme="http://www.fpml.org/coding-scheme/external/cftc/issuer-identifier">1031234567</issuer>
31          <tradeId tradeIdScheme="http://www.fpml.org/coding-scheme/external/unique-transaction-identifier">71234567890123456789013
32        </partyTradeIdentifier>
33        <partyTradeIdentifier>
34          <partyReference href="party1" />
35          <tradeId tradeIdScheme="http://www.partyA.com/swaps/trade-id">PARTYAUS33</tradeId>
36        </partyTradeIdentifier>
37        <partyTradeIdentifier>
38          <partyReference href="party2" />
39          <tradeId tradeIdScheme="http://www.db.com/swaps/trade-id">DEUTDEFF</tradeId>
40        </partyTradeIdentifier>
41        <tradeDate>2002-01-23</tradeDate>
42      </tradeHeader>
43      <fxSwap>
44        <productType>FxSwap</productType>
45        <nearLeg>
46          <tradeIdentifierReference href="nearLegId" />
47          <exchangedCurrency1>
48            <payerPartyReference href="party2" />
49            <receiverPartyReference href="party1" />
50            <paymentAmount>
51              <currency>GBP</currency>
52              <amount>10000000</amount>
53            </paymentAmount>
54          </exchangedCurrency1>
55          <exchangedCurrency2>
56            <payerPartyReference href="party1" />
57            <receiverPartyReference href="party2" />
58            <paymentAmount>
59              <currency>USD</currency>
60              <amount>14800000</amount>
61            </paymentAmount>
62          </exchangedCurrency2>
63          <valueDate>2002-01-25</valueDate>
64          <exchangeRate>
65            <quotedCurrencyPair>
66              <currency1>GBP</currency1>
67              <currency2>USD</currency2>
68              <quoteBasis>Currency2PerCurrency1</quoteBasis>
69            </quotedCurrencyPair>
70            <rate>1.48</rate>
```

(Continued)

(Continued)

```
71              </exchangeRate>
72          </nearLeg>
73          <farLeg>
74            <tradeIdentifierReference href="farLegId" />
75            <exchangedCurrency1>
76              <payerPartyReference href="party1" />
77              <receiverPartyReference href="party2" />
78              <paymentAmount>
79                <currency>GBP</currency>
80                <amount>10000000</amount>
81              </paymentAmount>
82            </exchangedCurrency1>
83            <exchangedCurrency2>
84              <payerPartyReference href="party2" />
85              <receiverPartyReference href="party1" />
86              <paymentAmount>
87                <currency>USD</currency>
88                <amount>15000000</amount>
89              </paymentAmount>
90            </exchangedCurrency2>
91            <valueDate>2002-02-25</valueDate>
92            <exchangeRate>
93              <quotedCurrencyPair>
94                <currency1>GBP</currency1>
95                <currency2>USD</currency2>
96                <quoteBasis>Currency2PerCurrency1</quoteBasis>
97              </quotedCurrencyPair>
98              <rate>1.5</rate>
99            </exchangeRate>
100         </farLeg>
101       </fxSwap>
102     </trade>
103     <party id="party1">
104       <partyId>PARTYAUS33</partyId>
105     </party>
106     <party id="party2">
107       <partyId>DEUTDEFF</partyId>
108     </party>
109   </requestConfirmation>
110
```

The traditional contracting process uses descriptive language and a common understanding of the contractual language, the rules of contractual interpretation, contract law (and other relevant areas of law) and regulation in order to document within the contract (which will typically, but not necessarily, be in written form). Often the contract will create 'defined terms'/'definitions', which are used to make interpretations of a contract easier, the contracts themselves more precise and concise – and reduce risks of ambiguity if used properly. In a similar manner, to move from an unstructured to a structured data-orientated contract, meaning must be ascribed to the structured data variables and allowable values of those variables. The ascribing of such meaning, however, may only need to be done by one of the parties to the contract (although this may involve multiple internal stakeholders with multiple objectives and needs from the contract data), if the data form is only to be used by one side of the contract for its own purposes. Where both the contractual parties intend to be bound in some manner by the structured data representation, it will be necessary for the definitions of the structured data representation to be mutually agreed (however, this moves the discussion into areas of 'computable contracts' and 'smart contracts' – see Chapter 12).

It can often be quite difficult to upfront agree (even where this is an internal single contracting party exercise) on the structured data representations and meaning. Accordingly, this is often best done by the analysis of a number of actual natural language contracts in order to determine the relevant variables and possible allowable values for such variables. This assists with the process of defining the meaning of the data by access to real commercial examples and business outcomes from the language, as well as the development of processes for handling exceptions (and a means of identifying them within the data representation). In many cases, it may be possible to shortcut such steps through the use of existing data standards, which – through their development – have effectively gone through such a process. An example of this are the various ISDA credit derivative definitions and their incorporation into the FpML standard. This is an efficient manner in which to provide meaning to structured data, with the added benefit of broader acceptance and operability.

Further Consideration of the Benefits of Data-Orientated Contracts

Data-orientated contracts can have a large number of analytical processes applied to them, unlocking a number of different business benefits. For example, one would be able to detect conflicts between opposing contractual obligations within a contract portfolio and make business decisions as to how to deal with them. Risks can be better monitored, such as rating downgrade provisions in contracts, which can have a significant impact on future liquidity (see Chapter 9). In this case, one can even combine the contractual data with market data, such as actual party credit ratings, in order to put business perspective to the commercial terms and their business impact.

One concern often raised centres around drafting, which is generic in form, rather than referring to things specifically – for example the use of terms 'acting reasonably' or 'in good faith'. This is often intentional to facilitate flexibility and discretion when assessing future conformance to the terms, or to allow the contract terms to evolve with the future development of the business (which is not completely understood or known at the time of entering into the contract). This does not become an issue unless the measurement of contractual performance, and possibly a resultant outcome, is sought to be automated. In some cases, assumptions can also be made to overcome this. For example, within the Deutsche Rahmenvertrag, it is market practice to insert a material reason termination clause, rather than a specific rating downgrade clause. Some firms assume in their models to assess contractual compliance and impact that this is equivalent to a downgrade of credit rating, by three notches.

A similar concern exists around legal uncertainty. In some cases, public policy, for example, may dictate a particular outcome in respect of contractual wording, which is perhaps outside the expectations of one (or all in some cases) of the contracting parties. That said, data-orientated contracts would facilitate the identification of contracts, and clauses within them, that are under risk of a new interpretation through a search of such terms.

It is difficult to demarcate precisely between the process of reaching agreement (the object of negotiation tools) and the design of the document wording (the object of drafting tools). Though the document records the agreement between the parties, it is often the case that what is being negotiated *is* the document itself, for example, in terms of the text that leads to the business outcomes as agreed between the parties.

There are many ways in which the same business outcome can be drafted for. For example, in the ISDA Master Agreement context, one might state:

(Variant 1) The 'Cross Default' provisions of Section 5(a)(vi) will apply to Party A and will apply to Party B

This could also be drafted in the following ways, which only really differ in terms of style rather than substantive difference:

(Variant 2) The 'Cross Default' provisions of Section 5(a)(vi) will apply to Party A and Party B
(Variant 3) The 'Cross Default' provisions of Section 5(a)(vi) will apply to both parties
(Variant 4) Section 5(a)(vi) will apply to both parties

It should be said that, in an increasingly data-driven world, with automated rather than manual processes, it is envisaged that, over time, the data representation of those business outcomes is key. This business-outcomes data representation should really drive the creation of the document recording the agreement of the parties.

Contract Negotiation Platforms

Contractual parties could use a contract negotiation platform in order to agree the commercial variables and seamlessly convert between the natural language contract and a structured data form. It can assist with the contracting process and provide a workflow for it. The platform is typically used to impose a number of constraints on the manner in which the contract information is entered. This has the advantage of capturing key commercial terms as structured data at the outset, rather than requiring the subsequent conversion to structured data. It does, however, require agreement between the contracting parties to the various constraints imposed on the drafting (although the aim is primarily to limit the legal expression rather than the commercial or practically required operational terms). In many cases, this is best facilitated by a trusted third party, such as an industry body or trade association.

The platform can present a user interface whereby there are a series of labelled entry boxes in which the contracting parties enter commercial and operational details. The constrained conduit of the contracting platform reduces uncertainty in communication and negotiation of the commercial and operational terms, ensures consistent formatting and style of structured data (e.g. date form of dd/mm/yyyy vs mm/dd/yyyy) and can also then generate a full-blown natural language representation of the agreed terms based on a series of predefined rules. Once the commercial and operational terms are agreed, the platform may include integrated e-signature software, which can facilitate the final step in the contract negotiation lifecycle.

Standard form contracts are particularly amenable to such development. Agreements such as the ISDA Master Agreement and its related collateral annexes (the various Credit Support Annexes and Credit Support Deeds) (see Chapter 7) are particularly suited, since not only do they create a standard agreement for parties to then tailor and negotiate with counterparties, they also break the agreement into a pre-printed form which is not intended to be negotiated, rather extracting out variables to be negotiated into a separate Schedule (in the case of the Master Agreement) or paragraph 11 or 13 (in the case of the related collateral annexes). This is also the case, for example, with the GMRA and GMSLA, published by the International Capital Markets Association and International Securities Lending Association, respectively. These agreement types certainly provide an excellent foundation for data-orientated contracting, however, the true goal of a negotiation platform and industry-wide data representation of the contractual terms has remained for the most part, certainly at the time of writing, an elusive goal.

Standardising Contracts for Document Assembly/Generation Purposes

Contracts are drafted at two levels: (1) the document level – the structure of the document sections and annexes, and location/interrelation of the provisions within it; (2) the clause level – at a more micro-level, considering individual paragraphs and sections of text (whilst maintaining consistency and completeness within the broader structure). The former tends to be more stylistic, but from a document assembly/generation perspective, very helpful if there is clear demarcation of where the different contractual provisions would logically be located within the document. Where there are clauses that could straddle multiple areas and locations, this can often be the cause of issues with the data perspective of the meaning of the contract.

Once the document-level structure is organised, the clause blocks are then used to construct the document in a similar manner to which a graphics designer would use basic geometric shapes to construct a picture, with the clauses forming the geometric shapes. Individual clause drafting can be handled through the use of a clause library to manage the different possibilities and fallbacks during a negotiation, and each variant can be assigned its correct 'data representation'. Many document assembly/generation systems allow any specific changes made to the clauses in the clause library to be stored for future use. It is often also possible to assign certain approvals, which can be initiated through a workflow, for certain variants or non-standard language. Given that the approvers are often concerned about the impact of particular language on them, either from an operational or business perspective – which is increasingly a data-driven analytical question – the data representation of the clause can be used to assist with this approval question.

Law firms have been using document automation tools to create drafts of documents for some time, with Allen & Overy using NewChange for loan documentation and Bryan Cave Leighton Paisner using Thompson Reuters' ContractExpress to offer its construction clients the ability to produce their own documents. Also, at the time of writing, 'ISDA Create – IM' is being jointly developed by ISDA and Linklaters, as a collaborative documentation platform to allow firms, in anticipation of the high volume of initial margin documentation in phases 4 and 5 of the margin reform regulation, to automate the creation and delivery of this documentation, and negotiate and execute with multiple counterparties simultaneously.

Legal Agreement Data Extraction

Although there is a growing realisation of the importance of legal agreement data capture as part of the process of putting legal agreement documentation in place, the reality is that in terms of important legacy contracts, this data has not been captured, or to the extent it has, there are significant issues over the accuracy and/or quality of the data. This has led to 'information retrieval' and 'data extraction' exercises from such legacy contract portfolios, although in many cases initially driven by regulatory demand (e.g. a review of rating downgrade clauses as part of bank stress testing), rather than the creation of a strategic infrastructure to support such exercises. One of the issues with this has been the tactical legal agreement data models used to store the data from such exercises, typically with insufficient design and thought given to data governance – in particular, the intended usage of the data and its definition. Where the data is obtained through large manual document review exercises, the data captured, without tight definition of the data attributes in the data model, has been subjectively (and individually), rather than objectively, captured – often by large teams of paralegals, disconnected from an understanding of the end usage of the data they are capturing. Attempts to rectify this have subsequently led to the exploration of the use of natural language processing, artificial intelligence and machine learning tools, in some cases originating from e-discovery use cases, to try and automate the extraction of such data from legacy contracts, rather than seeing this as a purely manual paralegal exercise.

With greater exploration into the use of technology-assisted data extraction tools, the data governance principles explored in Chapter 4 become even more important in eliminating the subjectivity obtained in manual document extraction. When given tight definitions of the data attributes in the data model from the early phases of such exercises, the software becomes a powerful way to unlock the business value from legal agreement portfolios. Not only can it overcome issues of human error by capturing the data in an efficient and accurate way, it can also achieve the process with a unified and consistent approach. For example, under manual extraction during first review of a large volume of documents, there is a strong possibility that with a number of reviewers, although they may have been accurate, they may present the data in slightly different (individualistic and subjective!) manners. Subsequently, this makes it more difficult for the data to be used meaningfully, as there will be variance in the way the data is presented, especially if – as is increasingly the case – it is to be consumed by a downstream system as part of a tightly defined business process. However, using data extraction software can assist greatly in a first review, as using a rule-based approach in the algorithm means that there will be a consistency to the way in which the data is captured, which can be used as a 'discovery exercise' to aid the parameters and data governance of any subsequent manual review.

As an aside, in the data extraction process in respect of legacy contract portfolios, there can be multiple versions of the agreement. This can cause problems in ascertaining which version of the document is the final version. However, through the use of e-signature software (see Chapter 13), contracts can be executed and stored in a single repository. This will be discussed in more depth later.

What is e-Discovery?

Disclosure is a step within a dispute resolution process where parties are required to make evidence available in relation to the parties' cases (note that it may support or undermine the disclosing party's case). The aim of this process is to enable the court, in the case of litigation, to ensure justice is done by having visibility of the relevant facts in the dispute in order to reach the correct decision.

The exponential growth in the volume of electronic documents created by systems (such as emails and other electronic artefacts) has exacerbated the problem of 'abusive discovery', with tales of increasing volume of electronic documents for discovery 'equivalent to a stack of paper 137 miles high' (see in *re Intel Corp. Microprocessor Antitrust Litigation*). It is against this backdrop that technology, in particular 'e-discovery', has been utilised to assist this disclosure process, given that there are otherwise just 'too many documents to review'. The objective of review in e-discovery is to identify as many relevant documents as possible, while reviewing as few non-relevant documents as possible (see *Da Silva Moore v Publicis Groupe*). e-Discovery software has moved far beyond keyword searches, which are inherently biased towards under- or overdisclosure. Two key metrics are typically considered: firstly, the recall level (the proportion of relevant documents identified during a review) and secondly, the precision level (which is the proportion of relevant documents within the reviewed set). Increasingly, predictive coding is used, which typically involves a lawyer initially training an algorithm on a 'seed set' (a collection of pre-categorised documents that is used as the initial training for a predictive coding system) of documents, which the algorithm analyses to identify trends and patterns through data and natural language analytics. The algorithms learn from the lawyer's decision-making and thereafter seek to identify similar documents and rank them by their likelihood of relevance. This can be done as an iterative process, until the algorithm has reached a desired level of proficiency in identifying relevant agreements. Leading e-discovery vendors at the time of writing include EMC Kazeon, HP Autonomy, Kroll, OpenText (formerly Recommind), Relativity (formerly kCura) and Ringtail.

As we have seen above, data extraction tools, when given well-defined data governance parameters, can be incredibly useful for obtaining important legal agreement data. However, legal agreement data contained in contracts may not always be in a machine-readable format, meaning that data cannot be extracted easily by the use of software. This leads us to discuss the use of optical character recognition (OCR) techniques as a way to overcome the issue, making sure that documents are machine-readable.

Optical Character Recognition

OCR is the electronic conversion of an image-based text (either typed or handwritten) into machine-encoded text – this might be from the image scan of a document or a photo of a document. It transforms analogue text representations into digitally recognisable characters (like ASCII text). Different OCR products use different methodologies to do this, and typically, in order to achieve high success rates, will rely on a number of pre- and post-processing techniques outside the core OCR process.

There are two core OCR approaches:

1) **Matrix (or pattern) matching**, which depends on precise matching to a store of character templates. When presented with an image version of a character, it attempts to identify with equivalent text-based characters within its library that it best matches within a certain degree of likeness.
2) **Feature extraction**, which searches for common elements like open spaces, closed forms, lines/diagonals intersecting and so on instead of depending on precise matching to set templates. By way of example, consider the letter A – if the algorithm sees two angled lines that meet at the top, and both lines are joined together by a horizontal line in the middle, that would be recognised as a letter A, regardless of the font in which it is written (provided that a high-level rule is true for that font) (see Figure 11.3).

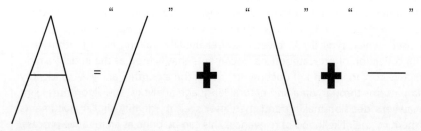

Figure 11.3 Feature extraction on the letter 'A', which can be thought of as the summation of two angled lines and a horizontal line

Pre-Processing to Improve Text Recognition

In order to recognise text effectively, the algorithm usually pre-processes the image using techniques (Figure 11.4) such as:

- **De-skew.** It is quite common for a skew to be introduced in particular during the scanning process of a physical document. Tilting the image as a pre-processing step by a few degrees in order to make the lines of text perfectly horizontal or vertical can greatly assist the effectiveness of the core OCR algorithm.
- **De-speckle.** Removing spots and smoothing the edges of the characters.
- **Character segmentation.** Splits touching characters that may have 'bled into each other'. This can be problematic, for example, in the case of a reference to a section in a document, section 5(a)(iii), where the closing and opening parentheses between the 'a' and the 'iii' may be close enough to be mistaken for an 'X'.
- **Layout analysis.** Identifying text positions, tables, columns and paragraphs.
- **Line removal.** Removing overlying lines; this can quite often be an artefact of the printing or scanning process. For example, where a printer or scanner roller has some dirt or Tipex, creating a vertical line on a document print or scan (that may be mistaken for an 'l' character).

Post-Processing Steps to Improve Text Recognition

More sophisticated software conducts post-processing steps after the core OCR algorithm as well, typically seeking to validate that the result is within the given context (see Figure 11.5). This could involve matching the transcribed output to a lexicon, that is, a

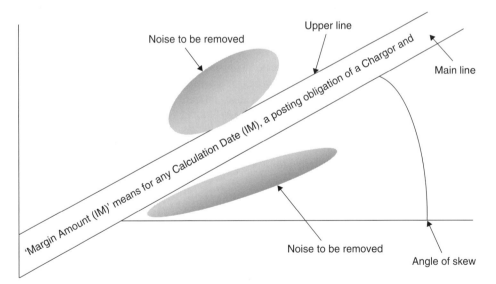

Figure 11.4 An example of OCR pre-processing techniques

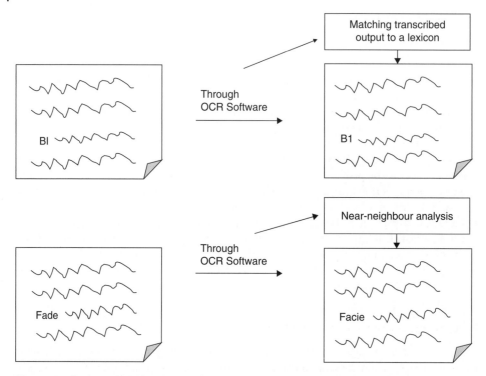

Figure 11.5 End-to-end OCR process and matching of the transcribed text to a lexicon

dictionary of allowed characters, which may be tailored for the particular type of documents (e.g. credit rating 'Bl' would automatically be corrected to 'B1', since this is a common word in the financial contract context and Bl is not a valid word) or conducting near-neighbour analysis to identify words or combinations of letters that are usually seen together (e.g. the word 'fade' might be automatically corrected to 'facie', since this is a common word in the legal contract context).

Rather than simply relying on algorithmic brute force to successfully digitise the image-based text into machine-readable form, it is important to take steps in terms of document preparation and storage, which would later assist any digitisation process (in many ways, to 'stop the bleeding' for the benefit of future exercises to digitise the contract portfolio). These include:

- Use of simple fonts with fixed character spacing (avoiding variable width or exotic fonts, as well as handwritten text – or manuscript amendments to a printed document).
- Avoiding page interruptions (such as multiple columns of text on a page) (see Figure 11.6).
- Reducing the number of times a hardcopy document is printed and scanned (e.g. for a document with multiple signatories, each party may print and scan the document, before passing it to the next signatory). Each such instance of printing and scanning dramatically increases the challenge of successfully digitising the document.

CONFIDENTIALITY AGREEMENT

This Confidentiality Agreement ("Agreement"), entered into and effective as of the ___ day of May, 2000 (the "Effective Date"), is by and between **InterGen North America Development Company LLC** ("InterGen"), a Delaware limited liability company with its principal place of business at 909 Fannin, Suite 2222, Houston, Texas 77010, and **Houston Pipe Line Company** and **Enron North America Corp.** (collectively the "Enron Companies"), each a corporation organized under the laws of Delaware, with their principal place of business at 1400 Smith St., Houston, Texas 77006. InterGen and the Enron Companies may be referred to individually as "Party" and collectively as "Parties."

Recitals:

A. The Parties wish to discuss information related to InterGen's 1100 MW Deweyville Power Plant located in Newton County, Texas and to the development of business proposals and pipeline interconnections involving InterGen's 1100 MW Deweyville Power Plant located in Newton County, Texas (the "Proposed Undertaking").

B. The Parties expect that, in furtherance of or in connection with the Proposed Undertaking, the Parties will receive Confidential Information (as defined below) from each other.

1. **Term.** This Agreement shall commence on the Effective Date and shall continue in effect for a period of one (1) year from the Effective Date.

2. **Confidential Information.** As used herein, the term "Confidential Information" means information that is of a non-public and confidential nature to the Party disclosing such information (the "Disclosing Party"), and is expressly identified as Confidential Information by the Disclosing Party.

3. Exceptions. Notwithstanding the provisions of Section 1, the term "Confidential Information" shall not include any information received by a Party (the "Receiving Party") from the Disclosing Party, to the extent such information: (i) was, prior to disclosure by the Disclosing Party, available to the Receiving Party on a non-confidential basis, or was otherwise in the public domain; (ii) is or becomes, at the time of or following disclosure, available to the Receiving Party or the public (other than as a result of disclosure in violation of this Agreement) from a source other than the Disclosing Party; or (iii) is independently developed by the Receiving Party without relying on the Confidential Information.

4. **Limitations on Disclosure.** The Receiving Party may not disclose Confidential Information received hereunder to any other person or party, EXCEPT that Confidential Information may be disclosed to (i) any third party to whom the Receiving Party is or becomes legally compelled by any

Figure 11.6 Problematic multi-column page setup

A common complaint about OCR technology is that even with the best devices, manual correction is still required. The cost of this manual correction is high, even when offshored to low-cost labour areas. For anything but a small quantity of text, correction involves a substantial amount of individual time, hardware, organisation and management. The costs are high monetarily as well as in terms of time. In a number of cases, this has led to decisions to manually retype documents rather than to OCR the documents and perform subsequent manual correction.

Since text is generally stored electronically for search and retrieval, the critical accuracy rate becomes the rate at which manual correction can be avoided without affecting retrieval results. The objective should therefore be to bring the text to a level which a retrieval system can cope with.

The accuracy of an information retrieval system is usually measured by precision and recall – precision is the percentage of retrieved documents (or text within) that is relevant, and recall is the percentage of relevant documents/text that are retrieved for a particular query.

Artificial Intelligence

Another relevant technology that has become important for the capture of legal agreement data is artificial intelligence (AI). Nilsson (2010) states that Artificial Intelligence is the '*activity devoted to making machines intelligent and intelligence is [the] quality that enables an entity to function appropriately and with its foresight in its environment*'. AI moves data extraction away from manual extraction to an extraction software that can apply predetermined rules as well as a system that can even train itself with and without supervision. In manual extraction, paralegals reviewing agreement data would be set a certain framework of rules, which they must apply. However, in certain cases, legal agreements can contain a large volume of documents. As we have already alluded to in this chapter, applying such manual extraction techniques to large-scale document extraction exercises can be time-consuming and highly prone to human error.

In contrast, AI systems can approach such a task with relative ease through a number of different techniques. Firstly, similar to the paralegal being given a rule to apply to a document, an AI system can also be programmed to follow such a rule. For example, if a reviewer is looking to find a change of control provision requiring consent, it is possible to create a rule stating that any sentence with 'change of control' and 'without the prior consent of' is a change of control clause. This is similar to Boolean algebra, which is used by the smart contracts considered in Chapter 12. The second technique that can be applied is machine learning, which can be separated into unsupervised machine learning and supervised machine learning. In supervised machine learning, software is trained with a restricted dataset of labelled examples. The software then learns what language is relevant and builds probabilistic provision models. These models are tested against a set of annotated agreements that the system is unfamiliar with. In contrast, unsupervised machine learning exposes the software to huge volumes of examples and data but without labelling. The AI then either 'clusters' data that is similar or highlights outliers that do not group together. Importantly, all of the above categories (rule-based, supervised or unsupervised) will use natural language processing (NLP), since they will require the ability to process words. Whilst most of the above techniques include NLP, only some of the categories will include deep learning. This is a less applicable AI technique in respect of legal agreement data, but in brief it is where the software algorithm is taught to analyse large data sets in what are called neural networks, as they seek to mimic the way the human brain works. Deep learning goes beyond machine learning – machine learning will, for example, learn whether an image is of a cat, whilst deep learning will attempt to determine what parts of the image make up a cat, such as the tail, whiskers or eyes.

Rather than simply relying on manual extraction, AI systems can extract data from agreements with greater speed, diligence and accuracy, far surpassing manual extraction techniques. With this realisation, there has been a rapid increase in the number of AI contract analytics vendors in the market, all trying to be classed as the front runner. In particular, vendors such as eBrevia, Kira, Neota, Seal, Luminance and Eigen have been in the spotlight from various stakeholders, such as law firms and legal technology PR outlets. For example, Artificial Lawyer.com, run by Richard Tromans, has closely followed such developments and even law firms have started to create legal technology incubators to host these vendors, such as Allen & Overy's Fuse, Mischon de Reya's MDR LAB and Slaughter & May's Fintech Fast Forward. With over $19.1 billion being spent on AI applications across multiple industries, there is a lot of interest around AI's capabilities to capture legal agreement data. Some commentators, such as Professor Richard Susskind, predict that AI will have the ability to be 'the end of lawyers'. One might even agree with Susskind if we look to the experiment carried out by contract review vendor LawGeex. In their experiment, 20 US-trained lawyers competed against an AI system to issue-spot legal issues ranging from governing law to limitation of liability in five non-disclosure agreements. The results of the experiment were that the AI system was able to spot the legal issues faster and more accurately – the lawyers achieved an average rating of 85%, taking on average 92 minutes, whilst the AI system achieved an average accuracy rating of 94%, taking on average 26 seconds. Clearly, this is an example highlighting an AI system's ability to analyse some legal documents with greater speed and accuracy over traditional manual techniques. However, it may, in the short term at least, be wrong to state that this is an example that AI will be 'the end of lawyers'. Rather, what this highlights is the potential that AI systems used in conjunction with human guidance and direction (otherwise known as 'augmented AI') can offer, to optimise tasks such as the accurate and efficient analysis of a group of legal agreements and the capture of legal agreement data from it.

Bibliography

'About FPML at a glance' (www.fpml.org/about/)

Allen & Overy, 'Advanced delivery: Fuse' (www.allenovery.com/advanceddelivery/fuse/Pages/default.aspx)

Cunningham, L. (2006) 'Language, deals and standards: The future of XML contracts', Boston College Law School Research Paper No. 93

Da Silva Moore v Publicis Groupe, Case No. 11 Civ. 1279 (ALC) (AJP), 2012 WL 607412 (S.D.N.Y. Feb. 24, 2012), *aff'd* 2012 WL 1446534 (S.D.N.Y. Apr. 26, 2012)

Datoo, A. (2018) 'Data-orientated contracts', *SCL*, 20th March 2018

IDC (2018) 'Worldwide spending on cognitive and artificial intelligence systems will grow to $19.1 billion in 2018, according to new IDC spending guide', *IDC*, 22nd March 2018

In re Intel Corp. Microprocessor Antitrust Litigation, 258 F.R.D. 280, 283 (D. Del. 2008)

ISDA (2018) 'What is ISDA Create – IM?' (www.isda.org/2018/05/24/isda-create-im/)

Kaplan, J. (2016) *Artificial Intelligence: What Everyone Needs to Know*. Oxford University Press: Oxford

Kemp, R. (2016) 'Legal aspects of artificial intelligence', *kempitlaw*, November 2016

LawGeex (2018) 'Comparing the performance of artificial intelligence to human lawyers in the review of standard business contracts', *LawGeex*, February 2018

Manning, C., Raghavan, P. and Schütze, H. (2008) *Introduction to Information Retrieval*. Cambridge University Press: Cambridge

MDR LAB (https://lab.mdr.london)

Miller, S. (2014) 'c-24-example-fpml', *GitHub*, 20th January 2014 (https://github.com/C24-Technologies/c24-example-fpml/blob/master/src/main/c24/demoware/FpML/SplitTradesLegsAndCashflows/FpML5-4-confirmation/Test%20Data/products/fx-derivatives/valid-fx-ex26-fxswap-multiple-USIs.xml)

Nilsson, N. (2010) *The Quest for Artificial Intelligence*. Cambridge University Press: Cambridge

Rebenchuk, S. (2018) 'Contract analysis software: The technology fundamentals', *Kira*, 26th April 2018

Roitblat, H. (2013) 'Introduction to predictive coding', OrcaTec LLC

Slaughter & May, 'Fintech fast forward' (www.slaughterandmay.com/what-we-do/legal-services/industry-sectors/fintech/fintechfastforward)

Surden, H. (2012) 'Computable contracts', *UC Davis Law Review*, 46, p. 629

Susskind, R. (2008) *The End of Lawyers? Rethinking the Nature of Legal Services*. Oxford University Press: Oxford

12

Smart Contracts

The regulatory changes that we have discussed in previous chapters have undoubtedly added considerable strain and complexity to the management of legal data. New technologies are emerging in order to reduce the issues created by large legacy contract portfolios where the legal data has not been considered adequately at the point the contracts are put in place. One technology in particular that is currently generating a lot of interest is smart contracts, invigorated by the advent of the blockchain. However, it must be acknowledged that both technologies are still nascent and there is a lack of standardisation (and therefore confusion and misunderstanding that plagues the two). This chapter explores smart contracts and the potential for them to address legal data in the banking context.

What is a Smart Contract?

At a very simple level, smart contracts are coded instructions which execute on the occurrence of an event. However, there is no clear and settled meaning of what is meant by a smart contract. Consequently, there is a lot of confusion. For the purposes of this book, we prefer to provide a timeline of the varying definitions to show how the thinking about smart contract technology has developed and how it might evolve in the future.

The first step in the timeline goes back to its conception in 1994. The idea of smart contracts was conceived by computer scientist and legal theorist Nick Szabo, defining it as '*a set of promises, specified in digital form, including protocols within which the parties perform on these promises*'. He describes this definition through the example of a drinks vending machine. When the money is paid, an irrevocable set of actions is put in motion. The money is retained and a drink is supplied. The transaction cannot be stopped in mid-flow and the money cannot be returned once the drink has been supplied (leaving aside reaching out to the owner of the drinks vending machine and attempting to reverse matters through them). The terms of the transaction are in a sense embedded in the hardware of the drinks machine and the software that runs the machine. In summary, a smart contract under Szabo's description is both an instance of computer code and a running software program that interprets code, accepts input conditions and decides an outcome.[1]

However, from 1994, smart contracts remained a somewhat abstract term and of limited value, because ultimately they relied on stakeholders trusting another entity to execute the smart contract. In Szabo's example, the buyer would have to trust the drinks machine software to execute the intended contract. In other words, it would require a trusted intermediary and therefore smart contracts are not distinguishable from other executable software. However, with the advent of distributed ledger technology and blockchain, smart contracts are able to depart from their 'primitive ancestors', which were reliant on trust. At a high level, this is because distributed ledger technology (DLT) and blockchain rely on consensus algorithms rather than trust in an intermediary, such as a bank (this will be explored in more detail later in this chapter).

Consequently, this new form of smart contract began to resurface in 2009 with the creation of the Bitcoin blockchain – itself technically a limited form of a smart contract whereby each transaction includes programs to verify and validate a transaction (each is effectively a small smart contract). However, smart contract technology broke into the mainstream after Vitalik Buterin's White Paper entitled 'Ethereum: The ultimate smart contracts and decentralized application platform'. This paper introduced the idea of smart contracts as an entity that could send and receive currency. Consequently, the Ethereum network allowed more complex smart contracts to be developed through using a specified smart contract computer language known as Solidity. Therefore, the advent of blockchain and DLT was very important for the development of smart contracts as we understand them today.

What is Ethereum?

Created by Canadian–Russian programmer Vitalik Buterin in July 2015, Ethereum is an open software platform based on blockchain technology that enables developers to build and deploy decentralised applications (known as 'DApps'). Similar to Bitcoin, Ethereum is a distributed public blockchain. However, Bitcoin only offers one application of blockchain technology – a peer-to-peer electronic cash system that enables online Bitcoin payments. The Ethereum blockchain instead focuses on running the programming code of any decentralised application, which essentially allows smart contracts to function.

As lawyers have started to contribute their thinking to smart contracts (they are after all contracts of sorts, if only in name), the spectrum of what is understood as a smart contract has begun to widen. At one end of the spectrum, there has been the 'code is contract' school of thought, whereby the contract is fully expressed in code without any natural language. At the other end of this spectrum, smart contracts are simply natural language contracts which digitise the performance of business logic (e.g. payments).

---

1 Modern examples of a smart contract can be found in relation to AXA's Fizzy application (covered later in this chapter) whereby, if an insured flight is cancelled, the contract automatically self-executes to pay out flight delay compensation.

In the middle of the spectrum, we see two other potential concepts emerge: (1) a contract in code that is duplicated with separate natural language documentation; and (2) a split contract where non-human performance is encoded into computer code and wider human obligations are written into natural language. Lawyer and head of operations at Ledger, Josh Stark, defines this spectrum in two schools of thought: 'smart contract code' and 'smart legal contracts':

- **Smart legal contracts.** Legal contracts, or elements of legal contracts, being represented and executed by software.
- **Smart contract code.** Pieces of code that are designed to execute certain tasks if predefined conditions are met. Such tasks are often embedded within and performed on a distributed ledger.

This intersection with contract and code has generated a lot of the siloed thinking over smart contracts, particularly amongst computer scientists and lawyers, but as joint ISDA and Linklaters white paper notes, rather than seeing smart legal contracts and smart contract code in separate domains, there is a relationship between them. They clarify that:

> *[for a] smart legal contract to be implemented, it will need to embed one or more pieces of code designed to execute certain tasks if pre-defined conditions are met – that is, pieces of smart contract code. Smart legal contracts, therefore, are functionally made up of pieces of smart contract code … [h]owever, every smart legal contract can be said to contain one or more pieces of smart contract code, but not every piece of smart contract code comprises a smart legal contract.*

Whilst this provides some clarity as to Stark's two schools of thought, we are no closer to a basic definition of what a smart contract is. Until there is a unified view of what a smart contract's definition encapsulates, there is use in readers understanding its basic characteristics, as provided concisely by Clack et al. (2016):

> *A smart contract is an automatable and enforceable agreement. Automatable by computer, although some parts may require human input and control. Enforceable either by legal enforcement of rights and obligations or via tamper-proof execution of computer code.*

This definition is broad enough to encapsulate a wide spectrum of smart contracts, including both smart code contracts and smart legal contracts. More importantly, it captures the fundamental essence of the technology – the automation and self-execution of a preset conditional action.

Further Misunderstanding – Ricardian Contracts

One further area of confusion in the realm of smart contracts is their relationship with Ricardian contracts (Figure 12.1). This type of contract was created by Ian Grigg, a specialist in financial cryptography, in the mid-1990s. According to Grigg, a Ricardian

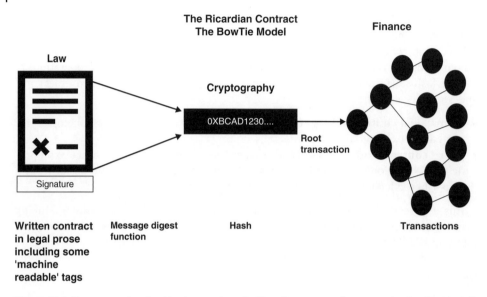

Figure 12.1 The process involved in the creation of a Ricardian contract known as the 'BowTie Model'

contract is '*a digital contract that defines the terms and conditions of an interaction, between two or more parties, which is then cryptographically signed and verified. Importantly, it is both human and machine readable and digitally signed*'.

A Ricardian contract registers a legally valid and digitally connected document to a certain object or value. It places all information from the legal document in a format that can be executed by software. This way, it is both a legal agreement between parties and a protocol that integrates an agreement offering a high level of security because of cryptographic identification.

Whilst both smart contracts and Ricardian contracts share a number of similarities, they are independent notions in their own right. Smart contracts are automatable sets of instructions that can self-execute on certain events and conditions. Ricardian contracts are documents that outline the intentions and actions relating to a contract, no matter whether it has been executed or not. In other words, Ricardian contracts are the 'best effort' to record the agreement and smart contracts are the execution of these agreements.[2]

How Does a Smart Contract Work?

Put simply, a smart contract operates through Boolean algebra. Boolean algebra, named after the nineteenth-century mathematician George Boole, is a form of mathematical logic that reduces its variables to true and false. This form of logic lends itself nicely to smart contracts' self-executing and event-driven characteristics. It can be summarised linguistically as 'if this happens then, then do that'. As will be detailed later in this chapter, the nature of Boolean logic has its limitations when trying to 'code' for subjective legal language.

---

2 Research is being undertaken to try and merge Ricardian and smart contracts together (e.g. EOS Canada) in order to resolve some of the limitations of smart contracts.

Boolean Logic

Assume a statement or hypothesis 'H' is either true or false, it can't be anything in between (this called the law of the excluded middle). From this basis, it is possible to form other statements, which are also true or false, by combining these initial statements together using the fundamental operators *AND*, *OR* and *NOT*. For example, if H is true, then NOT(H) is false. So, if 'it is raining today' is true, then 'NOT(it is raining today)' is false. We often translate the logical expression into more natural language, such as 'it is not raining today'. This can, as the example develops, become convoluted and difficult to follow, which is why a symbolic representation of the Boolean logic, which is clear and precise, can be very helpful.

Truth Tables

The rules for combining expressions are usually written down as tables listing all of the possible outcomes. These are called truth tables and for the four fundamental operators they are:

H	Q	H AND Q
F	F	F
F	T	F
T	F	F
T	T	T

H	Q	H OR Q
F	F	F
F	T	T
T	F	T
T	T	T

H	NOT H
F	T
T	F

P	Q	P XOR Q
F	F	F
F	T	T
T	F	T
T	T	F

For example, if one wanted to build logic such that a payment is made under an interest derivative transaction when the 3-month GBP LIBOR rate exceeds 2% and the maturity date of the transaction has not been reached, the truth statement could be symbolised as:

H = 3m GBP LIBOR is greater than 2%

Q = The Maturity Date of Transaction ABC is in the past

If R is a representation of whether the payout should be made:

$R = H \text{ AND NOT}(Q)$

That is, the truth of 'Payout can be made' is given by the following truth table:

H	Q	NOT(Q)	H AND NOT(Q)
F	F	T	F
F	T	F	F
T	F	T	T
T	T	F	F

From this you should be able to see that the payout is only made when the maturity date has not been reached and the 3-month GBP LIBOR rate exceeds 2%.

AXA's Fizzy application is an example of a smart contract application for flight insurance, whereby the terms of the contract between the holder of the insurance and AXA is based around insuring against a flight delay of greater than 2 hours. The smart contract operates on the Ethereum blockchain network and it continuously checks data from oracles in real time (a trusted third-party source); once the delay exceeds 2 hours, the compensation terms are automatically triggered and given effect to. Putting this into colloquial Boolean algebra, 'if the plane is late by more than 2 hours, then compensation must be paid out'. The key code representing this logic is shown in Figure 12.2 (note that the variable limit 'limitArrivalTime' is defined as 2 hours elsewhere in the code, the full version of which is reproduced in Appendix C).

```
138        // if the actual arrival time is over the limit the user wanted,
139        // we trigger the indemnity, which means status = 2
140 ▾      if (actualArrivalTime > insuranceList[flightId][i].limitArrivalTime) {
141          newStatus = 2;
142        }
```

Figure 12.2 The core logic code for the Fizzy smart contract application

```
117 ▾   /**
118      * @dev Update the status of a flight
119      * @param flightId <carrier_code><flight_number>.<timestamp_in_sec_of_departure_date>
120      * @param actualArrivalTime The actual arrival time of the flight (timestamp in sec)
121      */
122     function updateFlightStatus(
123       bytes32 flightId,
124       uint actualArrivalTime)
125     public
126 ▾   onlyIfCreator {
127
128       uint8 newStatus = 1;
129
130       // go through the list of all insurances related to the given flight
131 ▾     for (uint i = 0; i < insuranceList[flightId].length; i++) {
132
133         // we check this contract is still ongoing before updating it
134 ▾       if (insuranceList[flightId][i].status == 0) {
135
136           newStatus = 1;
137
138           // if the actual arrival time is over the limit the user wanted,
139           // we trigger the indemnity, which means status = 2
140 ▾         if (actualArrivalTime > insuranceList[flightId][i].limitArrivalTime) {
141             newStatus = 2;
142           }
143
144           // update the status of the insurance contract
145           insuranceList[flightId][i].status = newStatus;
146
147           // send an event about this update for each insurance
148           InsuranceUpdate(
149             insuranceList[flightId][i].productId,
150             flightId,
151             insuranceList[flightId][i].premium,
152             insuranceList[flightId][i].indemnity,
153             newStatus
154           );
155         }
156       }
157     }
```

Figure 12.3 An example of the Solidity smart contract coding language (taken from the Fizzy smart contract)

As noted above, Ethereum developed a smart contract-specific coding language called Solidity, an example of which can be seen in Figure 12.3. Solidity was defined by Ethereum as an object-orientated high-level language for implementing smart contracts, influenced by other computer languages such as C++, Python and Java.[3]

Distributed Ledger Technology and Blockchain

Contrary to popular belief, DLT and blockchain are not two separate technologies – they are part of a family of technologies. Blockchain is just one type of DLT and is less a new technology than a clever combination of existing technologies (peer-to-peer (P2P) networking, distributed timestamping, cryptographic hashing functions, digital signatures – considered in the next chapter – and Merkle tress, amongst others). Based on the Hileman and Rauchs methodology, blockchain contains five key components:

1) **Cryptography.** A variety of cryptographic techniques are used, including cryptographic one-way hash functions, Merkle trees and public-key infrastructures.
2) **P2P network.** A network for peer discovery and data sharing in a peer-to-peer fashion.
3) **Consensus mechanism.** An algorithm that determines the ordering of transactions in an adversarial environment.
4) **Ledger.** A list of transactions bundled together in cryptographically linked 'blocks'.
5) **Validity rules.** A common set of rules of the network (i.e. what transactions are considered valid, how the ledger gets updated, etc.).

However, there is still a lot of confusion surrounding the usage of the terms blockchain and DLT, as often these terms are mistakenly used interchangeably.[4] Before looking at the operational aspects of blockchain, we now back up a little to consider the differences between distributed databases and distributed ledgers.

- **Distributed databases.** Distributed databases are a type of database with no central master database to unilaterally decide on updating the database state. Instead, multiple nodes collaborate to maintain a consistent view of the database. However, the database assumes that all the nodes are correct, as they are cooperating and freely sharing data with each other based on mutual trust. This may not be a correct assumption, and nodes may be incorrect, malicious or dishonest, particularly if there is some benefit from changing the true representation of the underlying data. This means that distributed databases are typically operated by a single entity which maintains strict access control to the network – thereby ensuring trust in nodes on the network.

---

3 It must be noted that blockchain networks, other than Ethereum, can also facilitate the creation and hosting of smart contracts.
4 It should be noted that, at the time of writing, an International Organisation for Standardisation (ISO) committee is engaged in examining standardisation issues for DLT and blockchain, with definitions being a priority.

- **Distributed ledgers.** These are a subset of distributed databases. However, the relationship between the nodes operates on an adversarial threat model, whereby the model mitigates the presence of malicious nodes on the network. This model is designed to be 'Byzantine fault-tolerant' (as explored below). The main difference between distributed databases and distributed ledgers is that the former rely on a trusted environment whilst the latter's individual nodes do not trust their peers.
- **Blockchain.** Blockchain is a special subset of distributed ledgers that shares the adversarial threat model but has additional characteristics. In the case of blockchain, a distributed ledger stores a list of transaction data through a series of 'blocks', where each block is identified by a cryptographic signature. Each block is linked to the previous block by referring to that previous block's cryptographic signature, creating a chain of blocks traceable back to the initial block created. As the cryptographic signature of a block uses details of previous blocks, even a small change to the blockchain will result in a different cryptographic signature, so fraudulent attempts to remove or change prior transactions are detectable. Rather than existing in one location, the ledger is distributed across participants in a network. There is no central authority to govern the ledger, rather the network's nodes verify and validate transactions before they are added to the chain based on a consensus algorithm.

Centralised, Decentralised and Distributed Networks

The focus of a centralised network is control. This is the 'traditional' network architecture, where all nodes send their data to one central node (a server), which then sends the data to the intended recipient. In this way, the network can control speed, user service and flexibility within the network. An example of a centralised network is an online platform such as eBay. There can, however, be a number of disadvantages of such a network. The centralisation of power and control means that there is a risk of complete failure if that central node fails. Centralised systems require users to access information on the network uniformly, using the same processes. This type of network, therefore, may not support the flexibility required by multiple users with varied needs. Centralised systems also create centralised targets and are easier to attack from a security perspective.

In a decentralised network, not all the processing of the transactions is done in the same place, however, the network still relies on a central authority that controls and governs processing over all other nodes of the system. The network is, therefore, still centralised in nature. A bank's electronic system is a good example of a decentralised network, where the bank remains the central controller.

With distributed[5] networks, no one single entity has control over all the processing. By its very nature, this implies that the control is distributed amongst many nodes.

---

5 Confusingly, Vitalik Buterin, one of the founders of Ethereum, has used the term 'decentralised' to refer to the network system associated with blockchain, whereas most industry experts refer to it as 'distributed'. We adopt the latter here.

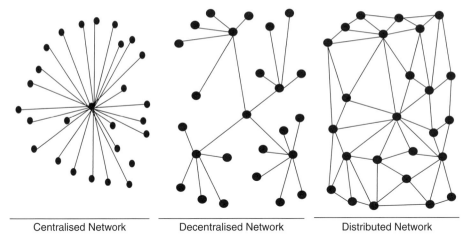

| Centralised Network | Decentralised Network | Distributed Network |

Figure 12.4 A comparison of centralised, decentralised and distributed networks

Blockchain is a distributed network whereby collective control is achieved over the network through the use of a consensus-based algorithm (see Figure 12.4).

Transactions, Blocks, Merkle Trees and Mining

In a blockchain, a transaction is the act of transferring ownership from one owner to someone else. This act of transferring ownership relies on data that describes the intended transfer. This data contains all the information necessary to execute the transfer of ownership. The blockchain maintains the whole history of all transactions that have ever happened by storing this data in a 'blockchain data structure' in the order in which it occurred. Any transaction not being part of that history is regarded as if it never happened.

Transactions are grouped together in a chain of blocks in a blockchain, as shown in Figure 12.5. Each such block is connected to the previous block through the use of cryptography (see Chapter 13 on digital signatures, which provides some basic details of how this operates), by the header of the block detailing a cryptographic hash of the previous block. These cryptographic links provide a tamper-proof ('append only') audit trail back to the initial block in the blockchain (via a Merkle tree). If an attempt is made to change a transaction in a block, this would make the cryptographic hash details in the headers of subsequent blocks incorrect.

Merkle Trees

Developed by Ralph Merkle in 1979, a Merkle tree is a binary tree-like data structure that can be used to condense all the transactions to be hashed into a single block

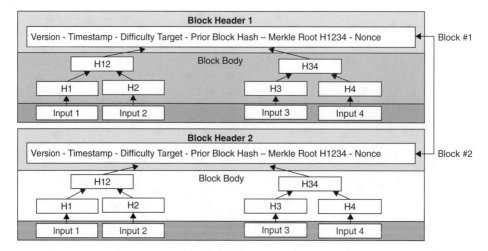

Figure 12.5 A representation of individual blocks (in this case, blocks 1 and 2) in a blockchain data structure connected through the cryptographic hash of the previous block

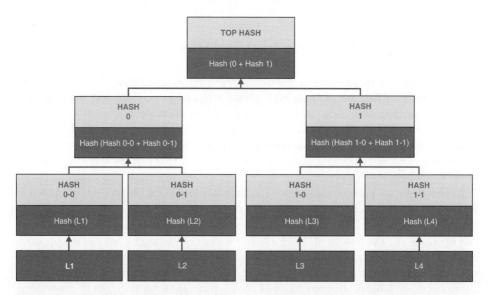

Figure 12.6 A Merkle tree condensing previous transaction hashes into a single 'top hash'

(see Figure 12.6). In a Merkle tree, every leaf node of the tree is labelled with the hash of a block and every non-leaf node is labelled with the cryptographic hash of the labels of its child nodes. It allows the grouping of many distinct pieces of data that are available at the same time, making them available via a single hash reference.

Consensus Algorithms

When a blockchain is being built, the fact that there is no central authority means that some sort of consensus needs to be reached on the state of the blockchain ledger, the order and uniqueness of the underlying transactions, as well as regarding governance in relation to how blocks are added to the chain. Blockchains rely on consensus algorithms in order to do this, even in a 'trustless' (or hostile) environment.

The Byzantine General's Problem

The Byzantine General's Problem is the classical computer science agreement problem that can be solved by consensus algorithms. This is a thought experiment proposed by Lamport, Shostak and Pease in 1982 regarding a group of Byzantine generals, each leading different parts of the Byzantine army, seeking to attack or withdraw from a city. They are facing a number of problems:

- The generals and their armies are very far apart, so centralised authority is impossible, which makes a coordinated attack very tough and the only means of communication between them is via a messenger.
- One or more of the Byzantine generals may be traitors and might communicate a misleading message or series of messages.
- The city has a huge army and the only way that they can win is if they all attack at once. The Byzantine generals need a consensus mechanism (or algorithm) which will make sure that their army can actually attack as a unit, despite all these setbacks.

This has clear parallels to issues that might be dealt with by blockchain. Blockchain is likely to be a huge network, raising questions around how one might trust the nodes (messengers) in a blockchain. There are a number of different types of consensus algorithms to resolve this:

- **Proof of work.** This was the first blockchain consensus algorithm, devised by Satoshi Nakamoto[6] for use in the Bitcoin blockchain. Nodes (typically referred to as miners, certainly in the Bitcoin context) solve hard, useless problems to create blocks. It relies on economics to avoid 'an attack', in terms of the sheer processing power (and associated cost) required to solve the problem.
- **Proof of stake.** This works on the basis that a node has enough stake in the system to make an 'attack' disadvantageous for the node itself. Nodes place their stakes to 'bet' on which blocks are valid.
- **Simplified Byzantine fault tolerance.** In this consensus algorithm, the block's validator is a known entity (e.g. a regulator in a business network). This validator creates and proposes a new block of transactions. A certain number of nodes must accept the block, depending on the number of faulty or malicious nodes. In order to be tolerant of a 'Byzantine fault', the number of nodes that must reach consensus is $2f+1$ in a system containing $3f+1$ nodes, where f is the number of faults in the system.

---

6 Satoshi Nakamoto is the name used by the unknown developer of Bitcoin.

Blockchain Protocols

Another important aspect of blockchain that has developed relates to the governance of the ledger. Blockchains can govern who has access to the ledger, who can read the ledger, who can send data to the ledger and also who can update the ledger through the consensus protocol. As a result, a variety of different blockchain variants have emerged, each with a unique governance framework. However, at the time of writing, it is possible to define the different varieties of blockchain in two main categories – open[7] and closed[8] – in reference to who can access the ledger. These two categories can be segmented further according to the differing governance framework configured into the network, as shown in Figure 12.7. This development in the variety of different blockchain networks has in large part been due to financial institutions wanting to utilise the technology. Uncomfortable with the unrestricted access in open blockchains such as Bitcoin and Ethereum, a lot of work has been undertaken to adapt the technology in order to make it palatable for highly regulated firms in the banking and finance context.

Furthermore, there are a number of different blockchain methods for storing data that have been developed, such as 'off-chain' and 'sidechain' methods. These have, to some extent, emerged due to the increasing data privacy requirements (e.g. as required under the GDPR; see Chapter 4).

- **Off-chain.** On public blockchains, off-chain mechanisms store confidential information separately on another system with access control restrictions. The use of the hash function serves only as a reference point and link to an off-chain database. The system can be set up to restrict access to the transaction details to authorised personnel only. However, this negates some of the advantages of using blockchain, as parties will be required to maintain their own records.

Blockchain Types			Read	Write	Commit	Example
Open		Public Permissionless	Available to any user	Any user	Any user	Bitcoin, Ethereum
Open		Public Permissioned	Available to any user	Authorised Blockchain participants	All or some authorised blockchain participants	Ripple
Closed		Consortium	Restricted to a limited set of participants	Authorised Blockchain participants	All or some authorised blockchain participants	Multiple firms operating on a shared ledger
Closed		Private Permissioned	Open	Network administrator only	Networks administrator only	Internal firm ledger shared between parent and subsidiary companies

Figure 12.7 A comparison of blockchain types and differences in governance

---

7 Open blockchains have also been referred to as 'public' blockchains.
8 Closed blockchains have also been referred to as 'private' or 'permissioned' blockchains, to refer to networks that have limited access to known and vetted participants. However, in practice, such terms are used interchangeably.

- **Sidechains.** A sidechain is a parallel blockchain that sits alongside the primary blockchain. These sidechains operate independently (therefore if the security is compromised, e.g. if they are hacked, they will not damage other chains).

As the technology continues to develop, it is increasingly difficult to have a clear distinction between open and closed blockchains. Firms are looking to overcome the issues of interoperability between different DLT network models. For example, Applied Blockchain, Polkadot and the Cosmos network are all developing proof of concepts to develop integration with inter-ledger technology in order to utilise the features of open blockchain with the more trusted closed blockchains, for example, through the use of 'parity bridges'.

An Alternative Future for DLT – Hashgraph?

Whilst much of the noise being generated by the industry has revolved around the specific DLT of blockchain, it would be wrong to assume that it is the only notable DLT. One DLT in particular is Hashgraph. Developed by Leemon Baird in 2016, Hashgraph is a consensus algorithm with P2P architecture. However, Baird has argued that Hashgraph is less technically restrained than blockchain and is able to rectify some of the so-called 'genetic' flaws of blockchain.

The major difference between blockchain and Hashgraph is that whilst blockchain organises its data structure into a series of interconnected blocks, Hashgraph comprises data in events, with each instance containing the transactions associated with its timestamp and the hash of both of the parent events that created it (Figure 12.8).

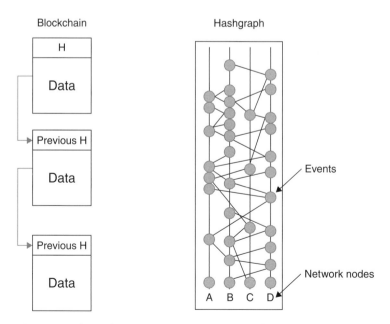

Figure 12.8 The Hashgraph data structure organises data into events rather than connected blocks

However, both DLTs do share some commonality by the fact that they propagate information in the network by relying on the 'gossip protocol'. This protocol implies that a node in the network conveys information regarding transactions to the other nodes, sending the hash codes associated with the transactions to all nodes in the network. However, this is where the two DLTs diverge in nature. In a blockchain network, this would require a proof-of-work algorithm to solve a complex mathematical problem. However, Baird's Hashgraph combines the gossip protocol in the form of 'gossip about gossip', with a voting algorithm to reach consensus securely and without a proof-of-work algorithm. This means that the gossip protocol shares new information that the other nodes do not know, and the 'gossip about gossip' includes where that new information originated from in the consensus timestamp. When the new messages combine the hashes of previous messages into one, there is an entire history of who 'gossiped to who' in the network and in what order. Effectively, the algorithm irons out the trust issues between the participating members when there is a trust deficit, making it exponentially faster than blockchain. To illustrate this speed advantage, Bitcoin and Ethereum can currently process between five and seven transactions per second through the proof-of-work architecture. In contrast, Hashgraph's consensus algorithm, called Swirlds, showed in a speed test that 30 computers can achieve '50k transactions a second across eight global regions in three seconds, or merely 1.5 seconds across 2k miles, or .75 seconds in a single region'. Hashgraph is therefore able to use consensus timestamping whilst retaining the functionality of blockchain in an efficient fashion.

Hashgraph reminds us that blockchain technology is not without limitation and that attention should not focus solely on one form of DLT, given its early stage of development. Any early technology is likely to evolve dramatically for a number of reasons, such as the development of standards, developments in important related fields (in this case, big data, artificial intelligence, machine learning and cryptography), as well as brute increases in underlying processing power (consider Moore's Law).

Moore's Law

In 1965, Gordon Moore, an Intel scientist, made a prediction based on his observation that the number of transistors per square inch on integrated circuits had doubled every year since their invention. His law (known as Moore's Law) predicted that the growth in computer processing power would double roughly every 2 years, while the cost of that computing power would go down. Moore's Law proved accurate for several decades, and has been used in the semiconductor industry to guide long-term planning and to set targets for research and development (Figure 12.9). The rate of increased processing power predicted by Moore's Law has helped to drive advances in big data, AI and machine learning. That said, it is now acknowledged that the rate of increase is slowing. Gordon Moore, interviewed in 2015, stated:

> We won't have the rate of progress that we've had over the last few decades. I think that's inevitable with any technology; it eventually saturates out. I guess I see Moore's law dying here in the next decade or so, but that's not surprising.

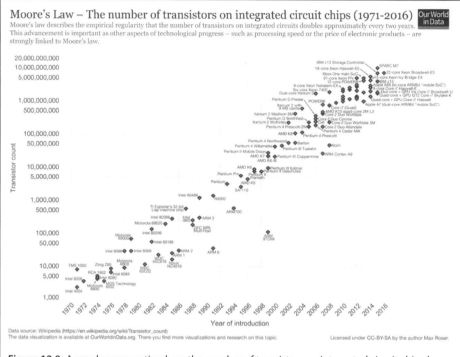

Figure 12.9 A graph representing how the number of transistors on integrated circuit chips has doubled each year

Source: https://commons.wikimedia.org/wiki/File:Moore%27s_Law_Transistor_Count_1971-2016.png. Licensed under CC-BY -SA 4.0

DLT and Smart Contracts

Going back to the simplicity of Szabo's drinks vending machine smart contract, it is simply a computer program to automatically execute an event, such as payment under a contract upon satisfaction of predefined conditions – or purchase of a fizzy drink from a machine. The drinks vending machine controls and executes the basic elements of the contract. It offers goods for sale and if a person selects one of those goods (i.e. accepts the offer) and enters the correct amount of money (consideration and demonstrating intent to create legally binding relations), then the machine will deliver the fizzy drink. The 'else' Boolean logic comes in where an incorrect amount is entered (the rejection of the counter-offer!).

In a commercial contract, the parties may want to program a contract that will automatically execute on a certain condition (i.e. an asset to be sold on reaching a certain price threshold). However, in the drafting process, they may not be willing to rely on another party's view on that price threshold being reached – there may be a lack of trust. This determination could be made algorithmically by the parties, although, given the lack of trust, they might choose to have separate algorithms (running on different systems) in order to assess whether the event condition has occurred. This introduces a risk that the contract's 'implementation' will differ between the parties. The lack of trust between the two parties is where the strength of DLT and blockchain comes into play, whereby smart contracts can be embedded on a DLT platform, meaning there is only one 'golden' version to bind both parties. Furthermore, neither party will require any further action to be taken when the smart contract is embedded, as it will self-execute.

Applying this to OTC derivatives, there may be multiple parties who do not fully trust each other, each comparing their version of events with the others (e.g. consider a credit event on an underlying reference obligation in a credit derivative transaction). Both parties will have the original transaction documentation and they both have a view on the external market variables affecting the transaction. Ideally, they should both agree on the outcome of the transaction given a set of facts, but the reality is that this is not always the case. With a smart contract operating on a distributed ledger, however, there is only one set of transaction terms that are agreed upfront and any external dependencies (such as the occurrence of a credit event, price of oil, share price, etc.) can be fed in via 'oracles' (simply a separate data source that is external to the blockchain). Therefore, the smart contract will exist on the blockchain and execute when a relevant event happens, or when the term of the contract reaches an end (Figure 12.10).

As mentioned previously, it is important to view smart contracts and DLT as two complementary, albeit distinct, technologies. With this in place, we can start to see a greater understanding of the two technologies together, as helpfully summarised by Hansen et al.:

- Smart contracts are software programs running on certain DLT protocols.
- Smart contracts are usually part of an application running on DLT, rather than standing alone as a DLT application.
- Smart contracts offer event-driven functionality (which may or may not require human input), triggered by data inputs (which may be internal or external), upon which they can modify data.
- External data can be supplied by 'oracles' (trusted data sources that send information to smart contracts).

Image - Smart Contract 5

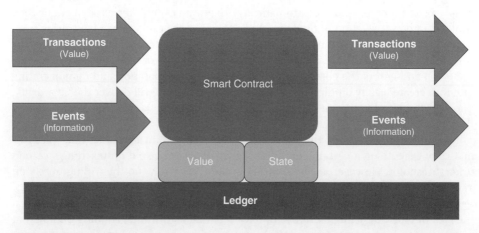

Figure 12.10 A model showing how a smart contract operates on a blockchain network (adapted from Gendal-Brown's 'A simple model for smart contracts')

- Smart contracts can, acting on information provided by oracles, 'enforce a functional implementation of a particular requirement, and can show proof that certain conditions were either met or not met'.
- Smart contracts can track changes in 'state' over time.[9]
- Smart contracts are autonomous in that the software developer who created them need not actively maintain, monitor or even be in contact with them while they operate.
- Once executed, smart contracts may be self-sufficient in that they can be programmed to 'marshal resources' – that is, raise funds by providing services and spend them on resources, such as processing power or storage.
- Smart contracts are distributed, because they exist as software running on a DLT protocol which is itself distributed across a variety of network nodes.
- Smart contracts guarantee execution of the contemplated transaction once the required conditions are met.

In theory, the self-executing and self-enforcing nature of a smart contract can pave the way to reduce the need for lawyers to draft, negotiate and even adjudicate agreements between parties under a natural language contract. By occurring through a smart contract, there is a clear opportunity to make the process for entering into contracts more efficient and, in theory, reduce the risk of disputes arising from non-performance of the contract because the code, applying Boolean logic ('if, then, else' logic), will simply execute the parties' intent without any need for manual steps or intervention.

Coupled with legal agreement data management possibilities, where the data resulting from a legal agreement is not only provided to stakeholders with an interest in the contract but also combined with other related data (e.g. market or counterparty data combined in the operational and business needs of those stakeholders), this demonstrates the ability of smart contracts to be the next generation of contracts as we move towards an increasingly digital world and economy, where 'data is the new oil'.

However, whilst smart contracts are capable of self-executing, we must revert to basic principles of contract law – as laid out in Chapter 2 – to decide whether a smart contract is capable of being legally binding.

Smart Contracts – Legally Binding?

> *Smart contracts are neither particularly smart nor are they strictly speaking contracts.*

It would be wrong to assume that because the technology uses the word 'contract', this is automatically legally enforceable – a smart contract is not the same thing as a legal contract. To be a legal contract, it must satisfy the four requirements listed in Chapter 2 (and restated below). Stark's smart legal contract would have to meet these conditions, but the code embedded for part of the contract would be electronically automated. So, with respect to smart code contracts, is there no legal contract?

At the time of writing, the legal status of smart contracts technology is yet to be tested by the courts. However, this does not mean that the current law is not applicable to the new technology. The common law has been adept at applying to other ways of forming

---

9 Where 'state' refers to all or part of the data that a program deals with.

a contract (e.g. by email: see *Bieber and others v Teathers Ltd* (In liquidation) [2014] EWHC 238). Therefore, we must refer back to the basic contract principles laid out in Chapter 2: offer and acceptance, consideration and intention to create legal relations.

This analysis has been detailed in a White Paper by R3 and Norton Rose Fulbright. Firstly, through Article 9 of Electronic Commerce Directive 2000/31/EC, contracts can be concluded through electronic means. The legal analysis can be summarised as follows:

- **Offer and acceptance.** Drawing on Szabo's seminal smart contract idea about a vending machine, English law has looked through an automated machine acting as an intermediary between the parties. For example, in *Thornton v Shoe Lane Parking*, the court equated a ticket vending machine at a parking lot to an offer. This reasoning was also applied in *Software Solutions Partners*, where insurance broker input the relevant data into his computer – an offer was automatically generated. The court further noted that, just because the offer had been made through electronic means, it did not alter the application of the basic principles.
- **Consideration.** In relation to smart contracts, this would not be a contentious point, as long as some value has been given in relation to the formation of contractual obligations.
- **Intention to create legal relations.** If the other requirements for a legally enforceable contract are present, it may be difficult for a party to assert that there was no intention to create legal relations. However, the White Paper discusses the potential issues with 'follow-on' contracts and the issues of smart contracts were deemed to be thought of as electronic agents. The court is yet to deliver any authority in this area. However, the court in Software Solutions Partners did seem to reflect the opinion that an electronic agent should be regarded as a mere communications tool – meaning that the agent's program logic must be equated with the actions of the party that put it in motion. However, this point remains open.
- **Certainty/completeness of terms.** The way the court interprets this is likely to ultimately fall on the facts of the contract. If there is a lack of certainty relating to the smart contract code, the court would likely hear expert evidence as to the meaning of the code (until this is the expectation of the judiciary!).

Therefore, the courts will be able to apply the same doctrinal reasoning as done in the past, and will depend on the specific circumstances to determine whether a smart contract will be legally binding or not.

Benefits, Limits and Risks of Using Smart Contract Technology

As we now have better understanding, we can start to see how smart contract technology could offer a number of benefits.

- **Speed and real-time updates.** As a natural by-product of automation, smart contracts can increase the number of value-generating transactions per unit of time, reducing the hours spent on traditional business processes. As well as efficiency, smart contracts are capable of interacting with the data sent to the blockchain, either from internal or external sources.

- **Accuracy and certainty for transacting records.** As blockchain technology is a shared ledger across multiple nodes, deployed smart contracts are replicated and stored throughout the whole network. In a public blockchain with a proof-of-work consensus algorithm, any amendments to the ledger must be verified by the majority of the network. Not only does this certify transactions, it also provides a permanent record and audit of the transaction history.
- **Lower execution risk.** Blockchain and distributed ledger technology platforms – where smart contracts operate – reduce the risk of non-performance (since the code is automatable by the network), and can replace the need for central trusted authorities when it comes to performing operations such as custody, settlement and clearing.
- **Reducing the need for intermediaries.** A significant benefit of smart contracts is that they reduce the need for a trusted third party (except when oracles are used), as trust is already built into the network through the consensus algorithms. By removing such intermediaries from the process, the costs associated with business transactions are reduced.

Use cases are already being identified and developed across the financial services sector. Most applicable for the topic of this book, a timeline has already begun for the development of smart 'derivative' contracts as initial steps are being taken to develop an ISDA 'Common Domain Model' (CDM), which is a key foundation step in order to achieve this.

ISDA Common Domain Model

In 2017, the ISDA embarked on a project to develop the ISDA Common Domain Model, driven by efforts to reduce complexity and create greater efficiencies in the derivatives market. An initial version (CDM 1.0), covering interest rate and credit derivative products, was published in June 2018, providing a standard digital representation of events and actions (such as rate resets, terminations, novations and compressions) that occur during the life of a derivatives trade, expressed in a machine-readable format. Recognising that market participants use differing language for data and processes to manage OTC derivatives, the aim was to develop a common standard to facilitate interoperability across market participants and platforms, facilitating the uptake of new technologies such as distributed ledgers and smart contracts to offer greater automation and cost reduction for the industry. Some of the basic design principles underpinning the ISDA CDM are:

- stores data in one format;
- performs actions once;
- finds common solutions to different problems at different scales, using composite modelling for events and products;
- shares data stores across permissioned market participants and regulators; and
- no 'Extract, Transform, Transmit, Load, Transform, Store, Reconcile' processes.

(Continued)

(Continued)

Building on FpML

FpML (see Chapter 4) is a common messaging language, allowing confirmation of the trade details between trading parties and reporting of those trades to regulators. However, each party is likely to have slightly nuanced, and therefore different, interpretations as to what the various FpML fields mean, and accordingly, different processes, systems and data inputs in relation to the FpML messages. The ISDA CDM seeks to define each of the processing steps in the derivatives lifecycle and standardise these definitions (see Figure 12.11).

	Event Identifier	Party	Party	Quantity	Economics	Comments
Part Term						
Before	3fb9	P1	P2	Q	IRS(5dc4)	
After	3k9s	P1	P2	q1	IRS(5dc4)	Only change is quantity
After	3k9s	P1	P2	c,ccc.cc	Cash	Partial termination fee

	Item	Description	Comments
1	Before	IRS(5dc4) exists.	
2	Event Identifier	3k9s identifies the event that splits the notional	
3	Economics	There is no change in the terms IRS (5dc4)	
4	Quantity	The original quantity is reduced from Q to q1.	
3	Cash	A cash quantity c,ccc.cc is exchanged for the decrease in quantity of economics (IRS(5dc4))	The cash consideration for the reduction Q -> q1 is a negotiated event

Figure 12.11 An example of how the ISDA Common Domain Model might approach partial termination

From Figure 12.12, smart contracts have a number of potential use cases. Gartner has estimated that by 2022, smart contracts will be in use by more than 25% of global organisations. However, whilst we can be optimistic about smart contracts, one must also realise the existing limits and risks of the technology;[10] after all, as stated by Grant (2018), *'a smart contract is only as smart as the code in which it is written and the infrastructure in which it operates'*. This could refer to two concerns – one legal and the other operational.

---

10 Note that smart contracts and DLT each have their own specific legal and operational issues, which are somewhat independent of each other. For example, blockchain is facing issues of compatibility with the GDPR's right of erasure, with its immutability function. Therefore, problems with DLT and smart contracts should be kept separate.

Use Case		What the Smart Contract can do
Financial services	Trade clearing and settlement	Manages approval workflow between counterparties, calculates trade settlement amounts and transfers funds automatically
	Coupon payments	Automatically calculates and pays periodic coupon payments and returns principal upon bond expiration
	Insurance claim processing	Performs error checking, routing and approval workflows; calculates payout based on the type of claim and underlying policy
	Micro-insurance	Calculates and transfers micropayments based on usage data from an Internet of Things (IoT)-enabled device (e.g. pay-as-you-go automatic insurance)
Life sciences and health care	Electronic medical records	Provides transfer and/or access to medical health records upon multi-signature approvals between patients and providers
	Population health data access	Grants health researchers access to certain personal health information; micropayments are automatically transferred to the patient for participation
	Personal health tracking	Tracks patients' health-related actions through IoT devices and automatically generates rewards based on specific milestones
Technology, media and resources	Royalty distribution	Calculates and distributes royalty payments to artists and other associated parties according to the contract
Energy and resources	Autonomous electric vehicle charging stations	Processes a deposit, enables the charging station and returns remaining funds when complete.
Public sector	Recording keeping	Updates private company share registries and capitalisation table records; distributes shareholder communications
Cross-industry	Supply chain and trade finance documentation	Transfers payments upon multi-signature approval for letters of credit and issues port payments upon custody change for bills oflading
	Product provenance and history	Facilitates chain-of-custody process for products in the supply chain where the party in custody is able to log evidence about the product
	Peer-to-peer transacting	Matches parties and transfers payments auto-matically: lending insurance, energy, credits, etc.
	Voting	Validates voter criteria, logs vote to the blockchain and initiates specific actions as a result of the majority vote

Figure 12.12 Sample use cases for smart contracts

Legal Issues

With regards to legal issues, as discussed above, smart contracts, at the time of writing, operate on a conditional logic ('if X happens, then Y occurs'), meaning that it is difficult to draft smart contracts to deal with ambiguous terms. For example, returning to the example of AXA's Fizzy application, it would be hard for a smart contract to code for compensation to be paid out for a flight that was late due to an 'Act of God' because of the subjective nature of the term. Nor would it be easy to execute a code with contractual terms such as 'best efforts' or 'acting reasonably'. It must be noted that we are not suggesting, in theory, that we cannot code for these terms at a point in time in some constrained circumstances for every conceivable eventuality, but in practical terms it is likely to be simply too difficult and time consuming to achieve such a feat (never mind attempting this for something other than a particular point in time). Also, such terms are often purposely open-ended and ambiguous, allowing flexibility for unknown events or developments. Rather than trying to automate every part of a legal agreement, there needs to be careful consideration as to which clauses of a contract lend themselves to be executable by code and those that are not (or as described by Selman, 'which clauses should be "smart"?'). Our thinking about legal contracts must become more granular in order to inform our understanding about smart contracts. Applying this thinking, legal contracts can therefore be broken down into operational and non-operational clauses:

- **Operational clauses.** These types of clauses closely align themselves with Boolean algebra, as they often require an action upon the occurrence of a specified event or at a specified time. These often form the basis for most financial contracts, such as payments referencing a set calculation. Considering that smart contracts are able to utilise oracles, these operational clauses can be fed data to inform the calculation of the payment.
- **Non-operational clauses.** In contrast, non-operational clauses do not align themselves as easily with Boolean algebra, as these clauses often refer back to wider legal obligations. For example, a choice of law clause to determine the law used in case of a dispute is not easily put into code.

Therefore, operational clauses can be seen as more amenable to use within smart contracts, whilst non-operational clauses are less so.

A key component of smart contracts is the automated execution, but in some circumstances a contract may become void due to a number of reasons, such as insolvency of one of the contractual parties, or if performance has become illegal. The smart contract would execute regardless and could not be legally reversed (assuming these reversal scenarios were not 'coded for' within the smart contract). One could perhaps require the parties to contract on further transactions, reversing the result of the void contract. As a result, one may question the very suitability of the word 'smart' in the term 'smart contract'. In terms of intelligence, it simply executes pre-programmed steps; it does not 'convert unstructured information into useful and actionable information', nor does it know anything beyond the smart contract itself in terms of the consequences of performance of the code (e.g. it would be illegal).

Lastly, with the potential convergence of legalese with computer code (most importantly for relating smart legal contracts), it will be an important task to make sure that the legal layer and technical code layer align. If not, issues of liability will emerge. At the time of writing, firms such as Clause.io[11] are trying to overcome the problems that may occur in trying to draft legal language into code, through the creation of a specific legal smart contract language for lawyers, called Ergo.

Operational Issues

Smart contract technology, like most software, is subject to increasing cybersecurity concerns. The most notable example of the vulnerability of smart contracts occurred in June 2016, with what has been known as the 'DAO hack'. The DAO (Decentralised Autonomous Organisation) was an open-source smart contract investment fund, which operated on the Ethereum blockchain network. It had raised over $150 million in 2016 across an extremely short period of time. Unfortunately the code contained a software bug, that had been detailed in a public white paper, which the programmers were actively working to fix. Before being able to fix a vulnerability, a hacker was able to exploit the vulnerability caused by this bug, and through exploitation of a recursive function in the code, removing nearly $3.6 million Ether into a 'child DAO' held by the hacker. The hacker, however, wasn't breaking the code of the DAO. He or she had simply acted in accordance with the code and therefore, to some, was legitimately (per the code) obtaining the funds. In response to the attack, the Ethereum community decided to do a 'hard fork' (a rule violating change in the blockchain), which reverted the attack and returned the funds. The purist view was, however, that the power of smart contracts lies in their unchangeable nature. The ensuing controversy over the 'hard fork' led the Ethereum network to split into two chains. The unforked version, where the attacker received the funds (Ethereum Classic), and the forked modified version (Ethereum). Other incidents have occurred, but the point illustrates that smart contracts are not without operational, including cybersecurity, risks.

Learn to Walk, Before You Can Run

Like with any new technology that has attracted a lot of attention, it could be suggested that smart contracts and DLT may be purely hype. In a 2018 Gartner report, only 1% of companies were using blockchain, whilst 34% showed simply no interest in the technology (see Figure 12.13). David Furlonger, Vice President and Gartner Fellow, correctly stated that stakeholders should avoid rushing to deploy the technology as it could lead to 'significant problems of failed innovation, wasted investment, rash decisions and even rejection of a game-changing technology', Gartner (2018). In fact, it is often said that blockchain and smart contracts are 'solutions looking for a problem'.

In order for both smart contract technology and DLT to grow further, there needs to be greater effort to fully understand the technologies which will aid businesses to decide when it might be appropriate to deploy them. There is significant promise that the technology could prove to be useful, but like most technologies, they must learn to walk before they can run. If this can be achieved, then the hype can be turned into reality.

---

11 http://clause.io

Blockchain Plans

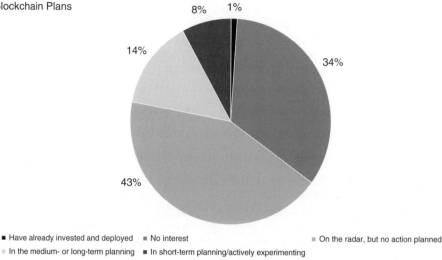

8% 1%

14%

34%

43%

- Have already invested and deployed   - No interest   - On the radar, but no action planned
- In the medium- or long-term planning   - In short-term planning/actively experimenting

Figure 12.13 The uptake of blockchain technologies by companies (from Gartner's 2018 CIO Survey)

As discussed in Chapter 4, one of the critical requirements is to create legal agreement data standards, as well as align contractual wording with actual business outcomes. The ISDA taxonomy and clause library project, launched at the time of writing by its Legal and Technology Working Group, is an interesting and vital first step in this direction.

Bibliography

Abraham, R. (2018) 'Can hashgraph succeed blockchain as the technology of choice for cryptocurrencies?', *The Hindu*, 25th March 2018

Aitken, R. (2017) 'Smart contracts on the blockchain: Can businesses reap the benefits', *Forbes*, 21st November 2017

Artificial Lawyer (2018) 'Hype killer – only 1% of companies are using blockchain', *Artificial Lawyer*, 4th May 2018

AXA (2017) 'AXA goes blockchain with Fizzy', 13th September 2017

Bain, P. (1964) 'On distributed communications networks', *IEEE Transactions on Communication Systems*, 12(1), pp. 1–9

Clack, C., Bakshi, V. and Braine, L. (2016, revised March 2017) 'Smart contract templates: Foundations, design landscape and research directions' (https://arxiv.org/abs/1608 .00771)

Clive Humby at the ANA Senior Marketer's Summit, Kellog School (2006)

Clyde & Co (2017) 'Smart contracts, blockchain and distributed ledger technologies: A legal overview for insurers', June 2017

Coindesk, 'How do Ethereum smart contracts work?' (www.coindesk.com/information/ ethereum-smart-contracts-work)

Courtland, R. (2015) 'Gordon Moore: The man whose name means progress. The visionary engineer reflects on 50 years of Moore's law', *IEEE Spectrum*, 30th March 2015

Disco, C. and van der Meulen, B. (1998) *Getting New Technologies Together: Studies in Making Sociotechnical Order*. Walter de Gruyter: Berlin

Drescher, D. (2017) *Blockchain Basics: A Non-Technical Introduction in 25 Steps*. Apress: New York

Dunlea-Peatross, T. (2018) 'Smart contracts for smart lawyers', *Bird & Bird*, 15th June 2018

Etherscan, Contract 0xe083515D1541F2a9Fd0ca03f189F5D321C73B872 (https://etherscan .io/address/0xe083515d1541f2a9fd0ca03f189f5d321c73b872#events)

Financial Times (2017) 'The mind in the machine: Demis Hassabis on artificial intelligence', *The Financial Times*, 22nd April 2017

Gartner (2018) 'Gartner survey reveals the scarcity of current blockchain deployments', 3rd May 2018 (www.gartner.com/newsroom/id/3873790)

Gendal-Brown, R. (2015) 'A simple model for smart contracts', *gendal.me*, 10th February 2015

Göthberg, D. and Azaghal (2012) File: Hash Tree.svg, Wikimedia Commons, 7th April 2015

Grant, A. (2018) 'Smart contracts 101: How this emerging technology works', *TripWire*, 15th January 2018

Grigg, I (2004) The Ricardian Contract. In Proceedings of the First IEE International Workshop on Electronic Contracting, *Institute of Electrical and Electronics Engineers*, 2004

Hansen, D., Reyes, C. and Rosini, L. (2018) 'More legal aspects of smart contract applications', Perkins Coie, March 2018

Hileman, G. and Rauchs, M. (2017) Global Blockchain Benchmarking Study, Cambridge Centre for Alternative Finance

Hogan Lovells (2017) A Guide to Blockchain and Privacy, September 2017

ISDA (2016) ISDA White Paper: 'The future of derivatives processing and market infrastructure', September 2016

ISDA and Linklaters (2017) White Paper: 'Smart contracts and distributed ledger – a legal perspective', August 2017

Koteshov, D. (2018) 'Smart vs. Ricardian contracts: What's the difference?', *EliNext*, 28th February 2018

Lamport, L., Shostake, R. and Pease, M. (1982) 'The Byzantine Generals Problem', *ACM Transactions on Programming Languages and Systems*, 4(3), pp. 382–401

Lewis, A. (2016) 'A gentle introduction to smart contracts', *Bitsonblocks.net*, 1st February 2016

Lloyd's Register Foundation and The Alan Turing Institute (2017) Insight Report on Distributed Ledger Technologies: 'Safety of engineered systems', September 2017

Monax.io, 'Smart contract explainer'

Moore, G. (1965) 'Cramming more components onto integrated circuits', *Electronics*, 38, p. 144

Orcutt, M. (2018) 'Ethereum's smart contracts are full of holes', *MIT Technology Review*, 1st March 2018

R3 and Norton Rose Fulbright (2016) 'Can smart contracts be legally binding contracts?', White Paper

Ream, J., Chu, Y. and Schatsky, D. (2016) 'Upgrading blockchains: Smart contract use cases in industry', *Deloitte Insights*, 8th June 2016

Selman, D. (2018) 'REALLY smart (and legal!) contracts', *Medium*, 28th March 2017

Software Solutions Partners Ltd, R (on the application of) v HM Customs & Excise [2007] EWHC 971

Stark, J. (2016) 'Making sense of blockchain contracts', *CoinDesk*

Stein, S. (2018) 'Hashgraph wants to give you the benefits of blockchain without the limitations', *Tech Crunch*, 14th March 2018

Szabo, N. (1996) 'Smart contracts: Building blocks for digital markets'

Thornton v Shoe Lane Parking [1971] 2 QB 163

'What is Ethereum? A step-by-step beginners guide', *Blockgeeks*

13

Electronic and Digital Signatures

In this chapter, we begin by considering the use of signatures as a method of contractual execution, before highlighting the various disadvantages of relying on 'wet-ink' signatures. The discussion then turns to the use of digital and electronic signatures, and the distinction between them. The chapter concludes by examining the current legislative approach to electronic and digital signatures.

Wet-Ink Signatures

The word 'signature' is derived from the Latin term '*signum*', meaning to 'sign, mark or seal', although in today's terms, it usually involves the writing of a name on a document. The signature at the bottom of a legal agreement is one of the foundational blocks of contract law, allowing an individual and/or entity to be bound by the terms of the contractual provisions contained in that legal agreement. It is traditionally viewed as a cursive scribble, representing the signatory's name for the purpose of providing authenticity regarding the origin of a document (the signatory's identity) and the voluntary intention of that signatory to be bound by the contractual terms of the agreement.

Signatures are used in many contexts where their legal effects are at best evidential, such as the signing of a birthday card. However, it is more with the context of signatures where they are intended to create legally enforceable rights and duties (whether immediately, or at some point in the future), through the signing of a legal contract, that this chapter is concerned with. It is the 'authenticating intention' which is often referred to as the defining characteristic of a signature for the purposes of the law, although in 2001, the Law Commission for England & Wales suggested that 'what is required therefore is something which is not purely oral and which evidences that authenticating intention'.

For a signature to be acceptable for the purposes of contract law, the process used to apply the signature to the document, and subsequently present it, is typically viewed through the lens of three key elements – authenticity, integrity and non-refutability. This confirms that the right person and/or entity applied the signature, that the signature can be seen as the signatory's intent to endorse the document and that the document has not subsequently been changed and/or tampered with (which would mean that the signatory's intent to endorse the document applied to a different version of the document).

The traditional 'wet-ink' approach to signing contracts and documentation does, however, have a number of downsides, especially in the context of the increasingly digital business agenda. During a business process, including that of putting documentation in place to be able to trade with a counterparty, documents change from digital to print format several times – with the loss of many of the advantages of digital form, which are expensive to later recover from a paper form (such as through OCR, as discussed in Chapter 11). Agreements are typically created electronically, printed for review and/or approval, then emailed in digital form to send to authorised signatories, printed for signing, scanned back into electronic form and printed again when needed for review. As discussed in Chapter 11, document generation platforms and document content management systems assist with reducing this heavy reliance on paper-based processes, however, ultimately paper is required, often at the very least, for the purposes of signing.

Issues that can be attributed to 'wet-ink' signatures

- Time spent printing (including formatting to ensure adequate printing style).
- Printing costs.
- Time to get multiple signatories to sign in person (who may sometimes need to sign in a particular sequence e.g. from a commercial point of view).
- Delay due to availability of signatories to physically sign.
- Scanning issues (e.g. poor quality, resolution and/or faintness of scan).
- Scanning costs.
- Time and cost of uploading the document(s) into an enterprise documentation content management system.
- Storage costs of hardcopy originals.
- Environmental impact of printing and use of paper.

Bridging the Gap to Computational and Smart Contracts

In the previous two chapters, the advantages of computational and data-orientated contracts and smart contracts were discussed. It is of course odd that any move towards data-driven contracts, recognising the valuable inputs from a contractual arrangement to business optimisation, regulatory compliance and operational management, should need to obtain contract data terms not from a digital source, but from an analogue one. A wet-ink signature does precisely this, meaning that the golden record, the contract itself, becomes a physical document with a wet-ink signature, or a scan of it. Even this is subsequently digitised through an OCR process, this almost always a 'lossy transformation'. Important information, above and beyond the text characters themselves – such as detail around paragraph headings, table headers and rows, which can be important when attempting to manage and use legal agreement contract data – is typically lost in such a process. Although tags are often used in the physical form by lawyers on hardcopy documents, the use of hardcopy paper is limiting in terms of how such information can usefully be shared, for example, for data analytics purposes. In many ways, electronic and digital signatures can be seen as a true bridge from the paper to the digital world, providing assurance around integrity, authenticity and non-refutability within the digital world, with its many advantages over an analogue and paper-based world.

Distinguishing Electronic and Digital Signatures

To begin with, electronic and digital signatures need to be understood in the context of 'electronic execution'. This is a broad term referring to a method of execution that does not involve physically signing a physical document, such as typing one's name into an email containing the terms of a contract, or at the other end of the spectrum, signing via an electronic signing platform.

Many professional standards bodies and regulatory bodies use the terms 'electronic signature' and 'digital signature' interchangeably, however, there are important differences between the two. An electronic signature can be thought of as *'an electronic sound, symbol, or process, attached to or logically associated with a contract or other record and executed or adopted by a person with intent to sign the record'.*[1] It is likely to be some sort of pictorial or bitmap representation of a wet-ink signature, or may even be a typed acknowledgement or acceptance. In a similar vein, the Electronic Communications Act 2000, in section 7(2), defines an electronic signature in a broad manner as *'anything in electronic form … [that is] incorporated into or logically associated with any electronic communication or electronic data and purports to be used by the individual creating it to sign'.*

In contrast, by referring to a digital signature, one usually means the provision of extra data in relation to a document which identifies and authenticates the sender and document data, typically through the use of public-key encryption. The Electronic Identification, Authentication and Trust Services Regulation (eIDAS)[2] effectively defines a 'digital signature', through the defined term 'advanced electronic signature', as *'one that (i) is uniquely linked to the signatory; (ii) is capable of identifying the signatory; (iii) is created using electronic signature creation data that the signatory can, with a high level of confidence, use under his sole control; and (iv) is linked to the data signed therewith in such a way that any subsequent change in the data is detectable'*[3] and a *'qualified electronic signature'* as *'an advanced electronic signature that is created by a qualified signature creation device and which is based on a qualified certificate for electronic signatures'.*[4] Accordingly, electronic signatures can be said to use various audit trail methods such as phone verification or email to authenticate the identity of a signatory, whereas digital signatures use certificate-based IDs for this, which are bound to the document via encryption techniques, demonstrating proof of signing. Many digital signature platforms link this 'extra data' with a digital signature having an associated pictorial representation of a wet-ink signature (see Figure 13.1).

Proposal accepted by:

Name: Mr Akber Datoo

Signed:..............

Position: Director

Date: .... 18 August 2018 | 07:33 BST

Figure 13.1 An example of a digital signature with an associated pictorial representation of the wet-ink signature

---

1 15 U.S.C. § 7006(5).
2 EU Regulation No. 910/2014.
3 Articles 3(11) and 26, eIDAS Regulation.
4 Article 3(12), eIDAS Regulation.

How Do Digital Signatures Work?

Digital signatures use public-key cryptography. Central to this is the use of hash functions, which take data sets of various length and size, converting them to a fixed length called a hash value. Good hash functions, typically used for cryptography, yield the same identical hash values for identical input data and it is highly improbable that distinct pieces of input data will result in the same hash value. Small changes in the input data result in changes to the output hash value (see Figure 13.2).

Cryptography can be thought of as a digital key to protect digital data and assets, in the same way that locks and keys are used to protect many physical day-to-day assets such as houses and cars. It involves two stages – encryption, whereby the data asset is converted using a hash function into a data character stream (called ciphertext) that is unintelligible without a digital key to unlock it, and decryption, where use of this digital key transforms the data back to its original pre-encryption form (see Figure 13.3).

Encryption can be symmetric or asymmetric. In the former case, the same digital key is used to both encrypt and decrypt the data. This, however, means that the one key can be stolen and allow anyone to both encrypt and decrypt data. With asymmetric cryptography, two separate but complementary keys (one 'public' and one 'private') that are mathematically related are used – one key encrypts the data, and the other one decrypts it. Crucially, the public key can be shared freely without endangering the details of the private key. Asymmetric keys can be used in one of two ways, depending on the direction of the information flow.[5] They do not protect the message from being read, but allow the sender's identity to be verified, since only the individual with the related private key can create the encrypted text that is capable of being decrypted by the related private key (see Figure 13.4). This also allows validation of the integrity of the document to which a digital signature is attached. The hash value is unique to the document – any change in the document, even by a single character, will result in a different hash value being obtained upon use of the public key. If the decrypted hash matches a second computed

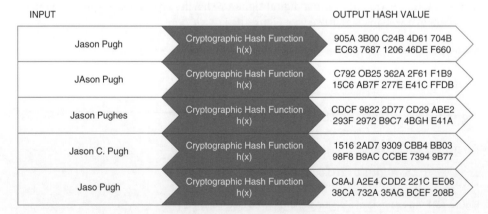

INPUT		OUTPUT HASH VALUE
Jason Pugh	Cryptographic Hash Function h(x)	905A 3B00 C24B 4D61 704B EC63 7687 1206 46DE F660
JAson Pugh	Cryptographic Hash Function h(x)	C792 OB25 362A 2F61 F1B9 15C6 AB7F 277E E41C FFDB
Jason Pughes	Cryptographic Hash Function h(x)	CDCF 9822 2D77 CD29 ABE2 293F 2972 B9C7 4BGH E41A
Jason C. Pugh	Cryptographic Hash Function h(x)	1516 2AD7 9309 CBB4 BB03 98F8 B9AC CCBE 7394 9B77
Jaso Pugh	Cryptographic Hash Function h(x)	C8AJ A2E4 CDD2 221C EE06 38CA 732A 35AG BCEF 208B

Figure 13.2 An example of both how a digital signature is converted into a fixed-length hash value and how small changes in the input data result in changes in the output hash value

---

5 In the case of public to private asymmetric cryptography, the data is encrypted using a public key but decrypted using a private key associated with the public key. Once the data is received, only the holder of the related private key can decrypt the data, which protects the message from being read by those without this private key.

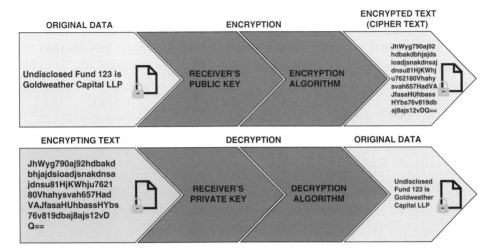

Figure 13.3 The process involved in the encryption and decryption of data through the use of private and public keys

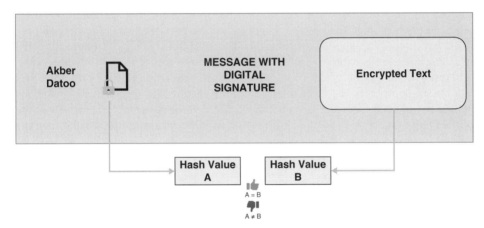

Figure 13.4 An example of how asymmetric cryptography can be used to verify if a document has been changed through a comparison of hash values

hash of the document, it proves that the document has not been changed or tampered with since the digital signature was applied. If, however, it doesn't match, then this is an indication that either:

a) the document has been changed; or

b) the private key that was used to create the signature does not correspond to the appropriate public key provided by the signatory for use.

Which Law Applies in Respect of the Formal Validity of an Electronic and/or Digitally Signed Contract?

Whether or not a legal agreement can be validly executed using an electronic signature is a matter for the law applicable to the formal validity of the contract, which includes matters such as the method of execution of documents. The principal EU regulation setting out the conflicts of law rule in this area is Regulation (EC) No. 593/2008 on the law applicable to contractual obligations ('Rome I'). Rome I determines the law which should be applied to ascertain whether a contract is formally valid. It provides that:

1) Where both parties are in the same country at the time of conclusion of the contract, the court will hold the contract valid if the contract satisfies the formal requirements of:
   - the law specified by the parties as the governing law of the contract; or
   - the law of the country where the contract is concluded.
2) Where the parties are in different countries at the time that the contract is concluded, the court will hold the contract valid if the contract satisfies the formal requirements of:
   - the law specified by the contract parties as the contract governing law;
   - the law of either country where the parties are present at the time of contract conclusion; or
   - the law of the country where the place of habitual residence of either contract party is at the time of execution.

Rome I is a helpful harmonisation tool for a party looking to enforce its contractual rights in an EU Member State court. On the other hand, non-EU Member State courts are not subject to a Rome I equivalent harmonising rule for determining which law should be applied to ascertain the contract's validity. Determining the governing law therefore must be established by reference to a country's individual laws. In Singapore, for example, the court will apply general common law principles and examine the contract to see if the intention of the parties with regard to the governing law can be inferred from the circumstances and determine which system of law the contract has its most real and close connection with before assessing the validity of the contract in accordance with that country's rules.

International Legislative Approaches to Digital Signatures

The legislative approaches to digital signatures can be divided into three categories:

1) **The minimalist approach.** In this case, the legislation is technology agnostic and does not specify techniques relating to ensuring the integrity of the electronic signature. Examples of such approaches are the USA and Australia. In many ways, this can be compared to the approach taken by legislation for wet-ink signatures, whereby the integrity of the signature must ultimately be proven in court.
2) **The specified approach.** The legislation is quite prescriptive regarding the manner in which the specified integrity of the signature must be achieved (e.g. specifying the use of PKI – public key cryptography). In such jurisdictions, digital signatures are usually assumed to be valid unless the contrary can be proved. Singapore and Japan are examples of such specified legislative approaches.
3) **The two-tier approach.** In such cases, the aim is to provide a framework regarding authentication (i.e. the minimalist approach), within which there will be greater legal recognition and effect if certain widely used techniques are used (i.e. not specifying one technology approach). This is the approach taken by the EU under the eIDAS regulation.

England and Wales – Legislation Regarding Enforceability of Electronic and Digital Signatures

The EU has created two major pieces of legislation in connection with electronic signatures: EU Directive 2000/31/EC (the e-Commerce Directive) and EU Regulation 910/2014 (the eIDAS regulation).

The first legislation was a 'Directive', which meant that it had to be written into each country's own law. In the UK this led to the Electronic Communications Act 2000. The Electronic Communications Act 2000 (ECA 2000) provides a framework for admissibility of electronic documents and signatures (see definition above) under English law. It does not distinguish between types of electronic signatures and/or digital signatures, and there is no legal requirement for a particular type of implementation. Sections 7(1) and 15(2) of ECA 2000 provide that electronic signatures are admissible in evidence before the English courts in respect of any questions of authenticity or integrity of the document, and whether it is intended to have contractual and legal effect.

The second legislation, as a 'regulation', applied immediately across Europe with no need for national legislative approval, and came into force on 1 July 2016. It provided confirmation of the status of advanced e-signatures, adding in a new category of 'qualified electronic signatures' (see above for definition) arising out of a cross-national model for identity and trust services defined at length in the regulation.

It should be noted that under the law of England and Wales, some document types are subject to specific formalities (see Chapter 2). An example of this is the fact that guarantees are required to be in writing and signed by the guarantor (or a person authorised by the guarantor to do so) – as per section 4 of the Statutes of Fraud Act 1677. Financial collateral arrangements, as defined in the Financial Collateral Arrangement (No. 2) Regulations 2003, must be evidenced in writing.[6] Certain documents, such as a mortgage where the mortgagee is to have a statutory power of sale, need to be made by way of deed.[7] It is regarded that the 'in writing' requirement is met by any electronic representation of an agreement, which results in the terms being legible on a screen. Where a document needs to be executed as a deed, this can cause logistical issues that need to be considered in the context of a document to be signed electronically, with particular regard to the requirement for the deed to be witnessed.

Bibliography

Casamento, G., Hatfield, P. and Hjörleifsson, M. (2009) 'Enhancing the admissibility and enforceability of electronically signed documents', *Bloomberg Law Reports – Technology Law*, 1(11)

Chhillar, N., Yadav, N. and Jaiswal, N. (2013) 'Enhances security reduces time: Digital signatures', *International Journal of Computer Science and Information Technology Research*, 1(1), pp. 51–57

Crosbie and Pickens v Pickens (1749) *Mor* 16814

---

6 s 3, Financial Collateral Arrangement (No. 2) Regulations 2003.
7 s 101, Law of Property Act 1925.

Curry, I. (2000) *Key Update and the Complete Story on the Need for Two Key Pairs*, Entrust Technologies, Version 1.2, August 2000

Harris, J. (2014) *8 Rules for E-Signature Security*, SIGNiX

Law Commission (2001) 'Electronic commerce: Formal requirements in electronic transactions', December 2001

MacQueen, H. and Garland, C. (2015) 'Signatures in Scots law: Form, effect and burden of proof', *Juridical Review*, 2015, pp. 107–134

Rennie, R. and Brymer, S. (2008) *Conveyancing in the Electronic Age.* Thomson/Green: Edinburgh

Appendix A

(h)(ii) *Party A Downgrade*

  1) *S&P Requirements*

  In the event that the short term unsecured, unsubordinated debt obligations of Party A (or its successor) cease to be "A-1" (or its equivalent) by S&P (an "**S&P Downgrade**") then Party A shall, within 30 calendar days of such S&P Downgrade, at its own cost, effect one of the following remedies:

  i) obtain a guarantee of its obligations under this Agreement from a third party with the Required S&P Rating; or

  ii) transfer collateral to Party B pursuant to the Credit Support Annex ("**CSA**") to this Agreement; or

  iii) transfer all of its rights and obligations under this Agreement to a replacement third party provided that such third party (or its Credit Support Provider) has the Required Ratings of all the Rating Agencies and is able and willing to make the Additional Tax Representation and provided the consent of the Note Trustee has been obtained whose consent should be given if S&P confirms that such transfer would maintain the raring of the Notes at or above "A-1"; or

  iv) take such other action as S&P shall agree with Party A as will result in the rating of the Notes by S&P following the taking of such action being maintained at or restored to the level it would have been immediately prior to the S&P Downgrade.

  If following an S&P Downgrade by S&P, Party A does not take one of the measures described in (i) to (iv) above within 30 calendar days of that S&P Downgrade, then such failure will not constitute an Event of Default but will constitute an Additional Termination Event, for which Party A will be the sole Affected Party and which Additional Termination Event will be deemed to occur on the 30th calendar day following that S&P Downgrade.

  2) *Further S&P Requirements*

  In the event that the short term, unsecured and unsubordinated debt obligations of Party A (or its successor) cease to be rated at least as high as "A-3" (or its equivalent) (an "**A-3 Downgrade**") by S&P then Party A will, within 30 calendar days of such A-3 Downgrade, at its own cost effect one of the following remedies:

  i) obtain a guarantee, a letter of credit (or equivalent) of its rights and obligations under this Agreement from a third party with a rating equal to the Required S&P Rating; or

ii) transfer all of its rights and obligations with respect to this Agreement to a replacement third party provided that such third party (or its Credit Support Provider) has the Required Ratings of all the Rating Agencies and is able and willing to make the Additional Tax Representation. For the avoidance of doubt, any collateral provided by Party A pursuant to the CSA shall not be returned until a replacement third party has been appointed pursuant to this Part 1(h)(ii)(2)(ii), and Party A shall continue to perform its obligations until such replacement third party has assumed its obligations.

If, following an A-3 Downgrade by S&P, Party A does not take one of the measures described in (i) and (ii) above within 30 calendar days of such A-3 Downgrade by S&P, then such failure will not constitute an Event of Default but will constitute an Additional Termination Event, for which Party A will be the sole Affected Party and which Additional Termination Event will be deemed to occur on the 30th calendar day following such A-3 Downgrade by S&P.

3) *Moody's Requirements*

In the event that the long term, unsecured and unsubordinated debt obligations of Party A (or its successor), cease to be rated at least as high as "A1" (or its equivalent) (an "**A1 Downgrade**") by Moody's or the short term, unsecured and unsubordinated debt obligations of Party A (or any successor), cease to be rated at least as high as "Prime-1" (or its equivalent) (a "**Prime-1 Downgrade**") by Moody's, then Party A will within 30 calendar days of such downgrade, at its own cost, effect one of the following remedies:

i) transfer all of its rights and obligations with respect to this Agreement to a replacement third party with the Required Ratings of all the Rating Agencies which third party is not deemed unacceptable by Moody's (acting in its reasonable discretion) and is able and willing to make the Additional Tax Representation; or

ii) procure another party with the Required Moody's Rating to become a co-obligor in respect of the obligations of Party A under this Agreement which third party is not deemed unacceptable by Moody's (acting in its reasonable discretion); or

iii) take such other action as Moody's confirm to Party A will remedy a Prime-1 Downgrade or an A1 Downgrade, as the case may be; or

iv) transfer collateral to Party B pursuant to the CSA to this Agreement.

4) *Further Moody's Requirements*

In the event that the long term, unsecured and unsubordinated debt obligations of Party A (or its successor) cease to be rated at least as high as "A3" (or its equivalent) (an "**A3 Downgrade**") by Moody's or the short term unsecured and unsubordinated debt obligations of Party A (or any successor), cease to be rated at least as high as "Prime-2" (or its equivalent) (a "**Prime-2 Downgrade**") by Moody's, then Party A will make best efforts, within 30 days of the occurrence of such downgrade and at its own cost, to effect one of the following remedies:

i) transfer all of its rights and obligations with respect to this Agreement to a replacement third party with the Required Ratings of all the Rating Agencies which third party is not deemed unacceptable by Moody's (acting in its reasonable discretion) and is able and willing to make the Additional Tax Representation; or

ii) procure another party with the Required Moody's Rating (as defined below) to become a co-obligor in respect of the obligations of Party A under this Agreement which third party is not deemed unacceptable by Moody's (acting in its reasonable discretion); or

iii) take such other action as Moody's shall agree with Party A.

5) Pending compliance with any one of Part 1(h)(4)(i), Part 1(h)(4)(ii) and Part 1(h)(iii) following the occurrence of an A3 Downgrade or a Prime-2 Downgrade, Part A will, at its own cost and within 10 Business Days of the occurrence of such downgrade, deliver collateral to Party B in accordance with the terms of the CSA.

6) If, following an A1 Downgrade or a Prime-1 Downgrade (as defined above), Party A does not take one of the measures described in Part 1(h)(3)(i) to (iv) above, then such failure shall not constitute an Event of Default but shall constitute an Additional Termination Event, for which Party A will be the sole Affected Party and which Additional Termination Event shall be deemed to occur on the 30th day following such A1 Downgrade or Prime-1 Downgrade.

7) If, following an A3 Downgrade or a Prime-2 Downgrade (as defined above), Party A does not take the measures described in Part 1(h)(5) above within 10 Business Days of such A3 Downgrade or Prime-2 Downgrade, then such failure shall not constitute an Event of Default but shall constitute an Additional Termination Event, for which Party A will be the sole Affected Party and which Additional Termination Event shall be deemed to occur on the tenth Business Day following such A3 Downgrade or Prime-2 Downgrade.

8) If, following an A3 Downgrade or a Prime-2 Downgrade (as defined above), Party A does not take one of the measures described in Part 1(h)(4)(i) to (iii) within thirty days of such A3 Downgrade or Prime-2 Downgrade, then, notwithstanding Party A's compliance with the provisions of Part 1(h)(5) above, then such failure shall not constitute an Event of Default but shall constitute an Additional Termination Event, for which Party A will be the sole Affected Party and which Additional Termination Event shall be deemed to occur on the thirtieth day following such A3 Downgrade or Prime-2 Downgrade.

9) If Party A delivers collateral to Party B pursuant to the CSA in support of its obligations under this Agreement following downgrade and at any time thereafter Party A (or its successor) has the Required Ratings of all the Rating Agencies, then an amount equal to the amount of any collateral delivered pursuant to such CSA shall be returned to Party A (and the provisions of Part 1(h) above shall apply in the event of any subsequent downgrade.

(iii) **Note Enforcement Event**

The service by the Note Trustee of a Note Enforcement Notice in accordance with Condition 11 of the Notes shall be an Additional Termination Event in respect of which Party B shall be the sole Affected Party (save that for the purposes of Section 6(b)(iv), both parties shall be Affected Parties).

...

(m) *Definitions*
  i) *In this Agreement:*

"**Moody's**" means Moody's Investors Service.

"**S&P**" means Standard & Poor's Ratings Service, a division of The McGraw Hill Companies, Inc. and any successor thereto.

"**Rating Agencies**" means Moody's and S&P.

"**Required Moody's Rating**" means, in respect of an entity, that its long term, unsecured and unsubordinated debt obligations are rated A1 or above by Moody's and that its short term, unsecured and unsubordinated debt obligations are rated Prime-1 or above by Moody's.

"**Required S&P Rating**" means, in respect of an entity, that its short term, unsecured and unsubordinated debt obligations are rated at least A-1 by S&P.

"**Required Ratings**" means in respect of Moody's, the Required Moody's Rating, (ii) in respect of S&P, the Required S&P Rating and (iii) in respect of all the Rating Agencies, each of the Required Moody's Rating and the Required S&P Rating.

Source: © D2 Legal Technology/Akber Datoo

Appendix B

Morgan Stanley

Liquidity Coverage Ratio Disclosures Report

For the Quarterly Period Ended March 31, 2018

Morgan Stanley

LCR DISCLOSURES REPORT
For the quarterly period ended March 31, 2018

Table of Contents		Page

1. Morgan Stanley

Morgan Stanley is a global financial services firm that, through its subsidiaries and affiliates, provides a wide variety of products and services to a large and diversified group of clients and customers, including corporations, governments, financial institutions, and individuals. Unless the context otherwise requires, the terms "Morgan Stanley" or the "Firm" mean Morgan Stanley together with its consolidated subsidiaries.

Morgan Stanley was originally incorporated under the laws of the State of Delaware in 1981, and its predecessor companies date back to 1924. The Firm is a financial holding company under the Bank Holding Company Act of 1956, as amended, and is subject to the regulation and oversight of the Board of Governors of the Federal Reserve System (the "Federal Reserve").

The Firm conducts its business from its headquarters in and around New York City, its regional offices and branches throughout the United States of America ("U.S."), and its principal offices in London, Tokyo, Hong Kong, and other world financial centers. The Federal Reserve establishes liquidity requirements for the Firm, and evaluates the Firm's compliance with such liquidity requirements. The Office of the Comptroller of the Currency (the "OCC") establishes similar liquidity requirements and standards for the Firm's U.S. bank subsidiaries, Morgan Stanley Bank, N.A. and Morgan Stanley Private Bank, N.A. (collectively, "U.S. Bank Subsidiaries").

For descriptions of the Firm's business, see "Business" in Part I, Item 1 of the Firm's Annual Report on Form 10-K for the year ended December 31, 2017 ("2017 Form 10-K").

2. U.S. Liquidity Coverage Ratio

The U.S. Liquidity Coverage Ratio rule ("LCR") requires certain U.S. banking organizations ("Covered Companies"), including the Firm and its U.S. Bank Subsidiaries, to maintain on each business day an amount of high-quality liquid assets ("HQLA") that are unencumbered and controlled by the Covered Company's liquidity risk management function ("eligible HQLA") sufficient to meet their total stressed net cash outflows over a prospective 30 calendar-day period, as calculated in accordance with the LCR. The Firm and its U.S. Bank Subsidiaries are required to maintain a minimum LCR of 100%.

The LCR classifies HQLA into three categories of assets: Level 1, Level 2A, and Level 2B liquid assets. The LCR provides that Level 1 liquid assets, which are the highest quality and most liquid assets, are included in a Covered Company's eligible HQLA without a limit and without haircuts. The LCR treats Level 2A and 2B liquid assets as having characteristics that are associated with being relatively stable and significant sources of liquidity, but not to the same degree as Level 1 liquid assets. Accordingly, the LCR subjects Level 2A liquid assets to a 15 percent haircut and, when combined with Level 2B liquid assets, they may not exceed 40 percent of the total eligible HQLA. Level 2B liquid assets, which are associated with a lesser degree of liquidity and more volatility than Level 2A liquid assets, are subject to a 50 percent haircut and may not exceed 15 percent of the total eligible HQLA. All other classes of assets do not qualify as HQLA.

To be included in a Covered Company's eligible HQLA, which is the numerator of the LCR, Level 1, 2A or 2B assets must meet a variety of specific standards designed to ensure that such assets have robust liquidity characteristics. In general, however, Level 1 assets include central bank reserve balances, both domestic and foreign, that are withdrawable by a Covered Company without restriction; securities issued or guaranteed by the U.S. Treasury Department or, in some cases, by other agencies of the U.S. government; and certain other securities that are issued or guaranteed by non-U.S. sovereign governments, multilateral development banks and similar institutions. Level 2A assets include certain investment grade securities issued or guaranteed by U.S. government-sponsored enterprises and certain other securities that are issued or guaranteed by non-U.S. sovereign governments, multilateral development banks and similar institutions that do not meet Level 1 asset criteria. Level 2B assets include certain corporate debt and common equity securities that are not issued by financial sector entities and that meet a variety of eligibility criteria, including market price stability in periods of significant stress.

The Firm's eligible HQLA under the LCR does not include our borrowing capacity at the Federal Reserve Bank of New York, the Federal Home Loan Banks, and non-U.S. central banks at which the Firm or its subsidiaries have borrowing capacity. In practice, the Firm could increase its available liquidity, if necessary, by exercising such borrowing rights on a secured basis against collateral meeting applicable standards, which vary by facility.

A Covered Company's total net cash outflow amount, which is the denominator of the LCR, is determined under the LCR by applying mandated outflow and inflow rates, which reflect certain prescribed, industry-wide stressed assumptions, against the balances of a Covered Company's funding sources, obligations, transactions, and assets over a prospective 30 calendar-day period. Inflows that can be included to offset outflows are limited to 75 percent of outflows to ensure that Covered Companies are maintaining sufficient on-balance sheet liquidity and are not overly reliant on inflows, which may not materialize in a period of stress. The total net cash outflow calculation also includes an add-on calculation that takes into account the largest daily difference between certain outflows and inflows with set maturity dates. The inflow and outflow rates mandated

1

by the LCR may be materially different from what actual inflow and outflow rates would be in a stress period.

The LCR recognizes that, under certain circumstances, it may be necessary for a Covered Company's LCR to fall briefly below 100 percent to fund unanticipated liquidity needs. The LCR establishes a framework for a flexible supervisory response when a Covered Company's LCR falls below 100 percent. Under the LCR, a Covered Company must notify the appropriate U.S. banking regulator (which is the Federal Reserve, in the case of the Firm) on any business day that its LCR is less than 100 percent. In addition, if a Covered Company's LCR is below 100 percent for three consecutive business days, the Covered Company must submit to its appropriate U.S. banking regulator a plan for remediation of the shortfall.

For a further discussion of the regulatory liquidity framework applicable to the Firm, see "Management's Discussion and Analysis of Financial Condition and Results of Operations ("MD&A")—Liquidity and Capital Resources—Regulatory Liquidity Framework" in the Firm's Quarterly Report on Form 10-Q for the quarter ended March 31, 2018 ("Form 10-Q").

3. LCR Disclosure Requirements

The LCR requires certain Covered Companies, including Morgan Stanley (but not the U.S. Bank Subsidiaries), to make quantitative and qualitative disclosures related to their LCR calculations and liquidity management practices on a quarterly basis ("LCR Disclosures"), beginning with the quarter ended June 30, 2017. This report contains the Firm's LCR Disclosures for the quarter ended March 31, 2018.

The Firm's LCR Disclosures are not required to be, and have not been, audited by the Firm's independent registered public accounting firm. The Firm's LCR Disclosures are based on our current understanding of the LCR and other factors, which may be subject to change as the Firm receives additional clarification and implementation guidance from regulators relating to the LCR, and as the interpretation of the LCR evolves over time. Some measures of exposures contained in this report may not be consistent with accounting principles generally accepted in the U.S. ("U.S. GAAP"), and may not be comparable with measures reported in the 2017 Form 10-K and the Form 10-Q.

4. LCR Qualitative Disclosures

The main drivers of the liquidity coverage ratio

Our LCR quantitative disclosures, shown in the chart in Section 5, reflect the average daily value of each disclosure category across the quarter. When discussing the main drivers of our LCR, we refer to these average daily values.

Our cash outflow amounts this quarter were principally driven by secured wholesale funding (referred to here as secured funding transactions) and asset exchange outflows, which constituted more than 50 percent of our LCR cash outflow amount and which were concentrated in our Institutional Securities business segment. Secured funding transactions include repurchase transactions, loans of collateral to customers to effect short positions, and other secured loans received by a Covered Company. Asset exchanges are transactions where the counterparties have previously exchanged non-cash assets and have agreed to return such assets to each other at a later date, but do not include secured funding and secured lending transactions.

Other outflow drivers are noted in the chart in Section 5. The Firm's main outflow drivers primarily arose in connection with our Institutional Securities business segment, except for non-operational funding and brokered deposit outflows, a substantial portion of which related to our Wealth Management business segment. These outflows reflect prescribed, industry-wide assumptions in the LCR about the liquidity risk in the Firm's business lines, activities and products, as measured for a projected 30-day stress period.

Our cash inflow amounts this quarter were principally driven by secured lending and asset exchange cash inflows, which constituted more than 70 percent of our LCR cash inflow amount and which were concentrated in our Institutional Securities business segment. Secured lending transactions include reverse repurchase transactions and securities borrowed transactions. Other inflow amounts are noted in the chart in Section 5 of this document. The Firm's main inflow drivers primarily arose in connection with our Institutional Securities business segment.

The composition of eligible HQLA

As shown in the following chart, Level 1 assets constituted a significant portion of the Firm's total eligible HQLA in the quarter, on both an unweighted and a weighted basis. The Firm's Level 1 assets primarily include cash on deposit with central banks, U.S. Treasury securities and other high quality non-U.S. sovereign securities. The Firm's combined Level 2A and Level 2B assets are below the 40% cap for such assets under the LCR, and the Level 2B assets are below the rule's 15% cap. The Firm's Level 2A assets primarily include U.S. government-sponsored enterprise securities and certain non-U.S. sovereign securities, and the Level 2B assets primarily include publicly traded corporate debt and equity securities that are not issued by financial sector entities.

HQLA Categories as Percentage of Firm's Total Eligible HQLA

	Average Unweighted	Average Weighted
Level 1 assets	81%	86%
Level 2A assets	10%	9%
Level 2B assets	9%	5%

Our liquidity management function dynamically manages the composition of our eligible HQLA, taking into account the Firm's liquidity risk tolerance, as approved by our Board of Directors; liquidity risk limits established by the Liquidity Risk Department; the results of liquidity stress testing; regulatory requirements; and other relevant considerations.

Derivative exposures and potential collateral calls

The Firm is a participant in global derivatives markets, with net derivative assets and net derivative liabilities of $20,482 million and $20,582 million, respectively, as of March 31, 2018, as measured on a fair value basis. In some cases, our derivative counterparties have contractual rights that require us to post collateral to them in the event that credit rating agencies downgrade our credit rating. In measuring collateral call risks, we consider all amounts of collateral that we could be required to post in accordance with the terms and conditions of the downgrade trigger clauses found in applicable legal agreements. The impact of potential collateral calls related to our derivatives exposures is inherently uncertain and would depend on a number of interrelated factors, including, among others, the magnitude of the downgrade, the rating relative to peers, the rating assigned by the relevant agency pre-downgrade, individual client behavior and future mitigating actions we might take. We manage the risk of potential collateral calls on our derivative positions by employing a variety of risk mitigation strategies, including modeling the impact of credit rating agency downgrades in our liquidity stress test program, diversifying risk exposures, hedging, managing counterparty and product risk limits and maintaining eligible HQLA and a substantial Global Liquidity Reserve to enable us to meet unexpected collateral calls or other potentially adverse developments. For a discussion of our Global Liquidity Reserve, see "MD&A—Liquidity and Capital Resources—Liquidity Risk Management Framework— Global Liquidity Reserve" in Part II, Item 7 of the 2017 Form 10-K.

Currency mismatch in the liquidity coverage ratio

A significant portion of our business is conducted in currencies other than the U.S. dollar, and changes in foreign exchange rates relative to the U.S. dollar, therefore, can affect the value of non-U.S. dollar net assets, revenues and expenses. Potential exposures as a result of these fluctuations in currencies are closely monitored, and

strategies can be adopted to reduce the impact of these fluctuations on our financial performance. These strategies may include the financing of non-U.S. dollar assets with direct or swap-based borrowings in the same currency and the use of currency forward contracts or the spot market in various hedging transactions related to net assets, revenues, expenses or cash flows. We actively monitor and manage risks associated with currency mismatch, and currency mismatch is not a main driver of our LCR.

Concentration of funding sources

The Firm has adopted a comprehensive risk management program to ensure the durability of our funding, including concentration limits on certain funding sources. As of March 31, 2018, our primary sources of funding were long-term debt (38 percent), deposits (32 percent), secured funding (15 percent), and shareholders' equity (15 percent)[1]. Our long-term debt instruments are diversified across tenors, currencies and channels, and our deposits are diversified across more than three million Wealth Management business segment household relationships. We execute our secured funding program in accordance with risk management principles that require a significant weighted average maturity, a maturity limit structure, and an investor limit structure to ensure no over-concentration in secured funding sources.

The centralized liquidity management function and its interaction with other functional areas

Our Board of Directors has adopted a formal liquidity risk management framework that imposes specific responsibilities on the centralized liquidity management function, including with respect to its interaction with other functional areas within the Firm. Under this framework, the Firm's Corporate Treasury and Bank Resource Management functions, together with our U.S. Bank Subsidiaries' Chief Investment Officer team, are the "first line of defense" with respect to liquidity risk management. Among other responsibilities, these functions are required to identify and assess the Firm's liquidity risks; incorporate identified liquidity risks into liquidity stress testing models and the risk management framework; conduct rigorous liquidity stress testing to measure liquidity risks over a range of scenarios and time horizons, enabling the Firm to determine liquidity and funding needs under adverse conditions; determine the size of the Firm's required liquidity in accordance with the Firm's liquidity risk tolerance and business needs; and dynamically manage the Firm's liquidity reserves, HQLA, and sources of funding, taking into account liquidity risk management limits and strategies, market conditions, client and counterparty behavior, monetary policy, legal or regulatory requirements and developments, or other factors in the markets in which we operate.

---

[1] Figures may not sum to 100% due to rounding.

The liquidity risk management framework adopted by our Board of Directors assigns "second line of defense" responsibilities to the Firm's Liquidity Risk Department and Model Risk Management function. Among other responsibilities, these functions are required to oversee the liquidity risk arising from business activities that are primarily managed by the first line of defense; review and approve all changes to liquidity stress test models, methodologies and assumptions; ensure the appropriateness and adequacy of liquidity stress test assumptions; and report the results of their independent identification, assessment and monitoring of liquidity risk and related limits across the Firm.

The Firm's Internal Audit function serves as the "third line of defense." Internal Audit's responsibilities with respect to liquidity risk management include auditing the Firm's compliance with internal guidelines set for liquidity risk management and liquidity risk monitoring; providing an independent assessment of liquidity and funding risks, controls and processes; and providing an independent assessment of whether the Firm's liquidity risk management function complies with applicable regulatory standards and supervisory expectations.

Changes in the liquidity coverage ratio over time and causes of such changes

Morgan Stanley is a global financial services firm with operations in all major financial markets around the world. The Firm's LCR will fluctuate over time in response to changes in our liquidity risk profile, market conditions, client and counterparty behavior, liquidity risk management limits, monetary policy, legal or regulatory developments, or other factors in the markets in which we operate. Volatility may be material and under some circumstances may result in a ratio of less than 100 percent.

The decrease in the LCR in the current quarter is due to an increase in net outflows (the denominator of the ratio) driven by the impact of an increase in lending commitments, primarily within the Institutional Securities business segment. The Firm remains in compliance with the U.S. LCR requirements.

5. LCR Quantitative Disclosures

In the following table, the figures reported in the "Average Weighted Amount" column reflect the prescribed, industry-wide assumptions and haircuts defined by the LCR to determine the Firm's eligible HQLA, cash outflow amounts and cash inflow amounts. The figures reported in the "Average Unweighted Amount" column reflect gross values that are not included in the calculation used to determine the Firm's compliance with LCR requirements.

Morgan Stanley

Period: January 1, 2018 to March 31, 2018	Average Unweighted Amount[1]	Average Weighted Amount[1]
$ in millions		

High-Quality Liquid Assets (HQLA)

1	**Total eligible high-quality liquid assets (HQLA), of which:**	**168,531**	**158,365**
2	Eligible level 1 liquid assets	136,643	136,643
3	Eligible level 2A liquid assets	16,511	14,034
4	Eligible level 2B liquid assets	15,377	7,688

Cash Outflow Amounts

5	**Deposit outflow from retail customers and counterparties, of which:**	**140,610**	**27,539**
6	Stable retail deposit outflow	-	-
7	Other retail funding	8,038	3,006
8	Brokered deposit outflow	132,572	24,533
9	**Unsecured wholesale funding outflow, of which:**	**52,707**	**34,488**
10	Operational deposit outflow	-	-
11	Non-operational funding outflow	47,409	29,190
12	Unsecured debt outflow	5,298	5,298
13	**Secured wholesale funding and asset exchange outflow**	**346,494**	**157,709**
14	**Additional outflow requirements, of which:**	**158,789**	**58,192**
15	Outflow related to derivative exposures and other collateral requirements	29,152	24,259
16	Outflow related to credit and liquidity facilities including unconsolidated structured transactions and mortgage commitments	129,637	33,933
17	**Other contractual funding obligation outflow**	**1,021**	**1,021**
18	Other contingent funding obligations outflow	191,456	6,344
19	**Total Cash Outflow**	**891,077**	**285,292**

Cash Inflow Amounts

20	Secured lending and asset exchange cash inflow	**388,305**	**113,730**
21	Retail cash inflow	**2,449**	**1,225**
22	Unsecured wholesale cash inflow	**21,042**	**20,364**
23	**Other cash inflows, of which:**	**20,809**	**20,809**
24	Net derivative cash inflow	5,164	5,164
25	Securities cash inflow	966	966
26	Broker-dealer segregated account inflow	14,678	14,678
27	Other cash inflow	-	-
28	**Total Cash Inflow**	**432,605**	**156,127**

		Average Amount
29	**Total HQLA**	**158,365**
30	**Total Net Cash Outflow Amount Excluding The Maturity Mismatch Add-On**	**129,165**
31	**Maturity Mismatch Add-On**	**1,816**
32	**Total Net Cash Outflow Amount**	**130,980**
33	**Liquidity Coverage Ratio (%)**	**121%**

1. Figures may not sum due to rounding.

5

Reprinted from https://www.morganstanley.com/about-us-ir/pdf/US-LCR-Disclosures-033118.pdf

Appendix C

Contract Source Code </>

```solidity
1    pragma solidity ^0.4.19;
2
3    contract Fizzy {
4        /*
5         * Potential statuses for the Insurance struct
6         * 0: ongoing
7         * 1: insurance contract resolved normaly and the flight landed before the limit
8         * 2: insurance contract resolved normaly and the flight landed after the limit
9         * 3: insurance contract resolved because cancelled by the user
10        * 4: insurance contract resolved because flight cancelled by the air company
11        * 5: insurance contract resolved because flight redirected
12        * 6: insurance contract resolved because flight diverted
13        */
14       struct Insurance {          // all the infos related to a single insurance
15           bytes32 productId;           // ID string of the product linked to this insurance
16           uint limitArrivalTime;       // maximum arrival time after which we trigger compensation (timestamp in sec)
17           uint32 premium;              // amount of the premium
18           uint32 indemnity;            // amount of the indemnity
19           uint8 status;                // status of this insurance contract. See comment above for potential values
20       }
21
22       event InsuranceCreation(       // event sent when a new insurance contract is added to this smart contract
23           bytes32 flightId,           // <carrier_code><flight_number>.<timestamp_in_sec_of_departure_date>
24           uint32 premium,             // amount of the premium paid by the user
25           uint32 indemnity,           // amount of the potential indemnity
26           bytes32 productId           // ID string of the product linked to this insurance
27       );
28
29       /*
30        * Potential statuses for the InsuranceUpdate event
31        * 1: flight landed before the limit
32        * 2: flight landed after the limit
33        * 3: insurance contract cancelled by the user
34        * 4: flight cancelled
35        * 5: flight redirected
36        * 6: flight diverted
37        */
38       event InsuranceUpdate(         // event sent when the situation of a particular insurance contract is resolved
39           bytes32 productId,          // id string of the user linked to this account
40           bytes32 flightId,           // <carrier_code><flight_number>.<timestamp_in_sec_of_departure_date>
41           uint32 premium,             // amount of the premium paid by the user
42           uint32 indemnity,           // amount of the potential indemnity
43           uint8 status                // new status of the insurance contract. See above comment for potential values
44       );
45
46       address creator;              // address of the creator of the contract
47
48       // All the insurances handled by this smart contract are contained in this mapping
49       // key: a string containing the flight number and the timestamp separated by a dot
50       // value: an array of insurance contracts for this flight
51       mapping (bytes32 => Insurance[]) insuranceList;
52
53
54       // ----------------------------------------------------------------------------- //
55       // MODIFIERS / CONSTRUCTOR
56       // ----------------------------------------------------------------------------- //
57
58       /**
59        * @dev This modifier checks that only the creator of the contract can call this smart contract
60        */
61       modifier onlyIfCreator {
62           if (msg.sender == creator) _;
```

Index

Page references followed by *f* indicate an illustrated figure.